A NEW HISTORY
OF THE COLD WAR

JOHN LUKACS, a ranking contemporary historian, is the author of numerous books and essays. His first edition of A HISTORY OF THE COLD WAR received exceptional critical acclaim here and abroad and has been translated into four European languages. Mr. Lukacs is a professor of history at Chestnut Hill and La Salle colleges in Philadelphia. He was recently visiting professor in the University of Toulouse, France.

Also by John Lukacs

THE GREAT POWERS AND EASTERN EUROPE

TOCQUEVILLE: THE EUROPEAN REVOLUTION AND CORRE-
    SPONDENCE WITH GOBINEAU *(Editor)*

DECLINE AND RISE OF EUROPE

HISTORICAL THINKING *(in preparation)*

A NEW HISTORY
OF THE
COLD WAR

by John Lukacs

THIRD EDITION, EXPANDED, OF
A HISTORY OF THE COLD WAR

Anchor Books
Doubleday & Company, Inc.
Garden City, New York

A *New History of the Cold War* is the third edition, expanded, of *A History of the Cold War*, originally published in a hardbound edition by Doubleday & Company, Inc., 1961 and revised for the Anchor Books edition, 1962.

Anchor Books edition: 1966

LIBRARY OF CONGRESS CATALOG CARD NUMBER 66–21017
COPYRIGHT © 1961, 1962, 1966 BY JOHN LUKACS
ALL RIGHTS RESERVED
PRINTED IN THE UNITED STATES OF AMERICA

Uxori dilectissimae

CONTENTS

PREFACE   ix

Part 1.   THE MAIN EVENTS

I   The Historical Origins   3

II   The Crystallization of the Cold War   40

III   The Division of Europe Becomes Rigid   67

IV   The Chinese Struggle and the Korean
      War   83

V   Stalin's Death and Dulles' Rise   104

VI   The Crucial Year   129

VII   To the Summits   155

VIII Decline of the Super-Powers   197

IX   The Cuban Comedy   226

X   Decrystallization of the Cold War   249

XI   Cold War or Cold Peace?   273

Part 2.   THE MAIN MOVEMENTS

XII   The Two Peoples:
      The Tendencies of Their Societies   281

XIII The Two Societies:
      The Tendencies of Their Political
      Theories   300

XIV   The Two States:
      The Development of Their National
      Interests   324

XV   The Two Nations:
      The Development of Their National
      Character   355

XVI   Conclusion:
      The Great Historical Movements of
      Our Times   390

INDEX   414

PREFACE

This is a *new*, and not a *revised*, version of *A History of the Cold War* which was first published in January 1961. Bringing it up to date I added a new chapter in December 1961 for the Doubleday Anchor edition which was published in the fall of 1962. The present book, to be published more than four years after the Doubleday Anchor and nearly six years after the original edition, includes five new chapters in Part 1, which is the historical narrative. It is therefore that I suggested the new title, *A New History of the Cold War*. There are many small changes throughout the rest of the text. Almost without exception these are inconsequential. I found little or nothing in the historical evolution of the last six years which would have made me revise my interpretation of the history of the cold war. This is, too, why I am retaining much of the text of the original preface.

It was in October 1959, shortly after the then Russian Premier's visit to the United States, that I interrupted work on a book with which I had been occupied for some years to propose a history of the cold war to my publishers. I began the writing of the book at Christmas time and finished it on the day the ill-fated Summit Conference met in Paris.

It is difficult to know why we write, just as it is very difficult to know the motives of any human action. Yet the aim, the scope, the approach of any kind of writing is inseparable from the purposes of the author. In introducing this book, therefore, I must say something about my original reasons for writing it that will also show the limits of its scope.

No history of the cold war in English existed in 1960. I believed then, and I believe now, that such a historical reconstruction may fill a rather obvious need. But I wish to make it clear that this book is concerned primarily with Russian-American relations in Europe and, to some extent, in the Far East; it is not a survey of the contemporary historical development of the world. During the past twenty years oceans of ink and mountains of paper have been spent on the topics of Communism, of Communist Russia, and of America In The World Of (whatever that means) Today. Yet surprisingly little has been written about the recent history of Russian-American relations.

I believe that history, as a form of thought, is one of the most precious and perhaps unique rational possessions of Western civilizations. The character of a person may appear best from the reconstruction of the history of his life; the same is true of the character of nations. The very history of a problem may reveal its essential diagnosis. There is no human problem, indeed, no field of human endeavor, that may not be approached and studied profitably through its history. This applies very well to the cold war.

Our future may be endangered by the progressive weakening of our sense of history. Meanwhile the limitations of contemporary history remain obvious. A lack of documentation exists, together with an oppressive mass of documents of largely insubstantial value. Yet these limitations are superseded by certain considerations.

First, the conscientious historian cannot altogether forgo the task of writing contemporary history on occasion. He must be more than a professional antiquarian. He has a duty to the present.

Second, because of the peculiar practices of publicity pursued by certain contemporary governments, there are documents, so-called primary sources, that governments publish hastily on certain occasions; they are even printed in newspapers; for the first time in modern history, too, vast advance payments and publicity boons are offered to certain authors of hasty and ponderous memoirs. On the other hand, the intrinsic quality of many of these sources is often so weak that the earlier professional distinction between primary and secondary sources fades away. The adage that History is something more than Documents has seldom been truer than in our times, when "documents" abound and when we also suffocate under mountains of worthless paper. Now the historian faces new difficulties together with new possibilities. It is still possible to write reasonably good, and perhaps even enduring, history without —or, perhaps, *beyond*—all of the documentation required in the past.

At any rate, this book did not and does not now claim to be a Definitive History. It presents but a historical approach to the so-called cold war. This should be obvious from its original title: not *The,* but *A History of the Cold War.* It is my approach, and my approach alone.

The character of this approach will also appear through the structure of this book. The scene of the cold war is very large; the actors are gigantic; their factors are complex. The historical evolution of Russian-American relations includes (but also transcends) the relations of Communism and Capitalism, of Marxism and Democracy, of "West" and "East." Because of these complexities my plan of approach called for the division of this book in two parts—1. *The main events* and 2. *The main movements.* I separated historical chronicle from historical analysis, in attempting to answer the questions of *how* things happened, first, and *why* things happened, second—even though, like every historian, I know that this separation is imperfect, since it flows from the very nature of human beings and of their history that in every description of the *how* the *why* is at least partly implicit.

I first thought of *A History of the Cold War* as a working model of some of the historiographical principles of my *Historical Thinking* (as yet unpublished). The organization of Part 2 especially illustrates my views on the relative hierarchy of modern historical factors.[1] I should not explain my approach further at this point. The structure of this book is such that this must unfold to the reader as he proceeds.

My principal purpose in this book was to contribute to the historical diagnosis of the Russian-American conflict. By "diagnosis" I do not mean some kind of cold and remote objectivity. I believe that just as the essence of the Christian heritage is the unique teaching of charity, the purpose of knowledge, and especially of historical knowledge, is understanding rather than certainty. This may go against the grain of our now widespread concepts of Scientific and Objective Knowledge: nevertheless, I believe it to be true.

The two unique achievements of European civilization in the last three hundred years were the creation of the scientific method and of history as a form of thought. We are at least becoming aware how human life and human reason may be endangered by the excesses of the former. Historical thinking, too, may be used to deceive and poison the passions of nations. But at least history tells us more about human nature than does science; it deals with perennial problems rather than with definite periods; its aim is understanding rather than certainty; and the quality of historical truth is such that it may be understood by anyone whose willingness to read or to listen reflects the willingness of his heart.

Christmas 1965

"Old Pickering School House"
Williams' Corner,
   near Phoenixville, Pennsylvania

[1] A few years after the first edition was published I was heartened to find a very similar approach in the organization of a very different book by a very different author dealing with a very different subject of general history: Christopher Hill in *The Century of Revolution, 1603–1714,* Edinburgh, 1961, Volume 5 of the Nelson *A History of England* series.

Part 1

THE MAIN EVENTS

CHAPTER I

The Historical Origins

(To 1945)

1

On the twenty-fifth day of April in the year 1945 advancing units of the American and Russian Armies met in the middle of Europe, along the banks of the Elbe River, near the German town of Torgau.

This symbolic event marks the principal condition of contemporary history that has remained essentially unchanged ever since. That principal condition is not the Atomic Bomb and not Communism; it is the division of Germany and of most of Europe into American and Russian spheres of influence. The so-called cold war grew out of this division.

We must not forget that the cold war has been a direct consequence of the Second World War, even more than the Second World War was the direct consequence of the First. Both of these wars began in Europe; first, and above all, they concerned Europe; but in the end they were ultimately decided by the tremendous might of the United States and of Soviet Russia. Above all, these gigantic struggles involved the political geography of Europe; and this, too, has remained the main problem of the cold war for two decades at least.

Neither the American nor the Russian people wanted the Second World War. Even their governments, with all of their faults, were less responsible for that war than were certain European governments, and particularly the government of the German nation. It was the Europeans, and particularly the central continental

Europeans, who ruined their continent by tearing each
other apart. Upon these ruins, then, by 1945, the armed
might of transatlantic America and of Eurasian Russia
came to preside.

2

The Second World War began between Germany
and Poland, Britain, and France, provoked by Germany; the real victors were the United States and
Soviet Russia. By 1945 they had become the two main
Powers on this earth. Russia, true, was bled white in
the war; more than six million of her sons were dead;
some of her largest cities were devastated; cold and
hunger continued to be the daily affliction of many
other Russian millions for many years to come. Still,
never in the history of mankind was the power and
prestige of Russia greater than in 1945. The rulers of
the world were awed by her resolution in war; the word
of her rulers was the supreme law from Vienna to
Vladivostok. Her sullen soldiers swarmed in the streets
of every town from Alpine villages in the heart of
Europe to Manchurian huts along the China Sea.

The power and the prestige of the United States of
America were even greater. From the middle of Korea
to the center of Berlin the benevolent system of the
American military was established in thousands of
places on five continents. About two of every thousand
Americans had perished in the war, compared with
about fifty out of every thousand Russians, about ninety
of every thousand Germans, about two hundred of
every thousand Poles, if we include the civilian population, who in America went entirely unharmed. The
stupendous wealth of the American wartime establishment fed, clothed, nourished, and furnished millions of
America's allies; it equipped the forces of Russia with
modern armor. The prosperity of the Arsenal of Democracy continued unbroken. In 1945, at a time when

the cities of Europe, half ruined, were shivering in darkness, the brilliant lights of America's great cities shone uniquely bright at night.

But already well before 1945 the map of the world suggested the primacy of America and of Russia. Already by 1850 the United States formed one of the greatest land empires of the globe, stretching from the Atlantic to the Pacific and from the Canadian frontier to the Gulf of Mexico and the Caribbean Sea; already by 1800 the Russian Empire, stretching from Manchuria to Warsaw, covered over one sixth of the entire land area of our globe. Already by 1850 there were as many Russians as there were Frenchmen and Englishmen and Germans; already by 1890 there were more Americans than Frenchmen and Englishmen together; already by 1900 the United States produced more steel than any other country in the world; already during the First World War the financial wealth of the world shifted to America. Well before 1945 the United States and Russia were becoming the two largest Empires in the history of mankind.

Even though their primacy in the political affairs of the globe was not yet fully established until that time, it could be foreseen how in an age dominated by materials, technology, and masses their resources might sooner or later bring them this kind of primacy, in times when numbers and material were to weigh more and more decisively in the ranking of nations, in the developing epoch of social democracy toward which the masses of the world—above and beneath the more dramatic changes of fortunes in the history of nations and of political systems—were gradually moving.

3

From the perspective of the present, two tremendous movements emerge from the history of the world during the past few hundred years. They are the dissolution of the aristocratic systems of governments and societies, and the disintegration of the great European Empires overseas. The rise of the American and Russian Empires is an inseparable part of these great developments.

Both modern Russia and the United States of America came into being during the eighteenth century. Their capital cities were named after their respective founders; but Washington did not exist before 1800 and St. Petersburg not before 1700. Neither did the town of Berlin amount to much at that time; London and Paris were the two capitals of the world.

Peter I, a willful ugly giant, brutally tore his people out of the semi-Asiatic darkness in which they had painfully squirmed and slumbered. His purposes were mostly European; his methods were often Asiatic. His aim was to introduce Russia into the European System of Nations. Unlike the dreadful record of Peter's successes, the record of the American Founding Fathers, and of Washington foremost among them, was unsullied by such brutalities. But, like that of Peter's Russia, America's fortunate geographical position was decisive: it enabled her to win her independence from England; and, like the Russians', the Americans' success was largely due to the profit they could reap from the wars that the European Powers fought among themselves.

The full establishment of Russia as a European Power is inseparable from the histories of Poland and Sweden and Turkey. Whereas the political map of Western Europe changed relatively little during the hundred years before the French Revolution, during that time the map of Eastern Europe had been transformed beyond recognition. Before 1700 the entire Baltic was a Swedish lake and the bright flag of Sweden flew over the shores of northwestern Russia; during the next hundred years Sweden lost not only her eastern

Baltic provinces but in the end even Finland went to Russia. Before 1700 the eastern frontiers of the Polish Kingdom stood closer to Moscow than to Warsaw; by 1815 Warsaw was but the capital of a Russian province; having been partitioned thrice among Russia, Prussia, and Austria, Poland disappeared from the map of Europe. Before 1700 the entire Black Sea was a Turkish lake; by 1800 more than the northern shore was Russia's, and her outposts were cautiously spreading toward the south.

The establishment of the United States, too, is inseparable from the histories of Spain and France and Britain. In 1700 the French and the Spanish had the most immense possessions and titles for possessions on the North American continent; little more than a hundred years later only a few specks remained for France; the final dissolution of the Spanish and Portuguese Empires in America had already begun, and the British held on to not much more than Canada. By that time it was evident that the United States was destined to be the dominant Power in the entire Western Hemisphere.

In the long run, the greatest developments in the political geography of the world in the last four centuries have been those imperial dissolutions that at least indirectly led to the great world wars of the last two hundred years. Toward the end of the sixteenth century began the decline of the Spanish Empire, toward the end of the seventeenth that of the Turkish, toward the beginning of the nineteenth that of the Chinese, and toward the end of the nineteenth that of the Austrian. Through these centuries the Russians promoted the decline of the Turkish and Chinese Empires; but their gains had been either impermanent or, except for certain Balkan and Caucasian acquisitions, unimportant in the long run. Before and during the First World War they (and also Wilson's United States) promoted the dissolution of the Austrian Empire; but it was Hitler's

Germany, not they, who was to gain from that dissolution.

The United States was more fortunate with the dissolution of the great Spanish Imperium. For the achievement of American independence was made possible by the great transatlantic world wars fought by France and Britain in the eighteenth century for the Spanish heritage. Indeed, without French help the War of Independence would not have been won. But it was twenty-two years before Yorktown that on another September day beneath Quebec the ascendancy of an English-speaking people in North America had been finally secured; and it was finally established in a treaty signed in Paris twenty years before another Paris Treaty in 1763 sealed the establishment of American independence.

It is therefore that from the retrospect of two hundred years, the year 1763 may be seen as a mark that may be even more important (though it is, of course, less dramatic) in the history of mankind than that central explosive date of 1789, which Europeans associate with the eighteenth century. For 1763 marks more than the conclusion of the greatest world war of the eighteenth century. It is a momentous milestone in the destinies of America and also of Russia. It was in 1763 that the clever Choiseul foresaw that though Britain had won and France and Spain had lost, the struggle against the British of the North American colonists was beginning, and that the latter were bound to emerge as the victors of the North American continent. It was in 1763 that the Treaty of Hubertusburg, after Russia's sudden unscrupulous withdrawal from the European coalition against Prussia, foreshadowed their coming alliance and the partition of Poland. It was in 1763 that Prussia emerged as a first-rate European Power. In the twentieth century, then, there is reason to believe that the establishment of the United States in America and of Russia and Prussia among the Great Powers in Europe may have been, in the long run, historical developments even more important than the storming of the Bastille in 1789.

Surely one hundred and fifty years after the French Revolution, Berlin and Moscow and Washington were centers of world history at least as important as London or Paris. Certainly by 1939 the political ideas and systems then incarnated in modern Germany and Russia (and also the gleam of American technocracy) attracted the imagination of young millions throughout the world to whom the scenes of the French Revolution were but copperplate engravings from an antiquated past.

4

In a stately little ceremony George Washington was inaugurated as the first President of the American Republic almost at the very same moment when in Versailles the grander, more dramatic, and less orderly French National Assembly came to meet. For decades thereafter the interest of the world centered on France and not on America. But it is evident that in 1789 the American Revolution was already accomplished; the American ship of state was successfully launched at the very moment the French Revolution began. Indeed, the American Constitution is an even greater accomplishment than the winning of the War of the Revolution. Like the United States, in the last two hundred years many colonial peoples have won their independence. Unlike the United States, few of them succeeded in erecting and maintaining a constitutional order of reasonable liberty. It is the fashion of Russian propagandists to compare 1776 with 1917, the Great American and the Great Soviet Revolutions; but this is no more than a half truth. The great achievement of the best among the American Founding Fathers is just that

What about the God-damned slaves?

they were moderate rather than radical, constructive rather than revolutionary; even though some among them believed that they did establish a New Order of Things, in every measure it is unjust to compare Washington, Hamilton, Adams, or even the democratic Jefferson with such unscrupulous terrorists as Lenin or Trotsky or Zinoviev or Stalin.

Nevertheless, the relations of Russia and the United States transcend these ideological considerations from the very beginning. Russia, represented by the most autocratic of all rulers, and the United States, representing the most republican and democratic system of the eighteenth century, had amicable relations very early. Even during the War of Independence, Catherine II refused the British, who, as with the Hessians, wanted to lease Russian troops for their American campaign; and the Russian government, associating itself with the League of Armed Neutrality, welcomed the weakening of British (and Spanish) power on the high seas and on the American continent. Already at that time a vague common feeling of youthfulness, of common pioneer tasks, similar puritanical and radical pretensions of a revivalist mission among the nations of the world, a common distrust felt at times toward the ancient established civilizations of Europe, were spinning themselves into a thin thread of instinctive and intellectual sympathy that from the history of Russian-American relations has never entirely disappeared.

On the edges of the then civilized world neither the young American Republic nor the Russian Empire could escape from being involved in the great world drama of the Napoleonic Wars. The United States almost went to war against France in the beginning; she went to war with Britain in the end. Russia fought France three times; she almost went to war against Britain once. The French burned Moscow in 1812 and the British burned Washington in 1814; yet the British knew from the beginning that they could not conquer all of North America, just as Napoleon knew that he could not occupy all of Russia, though he hoped to defeat her armies and conquer her Tsar. That perhaps most astute of all American diplomatists, John Quincy Adams, maintained excellent relations with the Russian Tsar Alexander: Adams encouraged the Russians against the French; Alexander encouraged the Americans against the British (his own allies). As so often in history, the Russians solicited American co-operation to the detriment of Britain and of Europe. Still the War of 1812 ended in a draw; indeed, the British, with the Treaty of Ghent, hastened to wind up their American war at a time when they needed reserve strength in Europe against the rapacious designs of Russia and Prussia, the two latecoming but most ambitious members of the victorious alliance against Napoleon.

In the long run, the few charred houses of Washington and the charred quarters of Moscow notwithstanding, Russia and America profited considerably from the long great world war launched by the French Revolution and Napoleon. The Russians were again back in Poland; they had acquired Finland; they gained border provinces at the expense of Turkey and became a Power at the gate of the Balkans: for a short time Alexander seemed the Arbiter of Europe. The United States acquired the vast Louisiana Territory and became a leading Power in the Caribbean. The disintegration of the remaining Spanish holdings in America was then to involve Russian and American ambitions and interests anew.

From the very beginning the United States, at times openly and often secretly, encouraged the various movements of revolt directed against the remaining European Powers in the Western Hemisphere. Toward the end of the French Revolutionary Wars ambitious groups in Latin America began to tear large provinces away from the Spanish Crown to establish new nations under their leadership. The ruler of Russia again showed some interest in the prospects of this disintegration; but it was Britain, not Russia, whose naval power and active consent made possible the independence of Latin America and whose politics and tacit consent made possible the historic functioning of the Monroe Doctrine. Like the United States, the government of Great Britain, with few minor exceptions, opposed the return of European influences to the Americas throughout the nineteenth century. Nor did Britain much oppose American expansion in the Pacific.

It is in that vast warm watery area of the globe that the American advance has been so astonishingly successful. As early as 1689 the Russians had reached China overland through Siberia; in the Treaty of Nerchinsk the Amur River was made the frontier between the Russian and the Manchu Chinese Empires; and today that portion of the Russo-Chinese frontier is still along the Amur. In 1689 the American frontier was but a few dozen miles inland from the Atlantic coast; today the American flag flies in Okinawa, Japan, Korea, across the Pacific everywhere and even on the Asian mainland. By the 1800s the enterprising sea captains coming from New England, half a world away, had a larger share of the maritime trade of China than had the Russians. It was not the neighboring Russians but the faraway Americans who "opened up" Japan in the 1850s. On the rainy western coast of North America, Russian settlements existed almost as far south as San Francisco in the 1820s but it was the Americans, not the Russians, who finally acquired all of that erstwhile Spanish territory. In 1867 the Russians, worried lest the British occupy it from Canada, preferred selling Alaska to the United States; they had also given up their half-hearted attempts to colonize Hawaii. Not until the aggressive rise of a modernized Japan did the rulers of Russia begin to comprehend the importance of the Pacific Ocean.

Still these great changes registered on the political

map of the world are transcended by—indeed, they are part and parcel of—even greater (though not always conscious) inchoate movements of peoples. These have been social as well as political, "horizontal" as well as "vertical." Though the first principles of modern political democracy had been set down several centuries before, and though the decline of the Spanish Empire began at least two centuries before, it was not until the end of the eighteenth century that the great momentum of these movements of peoples began. It was then that, for the first time in centuries, the populations of Europe and of America suddenly began to increase. From that time onward the barriers of social restriction rapidly crumbled; the blood and the flesh and the spirit of millions born poor swelled up into the remaining privileged classes. Though this vertical movement toward equality was swiftest and most advanced in the United States, it must not be thought that this was a movement unique for the new American democracy.

And millions moved also in a horizontal direction across the surface of the world to settle the remaining empty spaces of land. In the Northern Hemisphere these were mostly to be found within the American and Russian Empires, with their great plains, uninhabited except by a few primitive tribes.

5

For ninety-nine years after Waterloo the world did not experience another world war. The expansion of European Powers was directed no longer toward America but to Africa and Asia, southward and eastward. The expansion of Russia, too, was to her south and east. The expansion of the United States, on the other hand, moved away from Europe, filling the vast terrains of the American West and of the frontier. Thus no European Power would profit from America's own dreadful

Civil War. The world was spared an Atlantic War for a hundred years.

Europe was still the center of world events. Still it could be seen more than a hundred years ago that Russia as well as the United States was destined to play an ever larger role in the history of mankind; it was in the 1830s, when America seemed isolated and Russia for a time withdrawn from the great affairs of Europe, that Tocqueville, in *Democracy in America,* wrote his now famous prophetic paragraphs about the unnoticed tremendous growth of these two empires, Despotic Russia and Democratic America, each of them destined to sway one half of the globe.

The world was spared an Atlantic War for a century; meanwhile across the Atlantic developed the greatest mass migration of the last thousand years. In the century after Waterloo perhaps as many as sixty million inhabitants of Europe left their homelands. Spurred by misery rather than by politics, braving the lessening risks of cheap steamer passage, most of these millions came to fill the still spacious lands and cities of the United States.

It was not until the first decades of the present century that these large colonial and migratory movements came to a halt. It was a decade before the outbreak of the First World War that Japan thwarted Russia in the Far East by arms. It was a decade after the outbreak of the First World War that American congressional legislation put an end to the era of mass immigration to the United States. Meanwhile the great engineering achievements of the American transcontinental railroads, of the Russian Trans-Siberian Railway, and of the American Two-Ocean Canal through the Isthmus of Panama had been completed. Indeed, somewhat symbolically, the latter was officially opened in 1914 within a week of the great European war declarations —at a time, however, when the frontier era in the American West was already passing; when the metropolitan organization of the continental United States into States was already completed; and when in the far western parts of the Pacific the arms and fleets of Japan were already more powerful than the military and naval outposts of the nations of the white race.

During the nineteenth century, with few incidental exceptions, very friendly relations between the United States and Russia prevailed. During the Civil War, Russia (and Prussia, too) hastened to inform the Union that she actively disapproved of the British and French inclinations toward the Confederate States; a Russian fleet made a ceremonial and demonstrative visit of friendship to American ports. Toward the end of the century these amicable inclinations weakened somewhat. There were now many American immigrants from Central and Eastern Europe who had little liking for Russia; these included an increasing number of Russian Jews; the occasional pogroms and the cruel restrictions practiced by the Tsar turned liberal Americans against the Russian regime; and there were influential Americans who appreciated British warnings against the encroachments of the Russian Bear in the Orient. Still the pools of American Russophobia evaporated under the yellow glare of Japan's blazing successes; President Theodore Roosevelt was more than fair to the Russian side as he mediated excellently the Peace Treaty between Russia and Japan in Portsmouth, New Hampshire, in 1905; and the late flowering of Russian art and thought, particularly exemplified by the figure of Tolstoi, evoked a strong interest in Russia among educated Americans. The quick development of mass communications brought to millions of new readers some information about wonders as well as brutalities from hitherto faraway scenes and nations. But even though many millions of Americans knew something about the darker features of Tsarist Russia by 1914, it was not prejudice and dislike but rather a mixture of ignorance with a vague benevolence that marked the sentiments of the American and Russian peoples toward each other as the abysmal First World War opened in Europe.

6

Unlike in every other world war in which she had been or was to become involved, Russia chose to participate in the First World War from the beginning. The origins of the First World War are complex; but it may be said that Germany and Russia were perhaps more responsible for it than any other Power. We have seen that Russia attempted to profit from the disintegration of the Turkish Empire long before 1914. Three times in the hundred years before 1914 her armies moved, and on other occasions they threatened to move, south through the Balkans toward Constantinople. The concerted efforts of European diplomacy, and at times the naval power of Britain, thwarted these efforts on every occasion; and, except for the short Crimean War in the middle of the century, Britain succeeded without recourse to arms.

In the last three decades before the First World War, however, great changes in the European balance of alliances affected Russia's prospects and ambitions. Somewhat as with Communism in our times, the religious and racial ties of Pan-Slavism and of Russian Orthodoxy served at times as a secondary arm of Russia's ambitions; and these ambitions were now directed against the Austro-Hungarian as well as against the Turkish Empire. But Austria-Hungary, ever since Bismarck's achievement of a united German Empire, was now a German ally; and after Bismarck's demise no German statesman proved able to reconcile or to balance this commitment with the even more traditional friendship between the Prussian and Russian Empires. Thus Autocratic Russia entered into a mutual defensive alliance with Republican France in 1892. During the next fifteen years the aggressive naval, African, and Near Eastern policies and expansive ambitions of the German Emperor drove Britain first closer to France and then even to her century-long eastern opponent Russia.

On 31 July 1914, after a month of the sharply intricate negotiations that followed the Serbian assassination of the Austrian Heir at Sarajevo, Germany, as a preventive measure, declared war on Russia and threw her armies forward through Belgium against France. This priority of the German war declaration was, however, a consequence of the relative ineptitude of German statesmanship ever since Bismarck rather than evidence of outstanding German war guilt when compared to Russia: for Russia wanted war, too, in 1914.

A dreadful war; a dreary war; a disappointing war; for Russia it soon seemed hopeless, soulless, fruitless, endless. It was longer, much longer than expected; the Russian armies, equipped much worse than they had expected, fought with much less success than had been expected. The enormous rot of bureaucracy, the sickening lassitude of imperial government, the fever of recurrent intrigue, turned the initial gusts of patriotism into a gray miasmatic fog that seemed to envelop the lumbering giant of Russia, on the edge of which millions of peasant soldiers fired haphazardly at the advancing German armies. The alliance with France and Britain, the potential progress of Western European liberal democracy within Russia, the actual promises that Russian diplomacy significantly exacted from the Allies during the war, were not the kind of thing to capture or to refresh the dulled, painful imagination of the Russian millions: these things succored the souls of but a few urbane Russians. For what happened in 1917 was a much greater movement, of which the Bolshevik Revolution was only a part: it was Russia's great dreadful disgust with the European War and with their

Western allies,[1] whether foreign or domestic, with those rich Russian townees who came to talk to them about the promise of new freedoms and democracy. They sounded so foreign at times with lilting French

[1] I am saying this because of my conviction that the sentiments of *nations* toward or against each other may be even profounder motives of history than the relations of *states*. This has been seldom recognized by historians, even though the Russians' reaction to France and Britain during the First World War may have been one of the most powerful inner motives toward their subsequent break with the West. It was recognized, however, by no less a historian than Winston Churchill, in his condensed history of that war:

"The abandonment of Gallipoli dispelled the Russian dream. In her darkest hours, under the flail of Ludendorff, driven out of Poland, driven out of Galicia, her armies enduring disaster and facing death often without arms, the cost of living rising continually throughout her vast, secluded Empire, Russia had cheered herself by dwelling on the great prize of Constantinople. A profound chill spread through all ranks of the Russian people, and with it came suspicion no less deep-seated. England had not really tried to force the Straits. From the moment when she had conceded the Russian claim to Constantinople, she had not been single-hearted, she had lost her interest in the enterprise. Her infirm action and divided counsels arose from secret motives hidden in the bosom of the State. And this while Russia was pouring out her blood as no race had ever done since men waged war. Such were the whispers which, winged by skillful German propaganda, spread far and wide through the Tsar's dominions, and in their wake every subversive influence gained in power. Lastly, the now inevitable prolongation of the struggle was destined to prove fatal to Russia. In the war of exhaustion to which we were finally condemned, which was indeed extolled as the last revelation of military wisdom, Russia was to be the first to fall, and in her fall to open upon herself a tide of ruin in which perhaps a score of millions of human beings have been engulfed. The consequences of these events abide with us to-day. They will darken the world for our children's children." (From the one-volume edition of *The World Crisis* by Winston Churchill. Reprinted by permission of Charles Scribner's Sons and Odhams Press, Ltd.)

See also pages 309–10 and 366–67, about the existence of relative Francophile and of Germanophile factors in recent Russian history.

words mixed into their conversation; they looked so foreign in their morning coats.

The First World War, and not the appeal of Marxist ideas, was the great wave that carried everything and everybody to the crucial trough of 1917. The Bolshevik Revolution, at any rate, was but the third revolt in twelve years. In 1905 a wave of riots, mutinies, and strikes shook the Russian Empire; it led to the grant of a first, limited Russian Constitution by the Tsar. In March 1917 one broad wave of dissatisfaction swept away the Tsarist government in a few nearly painless and bloodless days; the proclamation of a Democratic Russia followed.

Lenin, rooming in exile in Switzerland, myopic like most political émigrés, heard the news of both of these revolutions with skeptical surprise. Like white-coated scientists experimenting with bacilli in airtight tubes, the German government then offered Lenin passage in a sealed railroad car to Russia through neutral Sweden. The experiment, as we all know, paid off only too well —to the ultimate detriment of Germany together with all of Western civilization. Still, the decisive factor was not so much the potency of the Bolshevik bacillus as the weakened resistance of the old Russian State and Society, a condition that was made desperate not so much because of Bolshevik underminings as it was due to the War. A state and a society where criminals and weaklings like a Rasputin, a Stürmer, or a Kerensky would have a greater influence than intelligent statesmen such as a Stolypin, a Witte, a Milyukov, seems doomed, at least in retrospect. It is true that it was not the old Tsardom but the incipient republican democracy of Russia that the Bolsheviks overthrew; but "overthrew" is not really the right word: by early November 1917 the order of the Russian state and government lay mostly in ruin. There is not much in the scene of 7 November 1917 that invites comparison with 4 July 1776 or even with the storming of the Bastille. Unlike those summery days in Philadelphia or Paris, the Petrograd scene was dark and dreary with freezing rain. It was but the beginning of a revolution—not even a *coup d'état* but a *coup d'une ville* in a foggy vacuum. Lenin and his Bolsheviks proclaimed themselves rulers of Russia not against determined resistance but amidst near universal chaos.

Still, their great trials lay ahead; and they were to endure through them. This is the one reason why we may regard 1917 the most outstanding year in the history of the twentieth century.

7

It was 1914 that, in retrospect, marks the end of an era; but 1917 was more of a turning point. First, the Bolshevik system and state in Russia endured. The Germans made peace with them in 1918. The Allies, stung with anger and fright by the prospect of a Germany relieved of the burden of her eastern front, attempted to intervene with arms against the Communist government that at times in 1918 seemed to hold hardly more than the few central cities of Russia; but after the Armistice the halfhearted Western intentions to intervene in Russia quickly evaporated. Without massive Allied support, quarreling among themselves, undistinguished by statesmanship, the anti-Bolshevik forces in Russia abandoned their armed struggles within a few years. Only the western border nations of the Russian Empire —the Finns, Estonians, Latvians, Lithuanians, and Poles —succeeded in establishing their national independence at the expense of Russian territorial holdings and Communist ambitions. Their independence was the political price that the new Russian regime had to pay for its survival. For by 1921 the new government of the "Union of Soviet Socialist Republics" was the sole ruler of the Russian Empire from Moscow. It ruled over a devastated, famished, torn, naked, and weakened country, but it ruled, nevertheless, over about one sixth of the continental areas of the earth; and it was so recognized by almost all of the world's Great Powers. This was the great accomplishment of Lenin and Trotsky and Stalin.

But 1917 marks an even more important turning point in the history of the world. For the first time in history, breaking with a long national tradition proclaimed by the First President, the United States chose to enter a European war. Soon a million fresh American soldiers were pouring into France; their arrival furnished the means for the last decisive campaign against Germany. The American intervention (a host of Latin-American nations and China followed the American move) in 1917 transformed what was previously an almost solely European war into a World War, in which the most decisive events were Russia's withdrawal and America's entry. It is true that the massive Russian retreat from the war did not help Germany enough to win the war, while the massive American intervention helped the Allies just enough to win their final victory. But, by 1917, the relative importance of these tremendous events already suggested the future, when not only would the balance of another European and World War be tipped by the weight of America and Russia but at the end of it America and Russia would be the two chief masters of the continent.

How and why the United States entered the First World War is a complex story, among the elements of which one of the most complex is the character of the outwardly so straightforward and yet so strange Woodrow Wilson. The clearest argument, that the United States could not tolerate the prospects of a German Atlantic victory over Britain, was not told to the American people in these words, and probably Wilson himself did not think about it in these terms, at least not consistently. It is a curious coincidence that his final agonizing decision for war came in the days when the news of the March Revolution from Russia was electrifying the dem-

ocratic imaginations of the world. This may have influenced (though it did not alone provoke) Wilson's
decision: for this dry and outwardly unemotional profes-
sor-President was deeply affected by sentimental and
ideological concepts of politics. He could proclaim and,
indeed, transform the character of this great war now,
when Russia, that embarrassing prospective ally, was
no longer ruled by a reactionary Tsar. Now it could be
the true alliance of Democracies against Empires; the
world could be made Safe for Democracy.

About Russia, Wilson's illusions were soon to be disappointed; but this did not alter the condition that by
1918 all of Europe, even the coming losers, looked to
Wilson with trust and hope. The author of the Fourteen
Points, like the Russian Tsar Alexander I the century
before, became the Arbiter of Europe.[2] Soon the

[2] "There is a curious parallel," wrote Alfred Duff Cooper
almost thirty years ago in his brilliant biography of Talleyrand, "between the position of the Emperor Alexander [in the
1810s] and that occupied a century later by President Wilson. Both represented enormously powerful nations called
upon for the first time to play decisive parts in the settlement
of Europe. Both had been nurtured in liberal principles and
were actuated by generous sentiments. Vague aspirations
played a larger part in their mental equipment than practical
experience. They believed that every nation should be given
the government that it desired, and they hoped, the one by
means of a Holy Alliance, and the other by a League of Nations, to secure the future peace of the world. Both these
men of brilliant attainments seemed for a short period to
dominate the world; both of them, a few years after their
moment of triumph, ended their careers prematurely in an
atmosphere of tragedy and failure."
There is even more to this American-Russian parallel during the First World War. The last outstanding Tsarist Foreign Minister, Sazonov, in 1914 formulated Russia's war aims
in a confidential Note in Twelve Points that in many ways
were similar to Wilson's Fourteen Points. Quite independently from each other, and for entirely different reasons,
Wilson's America and Tsarist Russia promoted the dissolution of the Austro-Hungarian Empire from the very beginning, even more consistently than had their French and

George Washington carried him across the gray Atlantic to an exhausted Europe, to occupy, if only for a short time, the Chairmanship of World Peace. It was not the Bolshevik Revolutionary Lenin, it was this Princeton professor upon whose ideas hung the hope of millions and the fate of ancient European nations.

It has been the practice of most American historians to blame the ensuing troubles and disillusionments, including perhaps even the next World War, on American politics that then led to the withdrawal of the United States from European affairs and even from Wilson's League of Nations. This understandable inclination of perspective must now be corrected from retrospect. The blame lies with the Allied peacemakers, including Wilson, for what they did, rather than with what the American people and their politicians did not do. In 1918 the Western European and Atlantic Democracies won the war; they were indeed the masters of the world. They had all the face cards in their hands. Unlike one hundred years before, at the end of Napoleon's Wars, when the victorious coalition led by Britain had to face the ambitions and the powerful armies of Prussia and Russia athwart Europe; unlike 1945, when the United States and Britain had to share the control of the continent with Russia, in 1918–19 the Allies had an opportunity unequaled in modern history: for the two Aggressive Empires, Germany and Russia, lay weak in ruin, revolution, and chaos. Had Germany and Russia been allies, their Alliance would have won the First (and probably also the Second) World War. Had the Bolshevik Revolution not occurred—and this is an important point—in 1918 large Russian Imperial Armies would have camped across Eastern Europe; the Allies would have had to honor most of their desperate and secret obligations made to Russia during the war; a Yalta-like situation would have existed by 1918.

British allies. About the later similarities between Sazonov's and Stalin's war aims see also below, page 333.

For we must consider that the Bolshevik Revolution weakened rather than strengthened the international power of Russia; it not only failed to extend, it could not even maintain Russia's domains in Eastern Europe; it reduced the power and the extent of the Russian Empire for at least two decades to come.

But the statesmen at the Congress of Paris in 1919–20 did not measure up to their great forebears at Vienna or at Utrecht. Whatever their personal virtues, the divergence of their essential concepts reveals the spiritual disintegration of European Civilization that deep down was the source of their mistakes and political tragedies. The chief Wilsonian idea of national self-determination, whose purpose it was to clarify the map of Europe, led to confusion and injustice in many places. Misled by confusing principles, by the confusing clamor of democratic press diplomacy, and by the confusing claims of a dozen eager and unruly new nations, the Peacemakers at Paris cut their work short by making a patchwork of illegitimate compromises. From this, Hitler and Stalin were about to profit.

8

For the next twenty years—called by some the Great Armistice between the First and Second German Wars —America and Russia lay withdrawn into isolation. American prosperity, although deeply rent by the Great Depression in 1929, nevertheless continued to be the main element in American prestige throughout the world. The American nation, in line with her old tradition against large standing armies, released her soldier-millions at home. The Navy continued powerful, principally because of considerations regarding the Pacific Ocean. In 1921 Britain made her fateful but perhaps unavoidable choice of making friendship with the United States an obligation superseding her Far Eastern alliance with Japan. At least up to 1931, the United States could limit Japanese expansion in the Orient. Except for marginal affairs, however, the power of the United States was not brought into the struggles of the world.

The new Bolshevik Russia, too, chose isolation. After two hundred years at their seat in Petrograd, the Russian window to Europe, the government moved back to Moscow, the city on the great Eurasian plain. The hopes of international Communism for a host of Communist regimes rising above the ruins of Europe's war-torn bourgeois Empires remained unfulfilled: the few such Communist attempts (in Budapest, Munich, and Berlin) sputtered out miserably. The Russian Communist attempts to spread their doctrine and system by the spirit failed miserably, too, in the former border provinces of the Russian Empire that now formed themselves into independent nations; and even when they attempted to spread it by the sword, as in Poland in 1920, they were defeated. Suspicious and fearful of what they wrongly believed to be the unscrupulous determination of European Capitalism to destroy them by arms at the first opportunity, the rulers of Russia, by 1921, had separated their large Empire from Europe by an iron curtain.

Withdrawn from Europe, like the United States, the rulers of Russia showed more interest in their Far Eastern prospects. For six years after 1921 they were somewhat more active in certain Asian countries, believing (as in the 1950s) that their support of nationalist and anti-European movements there would ultimately result in the victory of the local Communists; but there, too (in Turkey, Persia, Afghanistan, China), they were to be disappointed.

With Germany alone they entered into highly secret, unscrupulous, and significant political and military arrangements: the Pacts of Rapallo and Berlin suggested a community of German and Russian interests aimed against Poland and her ally, France; and clandestine

arrangements were made to train German tank, gas,
and air corps officers, outwitting the provisions of the
Versailles Treaty, in camps hidden within the vast
plains of Russia. But the governments of Germany had
no intention of staking too much on the friendship of
Russia; they were making arrangements with West and
East alike; and after Hitler became the German leader,
this significant military collusion between Germany and
Russia also came to an end.

Lenin and Wilson died in the same year, 1924;[3] Hitler and Franklin Roosevelt became leaders of their nations in the same year, 1933. Thus, at a time when
Germany and Japan had already left the League of
Nations, at a time when Germany, moved by anti-
liberal and anti-Communist fervor, chose to spurn her
potentially auspicious collaboration with Russia, the
liberal Roosevelt, in one of his few early diplomatic
moves of significance, proceeded with the long overdue
establishment of formal diplomatic relations between
the United States and the Soviet Union.

They were, after all, the two largest continental Empires of the globe; their populations and productive
capacities were almost as large as those of all Europe
combined. And yet it would be a mistake to attribute
too much importance to the otherwise significant American recognition of Soviet Russia in 1933. The center of

[3] Sun Yat-sen died in 1925. In the political ideas of this
founder of modern China, Wilsonianism and Leninism were
mixed. In China the equivalent of the Russian March Revolution occurred in 1912, a bourgeois coup even less dramatic
and less profound than the first Russian one. In Russia the
ensuing chaos lasted for four years; in China for almost forty.
In both countries the Communists and not the bourgeois
democrats became the masters in the end; both profited from
national passions, inclinations, and ambitions. Still, it is instructive that Sun Yat-sen's heritage is claimed by both so-
called Nationalists and the Communists of China, by Chiang
and Mao alike. To find such a national accord in Russia, we
must go back not twenty but two hundred years, to the figure of Peter I.

history was still Europe; and the main actors still Germany, Britain, and perhaps France, Italy, and Japan. Except for the usual minor crises and problems that arise in the relations between states of which one is avowedly revolutionary, between the two World Wars American-Russian relations continued largely uneventful. Inclinations somewhat similar to the traditional Russian suspicion and distrust for Europe that were renewed under Stalin, existed in America, too; toward the end of the 1920s both Kellogg and Litvinov extolled, each in his own way, the theory of Collective Security; but their reactions to the rise of Germany were still quite different. In Asia, however, a vague but broadening community of American and Russian interests developed against the aggressions of Japan. It is true that, unlike the United States, Stalin in 1931 and 1932 was considering collaboration with Japan; it is true that when, on the other hand, he proposed American collaboration against Japan in 1933, the State Department spurned the offer and, indeed, told it to the Japanese. Still, by the mid-thirties it was becoming evident that both Russia and the United States were to give principal encouragement to the Chinese resistance against advancing Japan.

We have now seen that, internationally speaking, Communism was a largely ineffective force at least for two decades. In the 1930s, for example, far more millions hearkened to Nazi or Fascist bugle calls than to the long-winded Communist trumpets. Dictatorial regimes, including some of the Fascist and even Nazi type, were in power in many places in the world, while for almost three decades after 1917 the Soviet Union (except for her only, remote satellite, Outer Mongolia) remained virtually the only Communist nation in the world. Meanwhile the expulsion of Trotsky and Stalin's growing terrorism within Russia weakened the already decimated ranks of international Communist revolutionaries all around the world—even though most of them knew how to close their eyes conveniently and pass over this kind of accumulating evidence.

Still, no history of our times can afford to neglect this ideological element in the movements of nations. Though the Communist Party in America was ridiculously weak, so weak, indeed, that, in 1932, at the deepest moment of the American capitalist catastrophe, it attracted hardly more than two out of every thousand American voters, an astonishingly large portion of American intellectuals and a significant number of the upcoming young American bureaucrats nourished broad sympathies for Communism and for Russia. Their national influence was limited (though on certain crucial occasions and in certain places it went at times dangerously deep); still, the rigid puritanical measures of anti-Communism with which the American people reacted to the Bolsheviks after 1919 were largely gone by the 1930s. But in Russia, too—notwithstanding the standard jeers against Wall Street and Monopoly Capitalism—the evidence of a certain naïve admiration for Americans and for their technocracy survived in the 1930s, and its gleam appeared at times among the ruling circles. The existence of these sentiments is at least worthy of record; soon, for quite different reasons, the coming Second World War was to bring the destinies of the Russian and of the American nation in close contact with each other.

9

The most extraordinary figure in the history of the first half of the twentieth century was not Lenin or Wilson or Roosevelt or Stalin, but Adolf Hitler. Even though his achievements were not more enduring, they were more dramatic and they changed the course of history more than those of any one of the others. This evil genius, from 1933 onward, concentrated in his person the evident energies, the half-hidden ambitions, and the hidden frustrations of the great German race, a solid propellant that rent peace with a crash and streaked through history with tremendous force until it was destroyed by madness in its course.

In the first six years of his rule Hitler's Germany became the master of Europe. In the next six years the world war that he began in order to secure the domains of what he called the Third (or the Thousand-Year) German Reich destroyed him and cut his Germany in half by bringing about the gigantic coalition of Britain, America, and Russia.

Taking advantage not only of the superb organizational talents of his nation but also of the weaknesses, irresolutions, and miscalculations of the great Western European Democracies, Hitler in six years armed Germany, broke the contractual limits of previous treaties, annexed Austria, conquered part of Czechoslovakia. Under the pretext of anti-Bolshevism he suggested alliance to Mussolini's Italy and to a Japan energetic with the ambitions of national expansion. A European diplomatic revolution culminating at Munich in 1938 dissolved the substance of the previous French system of alliances. The governments of Britain, as yet wholly unprepared for war, had gone to great lengths to appease and placate Germany's ambitions, part of which they, rightly or wrongly, considered reasonable and perhaps even just.

These ominous events and tendencies evoked foreseeable anxieties and reactions in the United States. President Roosevelt, who, with all of the faults of his view of history and of international affairs, possessed a mind that was more cosmopolitan than parochial, saw the danger relatively early: in October 1937, in his famous Quarantine Speech, he made a determined, though of course impractical, proposal to the nations of the world to coalesce against the Aggressors—who, at that time, were Germany, Italy, and Japan. Even though, for domestic reasons, his power was still limited —because of that strange time lag that tends to slow down the movements of American public opinion (the strict Neutrality Act, passed in 1937 and supported by provincial politicians as well as by most American intellectuals, was part of the belated isolationist reaction to the involvement of the United States in the First World War)—Roosevelt began to take a more and more active part in the affairs of the world. From January 1938 he began to encourage British and French opposition to Germany; he allowed measures supporting China and restricting Japan; he had already sent a very friendly Ambassador to Moscow. But above all, the American public elite and the press, though still rigidly opposed to the risks of international involvements, created and reflected an almost unanimous American indignation toward Hitler, Mussolini, and the Japanese Dictatorship.

The anxieties of the Bolshevik masters of Russia were equally foreseeable; their reactions were not. The shrill anti-Communist and anti-Russian claims of Hitler (and also of the Japanese) led to some Russian defensive measures as a matter of course. They, too, gave some support to the Chinese against Japan; they, too, believed in the necessity of a broader "Anti-Fascist" coalition, including Communists and non-Communists alike, on the ideological as well as on the international plane; thus, while the capital of Communism suggested the creation of "United Fronts" against Fascism, Russia entered the League of Nations and Stalin allowed Litvinov to enter into defense alliances with France and with Czechoslovakia. Yet the principal preoccupations of Stalin were domestic, not international. At the time when the attention of the world was directed to the dramatic successes of Hitler's Germany, the leadership of Stalin's Russia was consumed by the black terror of police purges, a brutal, Byzantine, and largely senseless reign of terror probably unequaled in Russia since a

similar phase in the rule of Ivan the Terrible. Whereas
the rise of Germany and Japan began to move America
more and more away from her previously rigid isolationist position, Stalin in 1938 isolated his muddy, harsh,
Eastern Russia from the rest of the world more than at
any time since the Bolshevik Revolution.

10

Twenty years after the Armistice, in September 1938,
Europe again came to the brink of war during the
Munich Crisis. The Czechs, threatened by the Germans,
had alliances with France and with Russia; but France
depended on Britain, whose Chamberlain was yet unprepared for war; he was also willing to give Hitler a
last strong token of British good will. The result was
peace but at a high price. The world breathed freely
for a moment; Hitler glowered after his triumph. The
world, and Hitler, took little notice of Russia, whose international obligations expired with the settlement at
Munich, to which her rulers were not invited and with
which they had nothing to do.

It was the weakness of the Western European Powers that relieved Stalin of his obligations, just as twenty
years before the weakness of a Bolshevized Russia had
relieved the Western Allies from their uncomfortable
wartime promises of territory to an Allied Russia. All
of the evidence indicates that Stalin was indeed relieved; contrary to what Russia's friends in the West
thought, Stalin had no intention of going to war for
Czechoslovakia. From Munich onward he believed instead—a suspicion that has run like a maddeningly red
thread through Russian and Communist minds ever
since Lenin up to the present day—that the Western
Powers, to gain relief for themselves in the West, were
offering Germany a free hand against Russia in the
East. This was what most Communists in the West, too,

believed; it sounded logical; but it was not true. What was true—and this the Communists and Russophiles in the West did not even imagine—was that Stalin could best avert this danger by improving Russia's relations with Germany—indeed, by establishing common interests with Germany. No matter how loud the noise of Communist anti-Fascist and Hitler's anti-Communist propaganda rantings, no matter how cruelly Hitler crushed German Communists in his prisons and concentration camps, the diplomatic relations of the Russian and German States remained frigid but correct throughout. Now the time had come to nourish these relations with the prospects of a profitable great partnership.

In March 1939, breaking his word given but six months before, Hitler marched into Prague to incorporate the weak remainder of Czechoslovakia. This foolish move suddenly electrified British determination to resist him. Almost at once British guarantees were offered to the next intended German victim, Poland, whose alliance with France, too, was revived. Throughout the summer of 1939 President Roosevelt (whose offer of a world-wide Non-Aggression Instrument was, of course, rejected by Hitler) privately as well as officially supported and encouraged determination in London, Paris, Warsaw. The direction—though not yet the extent—of American aid against German (and Japanese) aggression was already obvious.

Not so obvious was the direction of Russia. A British and a French mission were sent to Moscow to negotiate a mutual defensive alliance against further aggressions of Hitler. What they—and the world—did not know was that even before their arrival Stalin and his new Foreign Commissar, Molotov (the Jewish Litvinov had been dismissed), had already established very promising contacts with Germany. What the British and the French found out soon was that the Russian price for an alliance—carefully concealed under new diplomatic verbiage—was potential Russian control of some of the independent neighbor nations they had lost twenty years before. This the British and the French—it must be said, to their honor—could not grant. Hitler, the professed champion of Anti-Communism, did.

On 22 August 1939 in Moscow the infamous Pact between Hitler's Germany and Stalin's Russia was signed. Officially a Treaty of Non-Aggression, it contained a Secret Protocol providing for the partition of Eastern Europe—north of Hungary and of the Balkans— among themselves. With it, Poland was doomed and Germany's back was secured. The Second World War began within eight days of the Pact that stunned the world as did no other diplomatic event in a hundred years.

The German armies conquered Poland. Toward the end of the campaign Russia suddenly entered in the east and advanced to the demarcation line designated by the Pact and reconfirmed a month later (a line east of Warsaw that, by and large, coincides with the so-called Curzon Line proposed by the Allies in 1920 and is now the eastern frontier of the Polish Republic). Stalin demanded, and received, military and naval bases in Estonia, Latvia, and Lithuania. He demanded territory from Finland. The Finns resisted. In the winter of 1939–40, when fighting had ebbed to a standstill on the Western Front, a new White War flared up in the northern forests between Russia and Finland. The latter had the sympathy of the world, including some help from the United States (Roosevelt had offered mediation between Finland and Russia before the outbreak of the war); France and Britain were even ready to intervene on Finland's side and thereby turn the Scandinavian situation to their advantage when the initially poor Russian war effort improved and in March 1940 a Treaty in Moscow concluded the Finnish War. In April, Hitler's forces conquered Denmark and Norway. In May his armies were flung forward in the West. In June they crushed metropolitan France into submission.

President Roosevelt, still hampered by strong American isolationist inclinations and by the prospective presidential election, tried to move as swiftly as he could to establish far-flung American defenses in the western Atlantic and to strengthen the armor of fighting Britain.[4] The actions of Russia, the other great neutral, were not marked by any such generosity and foresight: they were parochial, narrow at their worst, ruthless and cunning at their best, impressed by as well as fearful of Germany, Stalin treated the British with a calculatingly insulting tone. Like Mussolini, he took the occasion of the German victory in the West to advance his own national ambitions and security: brutally he forced the three unfortunate Baltic nations to become member "republics" of the Soviet Union; he tore more than old Russian Bessarabia from a trembling Rumania. Thus he fully collected the share allotted to him by the Germans in the infamous Pact; and the frontiers of his Russian Empire in the West began to approximate the old lines of Tsardom before 1914.

In the summer of 1940 there arose a triangular relationship of greatest significance. After the collapse of France, Hitler was still willing to offer peace to Britain (if only the British would acquiesce in German overlordship over most of Europe); but led now by the indomitable Churchill and aware of increasing help from the New World, the British in their finest hour defied the German offer and the ensuing hail of German bombs. Churchill, in turn, cautiously suggested to Stalin that Britain and Russia, the two remaining Great Powers on the edges of a German-dominated Europe, might improve their relations somewhat; but Stalin, suspicious and fearful, spurned these British advances; instead, he turned to Hitler. In November 1940 he sent Molotov to Berlin. The parochial naggings of this extraordinarily

[4] Roosevelt's actions in 1940 do much to lessen the impact of his errors in 1943–45, which would otherwise overwhelmingly darken the historical reputation of his statesmanship.

steadfast but unimaginative Soviet diplomatist about Russian demands for military enclaves in Bulgaria and Finland aggravated Hitler, who, already allied with the Japanese, would have preferred to discuss the possibilities of a great division of Europe, Asia, and Africa among the Four Dynamic Proletarian Nations of Germany, Italy, Japan, and Russia. Upon Molotov's return from Berlin, Stalin ordered him to draft a Soviet proposal for the spheres of such a great division. But by that time Hitler had decided to attack Russia. Indeed, his decision originated earlier, at the very moment when he saw that Britain would not make peace with him: he believed that if he were to eliminate Communist Russia, too, the British (and the Americans) would see the senselessness of the war against his Germany.

From December 1940 onward the German armies began massing against Russia. Outwardly the good relations between Berlin and Moscow continued to prevail; and the sudden Balkan campaign in the spring of 1941 (where resistance against Germany was actively encouraged not only by Britain but by America) delayed the opening of the Eastern Campaign. But such a great military enterprise could not remain secret for long. Churchill and Roosevelt sent report after report to Stalin to warn him against the onslaught. The crafty Russian leader now proved himself to be not merely wicked but cowardly. He kept spurning the Western Allies, while with every means he tried to impress Hitler with his friendship and good will (even after the German war machine moved across the Russian frontier and bombed Russian cities, his Ambassador in Berlin mumbled that the German war declaration might have been a mistake). All of this did not help him. On 22 June 1941 the Germans and their allies invaded the Soviet Union. Immediately Churchill and Roosevelt promised every possible support to the Russians. But the Russian armies, considerably unprepared, retreated and lost battles all along the front; by October the Germans were deep in Russia, beyond the Crimea and at the gates of Leningrad and Moscow.

There was but one excellent diplomatic move that distinguished Stalin's statesmanship before the German attack. In April 1941 he suddenly offered to the Japanese a Non-Aggression Pact, which they accepted with some eagerness. To both Russia and Japan the Pact secured the relative advantage of a one-front war. Thus, like Hitler in 1939, Stalin in 1941 could face the prospects of a tremendous war at least with his back secured. From July 1941 it was slowly becoming evident that the principal ambitions of Japan were directed southward and not westward, at Indochina, Malaya, Singapore, and the Dutch East Indies as well as at the consolidation of their conquests in China. There was in Japan an underhand domestic tug of war between the radical nationalists and the relatively conservative party around the Emperor; by October 1941 the former won out, unwittingly assisted by the rigidity of American diplomacy that took restrictive measures against Japan.

By the fall of 1941 American outposts, having been moved forward into Iceland and Greenland, together with the United States Navy, which had extended its operations to the middle of the Atlantic, waged almost what was an undeclared war against Germany, whose leader, however, did not yet choose to declare war on the United States. It was Japan whose brilliant but unscrupulous surprise attack on Hawaii brought the great American Republic finally into the war on 7 December 1941, after all hopes for a diplomatic settlement between Washington and Tokyo had evaporated.

On the same day that tropical Pearl Harbor stood in flames, in the other part of the world in a snowstorm Russian divisions were first driving back the Germans from their advanced outposts near Moscow. On 7 December 1941, therefore, the gigantic Russian and American Empires became allies with Churchill's Britain. Even though the military fortunes of the Second World

War did not begin to turn until almost a year later, at Guadalcanal, El Alamein, Algiers, and Stalingrad, 7 December 1941 was the turning point of the Second World War. From that day onward the defeat of Germany, Italy, and Japan was assured. What remained were the questions: when would this occur and what form would it take?

11

There is no need to recount here the sequence of military events until the end of the Second World War. In 1942 the advance of Germany and Japan was reversed. In 1943 their conquests were reduced. In 1944 their forces were beaten. In 1945 their power was destroyed. Their wickedness and their follies insured that the Grand, and Temporary, Alliance of the Anglo-American Atlantic Democracies with Communist Eurasian Soviet Russia would remain unbroken to the end, even though it was not unvexed by suspicions and misunderstandings emanating almost always from the Russian side.

We must say something at this point about the Russian contribution to the Allied victory. It is true that Russia was thrown into the struggle not by adherence to principle but by the assault upon her by her equally unprincipled former German partner. But it is also true that the Russian nation rose to the occasion heroically; that Stalin employed the sentiments of patriotism successfully; that, as sometimes happens in the history of dictatorships, the latent repressed energies of the nation prospered in the colder, freer air when released for the purposes of a patriotic war. It is true that Russia came close to the brink of defeat and that American and British assistance to Russia accumulated into staggering amounts. But it is also true that the massive bulk of this aid did not reach Russia until after the Battles of

Moscow and Stalingrad, when the Russian armies had already reversed (though not yet conquered) the German might. Thus the American assistance was not the factor in these battles, though it was probably a main factor in the swiftness of the Russian armed movement into Eastern Europe later; and we must remember that when in 1944 the great Anglo-American armada invaded France, for every German division facing Eisenhower in the West three others were tied down in the great retreating struggle against the Russians in the East. It is true that desertion accompanied the great advance of the German Army into Russia, that many thousands of Russians, Ukrainians, and Tatars moved spontaneously over to the Germans' side. But it is also true that opportunism as much as conviction may have been the principal motive; for these tendencies current in 1941 and 1942 ceased after the Russian victory at Stalingrad. It is true that Russia, somewhat like a late giant scavenger, did not advance upon Japan until the very end of the war. But it is also true that it was the American General Staff that had eagerly solicited the Russian entry against Japan throughout. After the Second World War, especially in America, a myth about the unique warring powers of Russia prevailed. Within a few years the passions of the cold war changed this myth into the belief that the corrupt forces of a Communist Russia, racked by desertion, were rescued just in the nick of time by the unthinking serendipity of American aid. Both of these myths are nonsense.

We have already seen how decisive the American contribution was to the Allied victory in the Second World War. It did not alone save either Britain or Russia from disaster; but without American intervention British courage and Russian determination probably would not have been sufficient to insure Hitler's complete defeat. Thus throughout the war the power and the prestige of the United States rose in an ascending curve, surpassing the power of Britain by 1943 and even the land power of Russia by the end of the war. It is for this reason that the mishandling of historic opportunities by the United States around that time turned out to be regrettable; it was to lead directly to the tragic conditions of the cold war.

At any rate, the fate of Europe had already come to depend principally on Russia and America when their Armies, one coming from the east, the other from the west, sealed the fate of Hitler's Germany by meeting along the Elbe in April 1945.

On the banks of that river, carrying the flooded wreckage of spring and war, American and Russian soldiers, fired with friendly sentiments and with drinks, celebrated late into the night. Among the soldiers of the 58th Russian Guards' Division there were some whose home was Vladivostok, who came to the middle of Europe from the shores of the western Pacific; it is quite possible that among the soldiers of the U. S. 69th Division there were some whose home was Seattle or San Francisco; they, too, had been sent to conquer halfway around the world. Their first meeting took place not only in the middle of Germany; they met in the middle of European history; for Torgau is about midway between Wittenberg, where Luther's fire of great revolutions started, and Leipzig, where Napoleon's course of great victories ended. It may be another hundred years before historians—that is, if by that time the scientists have not destroyed the prospects of history—may see whether the meeting of the American and Russian Armies at the Elbe meant the end or a beginning of a new historical epoch. We, at this time, can only attempt to describe what followed that event during the next twenty years.

CHAPTER II

The Crystallization of the Cold War

(To 1947)

1

It is now possible to point out in time the beginning of the cold war, to identify the markers at the beginning of the dangerous new curve on the road of Russian-American relations. It all happened within two years, from the Yalta Conference to the so-called Truman Doctrine, from the spring of 1945 to the spring of 1947. In 1945 the first open misunderstandings arose; in 1946 the first important American countermeasures were taken; in 1947 the previously warm sentiments of the American and Russian peoples toward each other gave way to grimness and near enmity. By 1948, three years after Americans and Russians had toasted together the fall of Berlin, Americans spent their blood and took the risk of war in defense of the people of West Berlin against a Soviet blockade. By 1950, less than five years after American generals (including MacArthur) had solicited the entry of Russian armies into Manchuria and Korea against the Japanese, American troops supported from Japanese soil were fighting a war against the North Korean Communist satellite of Russia.

It is not possible, however, to treat these events apart from their immediate antecedents. History, unlike a book, is not formed by clearly separated chapters; its chapters overflow into each other; and the relation of causes to effects is human, manifold, indeterminate, and enduring rather than mechanical, predictable, accurate, and closed. What, then, were the reasons for this great reversal of alliances and sentiments? We cannot restrict them to a chronicle of the incidents and frictions that began to accumulate between Russia and the United States once their wartime alliance was over, as if the cold war grew out of a sudden series of deplorable accidents. On the other hand, it would be unreasonable to seek the origins of the cold war in a comparison of the theoretical texts of Marx or even Lenin with, say, those of Jefferson or Wilson, as if theory were stronger than history, as if the Russian-American struggle had been "inevitable" from the beginning. It is to the closing years of the Second World War that we must look to see the more or less direct causes of the great reversal—to the conflicting and confusing war aims of the three principal Allies, represented and exemplified by Churchill, Roosevelt, and Stalin.

Beyond survival, the British aim was to establish, after the reduction of Germany, a reasonable European and international balance of order. Beyond survival, Stalin's main aim was to establish, together with the reduction of Germany, his control over most of Eastern Europe. The survival of the United States was never seriously threatened in the war; but apart from certain considerations of American strategic interests, the officially admitted aims of the United States, beyond the defeat of the enemy, were pre-empted by vast and unrealistic legal drafts about the future function of the United Nations. Stalin (and Asia) were to profit, and Churchill (and Europe) to suffer, from the confusion of these American aims.

But the clarity of perspective must not distort the proportions of a historic landscape when viewed in retrospect. From the following pages the reader may deduce the impression of Russia the Brilliant New Villain, America the Thoughtless Young Dupe, and Britain the Tragic Old Hero in a historic drama toward the end of the last great war. Even if these impressions are transferred to the three great national representatives, they are not more than half truths: Stalin, while surely often villainous, was not always brilliant; Roosevelt, while often breezily thoughtless, was surely no dupe; and Churchill, the British hero, was voted out by his own people, while his spirit continued to be young rather than old: his tragedy and victory mixed. And we must consider the broad force of Momentum in history, a force that, even more than Foresight, governs the actions of mankind, especially in this age of democracy: for the reversal of sentiments and of opinions was much slower than the reversal, detectable in retrospect, of certain policies. We must keep in mind that though in retrospect we may discern the first British preoccupations and tentative moves against undue Russian expansion as early as 1942 (and American ones in 1945), admiration for Russia was a tremendous force moving British public opinion, her leaders, and her representatives even in 1945, and its predominant momentum continued in America (where the images of public opinion, policy making, and political leadership are even more involved with each other) well into 1946. We must remember that even Churchill at Yalta would not risk a break with Stalin; that, together with his anxieties and profound preoccupations about the plans of the latter, he continued to feel sympathy and admiration for the military efforts of Russia. It is with these considerations in mind that we must begin to trace the painful course of events from Moscow through Yalta and Potsdam and Berlin to Seoul.

2

There was no question even before the end of the war that Russia would emerge as one of the Great Powers of the world. There was no question that, even more than her prestige, Russia would increase her power and her possessions. There was no question that her main ambitions concerned not international Communist prestige but primarily Eastern Europe. All this was revealed by Stalin himself long before Yalta and early in the war. There was no question that, considering the great Russian contribution in the war and their own geographical situation, the Western Allies had no choice but to agree to some of these Russian demands. The tragedy was that they, and particularly the United States, did not face this situation until it was too late—until the Russians were in possession of more than their Allies, and perhaps even they themselves, had expected (and that they even now, after more than twenty years of largely undisputed possession, seem not to have been able to fully digest). Here was the source of the cold war.

Here, too, may be the source of great future eruptions. Here we must say something about the importance of Eastern Europe. The First World War erupted in, and mainly because of, Eastern Europe. The principal mistakes of the peacemakers after the First World War were made in Eastern Europe. The Second World War broke out in, and because of, Eastern Europe. Its development suggests that during the first half of this century the point of gravity of European and perhaps even of all world history may have been shifting toward the central and eastern parts of the continent, just as five hundred years earlier it shifted from the Mediterranean to western and northwestern Europe. The battles deciding the balance of Europe had been fought then in the Lowlands, at Rocroi, Blenheim, Fontenoy, Waterloo, Sedan; now they were fought at Tannenberg, Warsaw, Stalingrad, Budapest. Even so, the Western Allies up to now did not devote sufficient attention to Eastern Europe. The Russians, more naturally, did.

Still, it would be a mistake to attribute such long-range historical wisdom to Stalin's wartime calculations. His ambitions were expansive; but they were national rather than international, Russian rather than revolutionary; and his greed as well as his fears had a strong parochial element at their core. The stubborn consistency of his minimum demands reveals much in retrospect. In December 1941, when the dire noise of German guns rattled the windowpanes of Moscow, he would devote the larger part of his negotiations with the visiting Eden about Russia's European frontiers. At that time, resting on the principles of the Atlantic Charter drafted by himself and Roosevelt but a few months earlier, Churchill could refuse to discuss in detail such things as the Russian title to the Baltic Republics. Nonetheless, he knew that in the long run some satisfaction to certain Russian territorial demands, demands that resembled very much those of Tsarist Russia, could not be avoided. Consistently Churchill sought thereafter to make an agreement with the Russians, the sooner the better, to commit them before the victorious hordes of the Soviet Army would surge into Eastern Europe and Germany.

There were two ways to limit Russia's prospective conquest and the forceful Sovietization of large parts of Eastern, Central, and Southern Europe. One was diplomatic, the other military; and though the two ways could not be altogether separate, circumstances dictated the different emphases. The military way was to precede the Russians in Central and Eastern Europe where and when this was still possible: Churchill tried to convince his American allies a dozen times but always in vain about the military feasibility of small-scale Allied landings in the Adriatic in 1942 and 1943; about the exploitation of the Allied advance through Italy in the direction of Trieste, Zagreb, Budapest, Vienna in 1944 and 1945; and we shall see how he was to argue the necessity to push through Germany as far east as was possible in 1945, at a time when a ruthless and cynical Russian interpretation of the Yalta agreements was already evident. But throughout he met with the rigid and, indeed, suspicious rejection of his plans by

President Roosevelt and his circle as well as by virtually all American diplomatic and military authorities. The political way, suggested above, flowed from the recognition that Russia had a principal share in the Allied victory but that this share should be reasonably defined before the end of the war. Here, too, American distrust frustrated Churchill: Washington steadfastly refused to discuss such political particulars until the war was over and the peacemaking to take place. Preoccupied with the prospects of the British Empire and always refusing to quarrel openly with the United States, Churchill could not press his European policy to a successful conclusion.

What were the sources of this American attitude? We can sketch their outlines in brief. There was in them an almost engaging broad benevolent element of naïve optimism, complemented by the less attractive American habit of not wishing to think about unpleasant problems. We are fighting a war, said the American generals; leave politics out of this. There was the feeling that America should be the Arbiter of the coming World Peace; a new, Rooseveltian version of Wilsonianism.[1] There was the earlier mentioned sense of pioneer comradeship with Russia, unduly exaggerated by propaganda during the war years. There was the latent sense of distrust of Britain and of the traditions of Euro-

[1] Entire libraries have been written by now about Roosevelt and the war. Among the hundreds of their political, polemicist, and professorial authors there is but one who saw through Roosevelt's global plans with profound insight. It is General De Gaulle, on page 241 in the second volume (British edition) of his War Memoirs. We must keep in mind that Churchill's indebtedness to Roosevelt and his considerations of American friendship weighed heavily in the writing of his masterly volumes, while the insight of the great Frenchman could be expressed with greater independence. Hence the clarity of his description of Roosevelt's "will to power, cloaking itself in idealism," is indispensable and superb. For reasons of proportion and of space in this book I cannot do more than draw my readers' attention to it at this point.

pean politics, felt by Left-wing Democrats as well as
by Right-wing Republicans. All of these sentiments
coalesced in the American attitude, singularly exemplified by President Roosevelt, of seeing the United
States as an Arbiter, a Moderator, a Great Midway
Power between Britain represented by that admirable
old Tory imperialist Churchill and the new rough pioneer Communist Democracy of Russia represented by
that admirable crafty Uncle Joe. This American attitude—glossing over many of the crudities with which
the Russians treated not only British but American interests during the war—was the key to the great wartime conferences from Teheran to Yalta and Potsdam.

Meanwhile the appetite of the Russian Bear grew.
It was at Teheran in December 1943 that Stalin was
informed about the finality of the Western decision to
go ashore in Normandy and drive directly toward the
Rhine; it was there that he could see for himself Roosevelt's demonstrative efforts to dissociate himself from
Churchill on certain important issues. We have already
noted that Stalin had been amazingly consistent in his
minimum territorial demands even in the darkest days
of the war. It is not at all certain that his plans about
the rest of Eastern Europe were equally clear and consistent; what is certain is that after Teheran these ma-
tured quickly; and he exploited the divergencies between the American and British policies to the full.

3

The decisive phase of the Second World War in Europe developed after the Conference at Teheran; in
February 1945, by the time of the Yalta Conference, it
was already over. In the first days of 1944 the Soviet
armies, moving westward, crossed the eastern borders
of prewar Poland. Subordinating their main lines of
military advance to larger political purposes, in the

second half of 1944, postponing their final thrust from Warsaw to Berlin, they swept into Rumania, Bulgaria, and Hungary. By the time of Yalta their armies had already conquered most of the Balkans; they were pushing across western Poland, western Hungary, and Czechoslovakia. In the West the mighty Allied forces under the command of General Eisenhower did not invade Europe until June 1944. Together with the small armor of a renewed France they freed Rome, Paris, Brussels, from the Germans in the summer, after which the Allied advance bogged down at the frontiers of Germany, compromised further by the last desperate German counterattack in the Ardennes in December. Not until March 1945 did the by then predominantly American forces cross the Rhine in the West, to race across Germany until they were to link up with the Russians coming in from the East.

The future of Western Europe was no longer in question: there the victory of the Western Allies was to reinstate the exiled or renewed lawful and democratic national governments after the liberation. The future of Germany was yet to be decided by the last armed effort; at any rate, neither America nor Russia nor Britain would alone take responsibility for the future government of a defeated Germany, about which in 1944 joint Anglo-American-Soviet consultative commissions were set up. But would the rest of Europe simply fall into Russian hands? Preoccupied with their dramatic liberation of Western Europe and by the no less dramatic American successes in the Western Pacific, the United States viewed the Soviet surge into Europe with supreme unconcern. Yet it was in Eastern and Central Europe that the gravest political problems of the future lay.

By the end of 1944 no power existed in Eastern Europe that could effectively resist the Russian conquerors. Hitler's armies retreated in defeat. The tragic effort of some of the best sons of the German nation to overthrow the tyrant Hitler and save some German power and integrity had failed in July. The rising of the incredibly heroic Polish Resistance Army in Warsaw was crushed by the Germans while the Russians stopped their advance to watch this horrible extirpation with cynical impassivity. Throughout Eastern Europe the few native and émigré Communists emerged in the shadow of a million Russian bayonets. For we must keep in mind that the coming Sovietization of the Eastern European nations was nowhere spontaneous or popular. Except for Greece, Yugoslavia, and Albania, where considerable Communist-led partisan armies constituted themselves during the war, there were fewer Communists in Eastern Europe than in France or Italy, for example. It was not the appeal of Communists but the presence of Russian armed power that produced Eastern Europe's Sovietization and Europe's division.

We have already seen that among the powerful leaders of the world Churchill alone wished to correct this fateful tendency of events; but by 1944 he was the least powerful among the Big Three while his own national interests were divided world-wide. Vexed and deeply concerned with the noncommittal and insensitive policy of his American allies, in May 1944, when he finally knew that no Anglo-American troops would arrive in the Balkans, he turned directly to Stalin to propose a temporary division of the Balkans and Hungary into British and Russian spheres of influence. In a Percentages' Agreement he proposed that in Rumania and Bulgaria, Russian influences should prevail, while in Greece, British influences should be predominant; for Yugoslavia and Hungary he suggested a 50–50 formula. Stalin, cunningly pleading at first that the United States should be consulted (and insisting on a 75–25 ratio for Hungary), finally subscribed to this rough and ready scheme during his Moscow Conference with Churchill in October 1944.

This is how Churchill was able to save at least Greece

from falling into the Soviet sphere. There, in the wake
of the German retreat, a civil war was already developing between the Communist and non-Communist forces
of the Greek national resistance. In December 1944
Churchill sent British forces into Athens to defeat a
violent Communist uprising. It is significant that for this
decision he earned angry American strictures[2] but no
criticism from Stalin at all.

Thus the lines of the division of Europe were already
forming before Yalta and before the end of the war.
Except for Athens and Helsinki (aware of American
sympathies for that small country, Stalin stopped short
of conquering all of Finland) by early 1945, in all of
the capitals of Eastern Europe, Russian (or, as in Belgrade and Tirana, Russophile Communist) armed
power ruled supreme.

4

Still, all was not yet over. The government of Poland
and the status of Germany were about to be discussed by the Big Three at Yalta. "Poland," wrote
Churchill, "had indeed been the most urgent reason for
the Yalta Conference, and was to prove the first of the
great causes which led to the breakdown of the Grand
Alliance." It was in Poland, and because of Poland, that
the Second World War began. Poland was the ally of
Britain from the beginning; her heroism distinguished
her throughout. At Yalta, Poland was discussed during

[2] "We shall not pull Britain's chestnuts out of the fire"—
meaning that they will not involve themselves in European
quarrels to the benefit of Britain—this phrase crops up often
in the records of American public figures about 1944. It is
interesting that Stalin used the very same phrase in the spring
of 1939, justifying Russia's reluctance to ally herself with
Britain against Hitler. In little more than two years these
Americans, like Stalin in 1941, were to learn a hard lesson
about chestnuts and fires.

seven of the eight plenary sessions. The results were poor.

We have already seen that Churchill knew that a victorious Russia could not be expected to forsake her traditional ambitions of national unity and security: she would gain the lands of Eastern Poland with their mixed Russo-Ukrainian populations up to about the so-called "Curzon Line." Churchill's idea was to grant this to Stalin during the war, in exchange for a Soviet recognition of the independence of the rest of a democratic Poland, which, in turn, would be compensated for her eastern losses by territories from Prussian and Silesian Germany. But American noncommittalness, the intransigence of the Polish exiled government in London, and, above all, the growing appetite of Soviet Russia had begun to work against Churchill's plans well before Yalta. From early 1943 onward the Russians not only demanded their new frontier but began to form a subservient pro-Communist satellite group, the so-called Lublin "Government," as the future masters of Poland. By the time of Yalta they were installed in Warsaw.

Unlike in certain parts of the Balkans, the immutable conditions of geography allowed no prospect of Anglo-American forces getting to Poland by the end of the war. Indeed, during the war (as to some extent she is still now) Poland was the index to Russian political motives. Because of this great Muscovite emphasis on Poland it was in Polish-Russian relations that Russian ambitions and their fearful consequences appeared earliest during the war. We cannot trace their instructive development in detail here. It is enough to say that by the time of Yalta the best Churchill and Roosevelt could strive for was a joint agreement with Russia for a Polish government composed of democratic and Communist, London and Lublin elements together that would, in turn, guarantee free elections as soon as possible.

Concerning Europe the Yalta Agreements may be summed up as follows:

Poland. The new Soviet-Polish frontier was, by and large, confirmed. A new Provisional Government was to be formed. Free elections were to be held. The Allied Ambassadors would supervise this process. The new Poland would be compensated by territories from East Prussia and other former German lands east of the Oder River, details of which would be established by a peace conference.

Yugoslavia. Since the national Communist forces of Tito had emerged as the major power in that country, a Yugoslav government of National Unity, similar to the Polish pattern, was to be formed, involving a limited broadening of the Tito regime by inclusion of a few personalities from the Royalist exile government still in London.

Germany. No important new decisions were taken. The already demarcated occupation zones were confirmed. Upon British insistence France was included among the Four Allies and a French occupation zone was to be established. A permanent body of consultation, consisting of the four Foreign Ministers, was set up. The Russian claim to the East Prussian port of Königsberg was recognized.

The rest of Europe. A general but vague declaration of policy toward liberated Europe promised democracy and free elections to the peoples of the continent.

It was about the Far East that important and more precise secret agreements were made, primarily between the United States and Russia:

Within three months after the end of the war in Europe the Soviet Union promised to enter the

war against Japan. Russia would regain her losses
from the Russo-Japanese War of 1904–5: the
southern half of Sakhalin; predominant Russian
control in the Chinese Eastern Railway; a Russian
naval base at its terminal, Port Arthur, and Dairen.
The *status quo* of Russian-controlled Outer Mongolia was confirmed. In addition the Soviet Union
would acquire the Kurile Islands immediately
north of Japan. The provisions affecting China
were to be confirmed further by an agreement between the Russian and Chiang Kai-shek governments.

Concerning the future international world organization (that, too, was primarily an American concern),
the framework of the United Nations, already discussed
at Dumbarton Oaks in 1944, was finally prepared. Russia agreed to participate in the constituent meeting of
the U.N., to meet on 25 April in San Francisco in order
to establish the Charter of that organization. In turn,
taking into consideration the multiple vote of the members of the British Commonwealth, and the weight of
the United States among the states of the Western
Hemisphere, two additional seats were given to the
Ukrainian and Byelorussian Soviet Republics in order
to increase the Soviet Union's votes to three. The most
important body of the United Nations would be a Security Council, governed by the permanent constituents
of the Big Four, dependent on their unanimity. This
virtual introduction of the veto, soon to be abused by
the Soviet Union, was proposed by the United States
months before Yalta; it reserved the independence of
action for the Great Powers in matters vital to their national interests.

During the past twenty years we have seen bitter
criticism and even abuse of the Yalta Agreements,
stimulated by the passions of the cold war. This is no
place for an elaborate estimate of Yalta; let it be said

only that the trouble with Yalta, in many ways, was the opposite of what its critics have been charging. Except for the American-Russian agreements concerning the Far East, the trouble with Yalta was just that the agreements were vague and general rather than precise and secret instruments. It is, indeed, not so much the Yalta Agreements but the haste with which they were drafted that ought to be condemned; as always in human affairs, it was not the letter but the spirit that counted—the momentum of that American spirit that did not wish to face the realities of the Soviet prospect until it was too late and that, consequently, did not insist on the proper Russian interpretation of the Agreements until it was too late.

For even though at the time of Yalta the Russians were masters of Eastern Europe, there were still opportunities to correct the developing awesome balance. There was a way; but there was no sufficient will in the right direction. The surprisingly swift Western Allied advance through Germany in the last months of the war provided the way; misunderstanding on the part of America frustrated the will.

5

Soon after the Yalta Conference the last phase of the war began, with Germany the main battleground, the same Germany that soon afterward became the central scene of the developing cold war.

The political division of Germany was one of the favorite ideas of the prospective victors, in order to put an end to the Prussian-dominated era of a centralized Germany. Even Stalin went along with this idea almost until the end of the war while the United States seemed to have less enthusiasm for it throughout; for a while she advanced the rather senseless Morgenthau Plan of economic chastisement instead. But the division of Germany at the end of the war emerged not along historical lines; it came out of the military demarcation lines first set up by an Allied technical group, the so-called European Advisory Commission, in 1944. Roughly speaking, each of the Allies was to be responsible for the military occupation of about one third of Germany: the Russian Zone in the east, the British in the west, the American in the southern part of the country. At Quebec and Yalta these arrangements were confirmed with some modifications, of which the establishment of a French Zone was the most important one. A similar quadripartite scheme for Austria was agreed upon early in 1945. Berlin and Vienna, both within Russian Zones, were to be symbolically policed by all four Allies. If we consider that they were first drawn up at a time when the Western Allies were still much further than the Russians from Berlin, these plans were not unreasonable; and it is significant that in late 1944 the Russian member of the EAC urged, together with the British, that the United States accept an Occupation Zone in Austria. What was unreasonable was the American unwillingness to modify these arrangements as late as in the summer of 1945. For by that time the first skirmishes of the cold war had begun.

While the terrible drama of the war closed with a fiery curtain over Germany, the ominous signs could no longer be misread. The Russians showed every intention of interpreting the Yalta Agreement in Poland as if it meant little else than a confirmation of their sole dominion over the affairs of that country: they and their agents hunted down and lured into traps the independent elements of Polish political life. They intervened brutally in the affairs of Rumania. They hindered the function of Anglo-American observers in the Eastern European countries as much as possible. Their junior ally Tito threatened to break into Trieste at the risk of armed clash with the outposts of the Anglo-American armies in Italy. Having learned about secret surrender talks in Berne between the Allies and German commanders in northern Italy, Molotov and Stalin crudely accused Churchill and Roosevelt of betraying their alliance. For the first time even Roosevelt replied with indignation, a significant first change of his mood. But within a few days the President was dead. And what Churchill was to call the deadly hiatus "between the fading of President Roosevelt's strength and the growth of President Truman's grip of the vast world problem" had already arisen. For by that time Churchill had finally concluded that the advance of Soviet Russia had become a mortal danger to the free world.

In the history of democracies seldom had there been such a difference between the surface impression of historic developments and the deeper dark currents of their reality. While the glow of victory filled the hearts of hundreds of millions with hope and relief, in the secret communications between London and Washington and Moscow the dim dark streaks grew dominant. On the day when Western and Eastern armor met at Torgau, cutting Germany in half, the San Francisco United Nations Conference met in a Pacific metropolis of radiant sunshine, while in its padded hotel chambers of council the arguments of Eden and Molotov over Poland were marking a bitter deadlock.

Meanwhile, however, the last opportunity to redress the balance had already developed. After the crossing of the Rhine in March, the advance of the Western Allies was so rapid that by the time of the German collapse their units stood in many places within the Russian Zone; indeed, American armored troops crossed into Czechoslovakia and were approaching Prague. It was now Churchill's intention that the Western Allies should arrive as far east as they could, possibly including Berlin, Vienna, Prague. This, then, in response to the Russians' obvious violations and unilateral interpretations of the Yalta Agreements, would prove a valuable trump card in their hands.

But, as so often in this last decisive phase of the war, his wishes were not heeded by the American political and military leaders. Eisenhower refused to move quickly toward Berlin; indeed, he informed the Russian General Staff about the lines of his advance; and in early May, upon a Russian request, he ordered the withdrawal of American troops from western Czechoslovakia. These were momentous decisions. Hitler was dead, and the war was over; but the descent of the iron curtain over Eastern Europe was beginning. Once more Churchill begged Truman not to withdraw to the Western zonal boundaries before the coming Conference at Potsdam; but Truman, still listening to his advisers, refused.[3] Thus in July 1945 the American and British armies withdrew for a hundred miles to the west, abandoning yet another crucial area to the Soviets in the heart of Europe. All Churchill could exact was American concurrence to his insistence that the Russians should no longer ominously delay the entry of the Western Allied authorities and garrisons into Vienna. This was granted.

Thus by July 1945 the geographical conditions of the cold war were set. For more than twenty years after the end of the Second World War in Europe, up to this day, the United States, Great Britain, and Soviet Russia have not made a general Peace Treaty; they have not even been able to convoke a general European Congress of peacemaking. While in the Far East a Peace Treaty with Japan was made in 1951, and while in Europe a number of minor treaties confirmed the existing order of things, the status of Germany is still not settled. What happened after 1945 was that the military divi-

[3] Nevertheless, his realistic grasp of world affairs had begun to show. His advisers, together with Joseph E. Davies, proposed that he meet with Stalin before meeting with Churchill. It was upon the latter's angry but dignified refusal that the President did not persist; indeed, as he later revealed, Davies' proposal for such a Truman-Stalin meeting was made without his authorization.

sion of Europe, with Germany in the middle, expected
as a matter of course to be temporary by the Americans, but more or less permanent by the Russians, hardened into the Main Fact in the political order of the
globe. Around this cold rigid Fact, modified only in the
singular important instance of the Austrian State Treaty
in 1955, the conflicting passions and fears of East and
West crystallized into the frigidities of the cold war.[4]

In this Age of Democracy all this was done without
the least consent of the peoples involved. It is in respect
of the democratic principle, then, that this account of
political events cannot forgo mentioning the great migration of peoples that took place in 1945 and thereafter. Evidence exists that one reason for Stalin's disregard of the Allied promise of free elections was that he
saw in it but a sop to American public opinion; but it
was Lenin who triumphantly said that in 1917 there
had been no need for elections in Russia, for the soldiers
decided to quit the war: they "voted with their
feet." Millions of Germans and Eastern Europeans voted
with their feet in 1945 and, indeed, during the sixteen
years that followed. Before the advancing Russian armies, whose Asiatic misconduct and insensitive brutalities confirmed, alas, at least that part of Nazi propaganda, fled first three millions of Germans from the east;
there followed another five million Germans expelled by
the Czech and Polish governments from their regained
or newly conquered territories; there were to follow another four million East Germans and Eastern Europeans
during the next fifteen years. Some of them, risking

[4] Thus Europe was divided into a Western and a Russian
group of states—but, then, this was what Russian diplomacy
wanted and what it had exacted from France and Britain
before 1917, during the First World War. In this respect,
too, Stalin fulfilled the imperial ambitions of the last Tsarist
regime. As with the policy of the democratic Roosevelt, I
am not saying that this was what Stalin exactly and consciously wanted; I am only saying that this is what he did.

death at worst and homelessness at best, are still slipping through the iron curtain. It is this kind of testimony that may demonstrate best the unpopularity and the ultimate failure of Soviet rule in Eastern Europe for future generations to come.

6

The Potsdam Conference, the last meeting of the Big Three during the war, was held at the end of July; it did not produce important new agreements or changes. Upon generous British and American suggestions about the internationalization of the great waterways of the globe to the benefit of Russia, Stalin raised certain territorial demands at the expense of Turkey. This, together with all other European territorial questions, was shelved for the future Peace Conference. The Polish question still remained foremost on the agenda. The new Communist-dominated Polish provisional government was already recognized by the Western Allies; Stalin still promised free elections; now the main problem was the frontier between Poland and Germany, left open at Yalta. Churchill and Roosevelt had agreed to run the new frontier along the Oder and the Eastern Neisse rivers; Stalin and the Poles insisted on the Western Neisse. This meant the additional Polish gain of western Silesia and the city of Breslau (and Stettin in the north). Meanwhile the Russians had already turned over these territories to a Polish Zone of Administration. There was no agreement. The problem was postponed, even though Churchill, for the last time, wanted to make this point of principle a strong point at the risk of a break. He could not enforce his determination.

By the time of Potsdam the collapse of Japan was imminent, with her navy destroyed and the home islands under continuous aerial bombardment. Through Moscow the Japanese had made the first tentative steps toward suing for peace; but Stalin was not too eager to promote these efforts before his armies could enter to reap his Far Eastern share from the collapse of the Nipponese Empire, while the American news of the first successful explosion of an atomic bomb in New Mexico for the first time produced some American reluctance to share the fruits of Far Eastern victory with the latecoming Russians. An Anglo-American ultimatum to Japan was issued from Potsdam. Within three weeks thereafter two atomic bombs were dropped on Japan, Russia declared her war, and the Japanese surrender was made official and complete.

It was not the Bomb that defeated Japan. Its launching may have accelerated somewhat the progress of Japan's ultimate conviction of defeat. Still, we cannot record the event of the Bomb without reflecting briefly on the human and historic (rather than on the technical) aspects of that dreadful event. There are symbolic coincidences in its circumstances. It was European, and particularly German, Science that during the past hundred years produced progressive technical wonders, including hitherto incredible weapons of destruction. Before the Hitler era it was in the electric intellectual atmosphere of Weimar[5] Germany that atomic research was most advanced. With Hitler's coming, many of these scientists, most of them of Jewish origin, sought refuge in Britain and in the United States. There, spurred by the fear that Hitler might get from their German colleagues the developing secret of a nuclear bomb, some of them succeeded in mobilizing American scientific leaders so that President Roosevelt was willing to underwrite the great cost of the American experimental projects for an atomic weapon. While the eminent physicists of Germany, partly because of human reluctance, partly because of Hitler's lack of interest in that direction, did not develop such a program, their refugee colleagues, solidly supported by the re-

[5] Where Goethe created his Faust. That is symbolic, too.

spectable phalanxes of American scientific authority, succeeded. The first nuclear reactor at Chicago in December 1942, the explosion of the first atomic bomb at Alamogordo, New Mexico, in July 1945, and the bombs cast on Hiroshima and Nagasaki in August 1945 are but outstanding stages in the progress of this awful movement; but the technological character of these stages should not obscure its real motives, which, as in every historic endeavor, were formed by the human factor, by personal motives and choices, conditioned by the political, racial, religious, national inclinations of responsible men. Quartered secretly under the most rigid restrictions of military conformity, this feverish group of men led a fantastic and totalitarian existence in the Indian desert of America, where in the dark dawn hours of 16 July 1945 the inhuman Bomb burst first with its inhuman blaze. On that very day opened the Conference at Potsdam.

Alamogordo and Potsdam: the new ruin wreaked atop the primeval American desert and the meeting atop the ruins of the desert of historic Prussia. Like the Battle of Moscow and Pearl Harbor, like the meeting at Torgau and at San Francisco, there is something symbolic in the coincidences of these great events, historical turning points provoked by Germany and consummated by Russian and American might in the Western and Eastern hemispheres almost exactly half a world apart.

7

After some hesitation, it was decided to tell Stalin about the Atomic Bomb at Potsdam. There is evidence that he did not appreciate its portents at that time. But this was, of course, a weapon with the greatest potential political impact. By the autumn of 1945 the Prime Minister of Canada revealed the first serious evidence of Soviet atomic espionage to the American President and the British Prime Minister during a specially arranged hurried visit. For four years thereafter the United States possessed a monopoly of the Atomic Bomb. It did not exploit this great advantage at the expense of Russia; indeed, in 1946 it offered, through the United Nations, to abolish atomic weapons through a system of international inspection. The Russians, beginning to work on their bomb at that time, refused.

The wake of a modern war may be in many ways more depressing than war itself. During 1946 many millions of Europeans were still living in half-ruined houses, hardly heated in winter, wearing thin clothes, having little to eat. In France and Italy the Communists, now the monopolists of popular radicalism, managed to attract one fourth of the electorate. Meanwhile the first skirmishes between East and West increased and intensified. In Greece civil war threatened to flare up again, as Communist guerrillas appeared all over the north. In Persia, which had been occupied by Russian and British forces jointly for four years before the meeting in Germany, Stalin was unwilling to evacuate the important border province of Persian Azerbaijan; Communist Albanian mines sank a British warship; Stalin demanded from Turkey the province of Kars and Ardahan, won by the Tsar's Russia in the nineteenth century; Molotov requested a Russian share in the former Italian colonies in North Africa; the dreary wranglings of American and Russian authorities in Korea and within the United Nations had begun; the Russian Veto was used over and over again, while throughout Eastern Europe (and also in East Berlin) the highhanded assertion of unilateral Russian domination continued. But the suspicious Stalin, no matter how aggressive and malevolent, felt that he could not always and altogether risk a complete break with the United States. He, as Tito was to reveal later, was unwilling to support the latter over Trieste at the risk of war in 1945; American pressure made him recoil in Persia in 1946; to Turkey

warships of the American Mediterranean Fleet were
sent for a brief demonstrative visit; and even in Eastern
Europe the political picture was still not uniform. In
Bulgaria the Communists were temporarily set back because of an American protest against obviously rigged
elections; in Poland and Rumania they postponed elections until 1947. Where reasonably free elections were
held, even under the shadow of Russian might the Communists failed to get a majority; their polling ranged
from 40 per cent in Czechoslovakia through 20 per cent
in Hungary to 3 per cent in the Russian Zone of Austria. But, even though some of his policies in Eastern
Europe were surprisingly cautious and gradual, Stalin
was determined to keep his Eastern European Empire
at no matter what the cost—short of war.

From Potsdam onward through 1946 the meetings of
the Council of Foreign Ministers, save for minor agreements, proceeded through one deadlock to another,
while Stalin went ahead with his plans to isolate his
newly won domains from the rest of the world. The reaction of American might to this was still developing
slowly and piecemeal. To understand this we must once
more cast a glance on the prevailing tendencies of
American public opinion in order to dispel those simplicist explanations by hindsight that have sought to
find in conspiracy, corruption, or stupidity the main motives of American behavior at that time. The inchoate
but deep and widespread inclinations of American isolationism had not yet been spent. Suspicions of Britain,
perhaps even more than of Russia, together with such
factors as American Jewish impatience with prevailing
British policies in Palestine and the general, though insubstantial, mood of ideological radicalism so current in
American intellectual and New Deal circles, continued
as the momentum of wartime public opinion still kept
on for a while. Save for the isolated Catholic press and
a few provincial exceptions, the American press continued with a Russophile tone. As late as March 1946 the

profound warnings pronounced by the visiting Churchill in his "Iron Curtain" speech at Fulton, Missouri, were disavowed by the American government, including Dean Acheson, the later Secretary of State; not until September 1946 did there come a break in the presidential cabinet that led to the resignation of the Russophile Henry Wallace; as late as 1948 Progressives and Communist sympathizers maintained some influence in the complex process of American opinion-making while the automatic Republican and Right-wing criticism against the Democratic Administration remained for years parochial and undistinguished by a single intelligent utterance of an alternative international policy. None of these evidences of mental and political lassitude should, however, obscure the principal condition: no matter what their motives, the people and the government of the United States showed generosity, patience, and understanding toward their Russian ally for a long time. Hitler, not Chamberlain, was alone responsible for the outbreak of the Second World War; Stalin, not Truman, was the principal architect of the iron curtain and the cold war.

We must not believe, however, that the supreme strategic interests of the United States were left unconsidered even during these last remnant years of the sentimental era of wartime illusions. We must keep in mind the peculiar double level of American statesmanship that is so often manifest in the discrepancy between announced policies and certain very significant actions. It is to the enduring merit of the American people that during all this time it did not care to turn its power to profit from the distress of a ruined world to build an Empire; but it must not be thought that the masters of the American ship of state were utterly unaware of those conditions that promised the development of the Pacific, the Atlantic, and even the Mediterranean into American-dominated strategic lakes of the globe. The Philippines received their promised independence in 1946, but American bases remained. After 1940 the United States acquired a host of British island bases in the Caribbean and in the Western Atlantic. While a neutral Denmark was compelled to cede the Virgin Islands to the United States in the First World War, subjugated by Germany in the Second, Denmark acquiesced in the establishment of American bases in Greenland and Iceland. On his way back from Yalta, Roosevelt summoned the potentates of the Arab Near East to his ship and received American commercial, industrial, and aerial privileges from them. And at points where the vital interests of the United States were felt, action was early and swift. At Malta, where, preceding Yalta, Roosevelt met Churchill only briefly and refused to go into important arrangements with the British about the prospective problems of Europe, he indicated that he understood the need of occupying at least as much of *Western* Europe as speedily as possible. His distrust of the independent De Gaulle, the American caution when it came to the problem of whether to tell the Russians about the Atom Bomb, the quickness of the secret American move to quarry the German rocket makers and scientists before these could be captured by the Russians, the swift American reaction to the first evidences of serious Soviet espionage about the atomic secrets of Canada and the United States, the instinctive and intelligent American decision not to let the Russians participate in the occupation of Japan, the determined establishment of American military authorities in Okinawa and other conquered Japanese islands in the western Pacific, the American support to certain aggressive native ambitions at the expense of the remaining colonial possessions of European Powers in the Dutch East Indies[6] and in certain parts of Africa, for example—all these are significant develop-

---

[6] In 1948. But already in 1943 Roosevelt had suggested that the French relinquish their rule in Indochina and that the British cede Hong Kong to China.

ments in retrospect. To this must be added the establishment of the United Nations' headquarters in New York, a location that not only symbolized but indeed characterized the American features and conditions of that organization.

A new and world-wide American expansion was beginning; and whether the accumulating evidence of Stalin's brutalities and ambitions between 1945 and 1947 alone caused this reaction or merely accelerated its development is not important—at least not here.

Up to this point in the narrative I have had to dwell in some detail upon the events of the Second World War, and particularly upon its decisive phase in 1944 and 1945. But now, when we can see how the principal conditions of the cold war have been formed, the inevitable encumbrance of manifold detail may be lessened somewhat. The conditions were set: and from now on the consequences developed so directly that except for a few extraordinary and unforeseen events no decisive change occurred in world affairs for the next decade to come. In 1943 it was by no means certain that the Second World War would end in so tragic a division of Europe or that the Grand Alliance between Britain, America, and Russia would, far beyond its expectable problems and crises, degenerate so quickly into outright enmity. By 1947, however, it was reasonably certain that Western Europe, West Germany, and Japan would depend more and more on American power; that the United States would continue taking over the burdens and the privileges of what previously had been principally British responsibilities in many places of the world; that the division of Europe was an accomplished fact; that the expectation of a German Peace Settlement within a reasonable time was out of the question; that the United States would not positively challenge the Eastern European *status quo;* that she would not employ her atomic bombs against Russia except in an unmistakable case of war; that, save for the contingencies of madness or extreme miscalculation, Stalin would not choose such a war. Thus the cold war began—or, rather, it grew into being.

CHAPTER III

The Division of Europe Becomes Rigid

(To 1949)

1

Even before the end of the war Stalin alone of the Big Three remained in power. Because of the unexpected electoral victory of the British Labour Party, Churchill was replaced by Attlee during the closing days of the Potsdam Conference, where Truman had come to occupy Roosevelt's seat; soon thereafter General De Gaulle, disgusted with the new quagmire of French politics and parliaments, resigned and withdrew from public affairs. The conditions of defeated Germany and Italy were not yet auspicious for the emergence of important leaders; in China civil war was in development. Thus outside the Russian Empire the world suddenly seemed devoid of the impact of great personalities; but soon it became evident that Providence and political fortune had provided the English-speaking nations and, with them, the free world with two persons whose statesmanship proved adequate for halting the eventual spread of Russian Communist tyranny. Their integrity, bravery, and intelligence shines in retrospect through those murky years. They were Harry S. Truman and Ernest Bevin, the provincial Midwestern politician who through a stroke of fate became President of the United States and the erstwhile dock worker who became Foreign Secretary of Britain in 1945. They soon made a strong and confident impression. There were many reasons to believe that, unlike Roosevelt, the inexperienced Truman would let the

State Department and its Secretaries determine the ultimate conduct of American foreign policy; but Truman, who, unlike his successor, knew from the first moment the historic traditions and necessity of strong presidential leadership, soon grasped the master wheel of the American ship of state with both hands. Meanwhile in Britain the somewhat colorless Prime Minister Attlee left to the Foreign Secretary the main task of insuring the continuity of British foreign policy in the best interests of the nation; and as early as in August 1945 Bevin's first speech in the House of Commons, direct and critical of Russian actions in Europe, dispelled the fears (or the hopes) of those who believed that the new Labour government would go to great lengths to accommodate the Russians.

Still, the United Kingdom, victorious in principle but impoverished in essence by the war, was no longer able to maintain her far-flung imperial and political commitments in all parts of the world. The British decision to grant full independence to India, Pakistan, Burma, and Palestine was made; from 1947 on, the British flag was hauled down in many places, while elsewhere the relationship of Britain with her colonial dependencies was newly reformed to the benefit of the latter in the name of the democratic principle. Yet none of these great transformations, including the dramatic birth of the Indian and Pakistani Republics on a vast subcontinent, and not even the birth of the State of Israel, had, as yet, an important bearing on the dreadful balance of the developing cold war. It was in Greece, the historic ally of Great Britain, that the turning point was reached.

2

By early 1947 President Truman and the American government finally concluded that the United States would not further acquiesce in the Communization—

either by conquest, civil war, or subversion—of any portion of Europe or the Near East that lay outside the Russian imperial sphere in Eastern Europe. The so-called Truman Doctrine, the Marshall Plan, and the Containment Policy were the three principal instruments of this historic (though, in retrospect, hardly avoidable) decision.

In February 1947 the British government informed Washington that it could not alone sustain the armed struggle of the Greek state against the growing irregular tide of Communist guerrilla armies. Without hesitation Truman assumed the burden. His Message to Congress in March 1947 called for American military aid to a Greece and Turkey threatened by Russian pressure and eventual blackmail. After some debate congressional consent was given. Forthwith American military missions and abundant supplies were sent to these Eastern Mediterranean countries. In about a year the Greek Army defeated the Communist guerrillas everywhere. The prominence of American sea power in the Eastern Mediterranean, manifested by the Sixth Fleet, remained an important factor in world affairs ever since that time.

It was evident in 1945 that American statesmen were more responsive to economic than to political arguments when it came to the distressing problems of Europe. Predicated upon the belief that Communism would primarily prosper from economic chaos, fortified by strong inclinations of American common sense as well as by traditional American institutional generosity toward poverty and distress abroad, the so-called Marshall Plan was proposed in June 1947. The United States was willing to support, in the form of goods, gifts, and easy loans, the rebuilding of the war-torn economies of Britain and Europe. The aim of the Marshall Plan was the ultimate restoration of the balance in Europe by quickly getting the weakened nations of Western Europe to their feet again; but its purposes were broader politically and even more generous economically, since Marshall Plan Aid was offered to Eastern Europe, including Russia, too. But Stalin refused to take it; indeed, he forced his westernmost ally, the still semi-democratic republic of Czechoslovakia, to reverse its original acceptance.

His purpose of dividing Europe was now clearer than ever before. Peace Treaties were already signed with former German allies, Italy, Hungary, Rumania, Finland; but except for a few unimportant details these amounted to a confirmation of the respective Armistice instruments signed before; moreover, Russian forces were not withdrawn from Hungary, Rumania, or Poland, where they were to guard communication lines to East Germany and Eastern Austria, pending a German and Austrian Peace Treaty. About the latter the Council of Foreign Ministers was getting nowhere during interminable debates. Through a variety of methods the Russians took ruthless advantage of the subject condition of their captive European neighbors; and in 1947 Stalin speeded up the gradual Sovietization of his prospective satellites. With crudest methods, on occasion not shunning even the open involvement of Russian police organs, the representatives of the remaining democratic forces in Hungary, Rumania, Poland, Bulgaria, and East Germany were sometimes deported, at times imprisoned, on occasion silenced, and frequently chased into Western exile. In Yugoslavia and Albania, where no Russian troops were stationed, the police control of the Communist regimes was most complete. In some of the other satellites, particularly Hungary, the unpopularity and the occasional ineptitude of local Communist satraps were still an obstacle despite the power of their Russian masters. In June 1947 the semi-democratic government of Hungary had to be transformed by force; thereafter unabashed police tactics were the main instruments for insuring Russia's mastery in Eastern Europe.

Though, except for increasingly angry protests and

for individual actions of personal rescue, the Western Powers did little to intervene, Stalin's brutalities in Eastern Europe deeply affected the free world. There was, therefore, not much argument about the wisdom of the American Policy of Containment—in essence a political expression of the purpose that motivated the so-called Truman Doctrine and the Marshall Plan—formulated by the thoughtful American diplomatist George F. Kennan and first indicated in 1947 in an article under the cipher "X" in the American magazine *Foreign Affairs*. Since Communism preaches a perpetual struggle against the non-Communist world, in certain historical situations this preaching may be rationalized into ruthless expansion unless it is met by the force of determined resistance. At least in Europe, it was now the supreme interest of the United States to prohibit the further overflow of Soviet influence beyond the already swollen limits of Stalin's new Russian Empire. This is the gist of the Policy of Containment. It sums up the events of the year 1947. It also suggests the principal direction of American world policy up to the present day.

3

By 1948 the leadership of Soviet Russia and of the United States over their respective halves of Europe (and also of Korea) was an accomplished fact. While Russian domination was welcomed by but a small minority of people in the eastern, American predominance was welcomed by most people in the western half of the continent, including Germany, where events were soon to test the measure of American determination. The American response to the Russian threat in Berlin was one of the finest American hours in the history of the cold war. A sense of relief and of Western Christian unity was diffused in the hearts of millions of Europeans. It was in 1948 that the term "cold war" became popular currency (I think the phrase was Walter Lippmann's[1]). But it was also in 1948 that the term "West" acquired a new popular historical meaning: the cold wind of the Bolshevik threat from the steppes of Asia, instead of chilling the spirit into the mortal rigor of hopeless fear, suscitated significant new fires in the European spirit; and the unity of Western Christian civilization was first felt by thinking men in Europe and America together. In the American presidential election of 1948 (the first in a series of elections that were followed all over the free world with an interest that unconsciously reflected the knowledge that here the American people were choosing the leader of the West) foreign policy played no important part; and the unexpected victory of Harry Truman, no matter what its domestic electoral sources, assured the leadership of the free world of this vigorous personality for some years to come. In Western Europe the distressing aftermath of war and poverty still prevailed; but the spirit of people, especially of the young postwar generation, compared favorably with the radical and cynical mood of disillusionment that had followed the First World War. A genuine movement toward European Unity became current; together with constructive intellectual and religious tendencies, it was also manifest in politics through the broad emergence of Christian Democratic parties whose leadership was provided by the personal excellence of De Gasperi in Italy, Adenauer in Germany, Robert Schuman in France, Figl and Raab in Austria. Partly as a consequence of these developments and

[1] The term "cold war" (like "foreign affairs") is, in its way, misleading. The law of physics does not prevail in human affairs, where extreme tendencies may lead to opposite results. When relations grow cold and freeze into enmity this is but one step from the hot outburst of conflict. The division of Europe and the hostile spheres of interests froze into clear rigidity; but the passion of peoples, that main agent of democratic history, warmed up into foggy fervor.

partly because of the blunders of Stalin's own brutalities, the Russians now suffered their first important set-
backs in Europe.

Stalin's main blunders bear the names of Czechoslovakia, Yugoslavia, and Berlin: this order is chronological
as well as one of ascending importance. In February
1948, nine years after the rapacious Hitler broke his
word and incorporated the remains of a cowed Czech
state, not knowing that his easy subjugation of Prague
was an unnecessary act whose symbolic character gal-
vanized resistance against him in the West, Stalin acted
in a similar vein. The Czechoslovak Republic, whose
pliant leaders had done everything not to arouse the
ire or suspicion of their mastodon Russian neighbor, was
not to be given the least opportunity to maintain certain traditional contacts with the West. Even without the
pressure of Russian armies, a Communist *coup d'état*,
dramatized by the following suicide of the Foreign Minister, Jan Masaryk, effectively transformed Czechoslovakia into an all-out Soviet satellite. The Western Powers were not willing to intervene; but at least they took
immediate steps to close their ranks and proceed with
military preparations. A Western European military
and political Instrument was signed in Brussels in March
1948. American military preparations in Germany increased while the still existing gradual differences in
the Eastern European captive nations were being reduced to uniformity through drastic measures that indicated impatience and worrisomeness on Stalin's part.
But on 28 June 1948 a Communist bulletin brought to
the world the surprising news of a break between Stalin
and Tito.

Few events indicate more clearly the Russian national and imperialist, as distinct from Communist, motives and ambitions of Stalin than the dark (and at
times almost comic) story of Russian-Yugoslav misunderstandings. In no Eastern European country was there
a native Communist Party stronger than in Yugoslavia;

Tito was indeed the most radical of the Communist leaders. But he was a junior partner, not a satellite; he had won his civil war, if not wholly without Russian help, at least not as a carpetbagger suppliant following behind the mighty hordes of the advancing Russian armies. Frequently Stalin preferred submissive Russian agents to steadfast Communist leaders; he grew dissatisfied with Tito's Communist South Slav nationalism from 1945 onward. As often before in history, the crudities of Russia's interventions alienated those who had been her best friends in the Balkans. When his Russian agents proved unequal to the task of upsetting Tito, Stalin pronounced Communist anathema upon Yugoslavia; but his subsequent threats only united the still considerably divided Yugoslav nation behind their audacious leader, whose prestige, in contrast to Stalin's, now began to rise throughout the world.

In line with his policy to eliminate the last Western islands within his monochrome East European Empire, Stalin began to put pressure on Berlin in the spring of 1948. It will be remembered that Berlin, like Vienna, was divided into four occupational zones where for symbolic purposes all four Allies were keeping garrisons, an arrangement made in 1944 and which indeed had precedents going back to the occupation of Paris after Napoleon's fall.[2] Unlike Vienna, where a central Austrian government resided, Berlin was not the seat of a German government. In its eastern suburbs the Russians were setting up the rudiments of an East German satellite "administration," while the West German government, after some debate, made its home in Bonn in 1949. These arrangements consequent to the practical division of Germany were not yet advanced when in May 1948 the Russians began to suspend supplies and communications between West Berlin and the West-

[2] Another precedent was the plan for a quadripartite occupation of Constantinople, made between Russia and the Allies in 1915.

ern Zones of Germany. The object of this Blockade was the starving of West Berlin into submission. It was broken from the very beginning by the resoluteness of the population in concert with Allied military determination to stand fast. Along the official highway connecting Berlin with the Western Zone, General Clark proposed to break through the Blockade with an American military column; but President Truman chose instead to depend on American ingenuity of material supply: the famous Berlin Air Lift was created. Throughout the dark autumn and winter days of 1948 a Berlin still largely in ruins drew hope and succor from the drone of American transport planes, piloted often by the same men who but a few years before cast bombs on that same city. Almost a hundred American, British, and French airmen gave their lives for the cause of freedom in Berlin. Their sacrifice was not in vain. The Russian bluff was called. In May 1949 the Russians lifted the "Blockade."

By that time, however, outside Berlin the division of Germany had begun to ossify. In Bonn in the West and in Berlin-Pankow in the East two rival German governments were installed. The Russians were beginning to give arms to their East German police and semi-military forces, while in the West the American military emphasis grew. In 1947–48 arrangements were made for American bombers to be installed on airfields in Britain. Increasing amounts of American military equipment were given to Western European nations. The permanent establishment of American forces in Europe was finally sealed by the instrument of the North Atlantic Treaty Organization, signed in April 1949. It was already foreseeable that unless important changes were to occur in the political relations of Moscow and Washington, at least a partial rearmament of West Germany by the United States and its allies would be but a matter of time.

Thus four years after the end of the Second World

War within Russian Europe all resistance was crushed; but Russian and Communist expansion seemed to have come definitely to a halt. The Russification of Stalin's new Empire proceeded with its Communization; in 1949 a Russian Army Marshal was made Defense Minister of the Polish Republic, and the elimination of even proved and radical Communists who were not known Russian agents began in the rest of the satellite countries. Still, it was not Russian but American power that swayed the destinies of most of the world. The number and the extent of American—not of Russian—military, naval, and air bases was increasing. In Europe at least, Communism failed everywhere outside the iron curtain; strong American support insured the victory of the Christian Democrats in the important Italian elections of 1948. The European balance was becoming redressed—at the cost of the abandoned Eastern European nations, but at least altogether somewhat in favor of the West. In May 1949 Molotov, whose impregnable Soviet Russian conservatism was associated with a crucial decade of Russian history and expansion, left the Soviet Foreign Ministry; Stalin appointed Vishinsky in his place. This was at least a sign of his dissatisfaction with the way Russian foreign affairs were going.

Up to that time the United States had the atomic monopoly; but now in 1949 the Russians exploded their first atomic bomb—promptly monitored by American atomic agencies under whose aegis the plans for the construction of a Hydrogen Bomb had already begun.

4

At this point, with the first phase of the cold war closing, we must look at the ideas guiding the course of the now inimical Giant Powers of the world. Both the Russian and the American peoples were told by their leaders that the Second World War brought no real peace, that they might have to gird themselves anew for the dangers of war. This was possible without drastic interference with the domestic prosperity of America; it was not possible in Russia, where the regimen of privations continued well after the war. While the American people, relentlessly reminded of their new international responsibilities, tended more and more in an internationalist direction, Stalin's Russia became more national and isolationist than it had ever been since the Communist Revolution. By 1949 the similarities between Stalin's regime and that of Tsar Nicholas I, for example, were so obvious that pages and pages from books such as the Marquis de Custine's description of his travels in the Russia of the 1840s would apply to Stalin's Russia in the 1940s. Yet Americans sought the key to Soviet conduct in dogma rather than in history, in the internationalist, revolutionary, and agnostic doctrines of "Leninist" Communism, rather than in the nationalist, isolationist, and orthodox features that were emerging under Stalin, whose xenophobic, puritan, anti-Semitic terror suggested a Tsar rather than any international Communist revolutionary figure, and whose exhortations of Russian national pride had deep roots in Russian history but no source at all in Marx. The American reaction, concentrating on the dangers of international Communism rather than on the historical features of Russian aggressiveness, was of course only in part due to the myopic American intellectual tendency of taking dogmas and abstractions unduly seriously. It was also motivated by a strong domestic undercurrent, a political anti-Communist reaction against the more and more obvious falseness of wartime radical and Russophile propaganda. It was the reaction against the illusions of an intellectual and political generation now on trial: and such shocking developments as the evidence of amateur espionage practiced by people like Alger Hiss, an able young top organization man of the New Deal generation, now revealed to have been at

least a Communist sympathizer, were to carry this popular anti-Communist reaction far.

Thus we find a curious and corresponding duality in
American and Russian political tendencies by 1949. On
one hand, the Soviet Union was, more than ever, the
mighty leader of international Communism; but in reality the tendency of her tyrannical ruler was more national than international, more Russian than Communist, more isolationist than revolutionary; for example,
there were (and, to some extent, there still are) two
iron curtains, one separating the satellites from the rest
of Europe, the other separating Russia from her Sovietized satellites, and the latter was even thicker than
the first. On one hand, the United States was committing herself only to the defense of certain Western European and marginal strategic territories against the
eventual armed aggression of Russia; but in reality the
tendency of this American policy was becoming ideological rather than political, and world-wide rather than
limited to America's admittedly vast national and Allied
interests; for example, the United States, even though
she had written off Eastern Europe, assumed the role
of a co-ordinating center of Eastern European émigré
political and propaganda activities, while her military
intelligence organs were already involved in an underhand struggle with their Soviet counterparts throughout the whole world.

For on a vital point American intentions and purposes were not entirely clear. We have seen that while,
during and even after the war, the Anglo-American purpose was, broadly speaking, the reconstruction of Europe, the Russian purpose was the division of Europe;
now Europe was torn asunder, and Containment and
NATO were to keep any more portions from going. But
there was an important difference between NATO and
Containment that has remained obscured and unresolved until the present day. The original purpose of
Containment—at least in Kennan's concept—was to build

up Western Europe and commit the United States in her defense so that after a while Russia's rulers would see how their aggressive behavior was leading them nowhere. Thereafter the growth of a peacefully prosperous Europe would modify the unnatural division of the continent into Russian and American military spheres, so that ultimately a mutual reduction of the more extreme Russian and American commitments and of some of their most advanced outposts could follow. These were not insubstantial speculations. They rested on political and geographical realities. In 1949 there was still an important marginal area in the middle of Europe that was not yet fully ranged within either the Russian or the American military system (indeed, until 1951 the only line where NATO's territories bordered on Russia was the short stretch of the Russian-Norwegian frontier in the extreme North). Finland was under the Russian shadow, and the Russians insisted on binding Pacts with Finland; but Stalin told the Finns that their country could remain outside the Soviet political sphere if Sweden, across the Baltic, was to stay outside NATO and the American military sphere. In 1948 neither West Germany nor, of course, Switzerland and Austria, were part of NATO; the latter, a battleground of competing intelligence agencies, was, like Germany, divided between Eastern and Western Zones but, unlike Germany, not quite hopelessly: there was a central Austrian government sitting in Vienna, recognized by both Washington and Moscow. Further to the south neither Yugoslavia nor Greece nor Turkey belonged to NATO (the latter two were then included in 1951), while it is significant that the multiple military alliances that the Russians were tying among their satellite neighbors were not extended to Albania, the only geographically isolated member of the Soviet group of states. Thus a motley but unbroken middle European zone separated the Russian and American spheres from the Arctic to the Aegean. This was the design of Kennan, who was the head of Policy Planning in the Department of State at the time; but this subtle and reasonable policy was soon superseded by the simple and military anti-Communist concept of NATO. Where the original purpose had been the ultimate dissolution of the division of Europe and Germany, NATO was to contribute to the hardening of that division into permanence. Absorbed by this newer purpose, the necessary imagination of American statesmanship began to falter; and we shall see how thereby the character of the American state and society began to develop in a centralized and military direction.

The question, therefore, arises whether American policy had understood Stalin's ambitions well enough. It was formulated at a time when Russia in Eastern Europe proceeded with shocking brutality. Around the edge of the new Russian Empire conditions were uncertain: the Red froth bubbled in northern Greece; France and Italy seemed withering in political and economic weakness. It was of the greatest importance to halt what was considered "the Red flood" before it could trickle and flow into Italy, France, Western Europe. But was this analysis sufficiently profound? There is no sufficient evidence that Stalin in 1947–48 had planned to advance into France and Italy or that he had even contemplated the imminent victory of the Communist Parties in those countries; indeed, the evidence points to the contrary. His actions were aimed at consolidating, in some cases with frantic haste, his imperial realms in Eastern Europe; and it is quite possible that the American preoccupation with Western Europe may have suited his purposes: for thus American attention was diverted from Eastern Europe.

Perhaps it would be well to put ourselves into Stalin's position in, say, 1947. He regarded Eastern Europe as his; he also felt somewhat justified in this possession. Russia had won the war against the German invaders. Her cities were devastated, her armies bled white; with age-old Russian suspicion, Stalin was prone to underestimate the Allied contribution to the victory over Germany. Russia had carried the main brunt of the war, while the United States, without wounds, emerged as the greatest and most powerful nation of the earth. It was the Americans, now in possession of the Western European pastry shop, who a few years before let him have his Eastern European cake with such unconcern; why couldn't he eat it, after all? Now Stalin did not particularly contest American power: he did not challenge America's sphere; did it not seem to him, however, that the Americans were beginning to challenge *his* sphere? Always he was willing enough to go along with sphere-of-interest arrangements; he, again like Russian diplomacy in the past, was a *quid pro quo* politician of sorts. When Churchill, at Potsdam, complained about Rumania, Stalin would retort that he fulfilled their bargain by not intervening in Greece; when Churchill or Truman insisted upon Poland, Stalin answered that Poland involved Russian interests while he had not the slightest concern with how the British protected theirs in Belgium or Holland. But Churchill, that cunning old British Capitalist Enemy of Communism, at least understood him on that point; the Americans did not. Stalin did not really compete with them over Western Europe; but why were they now, after the war, two years after Yalta, getting worked up about Eastern Europe, protesting loudly about imprisoned Cardinals? He did not really challenge what to him amounted to the American domination of Western Europe; the financial assistance which Moscow had furnished the Italian Communist Party, for example, was far less than what the Americans poured into Italy before the 1948 elections. Why, then, the American meddling in Eastern Europe? Had they not won enough in the war? All of the Pacific and the Atlantic basins, plus Western and Southern Europe? With his narrow Oriental eyes looking westward from the Byzantine windows of the Kremlin, Stalin may have reasoned thus.

Thus an amused historian may say that the first few years, and perhaps even the first decade (I wrote this first in 1950) of the Russian-American crisis over Europe might have been due to a fundamental, mutual misunderstanding: Washington presupposing that the immediate Russian aim was to upset and conquer Western Europe, Moscow presupposing that the American aim was to upset and reconquer Eastern Europe—and that both presuppositions were wrong.

Thus a cynical historian may say (I added this in 1960) that Moscow and Washington did not make out so badly, after all. True, in 1945 and thereafter a more intelligent and imaginative American policy could have prevented the Russian advance into the very middle of Europe and thus spared much of the cost and the toil of the cold war; true, in 1945 and thereafter less crude and brutal Russian measures in Eastern Europe would not have provoked all of these countermeasures, including NATO, and Russian influence in Europe would not have been limited to the subject satellite capitals—but the cynic may say: so what? No cold war, no American dominion over one half, and no undisputed Russian dominion over the other half of Europe. No cold war, no rigid division of Europe—ah yes, a boon to Europe it may have been: but, if so, the Russians, for instance, would not be the masters of Hungary today, and the Americans would not be able to tie an armed Germany within their military system. Still, this imaginary cynic of a historian would not be entirely right— at least not yet. For, no matter how true is the maxim that one must want the consequences of what one wants, this maxim is seldom put into practice in the affairs of men and of nations; and it is especially true in democratic ages that the discrepancy between intentions and ultimate results is great, very great indeed.

CHAPTER IV

The Chinese Struggle and the Korean War

(To 1953)

1

During the first five years after the Second World War the situation of Europe thus hardened along definite lines of division. During the same time the weakened state of the European Powers resulted in national, populist, and Communist eruptions in Southern Asia, Indonesia, Madagascar, and Indochina. Of these racially inspired movements, advancing with weapons and political ideas borrowed from Europe, America, and Russia, the most important was the civil war that had developed on the vast mainland of China, ending only in 1949 with the victory of the Chinese Communists.

It is, however, not the record of the struggle between two Chinese armed factions but the record of China's relations with America and with Russia that primarily belongs to a history of the cold war.

Of all the nations of the white race, the United States and Great Britain had the relatively best record of benevolent and temperate behavior when it had come to colonial interests at the expense of China; and this ought to remain at least a matter of historical record, even though gratitude may be even less of a motive in the conduct of nations than in the conduct of persons. There may be no significant difference in the way American and European commercial, industrial, and maritime interests exploited a China languishing under her corrupt rulers during the nineteenth century. But at least during the first fifty years of the twentieth century the United States, moved by self-interest as well as by her traditional sentiments against colonialism, mitigated and indeed prevented the complete dissolution of the Chinese national state at least three times during the long confusion that followed the collapse of the disintegrating imperial government of China. In 1900, after China's defeat by Japan and the collapse of her Boxer Rebellion, it seemed that the partition of China was at hand; it was avoided in part because of the American declaration of the Open Door Principle. During and after the First World War, American prestige and power constituted the main instrument that limited the rapacious ambitions of Japan on the Chinese mainland.

Here we must again remember that, as in Europe, the large gains of Communism in Asia were consequent to the Second World War, which had been provoked by those two self-professed champions of anti-Communism, Germany in Europe and Japan in the Far East. It is one of the paradoxes of contemporary history that, notwithstanding the attributions of Machiavellian calculations to President Roosevelt by his domestic and Chinese critics, it was his insistence, upon Chiang's frantic urgings, that the Japanese clear out of China that proved to be the deadly stumbling block in the last difficult phase of Japanese-American negotiations in 1941.[1] Its immediate effects were the final deliverance

[1] At least the outline of these intricate events ought to be sketched here. There is no doubt that the Japanese Emperor and at least part of the Tokyo government really wished to avoid a war with the United States in 1941. Even though Roosevelt refused to meet Prince Konoye in Honolulu earlier, around 20 November the situation was such that a possibility for a compromise was discernible from the text of a so-called Japanese "Proposal B" that was not too far apart from an American *modus vivendi* proposal already drafted. But between 22 and 25 November it was decided in Washington not to present the *modus vivendi* to the Japanese; and the American note handed to them on 26 November contained conditions that, though excellent in principle, the Japanese

of the Japanese government into the hands of the Tokyo war party and the attack on Pearl Harbor a few
days later; its ultimate effects were the destruction of
the Japanese Empire and the emergence of a new Chinese one, whose master, however, was not to be Chiang
but the Communist Mao.

2

Much more involved, complex, Byzantine, and secretive is the history of Russia's relations with China: for
unlike the United States, the Russians attempted to
profit not only commercially but territorially from the
distresses of China, a tendency that recurs in the history
of Tsarist and of Soviet Russia alike.

Before everything, we must keep in mind that, as
other great land Empires, the Chinese Empire was

---

government could hardly accept: for they amounted to the
renunciation of almost all of Japan's successful conquests of
the past decade. The motives behind this American diplomatic reversal are still somewhat obscure. We know that
Chiang's friends, allies, lobbyists, and agents played a very
important role. Involved also were Owen Lattimore, at that
time President Roosevelt's representative with Chiang in
China; Harry Dexter White, a fellow-traveler in the government, an eager self-made Adviser in High Affairs of State;
and Lauchlin Currie, then on the White House staff, whose
Communist affiliations have been revealed since. We know
that through an unusually efficient and dedicated network of
Communist spies Stalin knew as early as October the details
of the planned Japanese attack southward in the Pacific, information that was of crucial importance for him at a time
when the fall of Moscow seemed imminent; it relieved him
from the fear of a Japanese attack; he could send his remaining divisions from the Far Eastern border to European Russia, where they may have helped decide the Battle of Moscow. Unlike Churchill and Roosevelt a few months before,
Stalin did not share this intelligence with his prospective ally.
Did his agents have some influence in the crucial American
withdrawal of the *modus vivendi* draft in November? Some
influence, perhaps; a decisive influence, probably no.

a multiracial and multinational one. During various phases of her long history she ruled Korea, Indochina, Tibet, Mongolia, and the Central Asian desert province of Sinkiang. The weakening of great Empires is usually marked by apoplexy in the center and anemia in the extremities. During the century before Pearl Harbor, China relinquished Hong Kong and other important maritime enclaves to European Powers; she lost Korea and Formosa to Japan; she abandoned the still largely uninhabited maritime provinces around the future city of Vladivostok to Russia as early as 1860. But China was seldom a great Pacific sea power; certainly not in the twentieth century, with the Japanese or American Navies dominant. More important, therefore, is what happened to the great outlying land provinces of this great Asiatic land Empire. Her sovereignty over Tibet and Sinkiang had become nominal; the influence of Britain hovered thinly above the first, and the influence of Russia prevailed within the second of these large desert provinces. During the First World War, China lost Outer (or Northern) Mongolia to Russia; well before the Second World War she lost the centrally important Manchuria to Japan, whose rulers erected a satellite state in the latter while the Russians had made their first Soviet satellite Republic out of the first.[2]

We have already seen that between the two World Wars the Russian attempt to spread Communism failed in Asia as well as in Europe; but in China the ideological defeat of Communism was not complete. In the early 1920s Soviet Russia supported the so-called Chinese Nationalists and the early Communists alike; but the guileful Chiang Kai-shek saw through the Soviet-inspired policy of temporary co-operation; in a preventive *coup* in 1927 he knifed the Communists to pieces in Canton. The Russian advisers and chief agents in

[2] To this we must add the smaller satellite "Republic" of Tannu Tuva. It was incorporated within the Soviet Union in 1944.

China scurried back to Moscow in obscurity and dismay. Thus China, and China alone, was the place where Stalin went along with the otherwise Trotskyan idea of actively promoting Communist revolutions abroad.[3] The sorry lesson of this adventure only confirmed Stalin's natural disinclination to further risk Russian security and prestige by extensive involvements in Communist movements abroad; surely it also contributed to his subsequent dislike of the Chinese. Consequently—eight years before his more famous Pact with Hitler—Stalin in 1931 and 1932 intimated to the Japanese the possibility of a Russo-Japanese partition of Manchuria (similar offers had been made by the Russian Tsarist regime to Japan concerning Korea a generation before). Later he even sold the traditional Russian share of the Manchurian railways to them. But the Japanese had no desire to share the conquest of northern China with the Russians. Their aggressive ambitions grew.

A few years later a Chinese Communist guerrilla army, led by the warlord Mao, unassisted and by and large unobserved by Stalin, began to gather after a long and arduous march in the remote western provinces of China. Thereafter Russia turned to promote a coalition of the Nationalist and Communist Chinese forces against Japan. For by 1937 Japan had joined the so-called Anti-Comintern Pact with Germany and Italy; the Japanese Army was not only on its way to conquer all the great cities of China but it began to probe by force the state of Russia's Far Eastern defenses on the Mongolian border. There, in 1938 and 1939, a hundred thousand Asian soldiers, Russian and Japanese forces with Mongolian and Manchurian auxiliary troops, fought two veritable battles near Changkufeng and Nomonhan in a limited war of the existence of which the rest of the world remained almost ignorant. The

[3] Mostly for domestic political reasons. He still needed the support of the wavering ex-Trotskyites within the Politburo.

Soviet forces repulsed the Japanese. The latter moved on with their conquest of eastern China along the sea. It was American, and not Russian, supplies and assistance that kept Chinese resistance going against the Japanese. Indeed, we have seen that Stalin concluded a Non-Aggression Treaty with Japan in April 1941 and that Russia remained neutral until the very last phase of the Far Eastern War. Significantly, one of the articles of the Russo-Japanese Pact, upon Stalin's insistence, was the recognition of the Soviet satellite *status quo* of Outer Mongolia.[4] Four years later, at Yalta, he put this first on the Far Eastern agenda, insisting upon American recognition of the same.

3

With Russia neutral, it was reasonable for the United States to be the most important provider and ally of China during the rest of the war. What seems less reasonable was the general American, and particularly President Roosevelt's, inclination to attribute exaggerated importance to the wartime effort and to the postwar influence of China. In this near obsession, sentimental rather than political elements were predominant (though, of course, the latter may not be altogether excluded). Roosevelt and his circle were fully imbued with the idea that the colonial possessions and privileges of Britain and of the European Powers were antiquated obstructions on the pathway of world progress. It is interesting that while Roosevelt did not seem to realize the extent and the ambitions of Russian colonialism, Stalin's policies and comments made to Churchill

---

[4] Already in 1922 there was irritation even among the internationalist Communists (Zinoviev) in Moscow because of Chinese Communist allusions to Outer Mongolia. In 1944 Mao expressed the hope that Outer Mongolia would rejoin the Chinese Empire after the war.

during the war do not at all indicate such a doctrinaire opposition to the colonial system. About China, Stalin stood closer to Churchill than to Roosevelt: Stalin, too, thought the American attribution of Big Power status to China nonsense. Indeed, if we consider the extensive strains under which Japan heaved during the war, struggling on far-flung oceanic fronts in many directions, the contribution of the Chinese armies—of Nationalists as well as of Communists—during the last phase of the Japanese War was disappointing.

In 1945, then, the entire Far Eastern scene was transformed by the Russian entry into the war against Japan. We have seen the Russian conditions for entering the war, granted by the United States at Yalta and confirmed at Potsdam.[5] These had nothing to do with international Communism. Even more than in Europe, they amounted to a reconquest of all of those territories and privileges that Tsarist Russia had lost to Japan forty years before. The official text agreed upon in Yalta said: "The former rights of Russia violated by the treacherous attack by Japan in 1904 will be restored"; and Stalin in his August speech spoke of the "shame of forty years" that was now expunged. In August 1945 a treaty between Stalin and Chiang confirmed the Yalta dispositions.

These Yalta Agreements about the Far East—more precise than those concerning Europe, and also more scrupulously kept by the Russian and American governments—thus brought Russian armies into Manchuria, Korea, and the Kurile Islands by the end of the war,[6]

---

[5] I said earlier that Russia entered the war somewhat like a giant scavenger. Still, it must not be thought that the date of Russia's entry was determined by the Atom Bomb one day before, or even by the swiftness of the Japanese collapse. Months before, Stalin had informed Washington that he would enter the war on 8 August, the date that he kept.

[6] For a few decades during the nineteenth century the Kuriles, too, had been Russian. It is interesting that upon the news of the Stalin-Chiang Treaty, a report of the Naval

while Truman's resolute words sufficed to make Stalin desist from his last-minute ambitions to bring Russian troops into the occupation of Japan.

We must now turn to sum up the development of the inchoate Chinese Civil War—or, rather, the last phase of a long series of Chinese civil wars—which developed anew by 1946. We must leave Korea temporarily aside, since different conditions prevailed there, with Russian and American troops installed and separated by only a temporary demarcation line of the 38th Parallel that, as in Germany, soon froze into a rigid political frontier of division. In China, on the other hand, neither Russian nor American armies were directly facing each other. True, the Russians made the withdrawal of their forces from Manchuria contingent on the American withdrawal from other parts of China; but they did not wish to be deeply committed and involved in China unless the United States were to do so. True, American marines and naval units helped to ferry advance troops of the Nationalist government up North to establish their authority after the Japanese surrender; minor American marine units remained, here and there, on the China mainland almost until 1949; but their presence was hardly more than symbolic. True, the invading Russians stripped and exploited Manchuria and contributed also in other ways to the evolving advantage of the Chinese Communist forces; but, after all is said, the Russians did evacuate Manchuria by late 1946, turning its cities over not to Communist but to Chinese Nationalist garrisons. Russian support to the Chinese Communists cannot be denied; but, on the other hand, this support was far less than American supplies to the Nationalists during the same period.

Indeed, until late in 1945 and until the very last

Affairs Committee of the U. S. House of Representatives, dated 18 August 1945, and unaware of the Yalta dispositions, urged that the United States establish bases in the Ryukyus and the Kuriles.

phase of the Chinese Civil War in 1949—when the victory of the Chinese Communists suddenly seemed incontestable and complete—Stalin's support of Mao was halfhearted. For a long time Washington as well as Moscow attempted to maintain tactile contact with both slices of the Chinese pie; but Stalin was careful with his Chinese finger—hadn't he burned it before in the 1920s? The American government tried mediation twice; and as late as 1949 it indicated its dissatisfaction with the corruption and conduct of its now defeated and suppliant Chiang regime, which fled to Formosa from the mainland. Stalin, on the other hand, refused to believe almost to the very end that the Communists could win such a complete victory; he advised Mao to go slow[7]—advice that Mao did not follow. As the Chinese Nationalist government began its gradual flight southward, Ambassador after Ambassador abandoned it during this sorry anabasis of defeat; significantly, only the Ambassador of the Soviet Union remained with it to the last.

Mao, like Tito, won almost alone. Almost, but not quite—for, as in Yugoslavia, the completion of the Communists' victory in China was made possible because Russian, and not Anglo-American, armies had arrived in Manchuria, as in the Danube Valley, at a decisive time. The analogy is not complete: unlike Mao's opponent Chiang, Mikhailovitch, Tito's patriotic opponent, received few Allied supplies and was sorrily abandoned in the end. Still, Mao and Tito were the only two leading Communists who won their own civil wars, facing not only Anglo-American hostility (which they themselves had provoked) but also certain signs of Russian

[7] Remembering the occasional enthusiasm of certain American officials for Mao during the war, until mid-1947 the Russians feared that the Chinese Communists would be unduly close to the United States. This was at least one of the principal reasons why Moscow refused to break relations with Chiang's regime even as late as in 1948.

distrust and suspicion (which they themselves had hardly deserved) from the beginning.

Not until May 1949—at a time when it was forced to acknowledge the failure of its Berlin Blockade in Europe—did the Russian government turn its full support to the Chinese Communists. In October 1949 the People's Republic of China was proclaimed. In a last attempt to influence Chinese radical sentiment on the mainland, the State Department, led by Dean Acheson, while condemning the Communist leadership as traitors to Chinese national interests, pointed out how the Russians were extending their rule over territories that formerly belonged to China. Possibly Russian sensitivity to such arguments was a principal factor that led to their subsequent broad agreements signed with the new Communist regime in Peiping. While the essence of the 1945 Yalta and Sino-Soviet agreements remained, the instrument of a Mutual Assistance Treaty was added. The Russians also agreed to release Port Arthur and the Manchurian Railway to China by the end of 1952. But the *status quo* of Outer Mongolia (from where Soviet troops were not yet withdrawn) was confirmed, and for a while it seemed that Russian instruments of influence would continue to prevail in Manchuria, Sinkiang, and perhaps even in Inner (Southern) Mongolia. All this was to change to the advantage of China in the decade to come. It was, however, not from these Chinese borderlands but in the then exclusively Soviet Russian satellite of North Korea that the next decisive turn of world history came.

4

It is an ironic paradox that along the global border of the American and Soviet spheres war suddenly burst out in 1950 in a country about which neither the United States nor the Soviet Union showed concern until well after the end of the Second World War. The so-called Cairo Declaration in November 1943 promised independence to the Korean nation after the war in a general and imprecise statement. The Yalta Agreements did not treat of Korea at all. During the following few months before the planned Russian attack against Japan, it was agreed that a liberated Korea would be governed by a Four-Power (American, British, Chinese, and Russian) Trusteeship. This was confirmed at Potsdam, where the American military representatives, upon a Russian query, said that their troops would not land in Korea until after the invasion of Japan. Korea, thus, fell within the Russian sphere of military operations; their forces entered Korea after the Japanese collapse. It was MacArthur's General Order No. 1 that established the demarcation line of the 38th Parallel between the Russian and American zones of occupation, a line to which Stalin himself agreed. It is interesting to note that the division of Korea along the 37th Parallel had been proposed by the Russians to the Japanese, who rejected it before the Russo-Japanese War of 1904–5; the American proposition of that line, however, seems to have been made not on historical but wholly on technical grounds.

Thus, even more than the division of Germany, the partition of Korea came about virtually by accident. Soon new developments made the Korean situation even more similar to the German one, and different from the other, more fluid scenes of the Far East. As in Germany, Communists came to occupy political positions in the northern half of the country while Syngman Rhee, the leading figure in the South, arrived from the United States. Yet it is significant that many of the leading North Korean Communists had come not from Moscow but from China. For about a year attempts were made to arrive at a mutually acceptable united Korean government; for a while the Russians spoke in favor of the Four-Power Trusteeship idea; but, as in Germany, by 1946 the division of the country along the wholly arbitrary and technical demarcation line began to grow rigid. By that time the Russians seem to have concluded that to keep one half of a country within their sphere was better than to risk the democratic process of unification. Thus along that abstract line of geometry the organic body of yet another country was cut in half.

This Korean tragedy was referred to the Foreign Ministers' Conferences and to the United Nations in vain. In May 1948 elections in South Korea, approved by the United Nations, confirmed the government of Syngman Rhee. That September (a year before they recognized the People's Republic of China) the Soviet Union officially recognized the North Korean Communist government. Again, as in Germany, the Russians now proposed a mutual withdrawal of the occupation forces. In January 1949 they announced the completion of their withdrawal from North Korea; after some hesitation, the American forces, except for a military mission, were withdrawn from South Korea during the next six months. Thereafter incidents between South and North Korean forces occurred more often. But it is significant that the usual satellite treaty concluded between the Soviet Union and North Korea did not include the provision of mutual assistance; and a significant speech by Dean Acheson in January 1950 suggested that both South Korea and Formosa lay outside the American defense perimeter in the western Pacific. Thus no Russian and American troops faced each other when on 25 June 1950 the North Koreans broke across the Parallel.

The origins of the North Korean attack are even now obscure. There is reason to believe that Acheson's address encouraged the North Koreans to believe that they could destroy the South Korean regime without active American involvement, since the United States seemed to have left the Korean problem in the lap of the impotent United Nations. More important, all the available evidence shows that the North Korean move caught Mao unprepared. It has been suggested that Stalin gave his blessing to the North Korean military adventure: he considered it relatively safe in view of what the Americans were saying and also propitious because of the rise of China and of the otherwise receding Russian influence in the central Manchurian-Korean-North Chinese theater in the Far East. But whatever the spring of the Russian motive may have been, the American reaction certainly caught the Communist world by surprise. President Truman, without hesitation, acted energetically, intelligently, with the sure instinct of bravery. He knew that no matter how remote the strategic value of Korea, the prestige of the United States was now involved together with the future determination of the entire free world in resisting the pressures of Communist Power. He ordered the immediate engagement of American naval and air forces against the invaders. In the United Nations fortunately the Soviet Union was caught napping; her delegate was absent from the Security Council on the very first day when an American resolution called for the members of the United Nations to come to the aid of the attacked. Thus, in the absence of a Soviet veto, the United States could claim that it acted for the United Nations; and, indeed, together with no less than 142,-000 American and more than one million South Korean casualties, 17,000 British, Australian, New Zealander, French, Belgian, Dutch, Greek, Turkish, Colombian, Ethiopian, and Siamese soldiers valiantly gave their lives or suffered wounds in the war that came.

Like Churchill's in June 1940 in the Second World War, June 1950 was America's finest hour in the cold war. Truman's resoluteness was more than commendable. It electrified the free world and gave it confidence —no matter how dreary the campaign in that remote country was to become, no matter how relatively inconclusive its results were to be.

5

Despite the virtually undisputed superiority of American air power during the first phase of the war, hordes of North Korean soldiers poured southward on foot, overwhelming the South Korean and American troops; soon the latter retreated within the pocket formed around the bridgehead of Pusan, suggesting a coming Bataan or another Dunkirk. American sea power then turned the balance. An American blockade of North Korea was proclaimed; and from Japan, American supplies and troops flowed into Pusan in increasing quantities, unvexed by enemies at sea. In September 1950 General MacArthur, the Supreme Commander, mounted a bold amphibious counterattack. At Inchon, behind Seoul, American marines landed in a brilliant, imaginative operation. Within a week the North Korean troops, threatened by encirclement, fell back in defeat. Seoul was freed; the American-U. N. Army crossed the 38th Parallel; it carried the war into the territory of the Communist invaders, whose capital, Pyongyang, fell in October. Victory seemed complete; and General MacArthur said that by Christmas the war might be over. It was now, toward the end of this decisive second phase of the Korean War, that political complications arose. There was some question within the United Nations and the Western Allies whether the mandate of this United Nations force justified their conquest of the whole of North Korea. Russia was bearlike, growling rather than restive, while American diplomatic and military moves strongly emphasized that the frontiers of the Soviet Union would be respected as a matter of course.[8] It was, however, not from across the Russian

[8] Truman emphatically forbade the United States Air Force to intrude into Russian territory.

but from across the Chinese frontier that new armed hordes were introduced into the war.

From early October onward Indian and other neutral diplomatists indicated that the Chinese Communist government, restless and anxious over the prospect of an American army nearing its borders, would intervene unless the advance were halted. These political warnings were not heeded by Washington and their military manifestations were unheeded by General MacArthur until in the first week of November large numbers of Chinese soldiers were crossing the Yalu River into Korea. Their masses soon overran the American spearheads, whose victorious advance now turned into a bitter wintry retreat.

During this third phase of the Korean Campaign, the Chinese with their revitalized North Korean allies drove south of the Parallel and conquered Seoul again; but by February the momentum of their drive was spent; the American-United Nations forces moved back into Seoul and, beyond it, pushed into the mountains slightly north of the 38th Parallel, where the front line was stabilized by the spring. We now know that this meant the end of the last important military phase of the Korean War; but this was not yet evident in the spring of 1951, when a great political crisis developed within the Western Allied ranks.

6

At the center of events stood General MacArthur, one of the great commanders of modern history, a Roman figure of the New World. He represented the old American inclination to see in the Pacific the main theater of American destiny and the future center of world history. When the stunning events of Pearl Harbor seemed to have silenced the voices of American isolationism, these inclinations were soon transferred to an "Asia First" war policy, contending that the war against Japan, and not against Germany, was the primary task of the United States. MacArthur, the Pacific Commander, naturally inclined in this direction. His audacious advance from island to island redeemed the early American defeats in the war. In 1945 he became Supreme Commander in Japan. This tall and impressive figure, surrounded by a devoted staff, austere, isolated on the pinnacle of power, combined the image of a Roman proconsul with the Oriental image of a great conqueror. But he was not only majestically isolated from the Japanese, whom this impressed profoundly; he was also isolated from his own country, where he had not set foot for more than a decade. Out of this kind of closed Oriental perspective troubles were bound to arise.

It was General MacArthur's passionate belief throughout his career that mistaken political influences in Washington handicapped America's Pacific and Far Eastern interests to the unjust advantage of Europe. This belief was now fortified by the conditions imposed upon the Korean War. Here, MacArthur believed, was the occasion to destroy the power of the Communists in China, whose victory he attributed to lukewarmness and corruption in Washington. President Truman and Acheson knew better the priorities of the now world-wide nature of the cold war; they were also aware of the conditions that, for the sake of American prestige alone, were attached to the United Nations character of the Korean campaign. It was, in essence, another conflict between Europe First and Asia First concepts of American destiny. By early 1951 these always latent inclinations, spurred by the frustrations of the Korean War, crystallized into two political camps, and the crisis broke.

We have seen that the allies of the United States, and particularly Britain, were not in favor of extending the armed advance to include the conquest of all of

North Korea. Their warnings were left unheeded while MacArthur's own intelligence staff discounted the Chinese danger. As the onslaught erupted, MacArthur immediately proposed the bombing of Manchurian strong points and Chinese bridges on the Yalu. After painful discussions, Truman decided against this. It is true that the massive introduction of the Chinese Communist element transformed the character of the Korean War. On the other hand (contrary to the universal chorus of Experts who after 1945 proclaimed that from now on there were but two alternatives in political history: Universal Peace or Universal Atomic War) the Korean War, no matter how extreme the opposition between the two sides and their ideologies, was a limited war indeed. The Soviet Union did not intervene; except for military supplies she helped the North Koreans but little (the first Russian jet airplanes were not given to them until 1951). Unwilling to risk the chance of a full-scale war, the Chinese engaged in the euphemism of calling their soldiers "volunteers." The decisive American domination of the Korean seas was left unchallenged by the enemy, while no attempts were made to bomb the decisive American bases in Japan; if Manchuria, as MacArthur said bitterly, was "a privileged sanctuary" of the Chinese attackers, so was Japan for the American defenders. It is, of course, easy to sympathize with MacArthur, who believed that he was waging a war with one of his hands tied. It is not so easy to sympathize, in retrospect, with his willingness to rally American political opposition to his side. The prospect of a change in the hitherto prevailing American war policy, the possibility of a sudden American air attack on Manchuria, arose. The British and the French came to Washington, trying to impress upon President Truman the incalculable consequences of a full-scale American war with China, an impression that the President largely shared. MacArthur was now becoming restive. Fully aware of his constitutional responsibilities, the American President dismissed him of his Supreme Command on 11 April 1951. A wave of political and sentimental clamor rose immediately in America.[9] It did not change the course of Far Eastern events.

For these were now further circumscribed by the geographical conditions of a limited war. By that time the very territorial objects of the war had become limited. The Communists saw that they would not be able to push the Americans out of Korea, while the American-U.N. command knew that, short of the risk of a full-scale war with China, they would not attempt to conquer all of North Korea again. The opposing armies were digging in; and the last attempt at a Chinese offensive was defeated soon after MacArthur's dismissal. Thus the commotion in American politics coincided, by and large, with the relative stabilization of the cragged front line running across central Korea. It was this latter condition that led to the practical end of the Korean War.

In June 1951 the Soviet Union, at the United Nations, proposed negotiations for an armistice. Interrupted on several occasions, soon thereafter negotiations began in Panmunjom on the 38th Parallel between the opposite commands. Seemingly endless wranglings about the fate of prisoners of war, exploited by Communist and Oriental chicanery, stretched these talks out for two years, during which still thousands of Americans, not to speak of the Korean population, gave their lives in bitter local

[9] At that time I found it very significant how upon the sudden news of MacArthur's dismissal dock workers in New York went on a protest strike, in a spontaneous demonstration. This expression of the political sentiments of these tightly unionized, New Deal-supported, and Democrat-organized workers in favor of this remote, right-wing, Republican hero of a general indicated the latent strength of that American popular tendency that was soon to gather around Senator McCarthy.

battles fought along portions of the front.[10] It was not until July 1953, when Stalin was dead and Eisenhower the American President, that the Korean Armistice was finally signed; understandably against bitter South Korean obstructions, since it sealed for a long time the division of that unhappy country.

7

The United States, led by Truman, had sprung to the defense of South Korea in the name of a principle that it maintained with honor through the end of the war. Still, the unpopularity of the remote, unspectacular, inconclusive Korean War remained an important factor. All of this contributed decisively to the emergence of a new American political climate, whose full effects we shall see in the following chapter.

Yet the balance of the Korean War must be seen from a wider perspective: for, apart from the sad record of American casualties, ultimately Russia emerges as the loser of this grim historic episode. The United States, after all, held its own. America maintained the freedom of South Korea; American troops stand even now north of the 38th Parallel. American naval power still dominates the entire Pacific, up to the very surf of the

[10] We must mention here two parallel propaganda campaigns; the change in the general texture of history in democratic times compels the historian to do so. We can see the relative caution of Russian statecraft throughout the Korean War. This does not mean, however, that this caution was imposed by anything but crass self-interest. For it was during this time that Communist organizations, on Moscow's orders, propagated the utterly hypocritical campaign of the so-called Stockholm Peace Appeal; and in 1952 they launched the utterly vile propaganda campaign accusing the United States of having spread millions of bacteria behind Korean and Chinese lines. Fortunately the influence of these campaigns was limited. And the reciprocal figures of the voluntary repatriation of the prisoners of war again indicated the relative minority appeal of Communism.

Chinese mainland. American control over Formosa, Okinawa, and over bases in Japan remained strong and undisturbed. In 1951, at San Francisco, the Japanese Peace Treaty was signed without Russia, whose observers could do little more than make grumbling public speeches. Moreover, it is obvious that a full-scale American involvement in a war with China would have suited Stalin well, to the detriment of Europe: as General Bradley said in 1951, MacArthur's plans might have led to the wrong war, with the wrong enemy, at the wrong time, in the wrong place.

The relative victor of the Korean War was not Russia but China; but her victory was one of prestige rather than of power, while her gains were made ultimately not at the expense of America but of Russia. To those who said: "We have lost China," the answer should be: When did we have China? We have already seen that except for the fifty years preceding the Second World War, the nations of the white race, including America, had no decisive influence in China at all; their colonial, commercial, and political influence was consequent to the disintegration of the Chinese Empire, which in the end America herself attempted to prevent. But now the power of China, with her hundreds of peasant millions, was rising again. Already in 1950 the Chinese conquered Tibet; and in Sinkiang not only British and American but also Russian influences waned as the new Communist military masters of China established their rule over that remote Central Asian province. North Korea at the beginning of the war was a Russian satellite; by the end of the war Russia had to share her influence with the Chinese, whose forces, after all, had saved the North Korean regime from extinction. It is true that the Invincible Communist Alliance of China and Russia was loudly proclaimed throughout; it is true that China depended on Russian technical and material assistance; but the latter was very moderate in extent. Even before the Korean War the Russians had to make concessions to the new Communist Chinese regime about their privileges in Manchuria, in Dairen, and in Port Arthur that had been established earlier at Yalta and with Chiang Kai-shek; in 1952 by "mutual agreement" the Russian evacuation of these important Manchurian places was postponed; by 1954, however, the Russians thought it better to go. Meanwhile the specter of Chinese energy made a favorable impression upon the yellow races of Asia. Unlike in Europe, where the appeal of Communism was low everywhere outside the iron curtain, its appeal in Asia was yet far from being spent; but its power was now incarnated in China as well as in Russia. Finally, like Britain on the side of the United States, Russia exercised a moderating influence on China during the latter phase of the Korean War; Russia, like Britain, was instrumental in promoting the armistice negotiations—a pattern that would recur in Indochina later.

Thus, while America, despite all of her toilsome frustration after 1945, did not lose a single speck of ground of her victorious conquests against Japan, less than a decade after 1945, and a half century after that Russo-Japanese War whose losses Stalin so much wished to recoup, Russia's domains in the Far East were limited again; her sovereign power along the shores of the northwestern Pacific was marginal, not central.

CHAPTER V

Stalin's Death and Dulles' Rise

(To 1955)

1

Stalin died on or about 5 March 1953, at the same time that a new Republican Administration, presided over by Eisenhower, was taking over the large and complex functions of American government. Though the world was promptly assured of the continuity of Russian and American policies, these were events of immense importance.

For almost three decades Stalin's figure and his massive shadow alone dominated the vast lands and affairs of the Russian Empire; for almost a decade, the fate of the world directly depended on his eventual decisions. Patient and yet often impetuous, stubborn and yet amazingly supple, brutally rude and yet occasionally sentimental, he advanced the frontiers of the Communist sphere far more successfully than Lenin; and yet he was more of a Russian figure, largely unacquainted with the affairs and uninterested in the ideas of Europe, reflecting more of Asia than Lenin, who had some Tatar blood in his veins. As with the Corsican Frenchman Napoleon and the Austrian Hitler, the few burrs under the Georgian Stalin's saddle included his desire to prove to be a great Russian. Unlike Napoleon and Hitler, he died near the summit of his power, ruling to his last days from the mysterious and awesomely isolated towers of the Kremlin. He reminds us of Ivan the Terrible, an earlier inhabitant of that orthodox Moscow fortress; and both Ivan and Stalin should remind us how the concept of Supreme Rulers in Moscow derived from the concept and practice of Tatar Khans even more than from the theories of Tsardom borrowed from Byzance.

After the short-lived glow of wartime victories, the Russian scene was full of darkness and fear again in the last years of this great Communist Khan. We have seen some of his mistakes in dealing with foreign affairs. We know how within the government of Russia his undisputed primacy produced, together with the efficacy of centralization and terror, the inefficiencies of sycophancy, nepotism, misinformation, and corruption. Though his lucid understanding of human motives seems to have prevailed until the end—for this master of half the world was a plotter rather than a planner, possessing above all the gift for an instinctive knowledge of men's weaknesses that marks the otherwise parochial genius of Levantine tradesmen or of American ward leaders—his paranoid inclinations toward suspicion mixed with brutality seem to have fatally shifted the balance of his mind in the end. Shortly before his death, the obscure Doctors' Plot, accusing eminent and mostly Jewish physicians of the earlier premeditated murder of his cruel lieutenant Zhdanov among others, cast the shadow of coming purges across Russia anew. There is some reason to believe—as with the demise of many Russian Tsars, we do not know and we may never know —that Stalin's death may have been hastened by fearful subordinates. There is no reason to doubt that his death was greeted with relief by millions outside and with mixed awe and relief by millions within Russia, including the leaders of the Soviet hierarchy.

A brighter scene, of course, was the change at the helm of the American ship of state. Carried by the wave of the popular sentiment for a change, the Republican Party, after twenty years of exclusion, had come back to power. Their victory was facilitated by that element of a popularity contest that in our times has become so large a part of American presidential campaigns: in other words, the candidacy of the benign and widely respected General Eisenhower was of decisive importance. It is, then, somewhat of a paradox that this popular General-President, accustomed to supreme military commands throughout his life but unacquainted with important American constitutional and historical traditions, immediately delegated, unlike his civilian predecessor, many of the decisive lines of command to his lieutenants, among whom the figure of John Foster Dulles stood out.

It is important, at this point, to say something about the character of this American statesman whose words and actions, for better or worse, influenced the course of world affairs more than those of any other person during the crucial years that followed the demise of Stalin. His incisive and categorical mind and the steadfastness of his determination reflected the best qualities of this American lawyer and patriot. Yet lawyers seldom make good statesmen: for the law, with its dependence on letter rather than on spirit, with its literal categories dependent on predetermined procedures of order, is seldom sufficient to the understanding of the vast open currents of world history. From his legal background, therefore, Dulles brought with him an unduly contractual inclination to extend American alliances, an inclination reflecting a rigid concept of the struggle with Russia, a rigidity that his admirers erroneously attributed to superior principles and his detractors, also erroneously, to mere prejudice. From his religious background, this Presbyterian brought with him the distressingly puritanical and at times even pharisaic inclination to see in the world struggle a national personification of good versus evil, mistakenly elevating the political ideology of anti-Communism into a superior moral principle. From his racial background, this Dutch American, an early admirer of the Boers against England, unusually sympathetic toward Germany, brought with him an enduring small core of distrust toward England together with the belief that alliance with Germany must now be the cornerstone of American policies. Keeping in mind, too, such characteristics as a certain native cunning, a certain American capacity of dissimulating statement, and a certain amount of personal vanity that made him stay in the powerful seat of Secretary of State long after the tragedy of cancer was sapping his powers, we may consider in retrospect that his occupancy of that seat had come at the wrong time, when perhaps great historic opportunities were missed, whereafter the United States continued on a now fateful course.

For the orderly and optimistic American scene of the inauguration of a new Administration early in 1953 was not without interior streaks of darkness. The passions of anti-Communism, together with the popular reaction against the frustrations of the Korean War, obviously provided potential political capital. Already in 1952, before as well as during the electoral campaign, this capital was increasingly tapped in the name of patriotism and exploited with easygoing demagoguery. Senator McCarthy's political career was the outstanding example. More important than McCarthy, however, was the condition that the heights of this American domestic ideological passion were reached just about the time when circumstances—among which Stalin's death was a prime, but by no means the exclusive, factor—were forcing the rulers of Russia to modify, to alternate, and on occasion and at certain points, to reverse their previously aggressive course. Thus once more a new American Administration was unwilling or unable to recognize important changes and opportunities until it was almost too late. Thus Dulles' rise, though coincident with Stalin's demise, obstructed rather than promoted the loosening of the cold war. Thus we shall see how he contributed to the continuation of its most important condition, to the division of Europe.

2

Long before the Korean War ended, it had become evident that Europe, and particularly Germany, was again the main area of Russian-American conflict.

While in the Russian sphere of Europe police rule and the attendant miseries reached their extremes during the Korean War between 1950 and 1953, in Western Europe two important developments took place. One concerned the economic and the other the military reorganization of the Western European nations, including Germany. The first development was marked by various instruments of economic co-operation, of which the Schuman, or Coal-Steel, Plan of 1950, promoted by Christian Democrats in France and Germany alike, stands out, leading a few years later to the formation of the so-called Common Market of the Six Nations. More important and, indeed, underlying these instruments of contract was the beginning of the material and industrial recovery of Europe. More surprising, it was ruined and divided Germany that had assumed the lead by 1950. Spurred by American economic aid, assisted by the intelligent West German currency reforms, by a relative absence of stringent regulations on free enterprise, but representing most of all the German national virtues of industriousness and organization that turned even the initially very burdensome and difficult presence of millions of German refugees to profit, material conditions and productivity in West Germany and Berlin not only improved but were creating a condition of astonishing prosperity. The Germans, of course, automatically benefited from the condition of their disarmament at a time when Britain and the other still war-torn states of Western Europe had to devote a large amount of their national incomes to the maintenance of their armed forces in the face of

the Soviet military threat. For some years the Germans
were spared that burden; and, indeed, in the second
half of the 1950s the other nations of Western Europe,
particularly France, began catching up with German
prosperity. At any rate, these material developments
suggested the resilience of European vitality even after
the Second World War on a divided continent.

These developments further reduced the already
weakened appeal of Communism in Western Europe
by the time of the Korean War (even though, contrary
to American expectations, the economic benefits of the
Marshall Plan hardly reduced at all the standard per-
centage of Communist votes in France and in Italy).
Within the Germanies the direction of refugees and the
increase of prestige moved steadily toward the West
German Federal Republic and away from the German
"Democratic" Republic in the East. Even in 1949,
under almost complete police domination, about one
third of the people in East Germany voted against the
Communist ticket. This did not, of course, prevent the
final formation of the East German state in October
1949, whose government, save for a few details, con-
formed to the Soviet satellite pattern. On the other side,
West Germany, guided by the strong and able hand of
Dr. Adenauer, strove to prove the value of a new democratic Germany within the Western community of
nations. From the beginning it put special emphasis on
a nearly absolute co-operation with the United States.
By 1949 this tendency was acquiring a military significance. There is some evidence that, during the slight
easing of the cold war that followed the end of the
Berlin Blockade, the Russians, seriously concerned with
the prospects of West German rearmament, still regarded the unification of Germany as eventually negotiable; at that time, during the Foreign Ministers'
Conference in Paris, agreement was nearly reached
about the mutual evacuation of Austria. But American
and Russian suspicions toward each other, and their com-

mitments to their respective German junior allies, were already too deep.

During the Korean War the American military organization of Europe and of Germany proceeded rapidly. In September 1950 Acheson told the Western Foreign Ministers that the United States made the defense of Europe contingent on the creation of a West German Army. At that time not only the British but even Chancellor Adenauer were unenthusiastic about this plan (the latter, quite rightly, would have preferred a militarized Federal police force, a counterpart of the East German force of that kind). A few months later the previous Western European united command was put under American direction as General Eisenhower occupied the supreme direction of NATO-SHAPE in Fontainebleau. At first this organization was evident in not much more than in the creation of a large polyglot military bureaucracy in buildings marked by a bewildering complex of abbreviations; but behind them grew the American determination to install American forces permanently in a European theater, preferably together with the forces of a renewed Germany. Between 1950 and 1953 various senseless and exaggerated estimates were made about the number of divisions in the NATO Army that would, at varying target dates, be ready to face the mythical hundreds of Soviet divisions poised for eventual attack on the plains of East Germany.[1] American plans were advanced for the creation of a so-called European Defense Community, within which the respective national forces would have been merged so as to lose their national identities on the level of higher command. These plans were gradually advancing together with the in-

[1] Though none of them developed into a serious crisis (until May 1960), from 1950 onward air and intelligence incidents involving Americans and Russians multiplied in Europe; significantly, most of them now took place in the vicinity of the Soviet border.

stallation of American forces and large American colonies in Italy, France, West Germany, and, after 1953, even in Turkey and in Spain. For by 1951 Greece and Turkey had been invited to join NATO (no matter how far these sunny countries were from the North Atlantic); the intricate talks for a Spanish-American alliance began; the decision for German rearmament was now irreversible; in 1952 the West German government introduced conscription.

A change in the hitherto very rigid Soviet position occurred at that time. Obviously impressed with the (to them) supreme danger of a German-American alliance, in March 1952 Moscow proposed the resumption of serious negotiations about Germany. Its published drafts for a treaty even included such unexpected Soviet concessions as Germany's admittance to the United Nations and the right of Germany to keep a national army; the suggestion of free German elections was raised; the unification of the Germanies was to take place under the guidance of all-German commissions formed by both West and East German representatives; a reunited Germany, on the other hand, would not be allowed to ally herself either with the American or with the Russian group of states. These proposals were not altogether unreasonable; their usual Russian loopholes could have been explored and perhaps even filled during negotiations; but now it was the State Department and Pentagon that, in view of the prospects of bringing West Germany fully into the American alliance system, did not really wish to explore them.

At any rate, these Russian proposals were made at a time when, during the 1952 electoral campaign, the Republican candidates called for a new American policy, promising not only the liberation of East Germany but all of Eastern Europe from the Soviet Union. All of this, however, indicates that a significant change in the direction of Russian foreign policies was developing even before Stalin's death in Moscow and that a broad change in the extent and temper of American policies was developing even before Eisenhower and Dulles took over in Washington.

3

Early in March 1953 the aged Churchill, once more Prime Minister of Britain, saw sufficient evidence of a changing atmosphere to propose, through confidential and diplomatic channels, a meeting at the summit between Eisenhower, Stalin, and himself. He may not have known that at that time Stalin was already dying. He was soon to know from reports from Russia that the death of the tyrant, even if it did not lead to dramatic changes, opened up new potentialities of vast import. Grimly and rigidly the new ruling group atop the Russian Empire claimed that through discipline and order the course charted by Lenin and Stalin would continue. But soon the conditions imposed by external as well as by domestic and personal factors began to show. New tremors, emanating from Moscow, loosened the rigid and artificial system of terroristic uniformity insured by Stalin. Within the Soviet Union, Beria, the powerful head of the police forces, was suddenly crushed by his colleagues, among whom the supple Malenkov and the flexible Khrushchev stood out. The experienced Molotov continued as Foreign Minister while Stalin's favorite lieutenant, Vishinsky, died grief-stricken and the war hero Marshal Zhukov, degraded by Stalin, was brought back into the supreme councils. Other changes were developing whose end is not yet. The description of this developing Soviet Thaw does not belong here, where we are concerned with Russia's relations with the rest of the world; but there, too, significant indications were soon apparent.

In the capitals of the free world Russian diplomatic

suggestions and tentatives soon indicated that a new and more fluid phase of relations might be opening, particularly in Europe. Certain suggestions about the renegotiability of the German problem were made. Unlike Churchill, Dulles (and Eisenhower) showed little interest in exploring them. On 11 May 1953 Churchill made an open proposal for a Summit Meeting of the Chiefs of States in a historic speech in the House of Commons that included important suggestions about the necessary reconciliation of Russia's security interests with the interests of a united Europe. But, as at Fulton in 1946, as during the war in 1944, as after Munich in 1938, his ideas were regarded as somewhat extreme; they were dismissed by the State Department and by influential American circles that went so far as to attribute them to the last ambitious attempts of a statesman grown senile.[2]

[2] He thus was often accused of undue softness toward Communism by the very same people and organs (among the latter the influential picture weeklies *Time* and *Life* stand out) who but a few years earlier accused him of undue British harshness against Russia (see above, pages 50, 63). And the same Eisenhower who in 1944 and 1945 had opposed the wily Churchill who through deft military moves had wanted to keep the Russian Ally out of Berlin, Vienna, and Prague, in 1953 and in 1954 opposed the same wily old Churchill who now wanted to do that through negotiations with the Russian Enemy. One need not be an admirer of Churchill to see whom the development of history proved right. At this point, too, we may say something about the time lag in American foreign policies. We have already seen how, in Greece and elsewhere, by 1947 the State Department adopted the same policy for which it criticized Britain two years earlier; we shall see how, by 1955, two years after he had dismissed Churchill's summit proposal, Eisenhower himself went to Geneva to sit down with the new leaders of Russia; and in 1958 American marines were to land in Lebanon less than two years after Eisenhower and Dulles threatened to take stringent action against the Anglo-French landing at Suez. One of the last dogmatic statements of Stalin was a curious prediction that the Soviet Union would profit from the next war that would break out among the capitalist

It would be unfair, however, to seek the motive of these melancholy misunderstandings in the personal inadequacies of the new American President and of his Secretary of State. They were inseparable from a climate of American popular sentiment and public opinion that was dominant in 1953 and in 1954 and that, to some extent, remained characteristic almost of the entire decade of the 1950s in America. What it amounted to was the adoption of anti-Communism for an official American ideology. We cannot explore here in detail the complex origins, the simplicist logic, and again the complex consequences of this new American anti-Communism, whose component elements of strength were different from the superficially similar "Red Scare" that affected the United States around 1920, at which time the political wrath had been directed against a small subversive minority of Communist immigrants and radical agitators of the working class. This time the sentiments were more general, popular, and they resided in the hearts of great masses of people. I have already suggested that it developed as a wide popular, political, and even intellectual reaction against the more extreme errors of liberal and radical tendencies of the 1940s, to which the frustrations of the cold war, the Korean War, and the inflated successes of Communism were attributed. Meanwhile the superficiality of propaganda and the sensationalism of magazines and films created a commendably strong and uniform but unfortunately abstract set of anti-Communist ideas. The struggle with Russia was a struggle not between nations and men but between good and evil; and thus every anti-Communist belonged to the American side (a simple belief exploited by elements and ac-

---

Powers, between the United States and Britain; and though the fallacy of this exaggerated projection is obvious, it is also obvious that Russia profited on every occasion from misunderstanding between Washington and London during the Second World War as well as during the cold war.

cepted by people who had never sympathized with the American involvement against Germany in the Second World War). Thus in the place of a clearer national purpose this blanket ideology came to substitute the more traditional concepts of American patriotism. This will at least suggest the reasons for the extraordinary career of Senator Joseph McCarthy. This spunky demagogue, a mediocre and vulgar politician, could rally most of the American nationalist organizations to his side; American officialdom bent before him while American liberal intellectuals wailed self-pityingly in his wake. His career was broken in late 1954, when the President, belatedly, moved against him. After his censure by the Senate, McCarthy retired to expire in morose and alcoholic isolation. His chunky dark figure, riding the wave of anti-Communism, was a symptom rather than a cause; but his career was not merely a domestic phenomenon; deeply, though indirectly, it influenced the conduct and the course of American foreign affairs, since his political presence and his potential popular support were formidably influential factors during a critical and perhaps potentially propitious phase of Russian-American relations.

For events, in 1953 and 1954, indicated a Russian retrenchment, partly of course by calculation, but partly also by the uneasy recognition of pressures on the new rulers of Moscow. On 17 June 1953 Germany and the world were electrified by a wave of strikes and riots in East Germany that culminated in a virtual workers' revolution in East Berlin. Here was the first European revolution against the Soviets' rule. When the miserable East German government was unable to restore order, the tanks of the Russian garrison moved in; and though order was promptly restored by force and a few executions followed, a certain extent of Russian moderation and uneasiness was also apparent. Worried by the possibility of similar eruptions in Eastern Europe, the Russian leadership summoned Rákosi, the hated Communist satrap of the Hungarian nation, and brutally ordered his dismissal. On 4 July 1953 the more moderate Imre Nagy was proclaimed Prime Minister in Budapest. On the same day the final arrangements for the Korean Armistice were completed. Throughout the next two years significant reforms eased police terror and restrictions throughout Eastern Europe. This policy was not over-all and uniform; the new rulers of Moscow, with their hands full anyhow, were letting their satellite leaders govern more on their own; and many of these leaders feared like the plague any policy of "liberalization" that would endanger their own domestic position. Still the iron curtain, especially across Germany, was opened here and there. Soon the Russian leaders, notably the ebullient Khrushchev, were to begin their extraordinary series of journeys outside their Russian sphere to capital cities of the world. All of these developments suggested a gradual improvement of relations between the two worlds, and perhaps the chance for preparing a European settlement. Not until 1955, however, was a positive American reaction forthcoming.

4

There were many reasons why the United States and, indeed, the Western Allies were insufficiently responsive to these new diplomatic conditions in Europe during this phase of the cold war. One of the prime reasons was that their attention was drawn elsewhere. In 1954, war, civil war, and the threat of war flared up high in many places in the world outside of Europe, and especially in Asia. Of these the crisis in Indochina came closest to a new Korean War.

Of all the great regions of the world, the affairs of Southeastern Asia remained longest fluid and confused after the chaotic consequences of the Second World

War. The British, having left India and Burma but not Malaya and Singapore, were engaged in a difficult small jungle war with native Communist guerrillas. The French, whose prestige and power were badly ruined there during the Second World War, returned to Indochina with an army but with little native support. Since 1946 in northeastern Indochina the Communist Ho Chi Minh had established an insurrectionary regime in Vietminh; in the South the French held on to a semi-colonial Indochinese government under the Emperor Bao Dai, while in the remoter western portions of Indochina the Laotian and Cambodian Kingdoms advanced to full sovereignty. After bitter struggles the Dutch by 1949 felt compelled to cede the remnant of their title over the Indonesian Archipelago to the violent and shrill nationalist government of those islands. This withdrawal of the European Powers—originally promoted by Japan and also supported by the United States—did not end the chaotic conditions in this large, fetid, motley, and multiracial part of the world. The large Chinese minorities hearkened to the successes of the new Communist China. The Chinese began to extend political, and some military, support to them, especially in Malaya and Indochina, where from 1952 on the battles intensified; and in 1954 a large Vietminh offensive was mounted against the French, besieging the now isolated fortress of Dien Bien Phu.

Concentrating on the evidences of organized Communist support, mistaking somewhat the proportion of the native and racial factors, the United States, led by Dulles, found it necessary to commit herself against these potential Communist advances even in that faraway part of the world. A Southeast Asian equivalent of NATO was formed (from which Britain was at first excluded). American aid and missions and arms poured into remote and muddy capitals. Already early in 1953 President Eisenhower announced, somewhat exaggeratedly, that the United States, hitherto committed but

to the defense of Formosa, was "unleashing" Chiang
Kai-shek's forces for an eventual advance across the
water against the mainland Communist Chinese; but
these Formosan Hounds, though increasingly well fed,
could not swim.

American military and political influence was already
superseding the French in southern Indochina (where
the throne of the aged Bao Dai was soon to be toppled
and the energetic and pro-American Diem was to be
the ruler-President) when the Dien Bien Phu crisis
broke: the French Army could not hold the fort unless
the Americans were to intervene.[3] It was at that time
that Dulles, as he himself said in a phrase later, chose to
commit America to the brink of war. His name has been
associated by bitter critics with this phrase, perhaps
inopportune in a world over which hovers the shade
of Hydrogen Bombs; and yet there was some wisdom
there, for Dulles knew how the Russians and Chinese
understand force better than anything else. Still, this
would have been again the wrong war against the
wrong enemy, in the wrong place and at the wrong
time. Russia was far from being directly involved; even
Chinese involvement was but indirect; and in view of
the experiences of the Korean War, it is strange how
Dulles and Admiral Radford could believe that the intervention of American air power alone could turn the
tide of this guerrilla war fought in millet fields and rice
paddies. In the last week of April 1954, Dulles had
about committed the French to this American plan of
intervention; but Churchill, who was aware of the
global risks but even more of the insufficiency of such
an aerial intervention, halted its full development. Dien
Bien Phu, marked by scenes of tragedy as well as of
heroism, fell in May. In June a conference met in
Geneva. Through British and Russian mediation on the
respective sides, it settled the Indochinese War; Viet-

[3] See below, Chapter x, pages 265 ff.

minh and Vietnam were separated along the 17th Parallel, a much shorter line than the Korean 38th; the former's territory under native Communist control was somewhat extended, while the latter now fell mostly within the American sphere of influence.

Meanwhile throughout the 1950s nationalist revolutions complicated and, on occasion, endangered the balance of the Russian-American cold war. In Egypt the corrupt King Farouk was chased away by a junta in 1952; in 1954 Churchill decided to withdraw the British garrisons from the Suez Canal Zone. In Cyprus guerrilla war was developing, with Greeks pitted against the British garrison and the Turks; the Spanish were agitating for the British abandonment of Gibraltar; in Algeria the guerrilla war of the Moslem nationalists against the French was beginning, while in Iran, Dulles, after a period of significant hesitation, came around to the British viewpoint and encouraged the restoration of the Shah against the histrionic nationalist dictator Mossadegh in 1953. In Guatemala in 1954 the United States more or less openly promoted the overthrow of a Leftist government with a vaguely pro-Communist tinge that was about to receive a smattering of arms from the Soviet sphere. Still, these eruptions outside the Western world were directed by native and racial ambitions rather than by central Russian command; they led to a reduction of British and European possessions together with a global increase not of Russian power but of American commitments and influence. In the central continent of Europe and in the Far East the *status quo* remained unbroken while in Southeastern Asia the Bandung Conference in 1955, proclaiming universally vaporous Principles of Peace and Coexistence, seemed to bring the "neutralist" Indians and Indonesians together with China in a warm but illusive gust of racial sentiment.[4]

[4] It passed generally unnoticed how these Five Principles of Bandung resembled the Five Principles of a Joint Declara-

5

In 1955, then, the first break in the division of Europe was made. Though the completion of the Austrian State Treaty involved but a small country in the middle of Europe, its significance was immense and enduring.

We have seen how Churchill's proposition for serious negotiations at the summit had been spurned by the new American leadership in 1953. For two years afterward the standard phrase of this Administration was that Russian deeds, not words, were wanted. In April 1953 rambling but important policy speeches by the President and the Secretary of State suggested some of the conditions that the Russians would have to meet before they could be trusted further: these included the agreement of an Austrian Peace Treaty, the re-

---

tion of the Assembly of Greater East Asiatic Nations that had been sponsored by the wartime Japanese government in November 1943 in Tokyo. Yet this was but another evidence how the Japanese war aim of destroying forever the Europeans' position in Asia lived on. In the first place, for the masses of Eastern Asia the psychic impact of the spectacle of the early war victories of the Yellow Race over the British, French, and other Europeans transcended the more remote later spectacle of Japan's defeat. In the second place, the Japanese successfully turned over instruments and institutions of political power to native nationalist and revolutionary movements in 1945, at the time of the Japanese surrender and before the first token detachments of the European Powers arrived. This happened throughout Indochina, where, somewhat ironically, the Japanese as well as Chiang's Chinese helped to establish the Communist Ho Chi Minh; in Indonesia the Japanese simply turned the government over to their wartime collaborators. For in the Far East race was even more important than politics. Later, from Siam to the Philippines many erstwhile collaborators of the Japanese came back to positions of political power, most of them under the pretext of anti-Communism.

lease of the remaining prisoners of war, the signing of
the Armistice in Korea. Unimpressed by the evident
change of mood in Moscow, or by the very condition
that, unlike Stalin, the new Russian rulers were obviously attracted or perhaps even flattered by the prospects of their amicable reception at the summit, this
American reluctance remained predominant until after,
under the pressure of events, the Russians fulfilled
these initial conditions one by one. Already in January
1954 a Foreign Ministers' Conference had met in
Berlin, where, though no definite settlements were
reached, certain Russian reactions indicated some hope
for a coming Austrian, and perhaps even for an eventual German, agreement. Soon these were to mature
into more tangible fruits.

For in the meantime certain European developments had begun to modify, slowly but significantly,
the hitherto almost exclusively bipolar balance of
power whereby the fate of Europe entirely depended
on America and Russia. Almost a decade had passed
since the Zero Hour of 1945; now the political importance of certain European nations was rising together
with the clusters of new buildings that marked the new
growth of European industry and wealth. This curious
European renaissance of power led to the first (though,
as we shall see, at best limited and at worst abortive)
moves toward a disengagement of the two great military powers on European soil. (Like "peaceful coexistence," "disengagement" thus became an actual reality
years before the later much abused phrase was coined.)
In the East, Khrushchev and Malenkov accepted the
fact of an independent Communist Yugoslavia;[5] they
made a noisy visit of reconciliation to Belgrade. In the
West, French national recalcitrance, over and above the

[5] American and British mediation meanwhile had settled
the long and painful Trieste frontier dispute between Italy
and Yugoslavia in 1954.

obscure wranglings of Parisian parliaments and politics, put an end to the American-sponsored concept of a European Defense Community with its supranational European army. Dulles threatened the French with the prospects of an "agonizing reappraisal" of America's position, involving the eventual withdrawal of American forces from Europe (which he really did not mean). Eden, who was now in full charge of British foreign policy, since the aging Churchill was to retire soon, patched things up in September 1954 by bringing West Germany within NATO.

Impressed by these developments, but even more influenced by their own need of a *détente*, the Russian leaders finally decided to go ahead with an Austrian peace settlement. They wrangled out certain economic concessions (which turned out to be politically inconsequential in the long run); they insisted upon the assurance that Austria, like Switzerland, would be neutral; but, after ten years of occupation, they agreed to a mutual withdrawal of troops from Austria. It is significant that in the last moment Molotov and, to some extent, Dulles, deeply suspicious of each other, were reluctant to let go of these Austrian zones of strategic deployment; but in the end wisdom prevailed in Washington and, perhaps more surprisingly, in Moscow. On 15 May 1955 the Austrian State Treaty was signed in Vienna amidst scenes of popular jubilation. More impressive and significant was the historic setting. The Austrian government had a sense of occasion. The Instrument was bound by the same firm that bound the Agreements of the great Congress of Vienna in 1815. There was a flicker of emotion even on Molotov's impassive face. The Austrian historian Friedrich Heer recorded Molotov's farewell visit to the Kahlenberg Hill, overlooking the towers and spires of historic Vienna, beyond which on that clear day his eye beheld the forests and mountains in the west and the great Hungarian plain stretching in silence to the east.[6]

As centuries ago, when her siege by Tatars and Turks had been broken, the redemption of Vienna may have marked a turning point in the history of Europe. For the first time in ten years the Russians and Americans agreed together to withdraw their troops from a central portion of Europe; they recognized the free existence of a Catholic and historic nation. The last Soviet troops left by 15 November; characteristically, the achievement of full independence was celebrated by the glittering opening performance of the rebuilt Viennese Opera. Vienna was now the capital of a free and neutral country, an event that could not but have certain consequences upon her neighbors, primarily upon Germany in the West and upon Hungary in the East. The disengagement of America and Russia in Europe had begun.

6

During this March-like climate in 1955 American reluctance against a Summit Meeting finally melted away.[7] For more than a year now the Foreign Ministers' Conferences from Berlin through Geneva to

[6] Molotov asked for a translation of the words engraved there: "Round from Kahlenberg these lands you must see/ To comprehend my thought, to understand me," written by the great Catholic and monarchist Austrian dramatic poet Grillparzer.

[7] We must again keep in mind that domestic political sentiments in America did not follow this change in the climate of world affairs, of which the overwhelming majority of the American people were left unaware by their press and government. In January 1955, for example, several American mayors and city councils protested to the State Department because the restrictions imposed by the latter upon the movements of Russian diplomatists in the United States were *not* extended to their cities.

Vienna were becoming more useful. Finally the four Heads of State—President Eisenhower, Prime Minister Bulganin (who came with Khrushchev, of course, and with Zhukov), Eden, and the inconsequential French Prime Minister Faure—met in Geneva in July 1955, with Chancellor Adenauer anxiously hovering in the mountains of the neighborhood.

This was a strange conference: not a success, not a failure; it was, really, nothing. The Russians showed some eagerness to discuss European questions: Eisenhower, upon the proddings of Dulles (who, in turn, was prodded by Adenauer), was reluctant to engage into any bargaining in detail; instead, he wished to arouse the imagination of the world with such sweeping (and impractical) proposals as his plan for an Open Aerial Inspection of America, Russia, and the world. The Russians were taken somewhat aback; they were obviously impressed with the benevolence and sincerity of this American President, but they had thought that, no matter how high the summit, the discussions would concern real estate and not air. As in Yalta, the main fault at Geneva was again that the meeting was unduly hurried and that the few agreements were vague. The Heads of State directed their Foreign Ministers to look for a solution of the German problem on the basis of free elections and considering the interests of Germany and of European security; but this formula was too general and too vague to constitute a definite commitment such as Dulles was later to claim. Soon after Geneva the Russians invited Adenauer to Moscow, but his talks there were inconclusive. Meanwhile the American armament and full political support of West Germany continued; in the ensuing Foreign Ministers' meeting later in the year, Molotov again proved recalcitrant and unyielding.

We must consider the German situation now, close as it was to the end of the first important phase of German rearmament. Behind it lay a more complex set of motives than immediately meets the eye. That West Germany should belong within the American alliance system was now an American axiom. The French, with their weak governments and with their army badly worn in Indochinese and Algerian campaigns, favored the close tying of Germany to Western alliances and armed systems in order to limit the freedom of powerful independent German action in the future. In other words, they were quite satisfied with the enduring prospects of a divided Germany. The British went along with this, too; they were, however, more aware of the dangerous influences that might follow in the potentially explosive area of Central Europe from an undue increase of West German power. The Germans, on the other hand, who but a few years before seemed reluctant to bear arms in any future war, were now more and more willing to rearm. In this prospect they no longer only saw their full reintegration within the democratic and defensive system of the West; but, rightly or wrongly, they regarded it as a step toward the future unification of Germany, and they began to relish the prospects of their position as the First European Ally of the United States, which Dulles himself suggested in his speech welcoming Adenauer to America in 1955.

Here we must say something about the role of Chancellor Adenauer, who, twice triumphantly reelected, was the undisputed master of German affairs during this decade. A principled and Christian statesman, fully sincere in his repudiation of Hitlerism, Catholic and strongly Francophile, a "Western" German par excellence, he was called by some the greatest German statesman since Bismarck, as with unswerving loyalty he led his defeated and distrusted nation back to trustworthy membership within the Western community of nations. Still, there are three conditions that we must keep in mind as we regard the career of this otherwise steadfast and excellent statesman. The first was Adenauer's evident dislike for the British, which greatly (though not exclusively) contributed to the deterioration of the important British-German relations later in the 1950s.[8] Second, we must admit that while Adenauer's loyalty to the West stood in noteworthy contrast to the policy of those statesmen of Weimar Germany who in the 1920s often attempted to balance East and West against each other to the benefit of Germandom, the brutal rigidity of Russian policy, at least under Stalin, hardly gave a West German leader any other alternative. In the third place, we must consider how Adenauer's anti-Communism was more of the rigid Dullesian than of the intelligent Churchillian kind; he outlawed the unimportant Communist Party in West Germany; he took it upon himself, time and time again, to prevent serious negotiations with the Russians that might have perhaps led to mutual concessions but perhaps also to a gradual promotion of the dissolution of the partition of Europe and of Germany; and here his advice prevailed over the British in Washington throughout. It is true, of course, that his opposition was well founded at least in part: the Russians were unprincipled and dangerous partners, and the power and prestige of his Bonn government would be naturally compromised in any process of reunification. On the other hand, we must consider how Adenauer's policy of negotiating with the Russians from strength has not succeeded throughout the decade: by 1960 German unification was further away than in 1953, before the German rearmament began and before the full American-German alliance was formed.

Compared with these complexities, the Russian attitude was relatively simple. Indeed, it was similar to the American proposals in 1945 and 1946, at the be-

---

[8] The psychological effects of the temporary defection of Dr. John to East Berlin (he had been proposed by the British for the position of West German counterintelligence chief) were deep and enduring.

ginning of the cold war, that Stalin had dismissed at the time. They offered a mutual withdrawal of troops from Germany; they remained ambiguous about the definition of free elections; they were unequivocal in their principle that a united Germany must be neutral and could not belong to either NATO or the Warsaw Pact, either the Western or the Eastern alliance systems. For a few more years the partial possibility still existed that the Russians might find a way of dropping some of their East German Communist leaders and commitments if this could be done without much loss of face and at the price of Western concessions. They had already recognized the impossibility of a Communist Germany; now they were striving for a neutral Germany; what they would not accept was the prospect of a united Germany allied with the United States.

Meanwhile the power and the prestige of West Germany grew. Its industrial influences and economic products appeared throughout the world. A triumphant nationalist campaign culminating in an electoral victory led to the French abandonment of the Saar in 1955. In the same year the Soviet Union recognized the German Federal Republic; we have seen, however, that their diplomatic contacts, marked by mutual suspicions, were unfruitful. The rearmament of West Germany now proceeded rapidly while American military, intelligence, and propaganda organizations of increasingly complex character operated throughout Germany, from which agents issued and broadcasts were regularly aimed not only at the satellites but at the nationalities within the Soviet Union proper.

Still, there was an improvement in the general climate. Stalin's policies and McCarthy's advocacies were no longer powerful; limited arrangements for tourism and scientific and "cultural" visits were developing between East and West in Europe and even between the United States and the Soviet Union. An agreement was reached between the two to sponsor the admission of

a block of states, Communist, anti-Communist, and
"neutral" ones together, to the United Nations. The Russians reduced their forces throughout Eastern Europe,
where, after the Austrian Treaty, they made the
Warsaw Pact a sort of counterpart of NATO. Such a
Pact was also necessary to establish their rights to
maintain troops in Hungary, where their earlier contractual rights, on the basis of guarding communication
lines to their garrisons in Austria, expired with the
Austrian State Treaty. We have already seen that they
withdrew their garrisons from the Chinese ports; now in
1955 they solemnly returned the Porkkala Peninsula,
a naval base acquired after the Second World War, to
a friendly and neutral Finland.

Meanwhile American commitments in West Germany and, indeed, all over the world increased in accord with the contractual and strategic concepts of
American security held by Dulles. Thus, from the death
of Stalin to the revolutionary year of 1956, the Russians
retreated and the United States advanced; but—except
for Austria—Europe remained divided.

CHAPTER VI

The Crucial Year

(1956)

1

A decade had now passed after Yalta and the consummation of Russian victory in Eastern Europe and in the Far East. On a world-wide scale the prestige of Russia may have diminished a little, while the reputation of her power remained largely constant. Yet we have seen how the new and still not quite entrenched rulers of Russia thought it better to retreat from certain outlying territories and positions. In the year 1956, then, this Russian retreat nearly turned into a rout of disaster. The most remarkable achievement of Nikita Khrushchev was that he proved able enough to arrest this rout; and that in a few years he could recover so much of his own prestige and power together with the prestige and power of his nation.

There is a strange Russian duality in the history of the Soviet Union during all of these years after the death of Stalin. On one hand, we may speak of a thaw, of a relative spring, of an opening of a few windows to the West, of a gradual increase of personal liberties, of industrial and scientific achievements, of the growth of a bureaucratic upper class, of the decreasing interest in the idea of Communism. On the other hand, there is the virtual absence of any conscious or serious political opposition to the regime of Communism in the Soviet Union. For these tendencies of a developing Russian society have been urban rather than urbane, materialist rather than moderate, technological rather than humanist, pragmatist rather than rational, opportunist rather than political, middle-class rather than bourgeois (in the traditional European sense of that much abused word), and passive rather than formative so far as important national and foreign politics have been concerned. It is this strange Russian duality that is reflected in the character and career of Nikita Khrushchev; and this habitual Russian political passivity made it possible for him to maintain his leadership even though the supremely dangerous events of 1956, which, in turn—and this, too, is very Russian—he himself had precipitated. A peasant and a *jouisseur*, at times hopelessly vulgar and at others amazingly subtle, astonishingly ignorant about certain realities but clear and lucid about others, puritanical but on occasion feckless, dogmatic but flexible, his figure suggesting that of an ugly dumpling but also of a powerful wrestler, his face ogre-like at times and babylike on others, his character exuding self-confidence while on occasion revealing a deep sense of the lack of it and even an abysmal Russian well of inner guilt—a Russian character, not without a certain peasant charm but also with a characteristic Russian unwillingness to face the distinction between image and reality, with an almost Oriental lack of the ethics of rhetoric.

This may be revealed to every careful reader of that extraordinary document, his speech in February 1956 to the Twentieth Party Congress. Despite the Communist problems and the Soviet jargon, its spirit is Dostoevskian as much as it is Marxist. Less than three years after the death of Stalin it represents the climax of the so-called "thaw" (let us remember that Russian thaws, though so welcome of course after the long icy rigors of Russian winters, tend to be short and muddy transitions between two extreme seasons); it represents the climax of the efforts of the new rulers of Russia to exalt the principle of "collective leadership," to inform the domestic Party that the Stalin rule, the "cult of the individual," was now over. The proceedings of the Twentieth Congress were started off by Mikoyan with startling and unusually courageous references to Stalin's cruelties; a week later, on 24-25 February, came Khrushchev's long and rambling speech to the closed Party session.[1] Khrushchev berated Stalin for many of his domestic crimes; and he even made a few references to Stalin's mistakes in the field of foreign relations. Though the speech was clearly directed against Stalin's memory (even though it did not condemn Stalin entirely); though it was principally directed for domestic Party consumption; though it was made with the sincere purpose of extolling the "classic" doctrines and purposes of Marxism and Leninism anew; though it was read at a secret session; though it sounded at times like the litany of a cowardly servant who could no longer keep within himself the fear and hatred (not unmixed with some respect) felt toward his now dead tyrant of a master, its effects were tremendous. They almost cost Khrushchev his rule—and, presumably, his life.

It was Tocqueville—a much more profound observer of history and of human nature than Marx—who in 1848 noted that the laws of physics do not always apply to politics; that, unlike in steam kettles, explosions in human affairs often occur not when the pressure is greatest but when it already has begun to lessen. In 1956 Khrushchev's speech and his policies of decompression may not have alone caused but they certainly contributed to the Eastern European explosions that were to follow.

2

We must, however, distinguish between the effects of the Khrushchev course in Russia from those within

[1] We should note that there were no Party Congresses during the long and crucial years from 1939 to 1952.

the once independent Eastern European nations. It is very significant—and an implicit judgment of Russian national character resides within it—that within Russia, where his terror had affected so many people, Stalin's memory still holds that kind of awe and respect that Oriental masses cherish for their great Khans. As so often in Russian history, the ruling circles close to the crimes and follies of a Tsar, even when they had been the accomplices or cowardly sycophants of his deeds, were more profoundly shocked and impressed by them than were the dark superstitious masses who continued to revere the Mysterious Ruler (and who were often attributing their sufferings not to him but to the very aristocracies who, after all, attempted to rectify matters for the very people's sake).

In the first two weeks of March 1956 serious riots occurred in Soviet Georgia—a reaction of students and people *against* the degrading of the Great Son of Georgia, of whom they were now so proud—even though, as Khrushchev himself pointed out in his speech, Stalin often cruelly suppressed and persecuted Georgian national aspirations in his self-appointed position as the Leader of All the Russias. Still Khrushchev succeeded in the end in re-establishing his authority within the Russias, while in Eastern Europe the rills and the rivulets of the thaw ran across historic landscapes less accustomed than the Russian plains to deep frost. In Eastern Europe, Stalin's dethronement created confusion and the appearance of ambitious new currents of reform even on the top, among the thin but powerful stratum of Communist leaders.

It is a mistake to believe that the rulers of Moscow have been always excellently informed on developments within their Eastern European Empire. There were few trusted leaders and strong personages on whom they could rely; and most of these now entrenched Communist leaders showed little willingness to endanger their own position through moderate and liberalizing

THE CRUCIAL YEAR 133

policies. Thus we find the paradoxical situation: in Russia the new Communist leaders were pushing moderate reforms while the great mass of the people remained passive; in the Eastern European captive nations, where popular hatred and disdain of the Communist system was far closer to the surface than in Russia, the leaders tried to keep things as little changed as was possible for them. Khrushchev's demotion of Malenkov in 1955, on whom certain hopes were pinned by reformist Communists in the satellites, led to renewed police rule and to retrenchments. Still, by 1956, in the wake of Khrushchev's speech (and also in the wake of his state visit to Britain), significant events indicated changes within Eastern Europe, too. Significant improvements were attempted by the Hungarian and Czechoslovak governments in their relations with neutral Austria and with Yugoslavia. In May the Communist Prime Minister of Hungary announced the dismantling of the iron curtain fortifications along the Austrian (and in August along the Yugoslav) border. The Russian reconciliation with Tito marked the latter's visit to Moscow, where he tried to convince Khrushchev of the necessity of getting rid of such unpopular satraps as the newly reinstated Rákosi in Hungary.[2] For a while the Russians hesitated; then events in Poland may have forced their hand.[3] In June in Poznan, Polish workers and youths besieged the Party and police headquarters in the presence of hundreds of Western visitors to a trade fair. Only after two or three days was order restored; and the Communist government acted with hesitation and with relative clemency. Meanwhile in Hungary the spirit of intellectual ferment rapidly rose. At the time of Poznan, during a hot and electric open session of the so-called

[2] "But he is a clever man, after all. And there is no one else we can rely on," replied Khrushchev.

[3] We must also keep in mind that from June 1956 to February 1957 the Russian government was saddled with a particularly incompetent Foreign Minister, Shepilov.

Petöfi Circle, public demands were made for the punishment and chastisement of the unpopular and hated Communist leaders. The audience cheered and asked for Imre Nagy. The national Communist Gomulka was released from confinement in Poland, while in Hungary, Rákosi was ordered to rehabilitate posthumously the national Communist Rajk, who had been purged and executed in 1949. Soon the popular Imre Nagy was to be reinstated within the Party. He was now supported by the Russians themselves. Mikoyan visited Budapest in the third week of July; the recalcitrant Rákosi was removed from office by direct Russian intervention; finally broken, he was spirited away to Moscow in a Russian airplane, in disgrace.

3

These were important developments of great significance. But meanwhile the attention of the Western Powers was diverted to and, indeed, absorbed by Egypt.

We have seen that after Stalin's death Russia retreated in Europe and also in the Far East. The Middle East, however, was an important exception; it marked a new course in Russian policies in what now, somewhat euphemistically, are called the uncommitted areas of the world. We have seen how after 1920 Lenin, whose revolutionary hopes had failed throughout Europe, began extending support to national revolutionary movements throughout the Near East and Asia. Somewhat similar was the policy of Khrushchev from 1955 onward. Evidently much impressed with the way in which American economic and technical assistance led to the establishment of American influence in many places of the world, he chose to imitate the United States in this respect, too. It is interesting in retrospect to note how the mighty Soviet Union under Stalin had no clear policy and exercised little practical influence in the turbulent lands of the Near East, so close to Russia's southern frontiers. Now all this was beginning to change. Russian economic, technical, political, and even military assistance was being offered to a number of countries, in line with the strange international tendency of our times according to which the creditor is the suppliant, not the debtor: it is a privilege for a Great Power to be allowed to give money (and often senselessly) to a smaller country far away. The traditional inclinations of thousands of years led Arabs, Egyptians, and others to exploit such a situation in a clever and natural way.

By June 1956 the last British forces had left Egypt. Meanwhile American and Russian missions competed against each other in the valley of the Nile. John Foster Dulles showed increasing anxieties about what he said was a new and infinitely insidious way of Soviet penetration. On 20 July he announced that the United States would not, after all, build the Aswan High Dam for Egypt. Within a week Colonel Nasser, the Egyptian Dictator, breaking the 1954 Treaty that the British had just fulfilled, proclaimed that his Egypt would nationalize the Suez Canal Company. Pretending to have acted out of a sense of deepest patriotic injury, in reality he had certain clever calculations in mind; he sowed the seeds of discord not only between the West and Russia but also between Britain and the United States, from which, as we now know, he would ultimately profit.

Stung by this cynical and perfidious action, the British and French governments, now having been exposed to a lessening of their prestige through a lengthening series of abdications, chose not to acquiesce in this Suez affair. They wished first to engage the pressure of world public opinion that could be made effective only with the aid of the United States. It was, of course, expected that the Soviet Union should cheer Nasser on. It was not expected that the United States should choose to frustrate British and French determination. During the intricate conferences that began in August it was becoming increasingly evident that Dulles, if not supporting the Egyptians openly, was unwilling to support the British. We cannot say with certainty whether his fear of Russian complications or his consideration of American oil and strategic interests played the predominant part in this increasingly devious policy of the Secretary of State to the advantage of Egypt and to the detriment of France and Britain (and, indirectly, also of Israel). There is evidence that, whatever their relative proportions, these motives were mixed and were important factors in his course. The more open and benevolent President, having recovered from a heart attack, was only following Dulles' lead. By the middle of September the true nature of Dulles' policy was unmistakably evident to London and Paris. Partly in concert with Israel, who put great emphasis on the Russian arms shipment to Egypt, the plans of a military operation against Egypt were secretly drawn up. Of this—despite Dulles' later claims—Washington was of course aware; by October her hortatory tone toward her Allies and Israel turned into one of suspicion mixed with warning and resentment. Subsequently the British and the French, who had already begun ferrying troops and assembling their navies in Cyprus, decided to strike alone. They kept the last phase of their military preparations secret from the United States. Egyptian military preparations increased in October; a unified Arab army command was set up against Israel. On 29 October, fortified with French fighter planes, Israel's army attacked Egypt across the Sinai Desert. Within a day its armored columns were approaching the Suez Canal in victorious clouds of dust. Next morning Eden announced that Britain and France were "intervening" between Israel and Egypt and that their forces would temporarily occupy Port Said, Ismailia, and Suez.

But on that very day even more dramatic scenes brought the cold war to a turning point in the frenzied streets of Budapest.

4

It is understandable why the Western Powers, and particularly Britain, devoted most, if not all, of their attention to this Egyptian Crisis. It is hardly understandable why they were caught without a policy by the onrush of Eastern European events in October 1956.

This was the most crucial month of the most crucial year, the most dramatic time in the entire history of the cold war. And while the onrush of dramatic events was sudden, it ought not have been unexpected. We know now how much political and intellectual fermentation was going on in Eastern Europe for more than a year before October 1956, by which time the boiling froth at the top was evidently rising, swelled by the wave of a popular tide.

This was most evident in Poland, whose history and national character had many a precedent for impatient and heroic revolt. The very Communist leaders were now riven asunder by the rising wave of national and democratic passions to which even their hearts and often even their Communist minds responded. Now Wladyslaw Gomulka, secretly released from prison in 1954, re-entered the national scene. This austere and patriotic Communist, a proletarian Pilsudski, was to prove the master of events. His personal impact was already strong on the Party when its Congress was about to meet on the 19th; from the Russian precedent great changes were expected. Suddenly Khrushchev, with a retinue of Marshals, swooped down on Warsaw in the morning.[4] In an extraordinary scene he barked accus-

[4] The incorporation of the Baltic Republics in 1940, the subordination of Rumania in 1945, and that of Czechoslovakia in 1948 were accomplished by such ominous aerial descents by eminent Russian personages. But by 1956 these days were over, at least in Poland.

ingly at Gomulka, who replied with determination, dignity, and disdain. Throughout that dramatic day Khrushchev and Gomulka, and the Russian and Polish Party leaders, argued bitterly in the closed meetings. More important, outside Russian armored columns were moving, and Russian warships took up threatening positions off Polish port cities in the Baltic. But Gomulka and his friends made it clear that they would not give in to the armed threat. The first shots were already fired; arms were distributed among the workers of Warsaw; for a moment the specter of a national war between Communist Poland and Communist Russia rose. Then Khrushchev gave in. Impressed not only by the necessities of the situation but also, in the age-old Russian way, by the force and determination of his opponent, he promised his support to Gomulka; he flew back to Moscow, chastened and pensive rather than determined to revenge his retreat, which, in turn, was to be made acceptable by the wisdom and restraint of Gomulka himself.

The Polish nation was unrestrained in its jubilation; still, it had been chastened sufficiently by the tragic experiences of recent history to act less impulsively than in the past—at least for a while. The passions for freedom and the sentiment of national independence were sweeping high, higher, highest during the days of the Hungarian Revolution that followed; but Gomulka, assisted by other men and other factors, could still maintain his control. The Polish October led to important modifications of Communist rule, to a restriction of police intervention, to a wide leeway given to intellectual liberty, to an almost complete lifting of the iron curtain to the West, and, most significantly, to the curtailment of Russian military authority within Poland and to the resignation of the Russian Marshal Rokossovsky from the position that had been assigned to him by Stalin seven years before.[5] Cardinal Wyszynski, released

[5] It must be remarked that Rokossovsky played a relatively

from prison, helped Gomulka in his efforts to establish national unity. He asked Catholic organizations and the people of Catholic Poland to support Gomulka in the elections that followed. Thus the chief Catholic churchman and the chief of the Communist Party of Poland together tried to solidify the gains of the Polish October in a somewhat extraordinary effort of co-operation.

Ever since 1956, thus, Poland has occupied a unique position among the Communist neighbor states of the Russian Empire. More independent and more sovereign than any of the others, she earned anew the respect of her friends. But it must not be thought that Poland had succeeded in wrenching herself away completely from Russia and from Communism or that her able new leader really attempted to do so. There is, moreover, a strain in the otherwise admirable Polish character, so heroic under attack, so valiant in defeat, that shows a certain amount of fecklessness and irresponsibility in times when not great national crises but the toil and frustrations of daily existence prove to be the main trial. Disorganization, continued poverty and corruption, and, in the end, disillusionment have cast their shadows in the rooms of this Polish Halfway House, the new western foundation walls of which, as we have seen, had been set up since 1945 in what was formerly a German piece of land. But now the roots of truncated German trees were growing again. From 1957 onward Gomulka, still a Communist, began to halt and, indeed, repress the full development of Polish intellectual, religious, material, and political liberties that would otherwise strongly pull Poland away from Communism. Gomulka, still a patriot, was always aware of Russia as

restrained role in Poland throughout. There is some evidence that this Russian commander, who had been jailed in the Moscow Purges of the thirties, did not relish his position. His position, his personal inclinations, and his conduct in Poland show a resemblance to that of the Grand Duke Constantine, whom Tsar Alexander I imposed as viceroy of a subjugated Poland (1815–31).

well as of Germany; he knew that Poland could not
defy Russia and Germany at the same time. When the
significant tentatives of his intelligent Foreign Minister,
Rapacki, about "disengagement," approved only half-
heartedly by Moscow, met with contemptuous rejection
on the part of Dulles as well as of Adenauer, Gomulka
may have felt it necessary to insure further the friendship and acquiescence of Russia in an at least partly independent Poland by restricting and, indeed, reversing
domestic developments of non-Communist and anti-
Russian unorthodoxy.

But we are running ahead of our story.

5

The Polish Revolution occurred on 19 October; its
success was consummated during the next few days. A
tremor ran across the entire Soviet Empire. It was not
strong enough to dislodge its foundations in many places
—except for Hungary.

For many reasons, in Hungary the unpopularity of
the Communist regime was greatest in Eastern Europe;
it was also in Hungary that the intellectual and political ferment of change was greatest in October 1956.
The eruption that followed shook the world. Its immediate impact shook the world probably more than any
revolution since the Bolshevik Russian one forty years
before. It was definitely more dramatic but also definitely less successful than the Russian revolution; unlike the Russian one, the importance of its occasion
lasted but less than a month, even though its significance, and not only for Hungary, still may prove enduring.

We have now seen how the Russians, belatedly, bun-
dled off the despised and hated Rákosi to Moscow in
July; but they compromised by appointing not the re-
habilitated Nagy but the rigid Gerö—like Rákosi, an-

other Jew, like Rákosi, another cruel remnant of the terroristic recent past but, unlike Rákosi, not a clever tyrant at all. During the first three weeks of October symbolic reforms and significant events in Budapest assumed a trend that was somewhat similar to that of Warsaw. But, even though events in Budapest were touched off by the news from Warsaw, in Hungary, unlike in Poland, a domestic revolution broke out on 23 October. On that day, when Gerö was still on his way back from a state visit to Belgrade, an almost spontaneous demonstration started by university students pulled the people of Budapest into the streets and squares by the evening. A large crowd of demonstrators appeared in Parliament Square, demanding Imre Nagy. A hasty, stupid, and snarling radio address by Gerö had the worst possible effects for the regime. Meanwhile demonstrators were besieging the building of the Magyar Radio, where the secret police opened fire. By that time workers from the industrial outskirts of Budapest were arriving in trucks, carrying a variety of weapons. Stalin's gigantic statue, erected on the site of a Catholic church only a few years before, was destroyed amidst frenzied scenes of jubilation and dragged into the center of the city. Throughout the night demonstrations, attacks on Communist press headquarters, and rifle fire went on.

On the morning of 24 October the world awoke to the news of a Hungarian civil war. The army, the police, the workers' organizations, were going over to the insurgents' side; everywhere in the city Hungarian flags appeared from the center of which the hated Communist emblem had been torn out. The remnants of the Communist government continued to broadcast pathetic appeals in which promises were mixed with threats; they announced the appointment of Imre Nagy as Premier. But the regime had already asked Russian troops to enter Budapest and to help restore order. The battle continued, even though Russian tanks were moving in.

It was soon obvious that they moved hesitantly, with
some reluctance. Groups of young people succeeded in
setting some of them afire. Crowds were decimated not
so much by Russian tank guns as by the unscrupulous
brigades of the secret police, fighting for their own
lives. Meanwhile the revolution had spread to the entire countryside. This was a popular and democratic
revolution, one of the few in history in the literal sense
of that last adjective: spontaneous, often heroic, largely
unrestrained, and almost entirely leaderless. Its passions were, of course, stronger than any political considerations. The concessions of the new regime trailed
sorrily behind this elemental surge of events; the tragedies of bloodshed increased the few concrete political
demands of the people to the point that within a few
days the universal cry was no longer the reform of the
Communist Party but the abolition of the one-party regime, no longer the withdrawal of Russian tanks from
the streets of Budapest but the withdrawal of Russian
troops from the entire country.

We know something about the Russian reactions to
these astonishing events. Already on the afternoon of 24
October, Mikoyan and Suslov—representing, significantly, the relatively liberal as well as the orthodox
wings of the Politburo—had arrived by rapid plane from
Moscow. Soviet armored cars took them to the building
of the Hungarian Communist Party, in the cellars of
which the remnants of the Hungarian Communist leadership were crouching in fear. These two Russian leg-
ates gave their support to Imre Nagy; the miserable
Gerö was to be spirited away to Moscow. Within a few
days, however, it appeared that neither the presence of
Russian tanks in Budapest nor the belated concessions
of a remodeled Communist regime could turn the popular tide. On 28 October the Russian tanks ceased to
fire in Budapest. They began to withdraw from the capital. Nagy, on whom now popular hopes were again
pinned, was announcing extraordinary reforms. To

weigh the situation and, presumably, to strengthen his hand, on 30 October, Mikoyan and Suslov flew to Budapest anew. On that day a long Moscow communiqué of extraordinary significance announced the withdrawal of Russian troops from all of Budapest and eventually from Hungary; more important, it suggested not only support to the Nagy government but a fundamental revision of the relations of Russia with her Eastern European "socialist" neighbor states under the Warsaw Pact.

On that day of 30 October 1956—with Hungary pulling loose, when Poland had already wrenched herself half free, when frantic fears gripped the Soviet satellite chieftains in East Germany, Czechoslovakia, Rumania, and Bulgaria, when an Anglo-French armada was moving toward Port Said, when the Chinese in the East, too, were publishing a statement against the previous Russian mistakes of "bourgeois chauvinism," it seemed—and not to John Foster Dulles alone—that the dissolution of the Soviet Empire was at hand. We shall now see how the capable Khrushchev, within the nick of time, could halt this seemingly fateful tide of events because of the incapacity of other world leaders to assay and to act intelligently upon them at this exceptional and opportune juncture.

6

At two o'clock in the afternoon of Wednesday, 31 October, a week to the hour when Mikoyan and Suslov first appeared in the besieged Party headquarters in Budapest, the leaders of the Russian Empire met in the Kremlin in an anxious and historic session of their Politburo. We do not know much about what happens during such Politburo sessions, whether historic or not. We know, however, that then and there the decision was taken to reverse the Russian policy prevailing up to that time and to crush the Hungarian Revolution by Russian arms, tacitly accepting all of the consequences that such an act would bring to international Communist prestige. We need not have the accounts of that Politburo session to know that this was not a pleasant decision to take; but obviously the national and strategic interests of Russia were more important than international Communist prestige. Even so, we know that there was some inconclusive debate; Khrushchev and the military then decided the balance. Within a few hours the necessary orders reached the Russian command posts on the Hungarian-Russian frontier. By the evening of 31 October the first sporadic news of halt and reversal in the Russian armored withdrawal from Hungary came in to Budapest.

Nagy, unlike Gomulka in Warsaw, was not the master of events; and the Hungarians, with less historical experience of the Polish kind, were not sufficiently aware of the limitations that world politics imposed on their newly won freedom. They rejoiced in the sympathy of the world, unaware of the distance that separated Western words from Western actions and only dimly aware of the consequences of the fateful coincidence whereby the chief attention of the leaders of the West was directed to Egypt rather than to Hungary. Nagy announced Hungary's "neutrality" and withdrawal from the Warsaw Pact. Meanwhile the reversal of Russian armed movements continued; a few Communist personalities significantly disappeared from the capital. Nagy decided to appeal to the United Nations; but all of this was too late. At midnight on 4 November the Russians struck. Relying on a traditional Oriental and Russian method of treachery, under the guise of negotiations they lured into a trap the brave and popular defender of the now legendary Kilian Barracks, the War Minister Colonel Maléter. He was arrested personally by the chief of the Russian Secret Police. Within a few hours Russian guns began to boom as columns of Soviet tanks converged upon Budapest. Nagy and his followers fled to the Yugoslav Embassy.[6] The radio announced the formation of a New Workers' and Peasants' government led by a Kádár. Astonishingly, though perhaps not surprisingly, the insurgents fought on for two more weeks in ruined streets and in certain places in the country while the new regime, aware of its desperately meager claim to existence, kept proclaiming that it would maintain most of the reforms achieved by the Hungarian Glorious Revolution. The frontier toward Austria and Yugoslavia[7] was still open; and during the next month 200,000 Hungarians, 2 per cent of the entire population of the nation, left Hungary in an extraordinary wave of mass migration. They were received all over the world with generosity and sympathy. None of this, of course, changed the main course of events. Khrushchev could leave unheeded resolutions of the United Nations and the bitter condemnation of his intervention all around the world. By the end of November the silence of a near-graveyard settled over the tragic scene of Hungary.

We must not believe, however, that, in a mood of superb and cynical unconcern, Khrushchev and his colleagues were unmoved by these events. The determined Russian reaction covered up many anxieties in Moscow. We must not overlook the few but significant evidences of reluctance in the ranks of the Rus-

[6] Three weeks later he was again treacherously arrested by Russian police forces. In turn, having broken their word for the third time, Soviet police organs brought Nagy, Maléter, and others to trial, announcing their condemnation and execution *post facto* to a shocked world in June 1958. There is evidence that certain Russian leaders, particularly President Voroshilov, disapproved of this; there is some evidence that Khrushchev himself, acting under pressure, had found this decision disagreeable but unavoidable.

[7] There is some evidence that Khrushchev informed Tito about the Russian decision to crush the Hungarian rebellion, which had gone "too far."

sian army sent into Hungary, nor certain muted protests by university students in Leningrad. As important
as these sporadic instances was the devastating effect of
the Hungarian Revolution on the last few intelligent
supporters of Communist ideology and prestige in the
Western world. More important was that in Moscow it
was the Army, not the Party, whose leadership virtually
unanimously supported the oppression of the Hungarian
revolt.[8] And even more important was the evidence
that, until 31 October, Moscow was willing to give in to
Hungary unless—and this was the decisive condition—
the new Hungary would not entirely break away from
the Russian to the Western sphere in Europe.

Why, then, the sudden reversal on 31 October?
Partly because of the potential great dangers of a Hungarian precedent but also because of the exceptional
opportunity of Suez: in Hungary not so much because
Nagy was not an orthodox Communist as because he
could not halt the tide of anti-Communist passions; in
Egypt not so much because the Anglo-French action
threatened Russian interests as because the attention of
the world, and particularly of the United States, was
now diverted there.[9] In Egypt, Russian prestige was
involved but Russian power was not much at stake; in
Hungary, Russian prestige could perhaps be saved by
moderation but Russian power was at stake. And power
was always more important for Moscow than prestige;
moreover, Hungary is closer than is Suez to Russia.
Thus just because of the extraordinary coincidence of
the Egyptian and Hungarian events, we should not fail
to observe the primacy of Hungary in these Russian

[8] It is significant that Russian armored units began moving toward Budapest as early as 21 October—that is, after
the Polish and two days before the Hungarian revolutionary
events.

[9] A study of the world's great newspapers revealed that on
2 November 1956 in the Western press on the average more
than four times as much space was allotted to the Egyptian
as to the Hungarian events.

considerations in October 1956. These were decisive considerations: and Russian action, on 31 October, was spurred by the knowledge that the United States was now actively preoccupied with Suez but evidently unwilling to act in regard to Hungary.

7

It is obvious that ideological calculations of international Communist prestige alone were not enough to let the Russian masters risk the eventual loss of their Eastern European buffer zone. It is obvious that Britain and France were in no position to make their weight felt in Eastern European affairs. It is obvious, therefore, that during this paramount Russian crisis the reactions of the United States alone were of decisive importance.

We can dismiss much of the policy announced since 1952 by the Republican Administration about "liberation" or the "rollback of Communism" in Eastern Europe as propaganda, mostly aimed as it was at anti-Communist opinion and at voters of Eastern European origin within the United States. But we cannot expect the unsophisticated and desperate people of Hungary to have discounted this propaganda accordingly, massively broadcast as it was from American-supported radio stations in West Germany to Eastern Europe. It is true that Washington behaved with some restraint during the first and unexpectedly successful phase of the Hungarian Revolution; but these developments should not have come as unexpected to Dulles,[10] whose

[10] They didn't (1966). In the second volume of his presidential memoirs, published in 1965, Eisenhower unwittingly revealed that on 22 October 1956, that is, the day *before* the explosive events in Budapest, "I held conference after conference—in fact, there were twenty-three of these . . . Prac-

agents were not inactive throughout Eastern Europe in
1956 and who himself said—and not without reason—
that the great crisis of Soviet Communism was approaching. Shortly before the Hungarian Revolution,
Dulles had visited Tito, and it seemed that this rigid
anti-Communist himself was not unwilling, for the first
time, to see Eastern European events develop in a gradual, national Communist, Titoist fashion. All of these in-
complete calculations were then washed away by the
torrent of Hungarian events. Again we must remember
that we cannot treat their impact in isolation from the
rest of world affairs. There was the simultaneous and
dramatic outburst of the Egyptian crisis. There were
the simultaneous, less dramatic, but more wearisome
preoccupations of the approaching American presidential election. There was, above all, a renewed aura of
anti-Communist distrust and impatience in the American attitude toward Russia, since Dulles and the President held that the Russians had been wholly insincere
at Geneva. Bulganin's (and also Zhukov's) correspondence with the President was inconclusive; their proposals for "coexistence" and for Non-Aggression Treaties
with the United States were dismissed as mere propaganda; as late as 21 October the President published
an impatient and curt reply to Bulganin's latest efflores-
cent and propagandistic missive, accusing the latter of
attempting to interfere with the American presidential
election. Then came the Hungarian explosions. Their
American echoes were listened to with utmost anxiety
in Moscow. The United States, together with Britain
and France, called for the Security Council of the
United Nations to treat with Russian intervention in
Hungary. The Soviet Union, of course, obstructed and
refused this procedure of the United Nations; still, it
was during the important session of 28 October that

tically all had to do with subjects directly or indirectly related to the developing Hungarian crisis." (*Waging Peace*,
pages 62–63).

the news came of the Russian withdrawal from Budapest. The astonishing Russian announcement of 30 October, promising a revision of Russia's relations with her satellites and a transformation of the Warsaw Pact, was greeted by Washington with satisfaction; the President made a statement cautiously welcoming the Russian announcement and insisting that the United States had no intention of interfering with the security of the Soviet Union. But this was not enough. There were no American counterproposals. Having now seen that America would not intervene, Khrushchev and the Politburo felt that they could strike—having also seen that Washington, responding to Moscow, was not willing to propose a corresponding revision of her Western European military and alliance system, they felt that they should strike—in Hungary.

We need not describe the expectable American indignation in detail. By the force of events they were mostly restricted to the impassionate and unpolitical oratory of Ambassador Lodge at the United Nations. It was in regard to Suez, not to Hungary, that, for a moment, war clouds accumulated; but there American action was swift and decisive. Jabbed to the quick by the news of the British-French action and prodded of course very much by his Secretary of State, the President picked up the telephone to call Eden down with harsh and angry words. On 5 November—not until they were certain that the United States would not seriously intervene in Hungary and not until they saw that the American condemnation of Britain and France was seriously meant (something that at first they were not inclined to believe)—the Russians suddenly made warlike noises of a calculatedly ominous nature. While Russian guns were pounding Budapest, a strident Russian note threatened Britain and France with Russian rockets, and a somewhat impudent (but historically significant) Russian note proposed that American and Russian forces together intervene to uphold peace in the eastern Mediterranean. The immediate American reaction was to tell the Russians to keep out; to demonstrate American readiness, crews of the American Strategic Air Command in Britain were put on a demonstrative alert. Meanwhile the progress of the Anglo-French expedition toward Suez was slow. It was, then, not the threat of Russian rockets but American intervention that saved Nasser in Egypt and put an end to the Suez Expedition.[11] On 6 November the Anglo-French command, heeding a resolution of the United Nations, announced a cease-fire. The rest of that story is well known; it flowed naturally from the now set pattern of forces and events. Having been stopped short of their final destination of Suez by the combining pressures of America, Russia, the United Nations, and British Labour opposition (of which the first was decisive), the British and the French withdrew from the great waterway that they had built and maintained for a century. After some wrangling, the Israeli Army, too, withdrew; a United Nations Emergency Force was introduced into the Canal Zone and the Sinai; soon the canal was cleared, mostly with American assistance, while Nasser, rescued but in the nick of time by Dulles and Eisenhower, lived on, ungrateful and calculating. A tide of indignation rose in Britain against America; Anthony Eden broke under its strain. It was now America, and not Britain or France, that was to be the dominant Power in the eastern Mediterranean; American marines were to come soon to the places where the banners of Saint Louis and the White Ensign once flew.

Thus we have seen that, in the estimation of Dulles and Eisenhower, Suez was more important than Eastern Europe; we have seen that, for Khrushchev and for Russia, of course the reverse was true. Perhaps this is the main point on which American policy deserves

[11] It is perhaps significant that of all the Western European nations only West Germany and Spain showed official sympathy for Nasser (and Dulles).

criticism: for, as ten years before, Washington seems to have underestimated the crucial importance of Eastern Europe, especially in relation to Russia. They showed some but not sufficient understanding of Russia's strategic interests and obsessions about her Eastern European satellite buffer zone; and they showed no willingness at all to turn the great occasion toward mutual accommodations with Russia in Europe. In plain English, when the Russians suggested that they withdraw from Hungary, the American response did not mention anything about a corresponding withdrawal from any other part of Europe. Nor was this occasion limited to the crucial twenty-four hours between the 30 October Moscow announcement and the 31 October Politburo session. As late as 17 November a significant Russian note still suggested the possible revision of the Warsaw Pact and a willingness to explore European divisions anew. The American government was obviously and sincerely affected by the specter of the brutal second Russian intervention in Hungary, but it preferred to demonstrate its sentiments in indignant rhetoric. It was on the same night during one of his Kremlin receptions that the excitable Khrushchev uttered the since famous words: "We will bury you."

Like so many Soviet phrases, these words have been quoted out of context ever since that time. We must keep in mind its date as well as the entire phrase: "If you don't like us, don't accept our invitations and don't invite us to come to see you! Whether you like it or not, history is on our side; we will bury you!!!" Considering the time, the occasion, and the character of the speaker, it does not require much psychological profundity to see beneath these flushed and impulsive words ebullience together with a lack of confidence, aggressiveness together with a sense of ostracism and even of inferiority. These are very Russian words; they are the words of a powerful but unsure man, shouting rather than whistling in the dark.

8

There was, of course, another means with which the
United States in October 1956 could have promoted
the dissolution of Russia's Eastern European Empire and
perhaps achieved a tremendous victory in the cold war.
This was the threat of American armed intervention,
including the threat of a hydrogen war.

But even for Dulles, with all of his previous talk
about "massive deterrence" or "retaliation," this was
obviously out of the question. We are thus approaching an issue of utmost importance. It is true, as Churchill and others have said, that the awesome specter of
atomic arms has hitherto spared the world from the horrors of a hot war. But it is also true that the very existence of these awful weapons contributed to the rigidity of the unnatural division of Europe and of the world.
Thus these weapons have served as a defense of freedom but also as a restriction of freedom; they were
(and still are) instruments of utmost potency as well
as of historic impotence. It is quite possible, it is even
probable, that the rulers of Russia in 1956 may have
recoiled before an American threat of a hydrogen war;
but there is no question that, at least in Europe, the allies of the United States would have refused their as-
sent to such a threat. The world already knew too
much about the effects of hydrogen explosions. The
American tests in the Pacific in 1954 maimed and
burned the crew of a Japanese fishing vessel; the gradual introduction of radioactive particles in the air, the
problem of fallout, was beginning to vex people beyond
the usual groups of pacifists and Left-wingers. Even
though within the United States the absence of physical
destruction during the last war, together with the sentiments of anti-Communism, have as yet had little effect
on the atomic policies of the government in 1956, an

atomic war, for the sake of Hungary, was politically unthinkable.

Thus, as the year 1956 closed, people in the free world could look on bitterly but powerlessly at the tragedy of Hungary, doing their best through their exceptional hospitality tendered to the 200,000 fleeing Hungarians who dispersed throughout the world.

We should not, however, overlook more permanent considerations that issue from the balance of the dramatic events of that crucial year. It was evident that the Russians were now determined to keep their domains largely intact. But it was also evident that, in contrast to the up to then unanimous pontifications of intellectuals and experts, a revolution *could* occur even under a totalitarian government. It was evident that the United Nations was woefully impotent in dealing with profound historical issues involving Western Civilization. But it was also evident that the United Nations could be at times a useful instrument of American (but not of Western European) policies. It was evident that the echoes of the Hungarian repression further decimated the already so often decimated ranks of Communist believers throughout the world, and especially in Europe. But it was also evident that, whatever was happening to Communism, even within the Soviet Union, Russia remained powerful and strong. It was evident, on the other hand, that no matter how great her power, Russia could not successfully digest her captive Eastern European nations, that she could not even expect to transform them completely according to her own Communist mold. But it was also evident that the United States was not going to, and, indeed, that it never fully intended to, challenge Russian overlordship in Eastern Europe.

Among all of these often opposite and countervailing considerations, perhaps the last is the most important one. For there is reason to believe that the American reaction to the Hungarian events in 1956 convinced

Khrushchev, and presumably also other leaders of Russia, of just that. Again we must attempt to look at events from the perspective of Moscow, taking into account not only the geographical situation but the characteristic suspicions that range from uneasiness to maniacal proportions among its rulers. In November 1956, for the first time, Khrushchev could tell himself and his colleagues that the United States was to be trusted at least to the extent of not interfering with the Russian Empire in Eastern Europe. Thereby, to him at least, the conditions of a future improvement of Russian-American relations were immediately set.[12]

Thus, in a paradoxical and melancholy manner, the Hungarian Revolution was a turning point in Russian-American relations. While in the United States indignation about Hungary's fate set back the thaw in the cold war for at least two years, from the Russian point of view the chances of Russian-American friendship (and, indeed, perhaps for a clearer and better Russian-American division of the world) were getting better. Thus, less than three years after the Hungarian Revolution, Khrushchev himself would arrive at a ceremonial visit to Washington.

[12] It is in this respect that the naturally abortive Russian proposal of 5 November 1956 about a joint Russian-American intervention in Egypt is so significant. Moreover, it had its historical precedent. In 1823 Alexander I, noting the popular American sympathy for the Greek insurrection against the Ottoman Empire, suggested that a joint American-Russian fleet be sent into the Mediterranean against the Turks. Forty years later, when Napoleon III suggested that the Union associate herself with France in condemning the Russian suppression of the Polish Revolution, the American government of course refused.

CHAPTER VII

To the Summits

(From 1956)

1

Neither the American term, Cold War, nor the Russian term, Peaceful Coexistence, adequately describes the historical atmosphere of the next three years. From the crucial autumn of 1956 through 1959 except for one brief critical week in July 1958, the prospects of war became a little more remote while the coexistence (a euphemistic term for the obvious) of the Two Great Powers did not become very peaceful: it remained uneasy, suspicious, and generally cold. Their relations and, indeed, the development of world affairs again reflected a strange duality. On the one hand, Russian-American relations were on occasion improving; on the other, Russian-American rivalries were extended to new countries of the world and to new areas of the universe. On the one hand, the iron curtain was opened here and there; international co-operation between Russia and the West became more frequent; the Russians took part and made certain significant concessions in disarmament conferences; they announced a general program of reducing their armies; they suggested that they did not support the expansive and aggressive policies of Communist China always and everywhere; the experimental exploding of large nuclear bombs was temporarily halted. On the other hand, Russia and America now engaged themselves in a spectacular race of rocket shootings; the number of rocket sites increased; the advanced installation of American bases went on; in Eastern Europe rigid Communist rule was reaffirmed; the American armament of West Germany continued while the Russian political commitment to the permanent establishment of an East German Communist state was hardening. In November 1958 Khrushchev reopened the question of Berlin, and even though he postponed unilateral action, his threatened reforms in the status of that divided and central city of the cold war sounded ominous enough.

The wish to improve relations proved, however, the more important factor of these two countervailing developments. For 1956 was not only the Crucial Year but the Turning Point in the history of the cold war—that is, in the relations of the two Super-Powers, of the United States and of the Soviet Russian Empire after the Second World War. And even without the—sometimes dubious—advantage of historical perspective, as late as 1958, that is, after about a decade of cold war, certain developments were becoming evident. It was evident that the American and the Russian leaders were no longer crediting each other with immediate warlike intentions. Even though meanwhile the armament race continued in an alarmingly frenzied pattern, it was evident that, perhaps except for the Chinese, not even the most extravagant Communists wished to consider the prospects of a hydrogen war. It was becoming evident to both sides that precisely because of the existence of these horrible weapons, some mutual accommodations in a shrinking world could not be avoided. Evidently impressed with what they saw as the success of certain international economic policies, the Russian leaders transferred some of their emphasis to economic expansion in many places throughout the world, trying to match the Americans in a game in which the latter seemed to have been ahead. Evidently impressed by the spectacle of Russian successes in atomic and rocket artillery, the government of the United States transferred what was probably excessive emphasis to an ex-

pansion of military and propaganda activities, trying to
match the Russians in a game in which the latter have
been regarded as masters. We shall see, therefore, how
suspicion and respect, envy and ambition together have
contributed to a certain "Americanization" of Russia as
well as to certain deplorable developments of the
United States toward a technological and military welfare state. More important, in the short run, was the
fact that the wish of the Russian government—or, rather,
specifically, of Nikita Khrushchev—to improve Russia's
relations with the United States had crystallized from
an underlying tendency into a definite commitment by
early 1959. Out of this came reciprocal visits of Russian and American statesmen, culminating in three Summit Meetings in three years, in Washington in 1959, in
Paris in 1960, in Vienna in 1961.

2

Khrushchev, severely tried by the events of Hungary
and Poland, had to face criticism and potential conspiracy by those of his colleagues who saw folly in the
policies of "liberalization" that this ebullient and erratic Russian leader followed after the death of Stalin.
There were, however, two major circumstances to
Khrushchev's advantage. One was that even within Russia a return to the police rule of former years was to
some extent unpopular; the other was that, outside of
Russia, Khrushchev and the Army did succeed, after all,
in restoring order in Hungary and throughout Eastern
Europe quickly and ably.

It is a mistake to see Soviet events and personalities
as if these would but incarnate various schools of
thought of Marxist dogma. Even though admittedly the
leaders of the Soviet Union had, and still have, varying
estimates of the character of Stalin, to speak of "Stalinist" and of "anti-Stalinist" groups in Moscow may

be a gross error. A struggle for power and for personal security, not a struggle between dogmatists of different ideological schools of thought, characterizes the struggles within the restricted circle of Russia's leaders. And while it is true that, especially in politics, personal inclinations and animosities are not separable from the different ideas that are rightly or wrongly associated with different persons, even these ideas concern ultimately the interests of the Russian State rather than the interests of Communism. We should recall that within Russia, Khrushchev could crush Beria and later Malenkov not only because of their domestic tendencies but also because these men had been considering certain unorthodox and far-reaching diplomatic plans of accommodation with the West regarding Germany and Europe. During and after 1956, thus, Khrushchev —in some ways like Stalin during and after 1925—felt that he could consolidate his power best by gaining the support of some of his potential domestic opponents through his handling of foreign affairs. Thus we should not seek ideological motives and we should not unduly attempt to detect ideological groupings behind Khrushchev's actions that in 1957 led to the successful consolidation of his power. Thus, for example, he drew on the two opposites, Mikoyan and Suslov, during the Hungarian crisis; and a year later he eliminated from positions of leadership relative "liberals" as well as relative "orthodox," Malenkov as well as Molotov, Bulganin as well as Kaganovich, together with the eminent military leader Zhukov. For once these men were not killed, maimed, or jailed but relegated to provincial positions of relative obscurity. Thereby the period of the Directorate that governed Russia after the end of the Stalin Terror came to an end.

This does not mean, however, that Khrushchev's rule in Russia was as secure and incontestable as Stalin's had been. He himself revealed this on a number of occasions; and he had to alter and pursue policies in ac-

cord with the potential strength of his domestic enemies. The Chinese, for instance who, as we saw, in 1956
had supported the development of "national Communism" in Eastern Europe (since they welcomed the
weakening of Russian absolutism within the Communist
sphere), soon after the Hungarian Revolution became
the most strident proponents of stern Communist orthodoxy (since they were uncomfortably impressed with
the revealed strength of anti-Communist and pro-West-
ern sentiments in Eastern Europe). Indeed, they were
the first who urged that punishment should be meted
out to Imre Nagy, kept carefully in captivity, whose
future early in 1957 was not yet clear. The Chinese
of course did not have a decisive voice in the councils
of Moscow, but they could strengthen Khrushchev's opponents on potentially decisive occasions. It is in consequence of these considerations that Khrushchev again
turned against Tito in 1957 and that he acquiesced in
the execution of Nagy in June 1958; thus, on the other
hand, he could keep his balance, depend on Gomulka's
Poland, maintain certain liberalizing measures within
Russia, and, most important of all, continue his diplomatic approaches toward the United States (that the
Chinese, of course, did not like at all).

Meanwhile fortune came to his side at a crucial moment. On 4 October 1957, at a time when conflicts
and intrigues within the Politburo were still unresolved,
a Russian rocket fired a metal object into the sky beyond the immediate sphere of the gravity of the earth.
This so-called scientific achievement, whose preparations had been laid of course years before, had an immediate impact on Russian pride and prestige that, in
turn, was to Khrushchev's great advantage; in his political speeches, whether at home or abroad, he went
ahead to emphasize these undoubtedly spectacular Russian rocket successes with a kind of rhetoric that was
often immature, strident, and boastful.

There is no question that as the stringent and martial

restrictions of Stalin's era were gradually lifted, the energy of the talented Russian nation blossomed out in hitherto neglected directions; that Russian material standards of life were on the rise; that, as Khrushchev had said over and over again, Russia would surpass the production of the United States in some fields though not (as Khrushchev seemed to believe) over-all, and not decisively. His domestic position could thus profit from the long overdue fruits of the toil and wealth of so great an Empire; his external prestige could profit from the spectacle of a Russia that was growing not only powerful but more prosperous. Still, not far beneath these amenable developments on the surface were brutal pressures and passions that were revealed to the world on occasion, as, for instance, in the execution of the Hungarians or in the affair of the novelist Pasternak in 1958. And there were many evidences that strong dark currents of xenophobia, primitive nationalism, corruption, anti-Semitism, even though ignored by the world at large, continued to exist, influencing the actions of the masters of the Soviet Union, not far below the more agreeable bustling Muscovite aspect of a more self-confident and prosperous Russia—still Pugachev's and Potemkin's land—now open to small knotted groups of tourists traveling along prearranged routes.

3

We must now turn to sketch the outlines of a great American transformation, one that is more important than the Russian evolution after Stalin's death even though it has been seldom so recognized by the American people themselves.

By the second half of the 1950s an American generation had grown up that had been accustomed to what, with some exaggeration, may be called the centralized American welfare state. Moreover, for more than twenty years now, this generation has been accustomed not only to a military atmosphere abroad but to the establishment, even during peacetime, of American air, naval, and military bases on the five continents of the world.

We have seen earlier that, faced with Soviet aggressiveness, the reaction of the American government and people to the distress of Europe after the war was courageous, disciplined, and commendable. By the 1950s, however, a certain degeneration of the original purpose set in while the world-wide extension of American involvements continued.

In 1938 there were virtually no American possessions or military bases outside the Western Hemisphere; by 1958 there was an American world empire involving five continents and an overwhelming network of American military bases abroad. American troops were now stationed in the Mediterranean, in Central Europe, in Arabia, and in the Arctic even while the Russian Empire did not extend much beyond the frontiers of Tsardom of a hundred years ago. The United States now had alliances with about fifty countries (of which thirty were not in the Western Hemisphere) far beyond its oceanic frontiers while the Russians had virtually no binding alliances except with their Communist and satellite neighbors. By 1958 there were few Americans—including the majority of international "experts" and perhaps even the President—who could sit down with a pencil and list all the countries in which the United States had military bases around the world.

There is no question that many of these involvements were reasonable ones; they flowed naturally from the obvious American policy to contain Communist Russia. There was no question that, especially after the Second World War, the United States would be the leader of the free world. We have seen, however, that the limited purposes of the containment policy as drafted in 1947 by Kennan were extended to a world-wide string of contractual arrangements by Dulles. We have seen, and we shall have to return once more to the complications of American foreign policy that resulted from such extensive engagements; but here I am concerned with the effects of this world-wide transformation on American society. For this involved—and it still involves—great radical departures from previous American traditions.

Together with the development of a welfare state, the bureaucracy of the American government increased in tremendous proportions. The proportionate increase of the personnel and of the powers of federal investigative and intelligence agencies was even greater. More important, their "intelligence" activities were achieving a certain domestic glamour. The number of American men at arms, while not in itself exorbitant, was now supplemented by an ever increasing number of people in civilian and "defense" occupations. Abroad it was not only that the number of American bases increased, but that hundreds of thousands of American military families were now installed in American enclaves, forming American colonies in many places of the world from Spain to Asia; and for the first time in history the previously very homebound American soldiers and their families were beginning to experience the somewhat corruptive delights of luxurious living accommodations abroad. Meanwhile in scores of other countries where American military bases were not established, American technical, economic, and training missions were set up under not unsimilar conditions. An enormous bureaucracy was pressing American gifts and loans upon greedy people in five continents while, in line with the general advertising practices of a now heavily bureaucratized American business, the propaganda activities of the American government kept another swarm of bureaucrats in glassy offices all over the world. There is evidence suggesting that American intelligence, with practically unlimited funds, has had many potential agents at its disposal in many other places and occupations than people presume[1] while the State Department found it necessary to depart from the earlier American concepts of fair play, involving surreptitious practices by so-called "private" propaganda and political organizations, extending financial and organizational support to a sometimes fantastic variety of activities all over the world. Meanwhile at home the industrial corporations of the United States for the first time in history began to depend upon the increasingly complex "defense requirements" even in peacetime, involving hordes of middlemen and drawing upon the ambitions of active as well as of retired military officers. Thereby the earlier traditional American division between private and military establishments, and between civilian and military occupations was being washed away. Nor were these developments restricted to the industrial sphere: professional entertainers and professional intellectuals, from the greatest universities of America through basketball teams to jazz bands, were now willing recipients in increasing measure of federal "research" and "defense" funds on many "projects" of at least doubtful value.

I shall treat some of the symptoms of this new American development toward an imperial society in the second part of this book; here, at any rate, are a few figures that suggest the extent of this great transformation. Note that the two dates are 1948 and 1958: the comparison, therefore, is not between a peaceful and a critical year but between two critical years of the cold war of which 1948, the year of the Berlin Blockade, was probably the more critical one, when the chances of a hot war in Europe were probably as great as at any other time in the cold war. Between 1948 and 1958, for instance, the Russians did not conquer a single square mile of new territory: with this consideration in

[1] Written in February 1960, before the sensational revelations of the Spy-Plane Incident.

mind, the meaning of the following figures may be even more striking. In 1948 the total budget of the United States was about 37 billion dollars; ten years later it was nearly double, 72 billion. In 1948 military expenses amounted to about 14 billion, little more than one third; in 1958 they amounted to 45 billion dollars, almost two thirds of the entire budget. Thus by 1958 the military expenditures of the United States exceeded the entire expenditures of the nation ten years before, in 1948, when, unlike 1958, the United States had had to carry the burden of arming the West almost entirely alone. While the allocations to the Navy, traditionally the principal defense arm of the Republic, merely doubled from 1948 to 1958, the funds voted for the United States Air Force increased eleven times, from 1.7 billion dollars in 1948 to 19 billion in 1958. At home the federal bureaucracy grew from about 3.3 million employees in 1948 to nearly 5 million by 1958 (not including the employees of FBI, of the Central Intelligence Agency, and the mushrooming and not easily ascertainable number of people indirectly employed by the government). The total of personnel in the armed services rose from 1.4 million to 2.6 million. The staff of the State Department, consisting of less than 8000 people in 1948, multiplied fivefold in ten years, to about 40,-000, and this does not include the 14,000 employed by the United States Information Agency.

Obviously the developments of a decade justified some increases; surely they did not justify such overwhelmingly vast ones. Probably Russian expenditures may have increased, too, but hardly in so steep a fashion.

It is, in any case, significant that most of these increased commitments took place after 1952, under a Republican Administration formed by a party pledged to free enterprise and to limitations of governmental intervention, a party that is called, financially at least, "conservative" by its supporters while it is criticized as

being tightfisted, "reactionary," and "isolationist" by its
opponents. I wish, therefore, to draw my readers' attention to a symptom that, at the time of its occurrence, went entirely unobserved by the otherwise pains-
takingly attentive political commentators. It is Section
Nine of the Republican Party Platform that was proposed and accepted unanimously during the 1956 Convention. It called for nothing less than "the establishment of American bases strategically dispersed all
around the world." This statement by what even now
commentators call the "conservative" and "isolationist-
inclined" party illuminated, at least to me, the revolution of American political attitudes (and the absolute
anachronism of our accepted political categories) in a
flash.

4

And yet, within a year, the previously widespread illusion of American omnipotence received a painful shock
through the successful launching of Soviet Sputniks.

It is a melancholy paradox that the technological
and sensationalist inclinations of the American press
contributed to the Russian propaganda victory. In the
wake of two sensational "satellites" streaking through
the skies the common sense of the at first impassive
American public was besieged by the anvil chorus of
newspapers, commentators, educators, politicians, and
scientists, hammering away on the theme of *Sputnik
ante portas,* to which the eager German rocketeers now
in American pay were adding their own metallic tones.
Through the efforts of American military, educational,
and scientific propagandists, they made the issue of
Space Rocketry or the so-called "Missile Gap" into a
public mania, stoked by oceanic fuels of misinformation. Yet how limited was the core of realism in these
so-called "realistic" assessments! The "Missile Gap," just

as the earlier proposed "Bomber Gap," was not much more than an image decked out by various vested interests. True, in the two years that followed the first successful launching of the Russian "earth satellite"[2] American launchings lagged behind; but no one who knows the tremendous capacity of American technological determination could doubt that within a short time the American achievements would catch up with the Russian ones. True, these achievements of a Communist regime were impressive; and yet we must remember that for centuries the Russians have excelled in heavy artillery, upon which they put great, and often exaggerated, emphasis. True, highly electrified whirling rockets may, through powerful beams, assist military reconnaissance and disrupt certain military communications (radar, for example) on this earth; but even this is yet to be demonstrated. At any rate, history still concerns this earth and not "space" (a pompous and silly term); it still concerns "real estate" (a very telling term, at that). The eventual American "conquest" of the moon would hardly make up for an eventual Russian base, say, in Cuba; and even addicts of

[2] The quotation marks have a purpose. The careful reader of newspapers will find that the launchings of the first "satellites" were accompanied by wildly differing scientific estimates and by wildly varying telescopic confirmations. This is at least significant when we consider that these involved not Alpha Stars a billion light-years away but a visible metal object a few hundred miles above us. The unanimous opinion of scientists originally was that these "earth satellites" would circle along their majestic orbits above our globe forever; but by now it has become evident that their life expectancy is limited and that in some cases it hardly exceeds a few months. A question thus arises not only about the military importance of these haphazard objects hurled skyward but of the validity of the hitherto held scientific assumption that once a body is beyond the sphere of our earth's gravity it enters into an entirely new world of universal and eternal laws. It is perhaps too much to ask from our scientists to ponder this question.

science fiction must admit that it is (and it will always be) easier to bombard Key West from Havana than from the moon. If, on the same day, the world were to learn from the Russians that they planted the Soviet flag on Mars while they were compelled to haul it down in East Berlin, of the two events it is the latter that would affect not only Germany but millions of mankind, their lives and the history of the world.

We must, therefore, come back to earthly dimensions. We shall return to the problem of nuclear weapons and rockets in a moment; meanwhile we must look at those critical parts of the world whereto the American policy of containment was now extended without involving American military bases and rocket weapons.

5

Toward the teeming and corruptible new nations of the Middle East, Russia was now making strenuous gestures of friendship, foisting her aid upon their leaders, impressing their masses with her vociferous threats during the Suez Crisis. This evoked great anxieties in Washington. Thus in January 1957 the President enunciated his so-called Eisenhower Doctrine, a document strong in tone and intent but somewhat vague in particulars. It proclaimed that in the Near East American interests were involved against potential Communist aggression. Thereby, with Britain removed from the scene, the American government involved itself in the treacherous mire and maze of Arab politics, where, however, it was Nasser's, not Khrushchev's, ambitions that counted foremost. They culminated for a while in the creation of the United Arab Republic in 1957, putting together Egypt and Syria under Nasser's command, while in the neighboring Arab states Oriental intrigue, Moslem frenzy, and racial hatred produced rapidly

changing explosive situations whose ephemeral variations we need not recount in detail.

In the spring of 1958 violence erupted between two
political factions in the Arab republic of Lebanon. The
President of that state asked American intervention in
the name of the Eisenhower Doctrine; for a while,
however, Washington uneasily refrained from action.
On 15 July an Iraqi street mob, inflamed in part by
Nasser's agents, suddenly flooded the streets of Baghdad, murdering King Feisal of Iraq and his loyal conservative Regent and Premier in a most atrocious fashion while Nasser's radio in jubilant hysterical tones
called for a Holy War against the recalcitrant King of
Jordan. A world crisis was opening, with the Middle
East seemingly aflame, with American troops entering
a country not far from the southern borders of the Soviet Union.[3] The Egyptian dictator, on his way home
from a state visit to Tito, levanted off to Moscow. There
Khrushchev assured him of his support, showed him
impressive Russian air bases and rocket installations,
but, after all was said, he asked Nasser to be patient
and not to invoke Russian intervention. Washington, on
the other hand, wished to make it clear that the sudden American reaction was not aimed at the Soviet
Union proper. Unlike in Budapest or at Port Said two
years earlier, the intervention, though successful, soon
assumed a rather unserious aspect. The American Marines, wading ashore through the warm Levantine water in full battle dress, were greeted not with fusillades
but by the excited babbling of Lebanese soda vendors
and Arab bathing beauties. Khrushchev ordered a
"spontaneous" demonstration by a Moscow mob against
the American Embassy and proclaimed the need of a
Summit Conference with himself present. After a few
critical days Dulles sourly acquiesced in Khrushchev's
potential presence at a crucial United Nations meeting

[3] The neutrality of the Swiss and Austrian governments
was infringed by American military transport planes flying
over these Alpine countries from their bases in Germany.

in New York; but, after a hurried conference with the Chinese, Khrushchev changed his mind and refused to come. Meanwhile the Lebanese civil war literally fizzled out in soda pop. The ambitious Robert Murphy, the official State Department Troubleshooter in the Middle East, arrived and ordered the Lebanese to compose a government that would maintain some order. Subsequently Dulles (not without some reluctance) announced the eventual American withdrawal from Lebanon; and by the end of autumn the American Marines and the British airborne troops left Lebanon and Jordan.

This Levantine episode revealed a number of things, however. It showed again that Nasser and Arab nationalism rather than the Russians were the troublemakers here (within a year conditions akin to civil war erupted in revolutionary Iraq between partisan groups and the Dictator Kassim). It showed that the Arabs, no matter what their public rantings, were not altogether unwilling to turn the acuteness of American concern to their advantage (within a year it became apparent that Nasser could exploit the Russians better than the Russians could exploit him—a lesson not unlike what Lenin had to learn about the Near East in 1922 and Stalin about China in 1927). Soon Nasser, with his eye still upon Israel, having now found that American friendship might be more profitable in the long run than a Russian one, began to berate Russians and Communists. Khrushchev, whose rockets had attained the moon but who could evidently attain no decisive influence in Beirut or in Cairo, did little more than turn an amiable cheek. More important were the now sporadically emerging differences between Russia and China.

6

We have seen how, during and after the Korean War, Russian influence and the actual presence of Russia decreased at many points in the Far East. It was evident as early as 1954 that the Chinese leaders, surly, aggressive, nationalistic, and puritanical, did not show much gratitude for this Russian forbearance even though it is exaggerated to say, as many ideological commentators have said, that after Stalin's death Mao had become the dominant personality in the Communist orbit. Nor must we believe that the Chinese contributed much to Marxist doctrines that, like most ideas of the past century, came in a distorted and exaggerated form to China from Europe. Probably this explains why the Chinese rulers, too, partook in the vogue of liberalization in 1956. "A hundred flowers shall bloom," said Mao himself; but their bloom was shorter-lived than anywhere else in the Soviet sphere. Immediately after the Hungarian Revolution the Chinese changed their position, stridently insisting that the "nationalist" and "revisionist" Communists in Eastern Europe should be brought to task. There is reason to believe that their own experiences with the unexpected consequences of domestic liberalization were but one factor in this significant change. More important was the Chinese recognition after the Hungarian Revolution that a liberalization of conditions in Eastern European nations might ease the tension between Russia and America in Europe and that eventual mutual withdrawals of Russian and American forces now facing each other in certain crucial parts of Europe, might lead to a decisive improvement in Russian-American relations; to this the Chinese were grimly opposed.

Once more we must look at the greater, triangular relationships. Truman, and not MacArthur, was proved right in 1951, as he understood that an eventual war between China and America in the Far East might, after all, have served the ends of Stalin's Russia, which might have profitably stayed largely outside such a conflict. The Chinese, from 1956 onward, feared few things

more than a Russian-American settlement in Europe,
since they understood how in the Far East the interests
of Russia and of America, of these two remaining Great
Powers of the white race, occupying but marginal positions there, hardly conflicted at all. It does not, therefore, require a particularly sophisticated eye to perceive
the jealousies and anxieties of the Chinese Communist
leadership as they witnessed the strenuous Russian efforts toward a rapprochement with the United States
from 1957 onward. Indeed, for a while it seemed that a
curious, cautious, underwater race for American favor
had developed between the Chinese and the Russians.
The latter significantly proposed the opening of commercial air traffic between Alaska and the hitherto
closed areas of Siberia and the Soviet Far East (a suggestion to which Washington did not respond); the
former reopened negotiations about American prisoners
with American diplomats in Warsaw. From 1958 onward, then, the evidences of divergences between
China and Russia increased. The Chinese sharply attacked certain Polish attempts culminating in the Rapacki Plan;[4] they announced that they would build an
atomic bomb; they were manifestly unenthusiastic
about the Russian-American disarmament negotiations;
they were critical of the relative caution that the Russians showed during the Lebanon Crisis; they succeeded in keeping Khrushchev from flying to New
York for the ensuing United Nations debate. In turn,
the Russians were evidently unenthusiastic about the
sudden Chinese announcement of an impending invasion of the islands lying off the Chinese shore and protected by the American Navy.[5] Khrushchev dropped

[4] See below, page 177.
[5] The presence of the Navy was sufficient to deter and,
indeed, to make a Chinese invasion of these small pieces of
land impossible. Thus even now the government of the tremendous Chinese land empire of perhaps six hundred mil-

certain critical remarks about the extreme (and partly unsuccessful) rigid domestic commune policies of the Chinese; he did not wish to assist in the making of a Chinese atom bomb; he refused the transit of war material acquired from China by the Algerian rebels against France; the Russians remained painfully silent about the Chinese crushing of the Tibetan Rebellion in 1959; the Russian government assumed a significantly impartial position in the border dispute between China and India.[6]

At any rate, these events, together with other manifestations of aggressive Chinese expansionism, not only demonstrated the character of Chinese ambitions but led to a salutary diminution of that radiant image of Chinese prestige that but five years before was so benevolently contemplated by the leaders and masses of Oriental states. Again the Communist Powers, with their actions, were ruining their own reputation; and the West could gain some prestige from this. Meanwhile the Russians were admitting the urgency of their need to populate Siberia; they showed some symptoms of anxiety in front of potential Chinese pressures

---

lion people proved unable—indeed, it did not even dare—to reconquer a miserable group of islands lying but a few miles off their shore. In these times, when so much is being said about the alleged tremendous danger of six hundred million Chinese Communists to the United States and when so much military attention is attracted by the prospective invasions of planets, this elementary illustration of the continued historic efficacy of naval power ought to be kept in mind.

[6] In August 1963 the Chinese Government stated that in June 1959 "the Soviet Government unilaterally tore up the agreement on new technology for national defense concluded between China and the Soviet Union on 15 October 1957, and refused to provide China with a sample of an atomic bomb and technical data concerning its manufacture." On 9 September 1959 (only a few days before Khrushchev was to take off from Moscow for Washington) a TASS statement termed the Tibetan border incidents between China and India "deplorable."

(in Outer Mongolia, for example) on their thinly populated and multiracial Siberian borderlands.

All of this does not mean, of course, that a break between China and Russia was already imminent. In the face of the United States they still had many interests in common. But these developments indicate that, even from the distant aspect of Chinese-Russian relations, developments in Europe, where, unlike the Far East, Russian and American military interests and political spheres meet at direct and opposing points, were—and still are—of central importance indeed.

To the conditions in this central and still primary theater of history we must now return.

7

The center of the cold war is in Europe. The center of Europe is Germany. The center of Germany is Berlin. The central problem and issue of the cold war still is their division, and the central question, at least until 1963, was the development and the character of American-German relations. We know that from 1950 onward, and particularly during the Dulles era, the United States was determined to rearm West Germany and to make her indeed the principal European ally of the United States. This suited Chancellor Adenauer, who was determined to do nothing to compromise this unique German-American relationship. Believing also, and not without reason, that the Russians understand nothing better than determination and force, he continued to hold, even after the Hungarian events of 1956, that the eventual unification of Germany could only come about through an increase of American-German strength in front of Russia. This policy perfectly accorded with the design of John Foster Dulles, who, as we have seen, was completing the arrangement of a ring of American military, naval, and air bases imme-

diately outside the European and Asiatic frontiers of
the Soviet Empire. By 1957 the development of rocket
artillery had advanced to a point where the Soviet
Union would be vulnerable to medium-range transcontinental artillery (the so-called IRBM weapons), while
not until 1960 would the Soviet Union (and presumably also the United States) perfect their long-range
transoceanic artillery (the so-called ICBM weapons),
whereby they could hurl these tremendous rockets directly at each other from their respective homelands. It
is in view of these evident strategic calculations that we
must look at the development of these dreadful arms,
as follows:

	U.S.	U.S.S.R.	BRITAIN	FRANCE	CHINA
Atom Bomb	1945	1949	1952	1960	1964
Hydrogen Bomb	1952	1953	1957	1966	–
Rocket artillery capable of hurling objects beyond the immediate sphere of gravity of the earth	1958	1957	–	1965	–
Rocket artillery capable of reaching halfway across the world (ICBM)	1960	1960	–	–	–
Rocket artillery capable of reaching enemy territory from allied bases (IRBM)	1956	1956	1956*	–	?

* American-made rockets

Here on this earth what still counts in strategy is whose troops and ships and guns are where. Let us remember that, after all is said, even the long-range rocket is but a tremendous gun with a tremendously powerful projectile. Thus, considering the essential political geography of the cold war, it will appear from the above table that the key issue before 1960 was, and still is, the location of the intermediate rather than the long-range rocket stations. Between 1957 and 1960 the United States endeavored, with partial success, to commit some of her continental European allies, particularly West Germany, Italy, and Greece, to accept the installation of such rocket bases in their countries. These secret and important negotiations arrived, in the end, at diverse conclusions: Greece, for example, had shown sufficient reluctance so that in the autumn of 1959 Washington decided not to go ahead with rocket installations in that country—a significant decision in the light of what follows.

The Russians, even though delighted with their own successes in rocket artillery, have been considerably worried about these developments. We must understand their situation in front of this encirclement, even though they, like the Kaiser in 1914 or Hitler in 1939, have few grounds for complaints; it was their own aggressive behavior that led to this gradual American strategic reaction. Up to this day the Russians have not supplied nuclear weapons to any one of their satellite armies (including, of course, the Chinese); there were, too, few Russian rocket bases in Eastern Europe. It is interesting, for example, that Rumanian suggestions about a military neutralization of the Balkans as well as Yugoslav mediation played a certain role in the Greek decision not to accept American launching sites. It is more significant that after 1954 the extent of American armament of West Germany surpassed the Russian armament of East Germany in every possible way. To build up "situations of strength" was Dulles' key slogan.

When Adenauer visited Moscow in 1955, Bulganin said to him: "Don't think you can impress us by negotiating from strength." That the Russians, in 1955, should find it necessary to speak thus to the leader of a truncated nation whose population is less than one fourth of that of the Soviet Union, whose territory is less than one twentieth of the Soviet Empire, whose principal cities are within a hundred miles of the first Soviet outposts along the iron curtain, reveals the continued uneasiness of the Russians in front of Germany and especially in front of a German-American alliance. Their uneasiness increased subsequently.

This was one of the main reasons why Khrushchev, presumably prodded by his even more uneasy East German stooges and allies, reopened the Berlin "question" in November 1958, proposing a withdrawal of the Western (but also of the Russian) garrisons from West and East Berlin and offering a Russian guarantee of a Free City status to the former. If one overlooked his often careless use of words, Khrushchev's statement could be construed as if it had the character of an ultimatum. The Western reaction, however, was such that within a few months Khrushchev climbed down. Though not yielding on Berlin, he was willing to postpone action until the series of Summit Meetings that he finally succeeded in wrenching from Eisenhower by 1959.

Berlin, the central city of the cold war, a symbolic, reminiscent evidence of Soviet police rule and also of the radiant attraction of the Western way of life, a city of intrigue but where the movement of peoples was in one direction—westward; Berlin was still the center of the now great and historic triangular relationships of the three young giant nations of the globe, Russia, America, Germany. The struggle for Berlin has been centrally important as well as centrally symbolic from 1945 onward. The Russians lost the struggle for its spirit from the beginning, and the symbol was too powerful to make them attempt taking it by the sword. Still, we must understand that behind the Berlin dispute stood a much greater issue: Would the United States give nuclear weapons to the Germans in the West, even though the Russians have shown no inclination to give nuclear weapons to their German allies in the East?

About this question there were deep latent disagreements within the Western camp itself. The North Atlantic Alliance came dangerously close to such a revealing break in the autumn of 1957. At that time serious voices in Europe were raised in favor of what was subsequently called "disengagement," in other words, of the necessary exploration of the possibilities of a reciprocal withdrawal of American and Russian forces from their most advanced positions in Central Europe.[7] At the NATO Conference in December 1957 extraordinary powers of persuasion (together with certain subtle threats) were required by Dulles to push through at least in principle the establishment of American nuclear rocket bases on the territory of his European allies.[8]

---

[7] These included the plan advanced by the Polish Foreign Minister Rapacki (supported by Moscow, even though with reluctance) that went so far as to propose the banning of nuclear weapons not only from the two Germanies but also from Poland and Czechoslovakia, an arrangement certainly worth exploring but rejected by Dulles and the Germans. On the Western side, independently of each other, "disengagement" was suggested by Churchill and by Eden before 1956, by Field Marshal Montgomery, by Frank Aiken, the Foreign Minister of Eire, by Denis Healy of the British Labour Party, by George Kennan, and by a host of British and European commentators afterward.

[8] Dulles' attitude was not unlike that of his Soviet counterparts. Interdependence, yes, said Dulles; but the United States must preserve its freedom of choice. Thus, like the Russians, he suggested that beyond all the talk of fraternal co-operation, the United States' concept of Western defense (like the Russian concept of Communism) must prevail over all, *primus inter pares*.

Thus it was at this Paris NATO Conference in December

He could, however, count on the unqualified support of Chancellor Adenauer. More important, the political mood of West Germany had been changing. For almost a decade after the end of the war the Germans, chastened by their wartime experiences, demonstrated rather pacifist attitudes. In later years, however, they were willing to rearm with but few reservations; and an aggressive young Bavarian, Defense Minister Strauss, suggested on a number of occasions how the American rearmament of Germany might be a long-run political investment of great national value. By 1959 the German contingent became the strongest European army within NATO; the trump card of full German rearmament, probably prematurely played, was not held back in order to extract possible Russian concessions about East Germany; Adenauer's and Strauss' policy was overwhelmingly approved by the West German people. While the disarmament negotiations continued, the arming of the Germans with carriers of nuclear weapons went on. Nor was the West German government willing to make any important gesture toward Poland. When we keep in mind that the nuclear armament of West Germany and the question of the Oder-Neisse Line are two outstanding problems in Europe about which there was little agreement among the Western Allies themselves, these were, to some extent, disturbing. Meanwhile, too, the personal disagreements between Chancellor Adenauer and the British developed

---

1957 that for the first time the problem of American imperialism was faced by Western Europeans—dilatorily, not squarely but, still, faced. There occurred at that time a significant divergence between Adenauer and Spaak, the Belgian Secretary-General of the NATO Council. Spaak suggested that Europe should perhaps develop her own defenses, moving more independently from the United States. Adenauer rebuked Spaak; and thus the German-American concept carried the day.

into serious national misunderstandings and recriminations. These were reflected in the differences between the so-called Common Market and the so-called Outer Seven economic areas, with Germany and Britain as their respective protagonists. They appeared again during the Western political negotiations concerning Berlin as well as in the perhaps unduly severe British reactions to the sporadic occurrence of swastika paintings on West German walls in the winter of 1959–60.

But already by January 1958—after the fateful NATO decision, including Germany, to accept American rockets in principle—Khrushchev had begun to press for the recognition of the *status quo* rather than for disengagement or mutual withdrawal. Let us be frank, he dropped remarks on occasion: who wants Germany reunited? We don't; and neither do you. Thus the political reunification of Germany became as remote as ever; the Adenauer-Dulles policy of a "situation of strength" did not pay off.[9] After 1956 the United States at least as much as Russia regarded the maintenance of the German *status quo* as a primary aim, implying the acceptance of the division of Germany and of Europe. Within the two opposite alliance systems East Germany had become the most determined partisan of Russian rigidity and West Germany the most determined ally of the United States. Both of them were (and, at the time of this writing, they still are) determined opponents of "disengagement" and of an eventual loosening of their respective alliance systems.

[9] It was significant, too, that during the difficult and tortuous negotiations in 1959 in Geneva, the Western Powers did not effectively counter Soviet proposals by a counteroffer involving the internationalization or Free City status for *all* of Berlin, East Berlin included. This suggests how the Western Powers, and particularly the United States, by 1959 had come around to desire the freezing of the partition of Germany and of the present European *status quo*.

8

We must keep in mind that, no matter how widespread their reputation as international Communists
promoting the cause of world-wide revolution, the
rulers of Russia, including Stalin as well as Khrushchev,
have consistently tried to promote a Russian-American
division of the world. This evident inconsistency between Communist dogma and Russian policy should not
really surprise us, even though we need not believe
that the inconsistency is realized by the Russians themselves. In their attitudes appreciation and jealousy, admiration and envy are mixed. It is part of human nature, and perhaps especially of the Russian (and
Communist) character, that there is a large inconsistency between dogma and practice, between standards
of beliefs and tendencies of action. Behind every human action there are personal tendencies and many
motives; and though we can never judge the motives
of men with any degree of certainty, we can recognize
their evidences when these appear. There is certainly
much evidence that Khrushchev's admiration (a complex kind of admiration, of course) of the United States
was at least one of the principal motives spurring him
to seek a Russian-American accommodation, preferably
to be based on the prevailing territorial *status quo*.
For years he tried to have himself invited to the United
States. His atttempts were so obvious that they would
have counted against him in a more normal and traditional era of diplomacy; but by 1959 new systems of
international relationships and of publicity had come
to replace certain more traditional and tried diplomatic
practices. Highly publicized visits of statesmen,
whisked from airport to airport amid vast throngs
(and, at times, amid organized counterdemonstrations)
ordered out to cheer by governments, their numbers

eagerly counted, compared, and inflated by competing propagandists, form the new pattern of state visits at the present—even though during these so-called goodwill visits there is hardly any time left for important negotiations, and the image of publicity is counted more important than the realities of statecraft. Thus the American domestic practice of electoral campaigns has influenced the pattern of organized events throughout the world.

Ostensibly on a trade and commercial visit, in January 1959 Mikoyan virtually foisted himself on his still evidently unwilling and reluctant American hosts. Even though this able Armenian traveling representative was received by his official hosts in a reluctant mood that touched the limits of actual discourtesy, ultimately Khrushchev would have his way. Gripping the wheel of the American ship of state to the very end, in April the cancer-ridden Dulles finally felt he had to abandon his post. Deeply grieved by Dulles' departure, President Eisenhower after some reluctance nominated Christian Herter as Secretary of State. Dulles died in May. His funeral demonstrated the extraordinary power and prestige of the United States, with leading statesmen from virtually all over the world gathered in Washington during the impressive ceremonies. But already before his death there had been some evidence that Dulles himself was coming around to recognize the necessity of serious negotiations with the Russians. Now, in the last year of his presidency, Eisenhower assumed the leadership in a somewhat surprising spurt of energy: and the benevolence and the temperateness of his character together with his knowledge of the horrors of war were important factors in accepting the Russian bid for some kind of an armistice in the cold war.

The Mikoyan trip to America was followed by Macmillan's visit to Russia in February. There in a running and semi-public debate this British statesman acquitted himself honorably; he stood fast enough to make

Khrushchev's mind change at a point when their talks seemed to collapse under the accumulated weight of Russian misunderstandings and recriminations. We cannot say whether Macmillan's subsequent clever electoral claim of having thus secured the prospect of Summit Meetings was really so; still, Chancellor Adenauer's opposition was no longer sufficient to block the possibility of an American-Russian meeting on the summit. While scientific, geophysical, Antarctic, theatrical, musical, athletic, and commercial instances of Russian-American exchange and co-operation increased, in the summer of 1959 an American state exhibition was opened in Moscow and a Russian one in New York. Kozlov, a new Russian hierarch close to Khrushchev, came to New York to inaugurate the Soviet exhibit; Vice-President Nixon flew to Moscow to inaugurate the American one. There he got entangled in an extraordinary public shouting match with Khrushchev. Still it was then that the arrangements for the latter's American visit were made.

This visit, preceded by a hurried European tour by President Eisenhower himself—ostensibly to assure America's European allies, particularly West Germany (where he received his warmest public demonstrations), that no concessions or commitments would be made to the Russians at their expense—took place in the last two weeks of September. We still know little about what was said during the last crucial Sunday of Khrushchev's extraordinary tour as he finally went into seclusion with his host at the presidential mountain camp: the recently (1965) published second volume of President Eisenhower's memoirs, bland, non-committal and inaccurate as they are, tell the interested historian little that is new—except for the revelation of how uneasy Eisenhower had been in receiving the Russians, of how reluctant he had been to extend an invitation to Khrushchev; indeed, that to some extent the latter's invitation may have come about by mistake, by a kind of diplomatic slip committed in the President's name by the egregious Robert Murphy. "The spirit of Camp David"—this soon became a slogan in the Soviet press; but it is at least doubtful that any concrete or secret arrangements were made, save for a certain vague moratorium on the Berlin problem together with the promise of a Summit Conference and of President Eisenhower's visit to the Soviet Union during the following year.

There are, however, certain features of this extraordinary state visit that should be mentioned in this general historical account of the cold war. It was a beaming Khrushchev who waddled down from his gigantic Russian jet plane to American soil; and, notwithstanding extraordinary and complex experiences, it was a beaming Khrushchev who left at night in a flourish of good will (even though the President did not accompany him to the airport). Khrushchev was evidently determined to like America; he liked America; in a spiritual and psychological rather than in a physical sense (for American security services forbade him to visit "Disneyland") he saw in America what he wanted to see. He regarded it, as he himself said, a tremendous honor to the Soviet Union to stand beside President Eisenhower and accept the salute to the Soviet flag by a splendid American military band. As so often before, he thus inadvertently revealed his admiring sentiments toward the United States—even though he arrived brandishing a model of the Soviet lunar rocket that had just been hurled at the moon; even though, when cornered in press conferences, he burst out with savage and even brutal phrases. Unfortunately the conclusions drawn by the American press and public figures were not always reasonable: in turn, they revealed a somewhat alarming lack of American self-confidence. When Khrushchev was smiling, the American people were told that these were but the blandishments of a dedicated Communist; when

Khrushchev was growling and shouting (as, for example, during the press conference when to a question about Hungary he blurted out one of his peculiar Russian metaphors: "the Hungarian question is stuck in the throats of some people like a dead rat"), this blind and savage phrase was described as a masterly parry by a brilliant Communist dialectician. The American people themselves were slightly dazed; throughout the tour they acted, with few exceptions, in a curiously self-conscious fashion, like children who were not told clearly how to behave and what sentiments to demonstrate, accustomed as they had become by 1959 to such governmental admonitions. There were few demonstrations; Khrushchev was exemplarily protected by thousands of policemen; but at least during the first phase of his visit, with Ambassador Lodge detailed to accompany him, it was evident that he was supposed to be treated with reservations, as an inevitable but still not quite welcome guest; and several local politicians, like the Mayor of Los Angeles, took the occasion to make some political capital for themselves by introducing long anti-Communist tirades in their official speeches. However, after a Khrushchevian outburst, as the Russian leader threatened to break his trip and suddenly return to Moscow, the State Department immediately changed signals and ordered Lodge to assume a new standard of friendly behavior; the rest of the tour passed largely without recriminations and incidents.

After his return to Moscow, Khrushchev flew off to China to inform his uneasy Chinese allies. He had revealed by some of his phrases in the United States that all was not well with China; and it seems that his October 1959 meeting with Mao did little to dispel reciprocal misunderstandings between these two Communist Powers. The Chinese opened their frontier dispute with India; they began to quarrel with Indonesia; and throughout these developments it was made more and more evident that they could not count on Russian support at all. On the other hand, the outlines of American policy in this great Asiatic triangular relationship were not yet clear; Washington was surprisingly noncommittal about the Sino-Indian frontier affair while the Japanese, somewhat like the West Germans, chose to profit from their principal position within the American alliance system. In January 1960 the Kishi[10] government authorized Japanese rearmament together with the establishment of American military, naval, and air bases in Japan for another ten years, a step that aggravated Russian even more than Chinese susceptibilities; and President Eisenhower announced that after his tour of Russia in June 1960 he would return home via a state visit to Japan.

9

Remember Pearl Harbor. Remember not only the cunning, savage, unheralded Japanese attack but the complexities within the American government that preceded it.[11] The coming of the War of 1812, Matamoros in 1846, Fort Sumter in 1861, Havana Harbor in 1898, the Zimmermann Telegram in 1917, Pearl Harbor—remember them all. They are stories full of clandestine maneuvers, of spies and counterspies, deeply entangled and undergrown stories whose truthful reconstruction is among the most difficult tasks confronting historians. There are details about the origin of these American wars that are complex, dark, obscure, shot through as they were with confusing maneuvers aimed at luring the enemy into firing the first shots[12]—even though

[10] Kishi was Munitions Minister in the Japanese government that attacked Pearl Harbor.

[11] See above, pages 84–85.

[12] This is, too, why President Truman's decision to go to the defense of Korea in June 1950 will stand out as a shin-

nothing that Lincoln or Roosevelt may have done involved the ultimate and principal responsibility of those Southerners or Japanese who did fire them. The inner story of America's foreign relations is complex rather than simple, and never so complex as when it comes to the brink of war. Americans are not a simple people; and the texture of their history is at times very complex, too. Americans are a peace-loving people; but it is especially because of this that their governments are apt to do everything to avoid the impression of choosing war.

"Democratic Diplomacy," "Open Covenants Openly Arrived At"—few shibboleths stand up so badly as these Wilsonian ones in the record of modern history. There is this curious, paradoxical duality in the history of the cold war: on the one hand, diplomacy is more "open" and crude than ever before; on the other, it is more secret and hidden from the people than it ever was, now, in this very Age of Democracy. On the one hand, we have diplomacy by publicity, when diplomatic notes are broadcast and printed in the newspapers, when statements and proposals are made primarily because of their publicity value, a new and unorthodox and frequently false practice of playing to the world, taken up by the State Department and by the Russians, too, in the Khrushchev era. On the other hand, seldom has there been so much hidden and influential business of secretive provocations and spying as during the history of the cold war, and again especially after 1953, when John Foster Dulles began to extend the scope of American diplomacy.[13]

---

ing page in the history of the United States; for it was a uniquely honest reaction in the defense of freedom without second thoughts in what paradoxically then developed into the most unpopular war in modern American history.

[13] In the history of nations the influence of spying has been generally exaggerated. It is true that the secret services of states have played exciting underhand roles throughout

We have seen earlier how the character of American government became further transformed during the exigencies of the cold war. One of the consequences was the creation of a large Central Intelligence Agency, directed by the ambitious Allen W. Dulles, John Foster's brother. After 1952 its staff and operations mushroomed. The American people were told little about its operations; because of a mixture of prudence, indolence, and political opportunism. Congress gave free hand to this mammoth clandestine agency, unwilling as it was to be informed of its activities.[14] These were, of course, manifold; and they soon surpassed the expectable standards of gathering intelligence information; they included the setting up of revolutions in faraway countries, of clandestine radio propaganda stations, the floating of thousands of balloons into Eastern Europe in 1956, and, as we now know, the sending of fast-flying American aircraft across the very heartland of the Soviet Union. The Russian government, acquainted very well with the sordid practices of double agents and of their underhand

---

modern history. But their clandestine activities were seldom formative or decisive: what most of the dramatic achievements of secret agents amount to is the gathering of precious fragments of information that may or may not confirm but that do not formulate already existing diplomatic and strategic policies. Given the secretive character of Russia, the technological features and the world-wide scope of the cold war, hundreds of American and Russian agents have been struggling through involved networks throughout the world; but their activities have been symptoms and not causes of the cold war; as before in history, they reflected but they did not influence the course set by their nations—until now.

[14] We must at least note the geometric increase of American secret services in this century; the U. S. Secret Service was founded in 1900, the FBI in 1925, the CIA in 1950. The sorry necessities of the modern world called for their creation; but what is disturbing is the power and the prestige which their masters have acquired in American politics and government and before American public opinion.

guerrilla warfare, knew about these activities; because of higher reasons of political expediency, Khrushchev did not reveal what it knew about them to the world until the crisis of May 1960.

In the dawn hours of 1 May 1960 an American plane fell from the sky in the Urals. The pilot told his Russian captors that he was sent on a reconnaissance mission to fly across Russia, starting from a base in Pakistan and destined to land at a NATO airfield in northern Norway. A few days later Khrushchev broke the news to the world. The American government, caught first in a lie about an imaginary weather plane in Turkey, then turned around to admit the truth of what Khrushchev said; but blustering statements covering up the CIA by politicians and by the State Department followed. The latter, together with the President, announced that in the interests of American defense such flights would continue. A wave of self-righteous Russian indignation rose together with world-wide criticism. It was an anxious world that now awaited the Summit Meeting that was to open in Paris only a few days later.

Khrushchev came to Paris a day ahead of schedule. Accompanied by Malinovsky, a grim Soviet Marshal who dogged Khrushchev's footsteps throughout Paris, he demanded and hoped for an American retraction together with an apology by President Eisenhower. The President made a belated statement about stopping such flying missions during the remaining time of his presidency; beyond this, understandably under the circumstances of brutal Russian pressure, he was not willing to go. Khrushchev made a violent outburst; he refused to sit down with Eisenhower now; he suggested that the President cancel his visit to Russia. The Summit Conference was wrecked before it started. Khrushchev followed it up with an extraordinary news conference, during which he roared insults at Adenauer (probably aware of the vast relief with which the Chancellor of

West Germany must have greeted the collapse of the Paris Summit). The Russians were bringing the spy-plane affair before the United Nations. Khrushchev flew off to East Berlin. There the world was relieved to hear that he did not plan to aggravate the crisis further.

There are reasons to believe that internal developments in Russia forced Khrushchev's hand, a hand that he crudely overplayed because of the kind of man he was. There were, and still are, influential nationalist elements in Russia who did not share Khrushchev's inclinations to seek agreement with the United States or his optimistic interpretation of a friendly President Eisenhower; leaders of the Army fretted against the prospects of disarmament that Khrushchev pursued. Moreover, American statements and actions taken just before the Summit Conference played into the hands of Khrushchev's and of Mikoyan's domestic enemies. The American treaty with Japan, a statement by the President that he did not expect to stay in Paris long and that after six days Vice-President Nixon would sit in for him, an inopportune pro-German speech by Dillon of the State Department, and in the end the spy plane sent across Russia just a few days before the Summit Conference, convinced the Russian administrators that Khrushchev may have gone too far. There were some ominous evidences about personal changes and new controls in the highest positions of Russian leadership just before Khrushchev set out for Paris. And the violent and shocking maneuvers that followed may have been still concerned with the principal problem vexing the Russians, whether the United States would, secretly or openly, equip her West German allies with nuclear weapons. But no matter how much his hand may have been forced, Khrushchev's disappointment with President Eisenhower was certainly more genuine than false —which then illustrates how he misunderstood certain American realities.

For Khrushchev was wrong in thinking that the spy-

plane affair would divide America; and he was wrong
in thinking that the next President would, by necessity,
choose a new course toward Russia. A few intelligent
and serious public statements notwithstanding, it did
not seem as if American political opinion and popular
sentiment were deeply impressed with the mistakes and
the ultimate implications of flying over Russia in peacetime. At the time of the summit both of the then leading
presidential candidates, Kennedy and Nixon, were
among those who had been reluctant to condemn Mc-
Carthy in 1954; and we have already seen how the
number of people who had vested interests of one kind
or another in the maintenance of a vast military establishment has grown high in America and in Russia alike.
At any rate, the events of May 1960 revealed how, for
different reasons, neither the American President nor
the Russian Prime Minister was in full control of his
enormous and complex military machine.

Still, whatever the American mistakes may have
been the world was treated to a display of crudeness
on the part of the Russian leader that it would not easily
forget. Khrushchev may have worn a silk suit as he
left Paris in a silvery jet plane; but he represented,
after all, that old Russia, that peasant Russia, Tolstoi's
earth-crusted Russia, with all of its deep-seated feeling
of suspicion and inferiority.

Stupefaction and sadness marked the features of the
American President as he walked in Paris on the morrow of the destroyed meeting, on a suddenly empty
day. He was not alone: Macmillan and De Gaulle had
backed him up to the hilt.[15] It is not difficult, how-

---

[15] A sympathetic crowd, mostly of Republican dignitaries,
gathered at the airport to greet the President as he returned
from Paris while in the street schoolchildren held up signs:
"WE LOVE U−2." "Our Allies," said Eisenhower in his few
general remarks, with surprising emphasis, "were *magnifi-
cent*." There was a spontaneous burst of applause. I had
watched the scene on television; I was struck by the sense of
relief and gratitude that was reflected by the spontaneity of

ever, to surmise some of the latter's thoughts: indeed, it is conceivable that the scene of the American-Russian confrontation in Paris, this blind and groping clash of incompetence and brutality as demonstrated by the two Guest Giants lumbering in his house may have only confirmed in the mind of Charles de Gaulle what he tended to believe for some time anyhow: that the United States and the Soviet Union were far from competent in ruling the world; that the era of their near-absolute predominance was about to pass.

10

We have seen that Khrushchev, on the morrow of the Paris Summit disaster, announced—to the evident disappointment of his contemptible East German Communist underlings—that he would postpone the Berlin "issue" until a new Summit Conference six or eight months later, with a new American President. That was already the third of a series of postponements during recent years; but it suggested that, after all, Khrushchev was to persist in his attempts to improve Russian relations with the United States. Indeed, in a few months the passions and the rhetoric generated around the spy plane and its pilot largely evaporated; and in September 1960, in a surprising departure from earlier Soviet practices, Khrushchev decided to attend the United Nations Assembly in New York in person. Surrounded by the chieftains of certain Eastern European Communist states, he sailed forth on a small white Soviet liner into the turbulent atmosphere of New York. This time there was little to brighten his American visit; President Eisenhower refused to meet him; outside his

___

the applause and by the expressions on the applauders' faces; it reflected something new in American sentiment; a kind of dependence on European good will at a time of American anguish.

windows there were police whistles and the howls of demonstrators. The antiseptic and cacophonous mutter of the United Nations was, for once, enlivened by ridiculously vulgar scenes: an unkempt Cuban dictator, having left behind him a wake of chicken feathers in hotels whose managers wondered who would pay the bills, advanced across that supremely uninspiring hall and assembly to embrace Khrushchev who, in turn, a day or so later demonstrated his vigor by participating in the "debates"—atavistic memories of Russian parliamentary practices before 1917?—by taking off his shoe and pounding the table. To millions of Americans this clownish behavior obscured the occasional evidences of this shrewd peasant's statesmanship: for, after all, Khrushchev skillfully evaded Castro's invitation; instinctively aware of American susceptibilities, he declined to visit Cuba. His Soviet Ark sailed off into the autumnal North Atlantic, leaving behind a hot and confused America and one defecting Latvian seaman.

By that time the attention of the world had shifted to the oncoming day of the American presidential election; and on the first Tuesday in November the American people, with a surprisingly small margin, elected John Fitzgerald Kennedy for their President. This relatively young man, with his appealing features, and a well-earned reputation for great physical courage, was now not only the youngest among the leaders of the world: born in the crucial year of 1917, he was the first among the statesmen of the West whose memories could not include the great traditions and the enduring impressions of the era before the First World War. His patriotism, his energy and his mastery of domestic politics, reflected, as many felt, in the brevity and eloquence of his Inaugural Address, soon made a favorable and confident impression, further sustained through the external influence of an exceptionally charming young wife. Drawing upon the enthusiastically offered resources of certain intellectual Democrats, many of them from the President's own university, Harvard, Kennedy carefully picked his lists of what seemed an impressively intellectual and moderate administration; but he showed that he intended to be master of his own house by choosing, after some deliberation, Dean Rusk, a colorless foundation bureaucrat, for his Secretary of State.

All this was watched by Khrushchev with great attention and, for him, with surprising reserve. Having held aloof during the last stages of the presidential campaign, he sent exceptionally hearty messages of congratulation to the Democratic victor; and, while the Chinese were spitting out bile, he offered to send a high Soviet personage to represent Russia at the Inauguration ceremonies. Kennedy, having responded to these overtures with cautious courtesy, nevertheless declined to consider his election as an occasion for a turning-point in Russian-American relations. All of his domestic rhetoric of "The New Frontier" notwithstanding, the young President, still relying on the advice of Allen Dulles, had no strong inclination to alter the course of the American ship of state. Indeed, his political experiences and his knowledge of history were, all, restricted to American affairs; apart from his senior thesis on England, the young Kennedy's record of pronouncements on foreign and European affairs was spotty and sparse. Under these conditions the first serious crisis of his Administration broke with surprising rapidity. It was the Cuban Fiasco of the Bay of Pigs. We shall deal with the unfolding of the Cuban comedy in a later chapter; but there was little comedy that was comic in this sad sinking of an ill-concealed, ill-conceived, and ill-executed operation. Just about a week before this Cuban Fiasco the Russians announced that they "put a cosmonaut into orbit"—that is, a man in a steel can was shot up to whirl once around the globe —and a month later another beaming and impassive snub-nosed Russian successfully subjected himself to the same feat. Together with the confusing crisis within the Buddhist jungle kingdom of Laos, these events suggested a further decline of American power and prestige. But the Russians had problems of their own: Khrushchev was surprisingly restrained in Russian comments and actions pursuant to the Bay of Pigs, and he responded eagerly to the occasion of another meeting at the summit. Thus, after somewhat hasty arrangements, the chiefs of the United States and of the Soviet Union met—for the seventh time in eighteen years, for the fourth time during the cold war—in the first days of June 1961, at the end of President Kennedy's fast Western European tour, in Vienna. Their meeting was, again, inconclusive. The intelligent and resolute American President seems to have been plagued by something similar to the nervous bafflement which characterized his predecessor when he was being dragged to Summit Meetings; and even though Kennedy had few reasons to entertain illusions about Khrushchev, he confided to his staff that he found the Russian leader appallingly "tough," especially in regard to the problem of Berlin. On the other hand it was practically arranged in advance that their meeting would not be much more than an occasion to get acquainted with each other; and thus, apart from exchanges of statements by each side, there was, on purpose, no negotiation. Still, for a moment, the anxieties of the world were lightened by the scene of Jacqueline Kennedy and Nina Khrushchev, as they appeared on a balcony after lunch in a simple and sincere appearance of friendship: two different women, two mothers nevertheless. Thus the Vienna encounter between their two very different husbands was not necessarily inauspicious in itself. But they were not to meet again. Once more, in 1964, President Johnson suggested that he would be willing to meet with his Soviet counterparts: yet it was now the new, uneasy governors of the Russian empire who chose to shy away from the prospects of such an encounter.

It does seem, in retrospect, that the Vienna Summit Meeting may have marked the end rather than the beginning of a phase in the history of the cold war. Seven times in eighteen years the heads of the two Giant Powers had met: but 1943–45, Teheran, Yalta and Potsdam, belong properly to the history of the Second World War, at most to the historical origins of the cold war, not to the history of the cold war itself. At that time it was Stalin and the Russians who were stiff and distrustful of their more gregarious American allies; whereas during the cold war in Geneva, Washington, Paris, Vienna, the American Presidents and their entourage were warier and more pessimistic than the eager Khrushchev. In retrospect, the extent and the import of the decisions taken at all of these Summit Conferences appears smaller and less significant than the unwillingness of the protagonists—from Roosevelt to Kennedy and from Stalin to Khrushchev—to grapple with the principal and critical problem of the division of Europe and, specifically, of Germany: an issue which, for example, was skirted at Yalta when Russian-American relations were excellent as well as at Camp David when they were poor, and which was papered over by vague generalities at Geneva or at Camp David. On the other hand important agreements *were* reached on the Far East, for example, at Yalta as well and even in Vienna where, for example, Khrushchev and Kennedy produced an interim agreement on Laos.

In any event, soon after Vienna Khrushchev decided to seal the division of Germany for good by closing the half-open frontier between West and East Berlin. Thereby the process which began in 1943, the partition of the German state into Western and Eastern units, was completed. An ironic paradox resides in the fact that this closing of the last hole in Berlin was to occur at a time when the so-called iron curtain, dividing the rest of Europe, was beginning to rust away, with great patches corroding and flaking off, and with all kinds of little methodical windows sheared open elsewhere by the tin scissors of opportunist governments—at a time when the fifteen-year-old *status quo* imposed by the Russians in Eastern, and promoted by the Americans in Western, Europe was beginning to crumble in the most surprising places, indeed, all along the line.

CHAPTER VIII

Decline of the Super-Powers

(From 1958)

1

By 1958 the armory of the United States and of the Soviet Union had become enormous. The two governments had accumulated thousands of atomic bombs and hundreds of hydrogen bombs; in addition to their large armies, fleets, and submarines they possessed powerful and speedy air armadas, capable of attacking distant continents; they perfected the manufacture of gigantic rockets which could hurl horrible bombs from the heartland of one continent to another; they succeeded, too, in firing metal articles of increasing mass and number beyond the sphere of the earth; they were, indeed, preparing a race for the moon. At the same time the real power of the United States and of the Soviet Union was declining. This is not the place for a metaphysical disputation: but it should be evident that "real" power, in this world, involves the influence which men have over men, and that, historically speaking, this kind of power is more meaningful than the "material" power with which men can affect their environment. Nowadays when we are so often told that the Industrial Revolution was the greatest single event in the history of mankind, perhaps we ought to think a little about the historical conditions of that "Revolution." Wasn't the development of industry not only a cause but also a consequence of the development of democracy? Was it a mere coincidence that the industrialization of production nearly two centuries ago began not in Russia or

in Spain but in England and Scotland and the United
States? And in the subsequent development of the
United States, weren't the effects of her population on
her productivity even greater than the effects of her
production on her population? And could Russia, in the
twentieth century, have become an industrialized
Super-Power without a population of two hundred million? These are not rhetorical questions. Nor is population a mere matter of quantity. In this age of incipient
world democracy historical developments, contrary to
the now prevalent general beliefs, are not governed by
mechanical causalities. The intrusion of popular sentiments, together with the images of public opinion,
affects the tendencies of governments and the very
structure of events: it is not only that what happens is
influenced by what people think happens but that what
people think happens (and what people think other
people think happens) is often inseparable from the
very development of events. In other words, "power"
is involved with "prestige" even more intricately than
before while the vast mechanical noises of "publicity"
may confuse and retard but they do not essentially alter
the historical functions of public opinion.

After 1958 the very enormity of the weapons possessed by the two Super-Powers contributed to their
political impotence in many places of the world: in this
era of Hydrogen Bombs puny Central and South
American countries could blackmail and defy the
United States with relative impunity, something that
they dared not do in the gunboat era; certain neighbors
of the mighty and brutal Soviet Union, too, could defy
her with more safety and success than they could resist
Tsarist Russia when the latter had not yet become an
industrial power; and even where clear-cut political
defiance was not forthcoming, the prestige of the two
Super-Powers of the World showed many signs of wan-
ing. Indeed, Russia's Eurasian Empire began to show

certain signs of dissolution, while the American world empire entered on a long process of retrenchment.

2

If we look at a political map of the world—that is, at a map whose main features show the existing states and their frontiers—we shall find that the map of what we, somewhat loosely, are apt to call "the West" remained fairly constant during the last hundred years, and especially since the First World War. The greatest changes in the political map of the world occurred not in Europe and not in America but in Africa and, to some extent, in Asia. The European and British colonial empires largely ceased to exist. Forty new states were born. This was mostly the consequence of the Second World War. This development was applauded and, at times, hastened by the United States and, of course, by the Soviet Union. It certainly transformed the already formless and unwieldy composition and authority of the United Nations. By 1960 its membership had doubled; the number of its member states reached one hundred. The names of many of these states are even now far from well known; even intelligent students of world affairs have trouble at times in finding their place on the map. Nothing like this has happened in the entire history of mankind; a political transformation comparable only to the vast changes in the map of the Americas when the Spanish Empire dissolved in new components a century and a half ago.

Yet the historic consequences of this tremendous political and geographical transformation were not at all commensurate. The reasons for this are manifold. In the first place, what has happened especially throughout Africa was not so much the birth of new nations as of new states. Leaving aside the profounder question whether "nation," in the proper sense of that term, is not a particularly European phenomenon, and seldom applicable to the complex tribal and racial realities of African politics, there can be no question that, while these events electrified the lives of small and extremely ambitious minorities, the majority of African peoples was not very much affected by them. For, in the second place, the gradual reformation of colonial relationships had already begun in many places well before the last world war; so had the educational and technological revolutionary transformations of primitive life. In the third place—third in order but perhaps first in importance for our story—Africa and the Southern Hemisphere remained, by and large, outside the main theater of the strategic conflicts of the Great Powers. American, Russian, European, and Chinese competition increased; yet it seldom grew beyond propagandistic, ideological, and technical endeavors.

Still, it was in this vast area of the world that the Kennedy Administration moved fastest and furthest. The President proceeded from the notion that colonial revolutions were, by and large, welcome. He accepted also the theoretically concomitant but, in reality, curious notion of the new nations' "neutrality." This, in practice, varied from country to country. True, most of the new statesmen were aware of the differences between American constructive and Soviet subversive gifts; but their inclinations were conditioned by "anticolonial" sentiments, and by a very large disregard for political freedom. Thus, for example, few of the African and Asian nations found anything worth mentioning about the Soviet subjugation of Hungary or the Berlin Wall, while they were doing everything possible to oust the remaining European Powers—Portugal, for example —from their last responsible African and Indian territories. The tragicomic story of the Congo where, from July 1960 onwards, the journalistic phrase of a "bloody orgy of murder and rape" had, for once, become a reality, demonstrated the incapacity of certain African leaders to govern their peoples or, indeed, themselves. The so-called "Neutrals' Conference" in Belgrade, composed mainly of African and Asian nations, that was somewhat pompously convoked in September 1961 by the former bandit and now elder statesman Tito, showed the confused and dishonest double standards used by these leaders in regard to the Soviet Union and to the United States: extremely lenient toward the first, somewhat suspicious and severe toward the second, even though stopping short of actions that would halt the benefices issued by Washington with its now traditional bureaucratic *largesse*.

At any rate, as we have seen, the composition of the United Nations had become vastly different. Already from its very beginning the states of Europe had a reduced role in that originally very American organization; by 1961 the nations of the West and the peoples of the white race were a minority within it. Its hygienic and depersonalized atmosphere became also fantastically complicated and cumbrous; some consideration was given even to the possibility of eventually removing it from New York. At any rate, it turned out to be something quite different from the organization planned by Franklin Roosevelt and established on the grounds donated by a philanthropic generation of Rockefellers. The so-called Asian-African "bloc"—in itself an imprecise term—grew predominant; and in 1961, after Dag Hammarskjöld's tragic accidental death in Africa, a placid Burmese became the head of this (at least theoretically) most august organization of mankind. All of this, however, remained secondary to the historic realities of the world conflict: for Europe and, indeed, the middle of Europe was still the center of history and, consequently, of the rivalry of world Powers.

3

In 1860, with the partial exception of the Americas, the European Powers and Russia were the masters of the world. A century later, as we have seen, the European nations constituted a small minority within the United Nations (indeed, Germany and Switzerland were not even among its members); and they left their colonies at a quickening rate. By the end of 1960 the last Italian and Belgian colonial administrations were gone; even the once grandiloquent Franco thought it best to reduce Spain's African colonies to a minimum, while France and Portugal were entangled in an increasingly desperate struggle of what remained of Algeria, Angola, and the rest. Meanwhile, more than sixteen years after the termination of the Second World War, Europe and Germany remained as divided as ever; indeed, the division of Germany rigidified. No serious person spoke any longer about the possibility of "liberating" Eastern Europe; and in Western Europe, too, the prosperity of nations was hardly reflected in their military powers: they—including Britain—seemed to leave the major tasks of their defense to the United States.

At the same time this over-all picture of European weakness was countervailed by a new emerging background. If, by 1950, five years after the Zero Hour of the end of the war, the economic recovery of Western Europe had definitely begun, ten years later, by 1960, the renaissance of Europe was an accomplished fact. The rise in living standards was spectacular; for the first time in many decades the rates of industrial increase surpassed those of the United States; the quality of European goods and, more important, certain features of European life began to attract the envy or admiration of Americans, Russians, Asians. To be sure, ugly moral problems plagued the consciences of most European nations, consequences of the increasing purposelessness of life and of the social dissolution produced by the large-scale technological transformations of daily existence; indeed, the "mass culture" of Britain, Germany, Northern Europe, showed alarming tendencies of hopelessness and of anarchic violence. On the other hand the sense of a European consciousness, with its concomitant sense of distinctness from Russia and also, to some extent, from America, slowly began crystallizing on both sides of the iron curtain; and this may be something far more important than the economic and bureaucratic arrangements for European unity. At any rate, these arrangements—the Common Market, and Britain's consideration of her eventual entry—made a profound impression on the United States whose responsible planners, for the first time in its history, were beginning to consider the eventual inevitability of a closer economic union with Europe; a reversal of the world situation at the beginning of the cold war, when many sensible Europeans had hoped to move in an American direction, to join their remaining fortunes and institutions with those of the then uniquely prosperous United States.

The general tendencies of this vague European renaissance, then, were beginning to involve the eventual loosening of the Russian and American alliance systems. True, the Germans put almost everything on the American card; but Adenauer still remained a sincere, honest, and steadfast supporter of the movement toward European unity. More important was General De Gaulle's assumption of power in France in May 1958. Evidently De Gaulle strove for a truly independent and more powerful Europe, ultimately less dependent on either American or Russian military and political systems. He followed this policy even at the cost of military divergences between France and the United States and at the cost of political and economic divergences between

France and Britain. Although the ultimate German attitude to a policy of a truly independent United Europe was questionable, Adenauer remained loyal to De Gaulle, avoiding recriminations even when De Gaulle was taking certain measures to limit American military establishments on French territory and American command over the armed forces of France. More important, the United States herself felt that she could not afford to react to these French policies with manifest disfavor.

There existed, after 1958, a certain parallel between the Western and Eastern European evolutions. In the East, the relatively more independent Communist Gomulka; in the West, the relatively more independent anti-Communist De Gaulle; in the East, the Warsaw Pact; in the West, NATO with its headquarters in Paris —two central capitals not quite in line with their respective systems of military conformity. Just as Khrushchev with Gomulka's Poland, Eisenhower had been careful after 1958 not to alienate De Gaulle's France beyond a certain point; just as Khrushchev felt the need to consolidate his relations with Poland, the United States felt the need to consolidate to some extent her friendship, torn by the events of 1956, with Britain and France.

Meanwhile, even though quite out of proportion with the actual power of his nation, the impressive personality of Charles de Gaulle made its mark on the course of world events. We have seen that, in May 1960, De Gaulle stood stunned and silent between a frenzied Khrushchev and a fumbling Eisenhower. It is probably significant that it was barely a few days after the collapse of that ill-fated summit that De Gaulle thought it opportune to speak about the necessity of an independent Europe. On 31 May 1960 De Gaulle mentioned, for the first time in public, the need of a kind of European independence from the United States; he suggested, too, the prospective diminution of the Soviet

Empire; he spoke of the future dissolution of the division of the continent; he indicated the need for a united Europe which would include England. "The geographical barriers of the Rhine, the Alps, the Pyrenees, the English Channel are no longer obstacles to unity," he said.

It is De Gaulle's historic merit that he chose to present alternatives which previously had been slurred over by ambitious bureaucrats, obscured by myopic politicians, fudged by intellectuals dependent on various institutions and foundations: that any "Europe" worth talking about must be, by necessity, European; that it could not forever depend on the military power of the United States; that, if it was to be united, it must be also independent. He was coming around to state the alternatives: Common Market or Supermarket? A European confederation; or a North Atlantic federation governed by America? From 1960 onward De Gaulle rose to a kind of eminence which was in many ways comparable to the position of Bismarck exactly a century before; and, like Bismarck, who had known then that Germany would not be united by the twaddle of professors and abstract democrats, De Gaulle knew that Western Europe would not be united by the twaddle of bureaucrats and economists shuffling deadening statistics, dealing with the international tariff on frozen chickens. Yet at the same time De Gaulle remained first, and foremost, a Frenchman, just as Bismarck was always a Prussian; and there was not much to indicate, even after De Gaulle's painful and courageous amputation of Algeria from France, that the French nation possessed the energies and the wherewithal within Western Europe which, in the 1960s, was comparable to Prussia's situation within the Germanies in the 1860s. What is even more important, De Gaulle, unlike Bismarck a century ago, could not feel the presence of an elemental surge of a new and passionate movement of peoples behind him—at least not yet in the early

1960s.[1] To some extent it seemed as if the peoples of Western Europe were content with being bypassed by the mainstream of world history. If so, they were mistaken; for, as the Berlin and German crisis of 1961 showed, at least the leaders of Russia were supremely aware that Germany and Europe were, still, the centers of the world conflict.

To some extent this view was shared by Washington, too: but there the historical and geographical realities were somewhat obscured by the technological and ideological vision of the world that has grown to dominate the thinking and the expressions of American statesmanship through a rising influence of bureaucrats and scientists. This was even reflected in some of the pronouncements of the otherwise judicious new American President; in May 1961, after the Cuban fiasco, at a time when the problem of Berlin was ripening into a new crisis, when the most acute task of statesmanship consisted in defining, negotiating, and eventually revising minute geographical and political details of the greatest importance then crystallizing in Berlin and involving the division of Europe, the young President of the United States chose to tell the American people that they must put a man on the moon.

4

In the summer of 1961 the Berlin Crisis passed into its acute stage. Khrushchev, somewhat unexpectedly, handed a Soviet memorandum to Kennedy during their Vienna meeting, a memorandum stating the Soviet position on Berlin, inflexible and rigid on paper. Throughout June and July the Soviets and their East German satellites insisted that the "solution" of the Berlin prob-

[1] I have attempted to deal with some of the historical difficulties and problems of "Europeanism" in *Decline and Rise of Europe* (1965).

lem must begin before the end of the year; that the Western Allies must negotiate with the East Germans from then on. It was evident that probably very soon the Communists would make some kind of a move, lopping off Allied rights and the remaining free traffic between East and West Berlin. Consequently the trickle of the daily exodus to West Berlin from the East thickened into a flow. Hundreds and, in time, thousands of people crossed daily in July to the prospects of a better life in the West; the prestige of the hateful East German rulers was again badly shaken; and early in August, Ulbricht flew to Moscow to consult with Khrushchev. During the damp Sunday dawn of 13 August he moved. The border between East and West Berlin was closed in a flash; barbed wire was strung along quickly, mile by mile; militiamen and soldiers of the East German Army guarded the crossing points in trucks; the flow of the refugees ebbed away in a day, and afterwards petered out, punctuated by tragic shots.

More than fifteen years had passed since the opening of the Berlin problem; more than twelve years since the ending of the first Berlin Blockade; more than eight years since the East Berlin uprising; almost three years since Khrushchev's reopening of the new Berlin Crisis. One can imagine the mounds of policy paper and the hours of policy planners spent in NATO committees and in the chambers of Bonn and Washington. Yet, for this contingency of 13 August, "the West" was, by and large, unprepared. There was a slightly ominous flutter of a war scare in America (in July President Kennedy chose to call up army reserves in order to impress Khrushchev with the American readiness to resist a West Berlin *coup* with "conventional," that is, non-nuclear arms, while businessmen and community worthies plunged into the thickening promotion of Fallout Shelters). A great city, erstwhile capital of the greatest nation in Europe, a city with a skeptical, taut, clever, courageous population, presided over by a brave and intelligent Socialist Mayor, the center of the cold war, the chief connecting and focal point of East and West, was unnaturally, brutally, senselessly divided in two. Within a few days this division hardened into concrete. The East Germans erected a cement wall running mile after mile across the pavements of a once living unit of a city; the doors and windows of houses in certain streets were walled in; unfortunate refugees were shot swimming dark canals. President Kennedy sent General Clay, the American commander during the 1948 Blockade, to Berlin; together with the periodically injected American infantry he was cheered by an anxious, quivering population. At times along The Wall gunfire and tear gas bombs erupted. In October the East Germans began to interfere with the last remnants of the ambiguous legal status of Berlin, with the rights of Western military men to move through East Berlin; twice American armored cars and infantry were sent through the one remaining open crossing point to symbolically enforce these rights. Then Russian tanks were brought up on the Eastern, and American and British ones on the Western, side of The Wall; and, for a moment—for the first time in fifteen years of the cold war—American and Russian tanks uneasily faced each other at a distance of a few hundred yards. Then the Russians withdrew; and so did the Americans.

This was in October 1961; and we shall see, in a moment, how and why Khrushchev, once more, came around to modify some of his Berlin demands, easing off his pseudo-ultimatum of signing an East German Treaty before the end of the year. Larger and deeper events, evident in Moscow, were involved here. But before touching on the important developments within the Communist sphere during and after the Moscow Party Congress, let us once more cast a look at the Berlin and German situations, from Russian, from American, from German, and perhaps from "European" angles.

We may detect, in retrospect, two relative changes in the Russian position during the 1950s. We have seen how, from 1952 onward, they were suggesting the possibility of a neutral, unarmed but unified Germany, in all probability non-Communist but certainly one which would not be allowed to join the Western military alliance system. We have seen how the Allies, and principally the United States, rejected such a German solution. The other alternative, then, was the solidification of the Germanies' division: and this was the policy to which Khrushchev seemed to incline, from 1958 onward. What we must keep in mind, then, is the fact that from his viewpoint such a *de facto* settlement and the Berlin *status quo* were hardly reconcilable. What he had to face in 1961 (and even thereafter) was the existence of not two, but of three, Germanies. There was his East Germany: weak, drained of its people, ruled by unpopular and often disappointing rulers, an artificial state with an area, resources, and population just about one third of their West German counterpart. There was West Germany: populous, prosperous, and increasingly armed. And there was West Berlin: a Western island, a big Western fleck, connected to the Western mainland by an American concrete causeway and by bright airlanes through and over the gray Communist sea: a non-Communist, more, an anti-Communist focal point within it (in January 1961 he spoke of the necessity of "eradicating this splinter from the heart of Europe"). Moscow might be willing to acquiesce in the existence of two Germanies, *Germania Maior* in the Western and *Germania Minor* in the Russian sphere—but, then, the existence of this *Germania Minor* must be assured, secured, unbroken, acknowledged, and complete.

The American position, at least on the surface, was simple: the defense of the *status quo*. There was no Berlin problem, stated Kennedy (and, for different reasons, also De Gaulle) until the Russians created it.

This was, of course, legally true; but it was, also, begging the question. There *was* a Berlin problem, and there was a German problem, both involved with the problem of Europe: the anomalous division of a city and of a country and of a whole continent. They should not be reunited through war—at least on this Kennedy and Khrushchev seemed to agree. Would they be reunited through peace? The assumption of American foreign policy was that they might be—some day, because of the slowly accumulating difficulties of the Russians throughout their Eastern European orbit. (Of this American assumption the Russians have been acutely, and pathologically, aware.) The other, unspoken assumption, hardened into a reality by 1961, was that both Americans and Russians had come around to the conclusion that, for each, half of Europe was better than none; and that, thus, disengagement was further away than ever. On the other hand the American President and government, for domestic as well as international motives, could not simply agree to a solemn and final demarcation of the division of Germany and of Europe: for this would involve, among other things, a readjustment of the status of West Berlin as well as the prohibition of nuclear armaments in the Germanies. Kennedy was not inclined to compromise the Dulles brothers' policy of an alliance with a strong Germany as the main prop of America's defense and policy system.[2] Evidently important Russian concessions could be had only at the price of certain important American concessions; and the character of the President (who, extremely sensitive to domestic political opposition, withdrew even from the

---

[2] Despite the spy-plane and the Cuban fiascos, Kennedy maintained the highest regard for Allen Dulles; so did his closest confidant, his brother Robert. When Dulles finally retired, in October 1961, the President took his advice by appointing the Californian conservative John McCone to head the CIA.

planned diplomatic recognition of Outer Mongolia), together with the general direction of American policy, suggested that such concessions could not be expected —at least not for some time, at least not without the pressure of yet unforeseen combinations and events.

Thus Soviet Russia and the United States, deeply entangled and extremely sensitive about their respective Germanies and Berlins, felt unable and were unwilling to suggest anything decisive that would change the division of Berlin and of Germany and of Europe. The German reaction to these events was curiously slow. Chancellor Adenauer was now rapidly aging; his policy of the strong American alliance evidently bore few tangible fruits for German unity; the events of The Wall showed this clearly; while its construction had been a consequence of Communist weakness, its existence was a mark of Western indecision. Yet the West German elections of September 1961 indicated only a partial loss of popularity for Adenauer and his Christian Democrats. While the morale of the West Berliners was very slowly ebbing, the determination of the West German people to acquire nuclear arms on their own was growing, even though—at least officially—this policy was wrapped in the proposal of forming "an independent nuclear arm for NATO."[3]

[3] At the same time the Germans were plagued, to some extent, by a curious revival of anti-Nazi (and, consequently, Germanophobe) propaganda in the United States. This was, in part, a reaction to the public trial of the Nazi exterminator Eichmann, captured secretly in Argentina and spirited to Israel; but this coincided with a spate of books and motion pictures, involving other factors, at the very time when the earlier strong Germanophobe sentiments in Britain were slowly ebbing. Thus, in 1961, American liberals tended anew to believe that the German people are cunning and untrustworthily and nationalistically eager to profit from the antagonism between America and Russia. This is an unjust impression—exactly as unjust as the unspoken assumption of most American "conservatives" that Germany should have always been the main ally of America, and that Hitler

It appears, at the same time, that the foreign policy of West Germany was not particularly competent. While in the early fifties not only the status of East Germany (called by the Germans, significantly, *Mitteldeutschland:* Central Germany) but the status of the former German territories occupied by Poland seemed shaky, and ultimately negotiable, by the early sixties the Oder-Neisse Line had become less and less contestable, and the very existence of the East German state (now the Germans referred to it, more and more, as *die Sowjetzone:* the Soviet Zone) was becoming more stable and more solid. Not only Russia, but none of Germany's European neighbors, including Britain, wanted to change the *status quo* of a Germany divided; and the United States, too, showed symptoms of not wishing to tamper with the existence of an East Germany at all. Thus grew the realization within Germany, too, expressed in 1961 only by a few courageous intellectuals and spiritual leaders, such as the philosopher Karl Jaspers, that the best Germans could hope for was no longer reunification but more freedom for their Eastern brethren; that All-German Reunification and Western European Integration had become mutually exclusive policies; that German unity was becoming a failure, while Western European unity was becoming a success—something that was the principal, though seldom outspoken, assumption of the British and the French (though not yet necessarily of the American and West German) governments.

5

Meanwhile the Russians had great and growing troubles of their own; and it is impossible to separate

should have been let alone to defeat Communist Russia once and for all.

their Berlin (and their German and European and American) policies from the development of these.

We have seen how, from the very beginning, the relationship between the two Communist giants, Russia and China, remained suspicious and uneasy. These difficulties were historical, racial, political as well as ideological; they involved the governments of these states, and the ideological arguments, as almost always, were but rationalizations of their already existing disagreements. During the first phase of the cold war they involved the questions of Russian or Chinese primacy over important borderlands: after 1955 the Chinese began casting for foreign and Communist support all over the world, and their eyes were becoming narrower and angrier at any sign or improvement in Russian-American relations. They obviously welcomed the weakening of American prestige and power everywhere; and they were beginning to welcome the weakening of Russian prestige and power, too. Meanwhile they had pressing problems of their own. Their navy was still very inadequate; their armaments were backward; and their determined effort at collectivizing their agriculture led to spasms of sufferings and famine and to consequent retrenchments. Thus they felt that they must assert their power. They leaned heavily on the Himalayan ramparts of India (whose government was enjoying a pale sunshine of Russian sympathy, manifest in the offer of Russian armored equipment); and in the muddy maze of Laos the pattern of 1954 appeared again: Russia joined Britain in a sort of mediation between the American-led and Chinese-trained Laotian factions. Meanwhile all over the world of colored races, Chinese influence and "doctrine" (whatever that is) began to emerge beside and, at times, over the spasmodic influence of Russian agents.

But, again, it was not in Asia but in Europe—in Eastern Europe—that the Russo-Chinese rivalry became most evident.

Ever since the dramatic events of 1956, the Eastern European satellites lived through a curious twilight existence. Their political dependence on Moscow was, again, unequivocal; on the other hand, life and movement and certain personal liberties were better tolerated in Eastern Europe after 1956 than before. This was most evident in the four states bordering on Russia, in Poland, Czechoslovakia, Hungary, and Rumania —for different reasons, and strongly influenced by the various national characteristics of these peoples, involving even their minority Communist rulerships. However, probably this geographical factor was decisive,[4] since, on the other hand, the older, rigid (often mistakenly called Stalinist) dictatorial cliques remained strongest in East Germany, Bulgaria, and Albania. I have suggested some of the Russian dilemmas involving East Germany; in Bulgaria there were bitter and secret intra-party struggles early in 1961, settled for a time according to Soviet wishes; but in Albania the anti-Khrushchev (and anti-liberal, and anti-Tito) faction led by Hoxha maintained a grim upper hand. The situation and the passions in that small and backward Balkan country are, again, inseparable from historic factors, and foremost from the historic and tribal enmity between Albanians and Yugoslavs; but it was also evident that greater connections were at work. In 1960, like Tito's Yugoslavia twelve years earlier, Hoxha's Albania refused to heed Moscow's admonitions. First during a congress in Bucharest, and finally in Moscow, the two leaders came to a break. The Russian submarines abandoned their Albanian base; relations between the parties were broken; and finally, in December 1961, came the diplomatic break on a state level.

[4] Here, again, we may see an illustration of a principal axiom of the cold war which has not received the attention it deserves. It is that while the danger of *Russian domination* is greatest in the countries close to Russia, the *reputation of Communism* becomes greater the farther away we get from Russia.

Unlike Tito, however, the Albanian Communists could count on support not in the West but in the East. The Chinese took up their cause. They remonstrated with Khrushchev because of his harsh dealings with the Albanians; they refused to associate themselves with the Russian condemnation of the Albanian Party. These things came to a head during the Twenty-Second Congress of the Communist Party of the Soviet Union in October 1961. Two developments of glowing importance fascinated the world, emerging from the gloomy murk of interminable Byzantine formalities and dull speeches lasting for hours. One was the split between Russia and China, breaking around the Albanian issue (or, rather, pretext); indeed, one day, amidst the rhetorical proceedings, Chou En-lai packed up and left the congress and convention. The other—for reasons probably as much psychological as ideological, personal rather than politic—was the final step of reducing the remaining prestige of Stalin. It was taken more than five years after Khrushchev's historic but secret speech to the Communist leadership of All the Russias during the Twentieth Congress. Now the body of Stalin was physically removed from the Lenin Mausoleum in Red Square; the symbolic name of Stalingrad was changed to Volgograd;[5] and the old Molotov, still very much alive, was ordered back from Vienna to Moscow.

The motives of this historic and symbolic recasting of the image of Russian contemporary history were certainly not unconnected with the Chinese problem: they were certainly more complex than, simply, a struggle between "Stalinists" and "anti-Stalinists" (in the phraseology of imaginative Western journalists and "experts"). Whether it was his political sense or his strange but very Russian feelings of conscience that prompted Khrushchev to go that far we cannot tell: at any rate, these Byzantine events were, again, more typically Russian than they were Communist; at any

[5] The name reverted to Stalingrad again in 1964.

rate, they were much less popular with the mumbling
people of All the Russias than with the Communist
ruling elite who had been, after all, painfully aware
of Stalin's more dreadful characteristics; at any rate, no
one could tell what Khrushchev would reap in the end.
It is a curious thing: it is not impossible, with modesty
and with some hesitation, to anticipate how Khrushchev
would be judged by our history; but no one can
yet say how he would be judged by the Russian people
—or, rather, by their presumably new barbaric spokesmen of a future age.

The consequences of the Moscow events were world-
wide and almost immediate. The worsening of relations
between Russia and China at once led to definite Russian efforts to improve relations with America; Khrushchev, like Bismarck (and Stalin), could not face the
prospects of a conflict on both tremendous imperial
flanks. In late September 1961 Khrushchev initiated a
personal and private correspondence with President
Kennedy. The text and the circumstances of his first
letter were characterized by surprising scrupulosity
and tact; against the opinions of some of his advisers
President Kennedy chose to respond in a not unfriendly
manner; there followed a rambling series of private letters between these two statesmen, culminating in their
exchanges during the Cuban Crisis in 1962, and ending
only with the sudden and tragic death of one of the
principal correspondents a year later. This practice,
even more than the more sensationally publicized "hot
line" (a direct telephone connection established between the White House and the Kremlin in 1963) contributed significantly to the more peaceful evolution of
Soviet-American relations. While the last personal encounter between an American President and his Russian counterpart at the last Summit in Vienna, on 4
June 1961, marked the end of a phase, the inauguration
of the direct Khrushchev-Kennedy correspondence, on
29 September 1961, may have marked the beginning of

another phase in the cold war; indeed, perhaps the beginning of the end of the cold war, of the transition from the cold war to a kind of cold peace.

Once more Khrushchev dropped the year-end Berlin "deadline" (which, to be sure, had been somewhat ambiguous from the very beginning); once more he floated fat little diplomatic balloons in conversations with visiting worthies from the West; for the first time in history he sent an amiable congratulation to the Pope (John XXIII), to which the Holy Father answered with tact and courtesy; and he even had a significant conversation with the able and thoughtful Dr. Kroll, the West German Ambassador in Moscow, something that not merely the Chinese but presumably also Ulbricht saw with great distaste. Around this conversation a minor diplomatic storm blew up; and Herr Kroll narrowly escaped censure from the rigid pro-Americanists in Bonn.

The key problems for Russia were still the content and the purpose of the American-German alliance and the possibility of nuclear weapons in German hands. About this the Kennedy Administration was neither unequivocal nor clear. In an interview given to Khrushchev's son-in-law, Kennedy made a cautious suggestion about preventing other European powers from having nuclear weapons. On the other hand the plan supported by the German Defense Minister Strauss, of giving NATO an "independent" nuclear arm of its own, was gaining ground in Washington. To some extent this was a euphemism, for the Fourth Nuclear Power, for all practical purposes, would not be a shapeless NATO Thing but Germany; under the aegis of NATO, to be sure, in the SHAPE of NATO, but with dominant German content, nevertheless.

That the Russians were extraordinarily sensitive about this affair could be seen from the curious, and ominous, Finnish episode in November 1961. It will be remembered that Stalin in 1948 let Finland remain domestically independent at the price of Sweden staying outside NATO; and that in 1955 the Russians gave up their naval base in Finland during the period when the disengagement of America and Russia in Europe seemed to have begun. By 1961 a West German navy had grown up; not, of course, comparable in size and power with the Russian (or even with the Swedish) Baltic Fleets but, together with the American North Sea forces and the impending disposition of the Polaris nuclear-rocket submarines, something worth considering. In the fall of 1961 a NATO Baltic subcommand was being formed. From Moscow's viewpoint, the tacitly accepted Russian domination over the Baltic now seemed infringed, for the first time during the cold war, when the indefatigable Strauss traveled to Denmark and Norway to discuss the organization of an American-German-Nordic sea command. These events—together with the appearance of new anti-Communist political candidates in Finland—were pretext as well as cause for Khrushchev, who, probably spurred by the general uneasiness within the Communist camp of states, suddenly put pressure on Finland to join Russia in "military consultations." These events, and the Russian phraseology, were ominously reminiscent of Stalin's first demands to the Baltic republics in 1939–40. The Finnish President interrupted his global tour in Honolulu: from that tropical scenery he flew across the world to meet Khrushchev in the icy town of Novosibirsk. There Kekkonen, like his great predecessor Mannerheim, succeeded in impressing the Russian master of Finland's sincerity; Kekkonen's opponent dropped out of the presidential contest; and Finland's domestic independence could continue so long as her foreign policy would be molded in great general accordance with Moscow's supposed interests.

Cuba and the Congo, Goa and Katanga notwithstanding, the Finnish episode rather clearly indicated that Berlin and Germany were indeed the principal matters of the cold war, and of Russian-American relations. But, as the year 1961 closed, disagreements about Berlin and NATO and the future of Europe, complicated with the maddening affairs of the Congo, were evident in the councils of the West. Meanwhile, in the Communist half-world of the Northern Hemisphere, the primacy of Russia, too, was rumbling and shaking, even though she forcefully reminded Finland of her ever present shadow, even though she had strengthened her grip on East Berlin.

6

Something now emerges, not clearly but slowly, not in one overwhelming movement but in falling and surging currents, from the main flow of these events. After fifteen years (one half of an old-time generation) of cold war the division of the world into American and Russian spheres of power was gradually breaking up.

In 1945 the Russians were the undisputed masters of Eastern Europe. A broken, defeated, impoverished, shivering Germany and Western Europe stretched in front of them to the sea. They enjoyed good will and admiration from the British and American peoples. For a moment Communism was intellectually fashionable throughout the Western Hemisphere; and the revolutionary movements in East Asia had already turned in the direction of Communism. The government of China was desperately dependent on their good will and support; and in the East only Japan was denied to them by the supremacy of American arms.

Few of these conditions existed fifteen years later. In Africa and Asia most of those populist and revolutionary minorities who clambered into the seats of formerly colonial states and principalities were neither Russian-made nor Communist; and even when they were the latter, their principal inclinations were less

Russian than Chinese. The weak and torn China of 1945 had become strong, unified, Communist—and also anti-Russian. The Russian primacy of power and influence in North Korea, Sinkiang, Manchuria, even their monopoly in Outer Mongolia to some extent, were gone. In Western Europe the Communist parties were either inconsequential or stagnant; in Eastern Europe the vast majority of populations continued to despise and, on occasion, to hate the Russians (without, however, feeling inclined to challenge their mastery through uprisings), while even within the minority of Communist leaderships intricate factional and personal feuds were developing. The Russians no longer controlled Yugoslavia, Albania, Eastern Austria, and they abandoned their naval base in Finland. All of this was in great general contrast with what the spokesmen of frantic anti-Communism were telling the world, and particularly the American people, about the grand uninterrupted march of Soviet Russia to World Domination.

On the other hand, American prestige and power, too, suffered a general erosion during sixteen years of cold war, and particularly during the five years following 1956, the crucial year, perhaps the turning point. In 1945 the United States was the undisputed, and the undisputable, leader of the free world. By 1961 this leadership may have been still undisputed, but it was no longer undisputable. In her own Caribbean backyard, the word of the United States was no longer the law. In 1945 only Perón's Argentina, the far southernmost republic of the Americas could defy American political wishes; by 1961 the United States, after a halfhearted and abortive attempt, thought it better not to interfere drastically with the pro-Communist Castro dictatorship in Cuba. Elsewhere in the world the American alliance system was either unwilling or unable to recapture for the West any state or territory that had been conquered by the Russians and their allies in 1945 and after; and the only territories that could be saved from Communist domination were indeed those—like Finland or Laos—that remained outside the American or Western alliance system. The states of Western Europe were much less dependent on American support by 1961 than ten or fifteen years earlier; indeed, in 1961 it was the United States that began to consider cautiously how to avoid potential economic troubles in the future by associating itself with the economic union of Western Europe. Meanwhile, despite the always politic, and often generous American actions aimed at the easy liquidation of colonialism, the atavistic, unreasonable, and opportunist suspicions of Asian and African peoples still saw in the United States the Principal White Power. While the popularity of America, springing from curiously deep and sentimental sources, among the great masses of Russians remained very high indeed, a certain kind of disillusionment with American leadership and with American culture (sentiments motivated by envy and snobbery as much as by restored European self-confidence) grew everywhere throughout Western Europe, perhaps least in Germany.

In the second part of this book we shall see how these developments were, to a great extent, consequences of the radical and deep-going transformations of Russian and American society and ideas during the last two decades. At any rate, by 1961 it was obvious that, all claims of the Space Age notwithstanding, this earth was still a very large and complex human planet; that no single Power could remain omnipotent even within its sphere for a long time; that, apart from these physical and geographical conditions, neither America nor Russia were yet sufficiently mature, able, or perhaps even willing, to establish their complete mastery over their portions of the Northern Hemisphere.

To some extent this has been a propitious development; the slow movement of Western and even of Eastern Europe, for example, away from their absolute dependence on their erstwhile masters. On the other hand this evident weakening of American and Russian political power was counterbalanced by the fantastic increase in their armaments. While their political prestige was weakening, the power of their arms was increasing: the United States and Soviet Russia were, still, far from relinquishing their positions as the Two Greatest Powers of the world. Indeed, for the first time in the history of mankind, it has been within their power to destroy all human life on earth.

This apocalyptic possibility has, therefore, become a potentially historical event; and, perhaps, it *is* already the most important (and not merely the most profoundly significant) event of our times. If this is so, then the history of this ought to be written—how did this come about? Thus perhaps the greatest task for a historian of our times is not even the tremendous story of the world wars of our century, and not even the world conflict of the two giants, America and Russia, but this story of the mad progress of human science to its now inhuman stages—from the Sicilian Vespers to Auschwitz, from St. Bartholomew's Night to Hiroshima, from Canon Copernicus' first hesitant modern view of the universe to Dr. Von Braun's present view of the purpose of "space," from Descartes, the father of the scientific method, to Dr. Teller "the father of the H-Bomb"—this story of progress which, at least implicitly, gives the lie to those optimistic and narrow theories of man's constant evolution toward brighter and sunnier uplands of morality and happiness; for this story of scientific "progress" has already become a story of human degradation.

Still, for our purposes at least, that is too large a story. And, as I shall put it later in this book, the history of nations is still more important than the history of science (which, in turn, is nothing else than the history of scientists). But at least it must be kept in the back of our minds; and it must be, at times, considered together with the condition that there are certain men, certain people, certain nations whose history and character and culture and education have not yet taught them to be sufficiently skeptical about the new claims of Progress; who, in hailing its "successes," remain, at least for some time, unaware of their direction, that they are rushing not toward Heaven but toward Hell.

It is perhaps significant that the Japanese, whose cities went up in fire during the last war, who suffered the first atomic bombing in 1945, whose fishermen even in 1954 were burned by radioactive dust, whose Constitution, promulgated by General MacArthur after the war, promised the disarmament of Japan forever, by 1960 would be willing to go along with new and extensive measures of rearmament. For history, governed as it is at times by the undue sharpness of national memories, is even more often governed by their dull failing. No matter how horrible they might have been, as the memories of old wars recede, the potential dangers of new wars increase. It is therefore that we must sketch some of the outlines of the Armament Race.

We have seen that the United States exploded its first Hydrogen Bomb in 1952 and the Russians in 1953. Immediately afterward the United States turned to the construction of a super Hydrogen Bomb, together with the construction of transoceanic rockets, the former— "the ultimate weapon"—to be delivered by the latter. After 1953 the Russians were becoming somewhat less recalcitrant in the fantastically complicated disarmament negotiations that went on in fits and starts during the decade, and in May 1955, just before Geneva, Khrushchev ordered his chief negotiator, Malik, to turn around and accept the main principles of the previously offered Western plan (called the Anglo-French Plan).

But it was now the American turn to climb down; obviously surprised by the Russian move, Dulles and the Pentagon hesitated, and after Geneva, in September 1955, the United States went back on its earlier proposal and introduced new reservations. The intricacies of these disarmament talks cannot be followed here; let us only remark that they have been effects rather than causes of the political relations of the Powers on one hand and of their armament programs on the other. By 1959 it was becoming evident that both sides were capable of constructing transoceanic rockets of various kinds. It was at that time that the atomic disarmament negotiations in Geneva entered their most important phase. President Eisenhower maintained a ban on atomic tests in 1959; and the Russians began to suggest that, under certain circumstances, they might consent to the principle of international inspection. The British believed that this radical change in Soviet policy would itself bring political dividends worth considering, as it would further corrode the iron curtain, while the American attitude remained more rigid, demanding extensive facilities for inspection. The serious question, whether the international limitations of the guns (of rocket sites on land and at sea) was not really more important than the inspection of the bullets (of their atomic bomb loads), was left untouched throughout.

In 1961 the marathon negotiations on nuclear tests were suspended; in August the three-year-old moratorium on the tests was broken by the Russians; immediately they tried to impress the Western world (and, probably, the Chinese, too) with fantastic bombs of the so-called 20- to 50-megaton type, bombs whose explosions could be registered by simple seismographs around the world, by scientific instruments whose original purpose had been the registration of earthquakes. The United States resumed the big bomb tests in April 1962. At the same time the leaders of the United States and of Russia knew that they had developing common interests: to halt the spread of atomic weapons before these were to be stocked in the arsenals of more and more nations, including China.

CHAPTER IX

The Cuban Comedy

(From 1959)

1

Let us now pay tribute to the unpredictability of history. Through two decades Central Europe and, specifically, central Germany were the principal subjects of the cold war struggle between the United States and the Soviet Union: we have seen how, in October 1961, along certain streets in Berlin American and Russian tanks were staring at each other directly for the first time. Less than a year later, at a time when the cold war showed certain signs of settling down to a cold peace, a sudden huge crisis, replete with nuclear bombs and rockets, loomed out of the warm mist of . . . Cuba, of a subtropical island, bypassed not only by the principal shipping lanes of the world but by the world struggles of this century: a faraway languid place ignored by Stalin, an American vacation paradise, faintly known by the rest of the world in mid-century by the excellence of her cigars, by the repute of her rum and of a monotonous and frenetic dance step known as the *mambo*.

Once before during the political history of the modern age the affairs of Cuba had become rather suddenly the focus of world interest. Around 1895 the endemic riots of the island's mixed population against the Spanish occupiers were fanned into a guerrilla civil war, with American connivance, by Cuban exiles established in Florida. Three years later, employing various pretexts, the American nation, stirred by the first intoxicating and sentimental winds of world imperial ambitions, went to war over Cuba with the ancient and tattered empire of Spain. That this Splendid Little War, as some leading Americans called it, proved to be a very important turning point in the history of Cuba and in the history of Spain is obvious. Less often recognized is the condition that the Cuban crisis of 1895–98 marked probably the greatest turning point in a hundred years at least in the history of Britain and of the United States: for it was between 1895 and 1898 that the United States first chose to become a World Power, and that the British, after a moment of hesitation, chose to court the friendship of the United States over all other considerations, a policy which they have never abandoned since that time.[1]

Thus had Cubans and Americans together hastened, provoked, and profited from the dissolution of Spain's last weak empire. But it would be both unfair and exaggerated to attribute to the United States devious capitalist and imperialist designs on that island. True, the new republic of Cuba granted the United States a naval base of considerable extent, in Guantanamo Bay; American Marines were stationed elsewhere in Cuba for some time; and the so-called Platt Amendment, written into the Cuban Constitution in 1901, empowering the United States to intervene in Cuba wherever and whenever it wished, reduced Cuba in practice to an American protectorate: but this American protectorate was benevolent, easygoing, and never really oppressive; and the Platt Amendment (though not the Guantanamo Enclave) was canceled by the Roosevelt Administration as early as 1934. True, American and financial corporations had a large influence in certain fields of Cuban economic life, sometimes amounting to near-monopolies: but few people in Cuba objected to this American influence, especially since Cubans, on

[1] See notes 6, 7, and 25 on pages 206, 207, 216 of *Decline and Rise of Europe.*

all levels of life, were eager emulators of American habits, so much so that the Cuban Spanish language was penetrated by an astonishing variety of American words and expressions while the inhabitants of Havana prided themselves for having achieved some of the pinnacles of social and architectural culture usually associated with Miami Beach.[2]

During the Second World War and during the first decade of the cold war Cuba prospered with relatively little American interference: by 1958, for example, the previous near-monopoly of American control over the production of sugar in Cuba had diminished to the extent that hardly more than one third of this production was owned by American corporations. By 1957 less than one third of Cuba's imports came from the United States, and not more than one fifth of Cuban exports were destined thereto. Meanwhile it should be evident that the half-century of American influence over Cuba was beneficial rather than reactionary. It is significant, for example, that by the mid-fifties more than half (57 per cent) of the population of this earlier wholly rural island had become urban; that the per capita income of Cubans—of *all* Cubans—was the fourth highest of all the countries of Latin America; that in 1958 Cubans had more automobiles for the population (one for thirty-nine inhabitants) than highly advanced states, such as Sweden and Belgium, before the last war. True, nearly half of the population was still illiterate: but, then, the history of the twentieth century has amply demonstrated how much easier and faster (and, of course, how much more popular) it is to drive than it is to read.

[2] Those journalists and intellectuals who on occasion indulge in the bad joke of mentioning "Cocacolonization" by the United States ought to consider the origins of the ghastly mixture of iced rum and Coca-Cola, a libation compounded and propounded by enthusiastic Cubans after the historic events of 1898 under the name of "Cuba Libre," Cuba Free.

At that time the splendid skyscrapers of Havana gleamed soapy white along concrete esplanades during the day, blinking furious neons at night. Crammed with American tourists during the winter season, the city of Havana offered every kind of entertainment, from the usual casinos to unusual carnal adventures. Diplomatic relations with the Soviet Union had been broken long ago. Only a lunatic would prophesy that within a few years the marble veneers of these concrete halls would echo with the grimy lisp of the Russian tongue; that in peeling hotel rooms would sit not American tourists but Soviet engineers whose job, in the morning, would be to direct the bulldozing of earth-craters for rocket-guns capable of demolishing Miami Beach; that meanwhile extraordinary American warplanes would nervously crisscross the island, in preparation for an eventual American attack on Cuba and perhaps for a world war with rockets and atoms and all.

2

During the quarter century that followed the abrogation of the Platt Amendment the national life of Cuba was marked not only by increasing prosperity but also by what, among Latin-American nations, was an unusual degree of friendliness and loyalty toward the United States. During the Second World War Cubans were not only not allowed to be stirred, they were not stirred by the attractions of Axis Fascism or of Franquist Hispanism; during the first dozen years of the cold war they were not only not stirred, they were not allowed to be stirred, by the attractions of Communism. When, in 1952, the half-Indian and pro-American military figure of Fulgencio Batista re-established his dictatorship in Havana, it seemed as if this were but another episode characteristic of the political history of what is, with some inaccuracy, called Latin America. It was Batista who overturned the cruel dictator Machado in 1933; sooner or later someone would turn up to up- turn Batista who, as things went, was not of the lowest category of Caribbean dictators in that long list of tropi- cal statesmen whose colorful personalities form a chain from Toussaint L'Ouverture and Iturbide, the Emperor of Mexico at the start of the nineteenth century, to Papa Duvalier and Generalissimo Trujillo in the Mid-Century of The Common Man. Yet the advancement of democ- racy and of education did introduce a new element in the usual succession of events. The revolutionary spirit would no longer be incarnated by hordes of illiterate Indian peasants with honest cruelty shining on their coppery faces but by the sons and, on occasion, daugh- ters of the growing middle classes, all of them white by nature, university by education, Americanized by magazine, and bearded by choice.[3]

On 26 July 1953 Fidel Castro, a very young man at the time, led some kind of a confused attack aimed os- tensibly at a barracks of Batista's army. This was a complete failure: the ambitious and amateur insurgents were rounded up, and it was perhaps this amateurish- ness of the assault as well as the social standing of some of the participants' families that stayed Batista's hand from too many executions. Castro was "exiled" to Mex- ico. In December 1956 (there is some reason to believe that their resolution had been spurred by the then spectacular popularity of the Hungarian revolutionar-

[3] It is at least possible that it was not merely the absence of hot water in the Sierra Maestra that produced the dra- matic and very rapid sprouting of beards on Fidel Castro's face and on those of his followers. There may have been some coincidence in this sudden beardedness erupting among revolutionaries in Cuba and Beatniks in North America around 1957—one of those electric coincidences that reflect synchronized heartbeats and brainwaves over an entire hemisphere, perhaps the deep-felt sense that the smooth- faced era of the Batistas and of the Eisenhowers was draw- ing to its close.

ies)[4] eighty-two men took off from Mexico for the long
and unguarded Cuban coast on a motorboat which bore
the unspectacular name of *Granma*. In the end only
twelve of *Granma*'s charges followed Castro, disap-
pearing in the Sierra Maestra mountains, from where
they began their guerrilla campaign against the Batista regime with the accumulation of smuggled guns,
of young city people who joined the adventure in the
spirit of a patriotic lark, and of the publicity accorded
to them by idealistic journalists in New York. A year
passed. By March 1958 the State Department itself,
contrary to the previous tendency of American ambassadors, usually warm-hearted supporters of Batista,
thought it wiser to reduce his American support: it was
then announced that the latter would no longer get
American arms for free, an event whose publicity value
was rather more important than its logistical consequences, since the official armies of Cuba still possessed
an armed and numerical superiority over the Castroite
guerrillas which was overwhelming. Heartened by this
American action (even though he never admitted this
later) Castro proclaimed a Universal and General Strike
throughout Cuba: but the target date turned out to be
a breezy and sunny day in April 1958, and his call
went unheeded. However, Batista—mostly as he sensed
the gingerly retreat of Americans from his side—now
decided on Terror: his policemen started on a grisly
series of imprisonments and executions. In this Batista
misread the evolving psychology of his people: for terror, to be successful, must inspire not only fear but also
a kind of respect; and the dictatorship of a half-Indian
former sergeant and of his uncultured chewing and

---

[4] The later avowedly Communist Foreign Minister of the
Castro regime, Raul Roa, published a pamphlet in early 1957
which called the Soviet "invasion" of Hungary "criminal and
outrageous." This pamphlet, devoting considerable space to
the world-wide implications of the events in Hungary, was
reprinted in Cuba as late as in October 1959.

spitting henchmen now appeared to thousands of Cubans, including army men and government employees, as a soiled and backward kind of thing which looked bad all over the world and with which they did not want to be any longer associated. Consequently Batista's army and police forces melted away with surprising rapidity. As so often in history, the collapse of the old regime not only preceded but caused the victory of the new one, rather than the reverse. On 1 January 1959 Batista fled from Havana to Miami; while the new master of Cuba, Fidel Castro, was on his way from the eastern end of the island Havanaward in a kind of royal progress whose slowness was not, however, the result of ceremony but of the new ruler's proclivity to long hours of diurnal sleep alternating with long hours of nocturnal oratory, the very volume of which should have been sufficient to deter those commentators who still refer to his personality as enigmatic.

But we should not underestimate or ignore the courage and the resolution of Fidel Castro. His personal leadership provoked, after all, the revolutionary fantastic events which followed. The key to these fantastic events was not Communism but anti-Americanism: specifically, Castro's flowing and ebbing dislike of the United States. In addition to the usual feeling of inferiority which South Americans often evince for the Colossus of the North, Castro seems to have been influenced, too, by his father's often expressed hatred for Yankees, attributable perhaps to his Spanish ancestry: certainly, two generations after their "liberation" from Spain by Americans, most Cubans felt little gratitude for the latter while they tended to extol their Cultural Ties with the former.[5] It is not clear how and when

[5] It is significant that all of his so-called Communism and Franco's so-called Fascism notwithstanding, Castro kept maintaining active diplomatic relations with Madrid throughout the turbulent years of his reign; in turn, Spain diplomatically refused to take active part in the American sanc-

and why Castro (who, after all, had won his civil war without much Communist help) chose to proclaim himself a "Marxist-Leninist"; undoubtedly he was stirred by the belief, prevalent among half-baked intellectuals especially outside Europe, to the effect that Communism, because of its "scientific" nature, was something revolutionary and supermodern, a wave of the future, like contraceptives or the electric toothbrush. Still it seems that Castro's avowal of Communism was the consequence and not the cause of his Yanquiphobia: had he led a revolution, say, in 1940, when Germany and Italy were the principal opponents of the United States there is reason to believe that he would have proclaimed himself a Fascist, as indeed did some anti-Yankee Latin-American political leaders at that time.[6] Shortly after his assumption of power, in April 1959, Castro arrived in Washington for a riotous little visit, where a long private discussion with Vice-President

---

tions imposed on Cuba. Thus Castro's attitude toward Spain (and also his attitude toward the Roman Catholic Church) has been altogether different from the attitude of the radical and Leftist revolutionary regime of Mexico in the twenties and thirties, a government which had indulged in a vicious persecution of the Church, and which consistently shied away from granting official recognition to the Franco regime in Spain.

[6] On the other hand Castro's anti-Americanism was not altogether doctrinaire or categorical. He often talked amicably with American journalists; he professed a great deal of admiration for Ernest Hemingway, who had settled down in Cuba some years before to write million-dollar fishing stories; he has been an avid player of *beisbol*, apparently the Cuban national pastime; he has let himself be referred to by the Latin-American pidgin term of *El Líder Máximo*, whose German equivalent of "Führer" pales before the accurate English translation which could be rendered as "Jefe The Most"; he has shown a strong penchant for the color and cut of American army uniforms, including the peculiar boxy fatigue cap which the U. S. Army's own fashion designers borrowed from the German Panzer Korps sometime during the Dulles era.

Nixon produced the expectable results of reciprocal re-
pulsion. President Eisenhower refused to see Castro
(indeed, he had inquired whether it would be possible
to refuse him a visa altogether). Perhaps the President
ought to have extended his welcome and his broad grin
of global reputation; perhaps it would have made some
difference; perhaps not. There is evidence suggesting
that by that time Castro had already convinced himself
of the necessity to ignore the United States as well as
of the necessity to convince the world (and, presumably, himself) that he was a Revolutionary Marxist-
Leninist. The rest of the story is well-known: executions, nationalizations, censorship, terror, in mounting
waves through 1959 and 1960—with the expectable result that American eyes became rigidly focused on
Castro in his capacity as the first Communist dictator in
the Americas, a dubious category which obscured the
condition that he was, after all, one more among the
many tyrants in the colorful history of the Caribbean.

By 1960 the Soviet Union—whose rulers seem to
have been delightfully surprised as well as somewhat
baffled with this sudden and unexpected world-political
plum—officially established her diplomatic quarters in
Havana and the arrival of hundreds of ill-assorted Eastern European trainers and technicians in Cuba began.
In early 1961 American diplomatic relations with Cuba
were finally broken. The spirit of moderate innovation
which characterized the incoming Kennedy regime did
not extend to Cuba: as to Castro, during the electoral
campaign Kennedy's tenor of patriotic exasperation was
indistinguishable from Nixon's. Meanwhile the young
President, carefully coached and coaxed by Allen Dulles, inherited a Central Intelligence Agency plan for
the invasion of Cuba. This plan for the training of a
Cuban exile army was hatched by the CIA and sold to
the Eisenhower Administration (it seems that without
the knowledge of the then President) already in early
1960. Kennedy, like Eisenhower, found it politic to hide

the might of the United States behind this not merely
transparent but tattered pretense of a "Cuban force" of
exiles. By January 1961 (at the time when the out-
going Eisenhower decided to terminate diplomatic relations between Cuba and the United States)[7] the
existence of Cuban exile army camps, mostly in Guatemala, directed by the CIA, was so obvious that long
reports about them appeared in the American press.
Late in March bombs began to pepper the streets and
factories of Cuba. On 15 April American bombers, flying from Nicaragua, bombed Cuban airfields pretending that they were Cuban airplanes piloted by Cuban
Air Force officers who had chosen that day to defect
from Castroland.[8]

It now seemed that the beginning of the end had
come for Castro. But the Exile Invasion failed miserably. On 17 April fifteen hundred Cubans, trans-
ported aboard warm rickety ships, were put ashore in a
place called the Bay of Pigs. This ill-concealed,
ill-conceived, and ill-executed operation terminated
swiftly; without the expected internal uprising, and
without further American armed support,[9] the "bridge-

[7] It seems that Castro was not altogether eager to break
these relations with the United States, even at that time.

[8] On that day President Kennedy said in a television interview: "If we don't move now, Mr. Castro may become a
much greater danger than he is to us today"—a statement in
considerable contrast to his statement at his press conference
on 12 April: "There will not be, under any conditions, any
intervention in Cuba by the armed forces of the United
States, and this government will do everything it possibly
can—and I think it can meet its responsibilities—to make sure
that there are no Americans involved in any actions inside
Cuba . . . And I intend to see that we adhere to that principle . . . this administration's attitude is so understood and
shared by the anti-Castro exiles from Cuba in this country."

[9] On the excited Washington deliberations see Sorensen,
Kennedy, New York, 1965, page 299 *et seq*. In this matter,
too, Kennedy was somewhat woozy: he did not quite stick
to his only reservation of "principle" of not committing

head" sank from sight in a day or two. Before an astonished world Castro now jumped up and down, screaming about The Defeat of The Villainous Invaders; and a groan of uneasiness rose across the United States. Unlike Guatemala where, in 1954, the Central Intelligence Agency succeeded, in 1961, in the Bay of Pigs it failed.[10]

There remained now no limits on Castro's assertion of Cuba's Communist character. His original 26th of July Movement was to disappear in a great merger with the Cuban Communist Party[11]; and he tried everything to commit Khrushchev on his side. What Castro thought of the agreeable picture of the Khrushchev and Kennedy families appearing together in Vienna five weeks after the Bay of Pigs we cannot tell. What is evident is that he was now badly dependent on outside help. He maintained good relations with the British, with De Gaulle, with Franco, with Khrushchev, with Tito, and with neighbor Trujillo against whom American government organs were beginning to make ominous noises. He was, however, careful enough not to provoke the United States unduly at Guantanamo, this quadrangular American military enclave planted solidly on the coastal flank of Castro's island; and he showed

American forces to the invasion attempt. On the night of 18 April he "agreed finally that unmarked Navy jets could protect the anti-Castro force of B–26s when they provided air cover next morning." But the jets couldn't find the B–26s next morning; and in any case it seems, Sorensen notwithstanding, that the wallowing defeat in the Bay of Pigs was due to failure on the ground and not in the air.

[10] Despite its elaborate efforts in circular publicity. Sorensen, page 302: "The CIA even dictated battle communiqués to a Madison Avenue public relations firm representing the exiles' political front"—or, rather, the CIA itself.

[11] This Party which in 1944 had changed its name to "Partido Socialista Popular," PSP, now choose to abandon the whistling lisp of these euphonious initials to the more promising PURS.

that he intended to be the master in his house by kick-ing the obtuse Communist leader Escalante out of Cuba in early 1962. But he was dependent on the Russians: for he was sure—and, perhaps, not without reason—that another invasion was to come.

3

It was this threat of an American invasion and not the so-called Rocket Confrontation which culminated in the fantastic American-Russian crisis over Cuba in October 1962: the former led to the latter and not, as it is com-monly believed, the reverse. We have no evidence that Kennedy and/or the CIA were planning another go at Cuba in order to straighten out the crooked failure of Pigs' Bay; but neither was there evidence that they were reconciled to the continued existence of a Cuba under Castro. On the other hand there was some evi-dence that Castro, and especially some of his lieuten-ants, were toying with the exciting prospects of inciting guerrilla revolutions in selected countries throughout Latin America; but there was some evidence, too, that Castro, all of his public harangues notwithstanding, was not averse to a future normalization of his rela-tions with Washington.[12] His self-professed Commu-nism had to be taken with the proverbial pinch of salt,

[12] This kind of evidence includes some of Castro's remarks dropped to foreign diplomatists, his gingerly attitude toward Guantanamo, his release of the Pigs' Bay prisoners, despite his various declarations about Instant Death To Traitors and the *lucha de muerte*. (Possibly this relatively humane at-titude was stimulated by warnings from Kennedy; perhaps, too, by Castro's own memories of how Batista had let *him* go, after all, some ten years before.) The ex-prisoners were then flown to Florida where President and Mrs. Kennedy received them, first in Palm Beach, then in the Orange Bowl football stadium, with Mrs. Kennedy translating the President's re-marks into Spanish to the effect that here were "the most valiant men of the entire world."

especially as his famous full-fledged public confession
of having been now, and always, a Communist was
prefaced by his proclamation of having been now, and
always, a Melon.[13] In any event he had his troubles
not only with the Americans, not only with the 200,000
Cubans who left or fled Cuba since the Líder Máximo's
assumption of power,[14] but also with some of the more
ambitious Cuban Communists and, of course, with his
newfangled patrons, the Russians. For three years he
tried to wheedle an alliance, or at least an unequivocal
declaration out of them to the effect that they would
actively defend him against an American invasion: but
beyond certain loud but vague statements the Russians,
understandably, would not go. They couldn't, however,
ignore him very much: for one thing, this might mean
that the Chinese would replace them, and appear as the

[13] Castro on 26 November 1961: "The Melons are here
with you! The Melons are here! We are the Melons, and we
will continue to be Melons, because we will continue being
Green outside and Red inside!" In his five-hour nocturnal aria
of 1 December 1961: "Do I believe absolutely in Marxism?
I believe absolutely in Marxism! Did I believe in it on the first
of January? I believed on the first of January! Did I believe
on the 26th of July? I believed on the 26th of July! . . . Did
I have prejudices? Yes, I had prejudices! Could I call myself
a full-fledged revolutionary on the 26th of July? No, I
could not call myself a full-fledged revolutionary on the 26th
of July! Could I call myself a full-fledged revolutionary on
the first of January? I could not call myself a full-fledged
revolutionary on the first of January! . . . I am a Marxist-
Leninist! Until the last day of my life!" Somewhat earlier
in 1961, to one of his American admirers (quoted in Draper,
Castro's Revolution, Myths and Realities, New York, 1962,
page 125): "We had so many silly ideas. Man, I had so
many silly ideas, my head, there was so much crap in it."

[14] An extraordinarily large proportion of Cubans went into
exile between 1959 and 1965, something like 4 per cent of
the entire population of the island. In comparison the extraordinary hegira of Hungarians through the broken frontier in
1956 amounted to less than 2 per cent, the emigration from
Russia between 1918 and 1923 to about 1 per cent of these
peoples.

avenging angels and the patron saints of all past, present, and future Melons and Avocados and other fruits and advocates of Communism in Latin America. Thus Khrushchev's reluctance gradually melted away: and some time in the summer of 1962 he may have decided, in his capacity of a theatrical, rather than avenging, angel, that the Cuban comedy was worth a gamble.

We do not know. The motives of the Russian gamble of putting rockets in Cuba is not only shrouded in secrecy: but they are so much at variance with the record of Soviet foreign policy, whether under Lenin, Stalin or Khrushchev, that they are still incomprehensible. The most reasonable hypothesis, at least to this writer, is not the generally accepted one, the one to the effect that Khrushchev had thought that "he could get away with it," installing Russian rocket bases in Cuba without American interference, something which would at once alter the world strategical situation in Russia's favor. (Khrushchev, in 1962, seemed to have been interested in improving relations with the United States rather than humiliating that great power and adding fuel to the power and to the prestige of what he was wont to call the American "war party"; moreover, with his intercontinental rockets in hand it is questionable what good the extra bases in Cuba would have done for him, unless they were to serve as a bargaining device—this, of course, was a possibility—and the Russian insistence to the effect that these rocket stations must be manned by Russian personnel, without interference by hot-blooded Cubans, should be considered together with the condition that these stations were erected in the fall of 1962 in an ostentatious manner, without any attempt to conceal or disguise them.) It seems rather that Khrushchev, driven to the wall by Castro's demands and objurgations, and in view of what to him, too, seemed to be a real possibility of a second American try at upsetting Castro, felt that while he still ought to refuse a binding alliance to the Cubans, he could not refuse to supply them with important weapons. The latter would, by necessity, include the only kind of weapons with which Castro, in case of an invasion, could effectively hit back at the Americans: with rocket-guns whose range would include the southern cities of the United States.[15]

Thus after the first arrivals of propagandists and language teachers Russian engineers, technicians, and even numbers of soldier-technicians came to Cuba, in dribs and drabs, dripping with heat and fatigue. It was a fantastic and comic episode in the cold war and in the history of Communism, this unexpected presence of thousands of dour and stocky East Europeans on that subtropic island, sweating profusely, taken aback by the inconstancy and the inefficiency of the liberated people who were supposed to be building Communism with their help: but the comic aspects of this scene were then transformed into something dramatic and harsh.

On 11 September 1962 a Soviet government statement warned that American military action against Cuba could lead to nuclear war: but the language of the statement, though harsh, was still not altogether precise or binding.[16] It was disregarded by the United States whose U–2 spy planes crisscrossed the island three or four times each month, taking copious photographs. There were rumors about Soviet anti-aircraft missile (the so-called SAM) installations, and perhaps of even more: but most of this kind of information came from Cuban exile and underground organizations, so

[15] It seems that, contrary to President Kennedy's assertion in his dramatic speech to the American people on 22 October 1962, the rocket sites in Cuba were not altogether suitable for the 2200-mile-range "IRBM" rockets of which he spoke.

[16] In response, President Kennedy on 13 September warned the Soviets against establishing "an offensive military base of significant capacity" in Cuba.

that they were generally discounted by what was now being called, peculiarly enough, "the intelligence community" in Washington. But on the afternoon of 14 October a U–2 spotted what Kennedy's presidential biographer was to call "the first rude beginnings of a Soviet medium-range missile base." Thus the crisis began. It has been described so often that we need not trace the anxious and serious unfolding of President Kennedy's decisions in detail. He certainly acted with dispatch, courage, intelligence, and a measure of cool and prudent moderation. The deliberations on the highest levels of the government, presided over by Kennedy and, for once, successful in maintaining complete secrecy in Washington, continued for a week. In the middle of this week, on 18 October, the Soviet Foreign Minister Gromyko, Mr. Bad Deeds himself, came to Washington to pay a long call on the President. The latter held his hand, without disclosing what he knew.[17] At seven in the evening on 22 October President Kennedy addressed the American nation in tones of utmost seriousness. He announced an American naval quarantine (not quite a blockade) of Cuba; he made it clear that any nuclear missile launched from Cuba against

[17] In his speech President Kennedy strongly suggested that Gromyko had engaged in double-dealing and treachery. The latter had amply demonstrated his capacity for these things in the past: but it may be argued that the statement he read to the President contained at least a sophistic kind of truth. "I have been instructed to make it clear," Gromyko said, that Soviet assistance to Cuba "pursued solely the purpose of contributing to the *defense capabilities* of Cuba and to the development of its peaceful economy . . . (the) training by Soviet specialists of Cuban nationals in handling *defensive armaments* was by no means offensive. If it were otherwise, the Soviet Government would have never become involved in rendering such assistance." (My italics.) It was, and it still is, arguable that the Soviet installations in Cuba were, really, defensive ones: but the President of the United States, on the other hand, was fully justified not to abide by Soviet definitions of what was defensive and what was not.

any nation in the Americas would mean a full retalia-
tory response of the United States against the Soviet
Union; he called for the removal of the Russian missiles
from Cuba, not for the removal of Castro.

There followed now days and nights of agonizing tension in Washington and Havana and Moscow. The allies
of the United States, very much including De Gaulle,
gave Washington their unconditional support, probably
since they were reasonably certain that Khrushchev
wouldn't risk a nuclear war for Castro: but this was the
very point about which the American government was
much less sure. The Air Force and the awesome nuclear
rockets of the United States were put into readiness;
the Navy went out to sweep the Southeastern Atlantic;
armor and troop convoys were reported rolling into
Florida. Eighteen Soviet cargo ships were on their way
to Cuba, steaming somewhere between the Baltic and
the Caribbean. All of them were known to the United
States. As dawn broke over the Atlantic on Wednesday, 24 October, thirty-six hours or so after President
Kennedy's dramatic announcement, these ships either
altered their course or turned around. Two days later
the Navy stopped and boarded a Lebanese freighter
under Soviet charter, without trouble.

The turning point of this crisis occurred, therefore,
some time Tuesday or Wednesday, when the order
must have gone out from Moscow to this straggling
Sovietish flotilla to turn around. This was not, however,
Washington's view, where attention was still focused
on the missile sites, about which the CIA claimed that
in a few days they would become "operational." The
President was fortunately cool-headed and moderate
(also his brother, the Attorney-General, came out during one of the secret cabinet meetings to remind him
that a "surgical" American air attack on these Cuban
"bases" would not be very different from what had happened at Pearl Harbor—a surprisingly objective and reasonable assessment). There was no sign of Russian war

preparations either in Moscow or elsewhere in Europe, including Berlin (this is what the State Department had feared); and even within Cuba Castro's behavior, for once, reflected some prudence.[18] The decisive factor, then, was the existence of the private Kennedy-Khrushchev correspondence which the latter had inaugurated with so much circumspection the year before. The fact of this correspondence proved to be of inestimable value for the peace of the world. Three or four letters flashed back and forth until by Friday it had become abundantly clear that Khrushchev would dismantle these dubious Soviet installations in Cuba in exchange for a Kennedy pledge not to invade the island. For a while there was some talk of an additional American concession of removing American rocket bases from Turkey and, perhaps, Italy (where they were due for dismantling anyhow) but in the end this was not necessary. The President was wise in staying his hand. In his fifth letter, drafted some time around noon on Sunday, 28 October, in Moscow, Khrushchev accepted Kennedy's revision of his suggested terms. No serious observer believed at that time in war, though the rapidity of Khrushchev's acceptance may have been unusual. (The head of the CIA, however, caught on the steps of a Washington church, was heard to exclaim in public: "I can hardly believe my ears"—a curious statement for someone in so august and intelligent a position.) Very wisely President Kennedy instructed the government not to gloat or claim "victory." He wanted to spare Khrushchev from possible feelings of public humiliation. Of course he knew, too, what few Americans recognized at that moment of great relief: that

[18] The American spy planes went on flying, lower and lower, over Cuba, photographing everything without the least interference; on one occasion only was a U-2 brought down with a warning rocket shot, the only American casualty in this acute crisis. Meanwhile the usual horde of Cuban dayworkers went on doing the Americans' laundry in Guantanamo.

the price of the Soviet withdrawal from Cuba was the American promise not to invade Cuba, to live and let Castro live.

Few people, glancing into the future on that beautiful autumn day in Washington, could foresee that less than two years later Kennedy would be dead and Khrushchev gone, while Castro would be wallowing in power warmer and safer than ever. Few people, reflecting on the past, recalled the curious coincidence of another October week, exactly six years before, when the possibility of a Russian-American world conflict may have loomed over the explosive events in Hungary, and when the world had been startled by another announcement from Moscow, to the effect that the Soviet army was ordered to withdraw from Budapest: at noon on 28 October 1956, another Sunday. At any rate, the Russians soon returned to Budapest but not to Havana: they would risk war for Hungary but not for Cuba, whereas the very reverse was true of the United States. Thus the Cuban Crisis of 1962 demonstrated, again, that even in this era of global alliance systems and transcontinental missiles, the conditions of historical and political geography were decisive: in spite of the potential chances that the largely unexpected revolution in Hungary had presented to Americans in 1956 and that the even more unexpected Cuban situation presented to the Russians after 1960, despite the rhetoric about anti-Communism and liberation by the former and about anti-colonialism and Communist fraternity by the latter, Hungary wasn't worth a world war for Americans and Cuba even less for the Russians.[19]

[19] I say "even less" because anti-Communism, together with a measure of generous indignation, seemed to have affected the American people deeper in the case of Hungary than what was the effect of Cuba on the Russian people. An American intervention in Hungary, despite its potentially incalculable consequences, would have had wide popular support in America, whereas there is some evidence to the effect that it was not only the hapless and perpetually perspiring

4

The swift and breathless agreement between Khrushchev and Kennedy included the latter's provision that the uprooting of the Cuban rocket sites should be verified by the United Nations: but this Castro would not accept. Holding his hirsute head in both of his hands in one of his "cabinet" meetings he now aimed insults at Americans and Russians with a certain impartiality. The placid U Thant descended on Cuba, leaving after a few days without any results whatsoever. "Whoever tries to inspect Cuba," Castro proclaimed, "must come in battle array." There came now (as to Hungary, six years before) the chief salesman of the Soviet Union, the Armenian Mikoyan, unequipped for battle but with an enormous black briefcase under his arm. It would be interesting to read a stenographic record of his diplomatic encounters with Castro; it would be even better to have some kind of a photographic record of their facial expressions: but Clio, though far from being the most niggardly of the Muses, puts limitations on the potential bounties of even her most faithful servitors. For eighteen days the agile Mikoyan, whose constitution, unlike that of his predecessor Iron-Pants Molotov, was not particularly suitable for this kind of enforced patience, was either berated or totally ignored by Castro: but this had no effect on the rocket stations which were being leveled, uprooted, and plowed under by impassive Soviet technicians. There remained in Cuba a mediocre flotilla of IL–28 bombing planes which Khrushchev had given Castro earlier (these relatively slow

---

Russian technicians in Cuba but wide masses of the Russian people themselves whose attitude toward Cuba ranged from passive indifference to latent hostility. There are few reasons to doubt that the average Russian likes Americans more than he likes Cubans.

bombers were capable of hitting the southeastern cities of the United States). Kennedy, insisting on their removal, presented the tergiversating Khrushchev with a minor and unpublicized ultimatum, to run out at 6 P.M. of 20 November, when he would announce in public the issue of these bomber planes. A few hours before Kennedy's news conference Khrushchev gave in. Consequently Kennedy announced the end of the naval quarantine. Castro, who saw that the Russians meant business—that is, Business First, and with the United States—grumbled but held his peace. Mikoyan flew off to Washington, to tell Kennedy that the Soviet Union was ready to settle with the United States every remaining question that still divided them, suggesting that a new and fruitful era of Russo-American relations was just around the corner.

This was the end of the Cuban comedy or tragicomedy or comico-tragedy or whatever one wishes to call it. We have seen that the comic element was furnished mostly (though not exclusively) by the voluble Cubans themselves: but even during the more fantastic episodes Castro's rhetoric was more ludicrous than were his actions. From this serious crisis of October 1962 Castro emerged as something of a more chastened and pragmatic personage. He had demonstrated earlier that he did not lack courage and that he was not altogether willing to play the mere role of a Communist front man, of a puppet. There is reason to believe that, just as the bitterest episode of the Hungarian Revolution turned out to be, after all, a turning point of Soviet-American relations to the better, the Rocket War Crisis over Cuba may have marked a turning point in Cuban-American relations. No serious person spoke thereafter of an American invasion against Castro; and the latter himself made certain efforts to normalize relations with the United States. By Christmas 1962 he released the prisoners of the Bay of Pigs. A year later, shortly before he was cut down by the murderous bullet in Dallas, President Kennedy himself hinted that if only Cuba were to get rid of her binding ties with the Soviet Union, the United States would not be averse to a gradual restoration of normal relations.[20] Throughout 1964 the influence of the old Communists in Cuba slackened, and conditions within Cuba became a little more anarchic and relatively more liberal, until in the end the famous "Che" Guevara, a professional Argentinian Bolshevik, thought it politic to disappear from the island after having chosen, perhaps wisely, to leave his sullen wife behind. In October 1965 Castro announced that he would allow Cubans to leave, in order to join their relatives in the United States. A direct American-Cuban agreement to this effect was worked out through the efficient offices of the Swiss Minister in Havana; and it may not be farfetched to see in this agreement another step in the direction of more normal relations between Cuba and the United States at the time of this writing.

While the usual predictions of experts about the coming collapse of the Cuban economy did not, of course, materialize, there was also evidence that Castro was coming around to see himself more and more as a national, rather than as a merely revolutionary, hero: he expressed, for instance, his great admiration for Churchill for having withstood the threat of invasion alone, a kind of admiration not usually fashionable in Bolshevik circles. Evidently the old Tory imperialist's war memoirs had a deeper effect on Castro than the deadening tomes of Marx which, of course, he may not have read at all: but the very fact that he got around to reading Churchill was, after all, surprising. Irritated with Chinese badgerings, in March 1966 Castro threatened to break diplomatic relations with Communist China whose leaders barely stopped short of adorning him with the usual epithet of a lackey of American Imperialism. In the end, Castro did not turn out to be

[20] Speech at Miami, 18 November 1963.

either a Trotsky or a Stalin: and the recent history of Cuba once more defied the ponderous prophecies of all kinds of political experts, very much including the Intellectual Analysts of Totalitarianism, with their usual penchant for predicting the continuation of whatever seems to be going on. Let us, therefore, end this chapter by paying tribute once more to the unpredictability of history—or, rather, to the way in which the silent hand of God, moving through the loud perversities of men, levels the plains into hills and writes straight with crooked lines.

CHAPTER X

Decrystallization of the Cold War

(From 1962)

1

Throughout this book the term "cold war" has meant the conflict between the United States of America and Soviet Russia, not between Capitalism and Communism or Democracy and Totalitarianism or West and East. We have seen that the world struggle between these two giant Powers, the result of the last world war and, specifically, of the division of Europe, crystallized into the harsh realities of a cold war after 1946, which means that when this book is published we will have lived through two decades of cold war, half of an old-time generation, and that a new generation of young people will have grown up under its clouds. Yet there is, in retrospect, a certain symmetry in the history of the cold war during these past twenty years: growth of its passions during the first decade, their gradual abatement during the second. The fall of 1956, the Hungarian and Suez crises, marked the turning point in the history of the cold war; it was then that it became evident how neither of the two Super-Powers really wished to challenge the frontiers existing in Europe at the risk of a world war; and, just as the three year period between 1946 and 1949 could be regarded as the crystallization, the period after October 1962 could be described as the decrystallization of the cold war, which is the title and the theme of this chapter.

The sources of this "decrystallization" of the Soviet-American conflict were threefold: the reciprocal possession of transcontinental atomic rockets, Russia's troubles with China, and the corrosion of the iron curtain in Europe compromising somewhat the division of Europe, which had been, as we have seen, the principal origin of the cold war. There was only one statesman who had foreseen this last development more than twenty years ago. In November 1944 Churchill told De Gaulle: "At present, Russia is a great beast which has been starved for a long time. It is not possible to keep her from eating, especially since she now lies in the middle of the herd of her victims. But after the meal comes the digestion period. When it is time to digest, the Russians will have their difficult moments . . ." Alone and aged in his London house, Churchill did not live to see the end of the division of Europe and of the cold war.[1] He was a very old man, full of sleep. What is merely possible is that he may have glimpsed, however faintly, something like the beginning of its end.

2

We have seen that the Soviet government chose not to reimpose the earlier pattern of tyrannical uniformity on her East European satellites even after the Polish and Hungarian explosions of 1956. For one thing, Khrushchev's memory seems to have been so deeply impressed with the evils of Stalinism that he regarded the mitigation of its severities not merely as a moral, but as a practical, imperative. For another, the American reactions in 1956 seemed to have convinced him, as we have seen, that the United States would not seek to overthrow the Eastern European *status quo*. Thus the kind of "liberalization" which had actually preceded the

---

[1] Churchill died on 24 January 1965, forty-one years to the day Lenin passed away. He was buried on 30 January, thirty-two years to the day Hitler came to power in Germany.

dramatic risings of 1956 in Poland and Hungary, continued; it was to involve most of the Eastern European countries during the decade that followed, involving even the orthodox Bulgarians, Czechs, and East Germans by 1963. In Poland many of the promising buds of the "October Spring" of '56 withered away or they were nipped by the government: the austere Gomulka was wary of the volatile and the explosive potentiality of national passions and he was especially aware of the limitations that Poland's geographical situation imposed on her relations with the Soviet Union. Soon after 1956 it became evident that Gomulka was, in effect, perhaps the most trustworthy ally of the Russians in Eastern Europe: certainly he did nothing to compromise this situation, with the result that two years after the October Spring autumnal gloom reigned in Warsaw again, and this half-frozen, half-thawed situation, with variations, continued in Poland for most of the decade. Something like the opposite happened in Hungary. Whereas in Poland the hero of '56 fell in the eyes of the nation, in Hungary the villain of '56 rose. Compelled by his conscience even beyond calculations of popularity, János Kádár chose to put in practice gradually most, if not all, of the reforms that had been demanded by the 1956 revolutionaries, with the sole exception of maintaining his cramped subservience to Moscow in matters of foreign policy, but with the concomitant result that by 1962–63 life in Hungary was relatively the "freest" in East Europe. In that year the unimaginative and overcautious leaders of Czechoslovakia began to follow suit; in 1963 signs of "liberalization" multiplied in Bulgaria,[2] and some of them appeared a year later even in the East German land of the humorless minion Ulbricht. The leaders of Rumania chose a different

[2] Two years later the discovery of an ill-prepared minor *coup d'état* in Sofia revealed differences between at least three factions of the Bulgarian Communist Party. The pro-Soviet faction, for the time being, won.

course. Moved by the necessity of justifying their alien regime to the people, and even more aware of the opportunities that were available to them by the split between Russia and China, the potentates of Communist Rumania, led by Gheorghiu-Dej, announced a sort of Wallachian national Communism, the most significant feature of which was their rhetorical defiance of Russia on occasion.[3]

Twenty years after their conquest by the Russians, therefore, the states and nations of Eastern Europe had, in different ways, regained some of their independence; their national characteristics were emerging anew, even though their political leaderships and their social systems remained officially Communist. Yugoslavia and Albania had broken away from the Soviet sphere; other Eastern European countries, like Rumania, could no longer be called Soviet "satellites"; but they were, still, Communist and not Western European countries. On the other hand Communism within these states, too, was changing: it was not merely unpopular: it was becoming meaningless. The pale and uneven rise of prosperity which some of these countries experienced during the second decade of the cold war, and especially after 1960, was nearly always the result of the allowance of non-Marxist practices and techniques in economic and social life, even though much of this was obscured by elaborate Marxist doubletalk; and the relative stability of these regimes was due not only to political apathy but also to the condition that new industrial and intellectual bureaucracies were emerging who were largely uncommitted, politically speaking, and that Communist party membership was no longer necessary for important state positions or professional

[3] Less noticed by the world was their systematic persecution of the Magyar minority in the Transylvanian provinces of Rumania, a fact which should make those who hail the emergence of "national Communism" think twice. (They won't.)

advancement. Perhaps most important was the condition that the isolation of these peoples from the rest of Europe was coming to an end: for many reasons, including financial ones, the Eastern European regimes permitted and, indeed, encouraged tourism and trade with the West. By 1965 the volume of trade between the Western and Eastern states of Europe doubled, and the number of visiting tourists was five to ten times that of five years before. This was, of course, the consequence rather than the cause of political changes: as in the case of Spain, the yearly influx of millions of foreigners affected the political equilibrium of the regime hardly at all; but these developments were not merely symptoms, they were conditions. They were conditions of the gradual weakening of the division of Europe which was, after all, the principal source of the cold war; and, with the single exception of the East German frontiers, perhaps even the physical dismantling of the ugly "iron curtain" wire fences and minefields has become, here and there, a remote possibility by the time of this writing.

3

Meanwhile in Western Europe, too, the latent question of eventual independence came to a head. It was proposed by De Gaulle; it involved directly France, indirectly the future of NATO and the states of the European Common Market. This question of a European independence was obscured for a long time by the successful reconstruction of Western European prosperity and by the more-or-less successful development of institutions aiming at some kind of a Western European unity: De Gaulle, however, saw the alternatives with a kind of cruel clarity: in his view Europe, before she could become united, must become independent of the United States. He supported the Western allies, very much including the West Germans, on Berlin; he gave his full support to the United States, as we have seen, during the October 1962 crisis about Cuba. But he was extremely wary of the Atlanticist policies of the Kennedy Administration which, playing alternately the British and the German cards, in his view aimed at a loose Atlantic political system under the tutelage and the undisputed leadership of the United States. His suspicions were suddenly confirmed in December 1962 when Macmillan was either unwilling or unable to consider De Gaulle's suggestions for a joint Franco-British nuclear armament program: for, after their meeting at Rambouillet, Macmillan flew on to meet Kennedy in the Bahamas where it was announced that the British would receive certain "Polaris" rocket-firing submarines in exchange for the American cancellation of the "Skybolt" rockets which they had promised to the British earlier. Persuaded as he was now that, at least for the time being, the British would do little or nothing besides the Americans' bidding, on 31 January 1963 De Gaulle announced that France would veto Britain's entry into the Common Market—which, to be sure, could have been arranged at the time only at the cost of transforming the Common Market into a loose trading association in which the United States would eventually become the dominant member.

During the next three years De Gaulle asserted his independence from the United States in many ways. He recognized the Communist government of China; he reduced the French commitments to NATO; he refused to recognize the Soviet-American nuclear test ban; he cultivated good relations with certain countries in Eastern Europe; he encouraged many other states in Asia, Africa and, beginning in September 1964, of Latin America, to be independent of Russia and of America alike, and to assume that France represented a kind of Third Force in the world, the influence of which was bound to increase in the long run. Irritated, too, by what he saw as certain sly American diplomatic attempts to isolate France, in 1965 he suggested that American investments in France should be curtailed; that the necessary reform of world monetary standards ought to involve the dethroning of the dollar and the restoration of the traditional standard of gold; finally, he announced that France would revise or reconsider her membership in NATO.

These were significant steps in a new direction. We should not, however, exaggerate their importance. De Gaulle was able to defy the United States: but he could not replace American domination with a power which was his own; France found it hard to keep up even with the industrial productivity of West Germany, let alone with that of the Super-Powers; and it was not even certain that the French people were either willing or able to assume such an independent course of their own. Finally, while De Gaulle could defy the United States with relative impunity, he was not, as he himself said, willing to give up the alliance with the United States altogether.

The key not only of Soviet-American problems but of the problems of European independence was, again, Germany. As early as 1958 De Gaulle succeeded in establishing an intimate relationship with the old Adenauer, probably as both agreed on the possibly approaching danger of a Soviet-American agreement over their heads. By early 1962 a concealed diplomatic race for Germany was on between Paris and Washington. On 4 July 1962 in Philadelphia President Kennedy announced the American policy of "interdependence"—that is, the eventual transformation of Common Market and NATO into a North Atlantic, American-European organization. That very day on the other side of the Atlantic De Gaulle received Adenauer in the ancient and scarred cathedral of Reims, symbolizing the new European amity of France and Germany; there followed next day a joint Franco-German military parade.

In early 1963 France and Germany signed a Treaty of Amity, aiming at extensive co-operation between the two countries. But soon it became evident that the Germans shied away from extensive military co-operation with France; understandably, they would not give up their situation of America's favored ally for becoming the favored ally of France. For about a year the Germans tried to avoid "the choice" between Paris and Washington; by 1964 this had become less and less possible. The number of German "Gaullists" (a dubious term, at any rate) dwindled, as the French President seemed to turn more and more on an anti-American course. The aged Adenauer had to retire, and Erhard, who was not a Francophile, took his place. The memories of De Gaulle's triumphant German tour and of his carefully prepared German speeches (in September 1962) were eclipsed by Kennedy's one emotional sentence shouted before the Berlin Wall in June 1963 (*"Ich bin ein Berliner!"*). By the summer of 1964 De Gaulle felt it necessary to say: "The fact is that Germany does not yet believe that Europe's policy should be European and independent." In view of these developments, and also in view of the increasing German unwillingness to meet French desiderata about the agricultural unification of the Common Market, in early 1965 the further development of the Common Market in the direction of institutional unity was halted by Paris. In turn, De Gaulle made certain diplomatic suggestions to the British for closer relations with France: for he knew, as well as others, that France was far from being able to lead Western Europe alone.

On the other hand De Gaulle's increasing intransigence did not really drive the other Western Europeans closer to the United States—again with the exception of the Germans. It was becoming more and more evident that American power and American prestige—whether military, industrial, social or cultural—was slowly declining since the mid-fifties even in Western Europe.

Yet while in Eastern Europe the attitudes of peoples toward the Soviet Union were something close to contempt, in Western Europe popular attitudes regarding the United States were, at most, ambiguous: a mixture of admiration and of mild bewilderment, with the emphasis definitely on the former.

4

It was some time after the Pigs' Bay fiasco that President Kennedy convinced himself that he ought to meet Khrushchev in person;[4] and it was some time after the Cuban rocket crisis that he convinced himself of the need for a Soviet-American agreement, a kind of armistice or even peace, aiming at a kind of piecemeal termination of the cold war. It was about time, critics might say, considering the Soviet willingness to come to an accommodation ever since Stalin had died. Still, this was a remarkable decision, if one considers the narrow nationalism and the general ignorance of international history which had been reflected in the few statements of John Kennedy on foreign affairs before his election[5]; more important, if one contemplates the Himalaya of suspicions and of dogmatism which decades of anti-Communist ideological rhetoric have de-

[4] It seems that the first suggestions of meeting with Khrushchev were raised as early as February 1961 when Kennedy assembled four former Ambassadors to Russia (Thompson, Bohlen, Kennan, Harriman) to an important private conference; but it was the Pigs' Bay events which speeded his decision to go ahead with such a meeting.

[5] Sorensen, *Kennedy*, page 509: "Foreign affairs had always interested him far more than domestic." The "always" is untrue. "They were the object of a far greater change in his own attitudes, as he learned by experience, grew in wisdom and mastered those complexities he had previously oversimplified." Very true. This sentence, written by Kennedy's closest confidant in what is otherwise an uncritical and adulatory biography, is very revealing.

posited on the vast landscapes of American public
thinking and of popular sentiment. For the first time, a
President would address himself to the task of reducing
this large natural obstacle.

"Let us never negotiate out of fear, but let us never
fear to negotiate," he said in his Inaugural Address.
The rhythm of this sentence caught the ear of the
American public but otherwise it meant little. Khrushchev had now released two American fliers who had
been shot down over Soviet Arctic waters the previous
summer; in turn, Kennedy lifted the import ban on Soviet crabmeat. He was, still, very cautious in face of
public and political criticism: in face of the latter he
backed down from extending diplomatic recognition to
Outer Mongolia, for instance. What was not public but
significant was his decision to halt spy-plane flights over
the Soviet Union. By the end of his first year in office
he spoke to a university audience in a more serious and
chastened vein: "We must face the fact that the United
States is neither omnipotent nor omniscient," he said,
"we cannot impose our will upon the other 94 per cent
of mankind . . . there cannot be an American solution
to every world problem." These statements had not
much of a public echo. But privately Kennedy had
already chosen a series of significant little steps to improve relations with the Soviet Union: he had an intimate meeting with Khrushchev's son-in-law in Washington; two highly publicized spies were exchanged;
cultural and trade agreements were prepared between
the two Super-Powers—developments the maturing of
which were interrupted but not halted by the October
1962 crisis. That the American people approved his
leadership during the crisis was reaffirmed by the unusually good showing of the Democrats in the November congressional elections; subsequently Kennedy's
hand was strengthened, and he felt he could respond to
the significant suggestions which Mikoyan brought with
him as he arrived in Washington from Cuba. That was

perhaps the psychological turning point. It was now
evident that the Russians were not going to make up
with the Chinese; that they were not willing to face a
deadly two-front struggle in the Far East and in Europe at the same time; that they wanted to reduce the
duality of this threat to their national security; that, if
they had to choose between the Americans and the
Chinese they would choose the former not the latter.
On 10 June 1963 President Kennedy delivered the
most significant speech of his career.[6] To the audience
of American University he spoke in measured tones
against a "Pax Americana enforced on the world by
American weapons of war" and he spoke in intelligent,
though somewhat general, terms of the great interests
of peace that the United States and the Soviet Union
had in common. The speech did not make much of an
impact on the American public; but it was received
positively by Khrushchev who had been alerted of its
coming importance in advance.[7] The full text was
printed in a Soviet newspaper. By that time the so-
called "hot line" had been installed between the White
House and the Kremlin—a direct telephone connection
which was a peace-publicity gimmick, put into operation precisely when the dangers of war between America and Russia were receding—an inconsequential symptom but a symptom nonetheless. Only once, on 26 June
in Berlin, did Kennedy slide back to a somewhat aggressive rhetoric as he, carried away by the adulation
of the enormous Berlin crowds, thought fit to compare
them with the citizens of ancient Rome.[8] By that time,

[6] It was delivered exactly twenty-three years after Franklin Roosevelt's Charlottesville speech condemning Hitler and
Mussolini, a turning point in attitudes during the crucial
year 1940. In both years the speeches were delivered to university audiences, on 10 June, a Monday.

[7] "The best speech," Khrushchev said consequently to
Harriman, "by any President since Roosevelt."

[8] "Two thousand years ago the proudest boast was

however, the Russians themselves seemed to have understood that this kind of rhetoric was aimed at De Gaulle's as much, if not more, as at their German policy. Once more the Chinese tried to blackmail the Russians against signing the Test Ban Treaty which they (and, of course, De Gaulle) would not sign. Guided by the able diplomacy of Averell Harriman, this Treaty between the United States, Britain, and Russia was signed on 5 August 1963 in Moscow. It was ratified by the Senate after some grumbling. It was a milestone, closing the first long chapter of world history which had begun at Yalta and Potsdam as well as at Hiroshima and Nagasaki, in 1945. The principal world conflicts were no longer those between the two Super-Powers confronting each other. But this was not yet a reversal of alliances. It was, rather, a reversal of priorities, and a revision of rhetoric. The Peaceful Coexistence of the Soviet Union and the American democracy was no longer merely a disagreeable fact: it was an accomplishment of certain standards, an achievement, the crystallization of mature efforts toward a more permanent peace and a more stable world. This is how John Kennedy regarded the direction of world history in the autumn of 1963; and it was in this direction that he intended to influence and educate the American public opinion and popular sentiment. He had many reasons to believe that he would succeed. He was in the prime of his manhood and of his presidency when he was killed on 22 November 1963 in Dallas.

5

In Texas that morning Kennedy had glanced at a political advertisement in a Dallas newspaper accusing

---

'*Civis Romanus sum.*' Today, in the world of freedom, the proudest boast is '*Ich bin ein Berliner.*' "

him of being a weakling compromiser with Communism. A few hours later he was killed by a person who had sometimes proclaimed himself to have been a Communist and who had earlier tried to become a Soviet citizen and a resident of Sovietized Cuba. This irresponsible young man seems to have acted not out of totalitarian commitment but out of the deranged and envious fury of his own rootlessness: but one could not know this on that wild day and during the weeks that followed; and there were many reasons to believe that the assassination of this young and enormously popular President by a Communist would result in an oceanic tide of popular and emotional anti-Communism. That this did not happen suggested, at least to this writer, the increase in the emotional maturity of the American people, even though this might have been obscured by some of the events during the following year.

The new President of the United States was a Texan who had coveted this high office beforehand; his political progress thereto had been rudely blocked by the Kennedy clan; now, suddenly, through this explosive tragedy, Lyndon Johnson was catapulted into the seat of power. Many people regarded, and regard even now, this presidential replacement not merely as a personal tragedy but as something of a long-range national and international calamity, as they mentally compared John Kennedy's personal vitality and his intellectual acuteness with the broad, massive and somewhat wooden aspects of his successor's personality. These criticisms obscured some of the positive elements in Johnson's mind and character which were precisely apposite for an American President during the decrystallization of the American-Russian cold war in the mid-sixties. Less internationally minded than his predecessor, Lyndon Baines Johnson's aspirations aimed at his being a great national, rather than international, leader. True, this characteristic was inseparable from a certain parochialness of his views and of his tastes and from a certain

Texan shallowness of his booming rhetoric: but it was a powerful factor in his energetic domestic policies of legislation and reform: and it was not altogether inappropriate during this phase of the decrystallizing cold war when the United States, especially in Europe, would do well to embark on a policy of broad and cautious retrenchment. Older than Kennedy, Johnson was more set in his ways; this was not altogether a conservative characteristic, since it was not certain that Johnson possessed the intellectual self-confidence of his predecessor which enabled the latter to change his mind around important occasions: on the other hand, the formative personal and political memories of Johnson were so much rooted in the Franklin Roosevelt era that this has had a powerful effect not only on his vision of his domestic program but on his view of Soviet-American relations.

These policies were, then, challenged *in toto* by the new and transitory spokesman of the Republican Party in 1964: and for the first time since 1920 the nominees of the two great American parties offered to the American people two very different political programs, especially in the field of foreign relations. Because of the weakness of conviction that characterized most of the Republican leaders, the candidacy for the Presidency in 1964 was won by the forces of Barry Goldwater, of a self-professed "conservative"—that is, a radical nationalist—from Arizona. Whatever popular appeal his extreme anti-Communism may have produced was diluted by the shallowness of his statements and by the evidences of his political incapacity. As the spokesman of an anti-Communist crusade Goldwater did win the presidential nomination and thus the leadership of the Republican Party in 1964, something that was not even remotely within Joseph McCarthy's reach at the peak of his career, ten years earlier; but it would be wrong to deduce therefrom that the appeal for "American conservatism," that is, for an anti-Communist crusade, had grown during that decade; indeed, there is reason to believe that the social base of McCarthy's following was more solid than was Goldwater's. In any event, the latter was decisively defeated in November 1964, with Johnson carrying off the second greatest landslide victory of the presidential elections in a century. For once, the political cliché fitted the real situation: the American people had given their massive endorsement to the President. By the time of his election, however, new and ominous developments had already compromised the potential portents of this triumph of American moderation.

The first of these developments was a domestic one. Unhealthy symptoms appeared on the American scene: wild Negro riots broke out in those very cities of the North where the civil rights of Negroes had been legally assured for at least a generation; in the South the demonstrations for the enforcement of the long overdue civil rights were resisted by brutal murders committed by members of the reborn Ku Klux Klan; a general sense of malaise appeared in many manifestations of American life, suggesting that the problems of this great people were deeper and more widespread than it has been generally believed; that perhaps it was not only the lack of world historical experience but also the superficiality of domestic cohesiveness which might eventually reduce that American role of world leadership which had been so generously and eagerly assumed by the American people earlier in this century.

The second disturbing event was Khrushchev's sudden removal from power in Russia. On 15 October 1964 —less than three weeks before the American election— a terse announcement from Moscow told the world of the "resignation" of this powerful figure, and that his functions would be taken by Alexei Kosygin (as Premier) and by Leonid Brezhnev (as Party Secretary), the latter a drab Soviet bureaucrat. Thus did the person who, with all of his faults, was the most humane Russian leader of the Soviet era, disappear into domestic obscurity; and though the general line of Soviet policies would not change very much, Khrushchev's removal marked the end of an important phase in the history of Soviet Russia and of her relationships with the rest of the world. Like Kennedy's American successor, Khrushchev's Russian successors were more parochial in experience and less confident in their handling of foreign affairs. It is true that, for once, the fallen leader was not dragged in the mud, killed, flung into obscurity or jail; this was, to some extent, the mark of the evolution of the Soviet regime; but the reactions of the Soviet people on the morrow of the stunning news did not inspire confidence in their more humane characteristics: it seemed, rather, to confirm the old adage that people tend to get the government they deserve. Khrushchev had, after all, dethroned the memory of Stalin; he had made a kind of transition from cold war to cold peace; he had clipped the wings of the secret police—and now the Russian people seemed completely unmoved by his fall; as a matter of fact, their remarks to foreigners suggested that they disliked him, that they were ashamed of him, because Nikita had been "uncultured,"[9] heavy and gross. They did not seem to understand that it was precisely these earthy and non-intellectual Russian characteristics which made Khrushchev reliably human; that his heart was even more intelligent than his mind. Notwithstanding the continuation of a kind of mild ferment among the urban intelligentsia, these reactions of the Russian masses were not encouraging symptoms for the future; and the new Kremlin leadership, in any event, found it necessary to embark on a moderate restoration of the reputation of Stalin.

[9] Khrushchev—said many Russians on the morrow of 15 October 1964—was *nye kulturnyi,* "uncultured." Lenin or Molotov or Stalin, these impassive fiends who did not take their shoes off in New York to bang tables but who, instead, let their friends and followers be tortured, they, with their cold Oriental eyes, they—they were not *nye kulturnyi.*

The third disturbing development, weighing heavily on America and compromising the process of the cold war's decrystallization, was the evolving war in Vietnam.

6

It will be recalled that, after having been subjugated by the Japanese during the Second World War, the French had to share their colonial government of Indochina with the native princes of Laos and of Cambodia as well as with the more dynamic and determined Communist leader Ho Chi Minh in North Annam. When negotiations with the latter failed, there began a long-drawn-out guerrilla war, ending in 1954 with a French defeat at Dien Bien Phu and their subsequent withdrawal from the entire Indochinese peninsula. The fact that President Eisenhower, contrary to the advice of Admiral Radford and to the somewhat ambiguous advice of Dulles, was unwilling to commit American air power on the French side during the last and decisive phase of the Dien Bien Phu battle, and the consequent ability of Russia and Britain to appear as negotiators, led to the Geneva Agreement in the summer of 1954, whereby Vietnam (comprising the ancient kingdoms of Annam and of Cochin China) was divided in the Korean manner along the 17th Parallel, with Ho Chi Minh's Communist regime in the North (with Hanoi the capital) and a more democratic or, at any rate, anti-Communist regime under the leadership of the Catholic Diem in the South (with Saigon the capital). The United States was not a signatory of the Geneva Agreement, though it was amply obvious that she was bent on replacing the French as the tutelary power at least in the non-Communist South, a somewhat dubious undertaking wholly in line with the anti-Communist globalism of Dulles, the portents of which were foretold by a contemporary novel by Graham Greene.[10]

The Geneva Agreement called for free elections all over Vietnam, to be held in 1956. The regime of the South, with American support, repudiated this pledge, since they feared that they would lose such an election. Consequently, aided by some Chinese prodding in 1958 (when the Chinese had been thwarted in their bid to oust Chiang from the offshore islands), the leaders of North Vietnam (called Vietminh by that time) started out on a sporadic guerrilla campaign with the ultimate aim of overthrowing the Saigon regime from within. In a few years the Vietcong guerrillas could roam over large portions of the countryside; they seemed to have won the predictable allegiance of whatever goes under the name of "intelligentsia," while the Diem regime itself was threatened by the monthly succession of coups and countercoups as well as by the explosive hatreds and suspicions rife among various religious, tribal, and political groupings. Still, apart from the usual flood of money and materials, the Eisenhower Administration introduced only a few thousand troops into South Vietnam; but this American presence was already sufficient to have committed American prestige down along the line.

All of this was in line with the usual policies of Dulles who had shown little reluctance to commit the United States to any and every anti-Communist cause and place anywhere on the globe. This policy of the Dulles Bros. was inherited by Kennedy who did not seem to have given much thought to this smoldering and increasingly chaotic theater of political warfare; indeed, he greatly increased the flow of American dollars and strengthened the American garrison (officially: "military advisers") to South Vietnam. By the summer of 1963, however, the situation was getting more and

[10] *The Quiet American.*

more critical; whereupon the Central Intelligence Agency chose to overturn the ruling Diem family with the hope that a more democratic and efficient national leadership would result in Saigon. The result was only the predictably catastrophic turn for the worse. Kennedy who, if we are to believe the testimony of one of his self-appointed biographers,[11] was now deeply worried about the CIA coup against Diem, did not live to see the further devolution of this jungle morass. His successor, for calculations of American prestige rather than for reasons of power, chose to stand by the American commitment to South Vietnam; and in 1964 he began to commit more and more units of American soldiers to what was now a veritable American theater of war. Within a year the number of American troops in Vietnam rose from a few thousand to nearly two hundred thousand. Together with the massive employment of tactical air power in the late summer of 1965 it seemed that they had thwarted the Vietcong's campaign for conquest of the countryside and, ultimately, of Saigon; and the Marines were building up a large American shore enclave near Cam Ranh Bay. But the bloody containment of the Vietcong short of their victory did not at all mean that the Americans could do what the French had been unable to do more than a decade earlier: to defeat the Vietcong in the field and to eliminate the guerrilla warfare altogether. Reasonable estimates suggested that no less than one million American soldiers were needed to do the trick—perhaps.

There are no sufficient reasons to think that President Johnson was an adherent of the Dulles formula of anti-Communism, or that he wished to convert South Viet-

---

[11] Arthur Schlesinger, Jr. This intellectual supernumerary in the White House had practically no influence compared to that of Theodore Sorensen, the other Presidential aide who wrote one of the two hasty post-mortem biographies of the Kennedy Era; but he was the better writer of the two. His testimony must be handled with caution.

nam into a permanent American protectorate. (It is more difficult to say as much about the bureaucratic mind of his Secretary of State or of the technological brain of his Secretary of Defense.) Like the United States in the Korean War, Johnson simply wanted to keep the Northern Communists from taking over the Southern country: but the Indochinese situation was militarily as well as politically different from the Korean one. There was a regular frontline in Korea; there was no such thing in South Vietnam. There were no Communist guerrillas of any consequence in South Korea during that war; in South Vietnam there were guerrillas here and there and potentially everywhere. The most impressive political figure in Korea was the old patriot dictator of the South; in Vietnam it was the leader of the North. In Korea the United States, after an initial retreat, was about to conquer all of North Korea in a few months, whereupon the North Koreans had to be bailed out by the throwing into battle of hundreds of thousands of Chinese; in Vietnam the North and the Vietcong proved to be a match for the Americans without having to depend on the Chinese for their survival. Unlike the wretched North Koreans who haplessly fluttered between Soviet and Chinese satellite status, the North Vietnamese had a modest capacity for statesmanship. It was the great merit of President Truman during the Korean War that he refused the demands of the impressive military figure of MacArthur, America's Oriental proconsul, for bombing Manchuria: for the President knew that such a military involvement with China would only please Stalin's Soviet Russia which at that time was the principal adversary of the United States in Europe; besides, there is every reason to believe that the aerial bombing of Manchuria would have led nowhere. Unfortunately there was little to suggest that Dean Rusk in 1964–65 understood these historical distinctions better than had his predecessor, the other Dean (Acheson) exactly fifteen years earlier;[12] and it seems, too, that Johnson was not sufficiently aware of the singular inefficacy of strategic air power. In February 1965 the President ordered the strategic bombing of North Vietnam, except for Hanoi and Haiphong, in "retaliation" of the North Vietnam support given to the guerrilla forces in the South: but, like the strategic bombing of Germany during the last world war, or like the American air superiority during the first phase of the Korean War, this produced no worthwhile effects at all. It certainly did not produce a North Vietnamese suit for peace. It produced wide uneasiness throughout the world, including Moscow, and including, for the first time, more-or-less serious domestic demonstrations against the war in the United States, involving more people than at any time during the previous phases of the cold war. There were, however, many more Americans who, as in the Korean War, demanded a more vigorous American war effort, including the aerial "wiping out" of Haiphong and Hanoi. There were also some illusions on the American Left about the virtues of the Vietcong. Few are those Americans, Left or Right, even at the time of this writing (Christmas 1965) who would state, in unequivocal terms, that all of Indochina, South and North, Nam, Minh, and Cong, are not worth the bones of a single United States Marine.

We have dealt with the Indochina War in a summary manner here, for two reasons: the first being that this war is still in full swing at the time of this writing, the second that the principal theme of this book is not the relationship of Communism and anti-Communism but of the United States and Russia. There can be no question that the massive American engagement in Vietnam, coming also at the time when Khrushchev had fallen from the seat of power in Moscow, halted the propitious development of these relations, and the pro-

[12] See above, Chapter IV, page 94.

gressive decrystallization of the cold war. This is especially regrettable when one considers that American-
Russian relations, and the cause of peace at least in
Europe, could have profited from the exacerbation of
the Russo-Chinese conflict after 1964. A few days before Khrushchev's fall, in October 1964, the Chinese
exploded their first atomic bomb. The uneasy attempts
of the new Kremlin potentates to bring the Chinese
once more to a Moscow conference table failed.[13] Re-

---

[13] The stages of the Sino-Russian conflict on the *party*—
that is, world Communist—level were as follows:

November 1957. First conference of the Communist
parties of the world in Moscow (40th anniversary of the Bolshevik Revolution). Mao acknowledges the "leadership" of
the Communist Party of the U.S.S.R., but he sees difficulties.

June 1960. At Congress of the Rumanian Communist
Party Khrushchev openly attacks his Chinese comrades.

October 1960. A compromise meeting between party delegates in Moscow fails.

November 1960. Eighty-one Communist parties meet in
Moscow. The differences are papered over. Yet the Albanians
violently attack their Russian hosts.

October 1961. Twenty-second Congress of the Soviet Communist Party in Moscow. Khrushchev attacks the Albanians
who are defended by Chou En-lai.

1962. The Chinese openly attack Khrushchev and the
Soviet Communists as "traitors."

1963. Attempts toward a Chinese-Soviet party conference.
They fail.

1964. The Russians prepare for a new world Communist
conference, with the aim of the majority to condemn Chinese
extremism.

December 1964. After the fall of Khrushchev the conference, originally scheduled for 15 December, is postponed
until 1 March.

1965. New postponement of the conference. The Sino-
Soviet conflict is now irreparable—for the time being.

I have summarized these weighty (that is, ponderous)
developments in a footnote, because, the majority of ideological and Kremlinological opinions notwithstanding, it is
evident that the relations of the two States have been
throughout more important and also more significant than
the relations of the two Parties, and that the latter have

lations between Moscow and Peking grew, thus, worse and worse throughout 1965, Khrushchev's removal notwithstanding. Already in 1964 the Chinese had begun to reclaim territories from the Soviet Union proper; and their military incursions on the long Indian frontier were not unconnected with their eventual pressures aimed at the Asian borderlands of the Soviet Union. On the other hand they suffered many reverses in their extreme and stupid propaganda and political campaigns throughout Asia and Africa, while the Russians still felt compelled to proclaim their support to North Vietnam, since they couldn't afford to relinquish to the Chinese the monopoly of Asian Communist leadership.[14] Yet there was evidence that on occasion the Russians, unlike in Korea, were in favor of negotiations between North Vietnam and the United States; and when they suggested that they would send supplies and a few military instructors to North Vietnam via the only railroad through China the Chinese refused. But the latter themselves were not eager to assist North Vietnam in force; there was reason to believe that disagreements existed between the Vietnam Communists and the Chinese.

Perhaps this is the point where the wooden diplomacy of Dean Rusk deserves most criticism: for, given the by now undoubtedly impressive endurance of the Vietcong and of the Ho Chi Minh regime in the North, it seems that even in the not too likely event of a decisive American victory in the South the Americans' present adversaries may have earned their rights to become eventually the principal power in Indochina in the long run; that in no event would they become mere satellites or puppets of the Chinese but, rather, a countervailing influence to the latter in Southeast Asia, again

been merely the consequences—though they are symptomatic consequences—of the former.

[14] Mme. Sun Yat-sen in October 1954: "When we speak, we speak not only for ourselves, but for all Asia."

in the long run; that, indeed, Ho Chi Minh's people may one day become potential allies of the United States. We have seen stranger reversals than that in the history of the last thirty years.

CHAPTER XI

Cold War or Cold Peace?

(1966)

1

The term "cold war" which, as we have seen earlier, was invented by American journalists around 1948,[1] is not a very good one. Still we have had to abide by it since it had become public currency; also, its usage spread from the United States across the world. We have also seen that by 1962 this "cold war" between the United States and Soviet Russia gave way to a situation that may be characterized as "cold peace" (this, in any event, is the better metaphor of the two); that a direct military struggle between these two Great Powers became less and less likely; that the original and principal theater of their conflict has become a relatively peaceful and prosperous continent, and that the very iron curtain dividing it has been changing in character. Does this, then, mean that the cold war was an historical episode? that it forms a twenty-year-long parenthesis in the history of the twentieth century? Yes: and no. *Yes:* because neither the United States nor Soviet Russia, all of their fantastic armaments notwithstanding, is capable of ruling the Northern Hemisphere, let alone the globe; because these two Super-Powers are, still, very far from each other; because their vital concerns involve their relationships with other countries, including their neighbors, rather than their relations with each other; because their direct

[1] See above, Chapter III, page 72.

national interests do not much conflict at all. *No:* because the absence of war between the United States and Soviet Russia did not and does not mean the presence of a settlement between them; because the unhistorical philosophy of revolutionary Communism still commits the Russian leaders on occasion; because the principal obstacle to a real peace between America and Russia continues to be the absence of a settlement in the middle of Europe, in Germany. The fact that the situation has been relatively quiescent there for the past four or five years should not mislead us. Will the present division of Germany harden or weaken? Will the Germans acquire atomic weapons? Will they become more "American" or more "European"? Will the Germans profit from the eventual dissolution of the Soviet Empire in Eastern Europe? This writer cannot now tell.

The world has never been long without war; and human nature does not really change. At the same time human nature is infinitely adaptable; and wars have always sprung from some sort of calculation rather than from sheer madness. It is even possible that, after all, despite the dreadful tensions and misunderstandings of the cold war, the nations of the world may be now entering into a long period without great and destructive wars. But we may be sure of one thing: that violence and the desire for change will not thereby disappear from human sentiments and from the texture of history.

While it is the mark of the barbarian to believe that change in itself means progress, the mark of civilization has been its ability to keep change (including violent change and war) within certain bounds. In any event, it is spiritual rather than physical, political rather than technical change that really counts in the long run. For we must consider the paradox of the cold war: the movement of history seems very fast; and yet, in reality, it is amazingly slow, slower than before. While the powers and dominations involved in the cold war are gigantic; the speed of rockets and of certain communications near fantastic, there still has been little change in its principal condition, in the political division of Europe—because of the slowness in the change in the opinions and sentiments of great masses of men that are the motive forces in history especially in the democratic age in which we find ourselves. The obsession of millions of people in the United States, and in certain countries of Europe, in regarding anti-Communism as if it were synonymous with patriotism or, indeed, with virtue; and the squalid tendency of other millions elsewhere in the world in regarding Communism as if it were something dynamic and supermodern—these are formidable factors in our times when, unlike in the seventeenth century, it is not so much little wisdom, *parva sapientia,* but rather, accumulating stupidity, *magna stultitia,* which seems—but only seems[2]—to rule the world.

2

My reconstruction of history has reached the present moment; my description of the past and evolving history now merge. Thus I cannot break off abruptly at this—or, indeed, at any other—point. Thus every historian, whether he wants it or not, whether he admits it or not, is a prophet of some kind, even though historical prophecy is not only "unscientific" but presumptuous and dangerous. Still, in historical life it is safer to predict what is not going to happen than what is going to happen. There exist tendencies that have up to now formed the main course of certain developments; they are still going on; their evidences are there in the

[2] But this is no source of comfort—in the short run. Since, at least in the short run, what happens in history is inseparable from what people think happens, when people think that stupidity is the rule they will often act accordingly.

daily newspaper. I shall not project them but attempt only to describe some of them at this point, as a historian rather than a prophet, for they exist and flow before our eyes straight into the agglomerating moments of the future.

It does not seem as if Communism is triumphing all over the world but, then, neither is Capitalism. It seems that Russia may remain a Great Power long after the passing of Communism, but it seems that she will not be able to digest and incorporate her empire in Eastern Europe. The power of China, of Japan, of Germany, seems to be increasing and attracting anew sentiments, passions, and political combinations. The future of Western Europe, especially in her relation to the United States, seems as yet undecided. Neither a Russian nor a Chinese revolution seems entirely improbable; on the other hand, an eruptive political revolution in the United States seems inconceivable. But it seems as if the international involvements of the United States, together with certain phases of the Armament Race, are to continue; and that the principal and painful dilemmas of the American people and government would involve more and more revolutionary situations in the Western Hemisphere. Meanwhile the struggle of races has already begun. But the ideas of Western Civilization, albeit often in distorted, perverted, and transmuted forms, are still dominant throughout the world. While the technological transformation of world societies goes on, involving every continent, race, nation, and class of the globe, Europe remains the center of history and the most difficult problem of the cold war. At the same time within the United Nations and sooner or later within all international organizations the nations of Europe are becoming a tiny minority indeed.

The cold war was a consequence of the Second World War, and now the greatest guarantee against a Third World War is the memory of the Second. This is

why, no matter what their faults, people such as Eisenhower and Khrushchev will not be altogether condemned by future historians because of the single virtue that their recognition of the horrors of war was
sincere. But we must keep in mind that soon an entire
generation will have grown up—in the United States,
relatively untouched by war, as well as in the Soviet
Union, in Germany, England, France, Poland, Japan,
China—a generation in whose vision of past wars the
element of horror will fade quicker than elements of
excitement; a generation whose minds, in this age of
mass education and communication, may tend to be
dogmatic rather than rational; a generation from whose
hearts violence and national and racial passions will not
disappear. Thus it may be reasonable to expect that
even if the masses of the world continue their daily
appointed rounds without the fearful experience of
war for another decade, around that time the danger of
terrible outbursts through incident or otherwise may
again increase.

For the passion of change is an unsuppressible spark
in the hearts of men even in this age of mechanical
standardization; and there is no such thing as pure
chance, a pure accident in the infinite complexity of
human motives and actions.

At some point in the complex chain the free will of a
man enters; for men are free and moral agents, and it
is therefore that they are responsible for what they do;
and it is also because of this inevitable intercession of
the free will of men that in human and historic life,
unlike in science, effects are neither predictably nor
ever completely made by external causes.

At the same time tendencies exist that, affecting the
minds, hearts, and muscles of men, propel the movements (though not necessarily all of the important
events) of historic life forming the events of the recent

past and forming already a part of every event of the future. Thus now, when I have described some of the main events of the cold war, to the description of its main movements I shall turn.

Part 2

THE MAIN MOVEMENTS

CHAPTER XII

The Two Peoples:
The Tendencies of Their Societies

(The Social Element: The Development of Two Great Welfare States)

1

In the first part of this book I attempted to describe the principal events of the cold war in the manner of historical narrative. In the second part of this book I attempt to describe principal American and Russian tendencies and developments in a manner of historical analysis. Thus, while narration and analysis necessarily overlap throughout both parts of this book, I am now purposely changing the emphasis. The purpose of a history book is usually suggested by its title. But the title of this book, *A History of the Cold War*, reflects its scope rather than its purpose. For the purpose of this book is not so much the complete and accurate reconstruction of a now closed historical period as the description, through a historical approach, of important tendencies, convergences, conflicts, misunderstandings, and movements of the two great protagonists of the World Struggle. The cold war is not over; its tendencies, conflicts, and movements go on; and many of these tendencies, conflicts, and movements were in development of course long before the cold war began. History is the story of life, of movement; not a static account of past periods. And in this democratic age the texture of history has become so complex that the very structure of events is affected; it is, for instance, no longer reasonable to reconstruct the main lines of events by concentrating on political history alone. Thus already in the first part of this book—"The Main Events"—it was obvious that though the principal events were of a political character, social, ideological, material, and racial tendencies intruded, since they influenced and overlapped into political developments; and now, in the second part of this book—"The Main Movements"—I am attempting a comparative description of these historical elements, of the movements, developments, tendencies of the American and Russian societies, states, nations, concepts, and ideas, necessarily on separate and successive levels. Thus the order of this second part is as follows:

The Tendencies of the Two Societies
The Tendencies of Their Political Theories
The Tendencies of the Two States
The Tendencies of Their National Character
Their Spiritual Tendencies

This successive order is not an arbitrary one.[1] We shall proceed, by and large, from what is most obvious but least significant to what may be most significant and perhaps least obvious.

2

The aspect of American and Russian society has been very different from the beginning. This is a superficial impression; but, like certain superficial impressions, it remains considerably true. The habits, the institutions, the temperament, the laws, the character of the settlers of North America produced a society whose principal features were recognizable even before the revolutionary achievement of American independence.

[1] See Preface, page xi.

Few national societies of the white race show so great a contrast as these two peoples, say, five generations ago, when Tocqueville was here: democratic, republican, commercial, freewheeling America on the western; autocratic, hierarchical, Byzantine, restricted Russia on the eastern edge of the civilized world. Compare these two great land Empires with their great latent riches at the beginning of the Industrial Revolution: the material standards, the commercial prosperity, the conditions of labor, the variety of goods, the financial reputation, the domestic habits, and civic standards of Americans were much superior to those of the Russians.

All of this is obvious. We must, nevertheless, recognize certain similarities between Americans and Russians already at that time. A most powerful influence that has left enduring impressions on the peoples of America and of Russia was the vast and open lands within their Empires: the open frontier. Unlike in Europe, where land was scarce and dear, the empty prairies of America and the steppes of Russia invited large groups of settlers and more or less permanently affected their habits. There are early similarities in the habits, clothing, buildings, climate, temperament, popular culture, and even the music of the American open West and the Russian open East; the external aspect of Siberian towns even now reminds visitors of the American West of a few decades ago. There exist similarities, observed at times by perceptive sentimental or critical observers, that appear in certain American and Russian folkish characteristics. To this we must add the often intangible influence, through blood and through the soil, of the Indian element on the early American and the Tatar on the Russian settlers.

Still, the most important of these relative similarities flowed from the relative absence of the feudal tradition in America and in Russia. The power and prestige of the permanent possession of land, the peculiarly European concept of patriotism, the walled cities, the sharp separation of city from country in Europe, the existence of the aristocratic and patrician aspiration, are historical factors that from the Middle Ages onward influence European concepts and habits even to the present day, even in the British Isles with their otherwise unique social development. The corresponding Russian and American concepts and habits often reflect different original tendencies. Thus, for example, Russian "Tsar" and Russian "nobleman" do not quite correspond to the European "king" or "noble"; the Russian concept of the "merchant" is something different from the specifically European phenomenon of the "bourgeois"; in turn, there were significant differences between the European "bourgeois" and the American middle-class concepts from the beginning. In the relative weakness of the patrician family tradition, in the early separation of "business" from "residential" quarters in Russian as well as in American cities, in certain Russian as well as American habits of impermanent residence, in the extraordinary geographical and social mobility of Americans as well as of Russians, we may detect certain correspondences that are attributable to the absence of a strong aristocratic tradition on one hand and to the pioneer condition of vast empty lands with great natural resources on the other.

We cannot go into these in more detail. Nor should we exaggerate them unduly. For, in the end, these social habits are inseparable from their motive spiritual factors; but here I am attempting to describe not the spiritual tendencies but the developments of these two great societies. Whatever the motives, during the nineteenth century the spirit as well as the conditions of the Industrial Revolution suited the character of the American people almost perfectly. From this the vast superiority of American industrial society was to come.

3

After the Civil War the industrial energy of the American people, swelling with millions of laboring newcomers, plowed, mined, and hammered out the wealth of the American earth with almost incessant effort. By the time of the First World War this new republic was the wealthiest nation on earth. The size of American cities, the wealth of American industrialists, the value of the American money, the volume of American industrial production, were the greatest in the world. During the First World War the United States became, for the first time, a creditor nation also on a world scale. By 1920, for the first time, the majority of American workers were employed in industrial rather than agricultural production; and the majority of the population was urban, not rural. Not until 1960 did the Russians reach a corresponding stage of social transformation.

The wealth of America's plains and mountains alone, of course, counted nothing. The industry, the labor, the dedicated trust of the American people made it count. We must keep in mind how, together with the inherited or acquired Puritanistic ethics and habits of work, the partly Puritanical but very characteristically American tendency toward social democracy played an important and ultimately decisive role in this successful American development of material enterprise. The tendency of equality, the American practice of organized philanthropy, American habits and concepts together prevented the devolution of American democracy, even in the most ferrous and hardfisted times of American Capitalism, into an unduly class-conscious society where the lives of the rich and the poor would be separated by increasingly different standards. Not even at a time when the survival of the fittest became an accepted American doctrine was it conceivable that political democracy in America could neglect the powerful and even more typically American tendency of social democracy. Again we cannot go into the motives of this development in detail, save to mention that of all the great Empires of the world the United States, with its vast territories and population, was least in need of external commerce and markets; it was, therefore, in the interests of American industry, too, that this vast domestic market be nourished and capable of absorbing its swelling internal ocean of goods. Thus began the astoundingly successful American development of mass production. It is significant how the automobile, originally invented in Europe and for long a characteristic possession of the upper classes there, became an American popular possession and even an institution by the very year 1914, when Henry Ford had begun his then revolutionary mass manufacture of automobiles by paying high wages to workers, who then, in turn, could become buyers of automobiles themselves.

Thus, even though certain American pretensions to class consciousness grew more rigid especially during the period of mass immigration, even though at that time the outlines of an American patriciandom were strenuously asserted, the evolution of a mobile and classless American society was already in full development long before legislation, ideas, and taxation were to reduce the power and, to some extent, the prestige of the American upper classes. There were, of course, remnants of cruel practices, discriminations against workers and immigrants, astonishing evidences of financial corruption here and there; but, by and large, American society weathered the hazards of the Industrial Revolution very successfully indeed. By 1920 the material benefices of industrial democracy were diffused throughout American society.

There is no need here to describe those historical and political conditions that kept Russian social and material developments so much behind. We must mention, however, that serfdom was officially abolished in Russia in 1861, almost at the same time that slavery was abolished in America. Even though it is true that the practical consequences of these emancipatory declarations were often slow in coming in America as well as in Russia, while large portions of Russian wealth still depended on the labor provided by peasants on vast fields and estates, in America even the South was no longer dependent on slave labor. It is true that the industrialization of Russia began long before 1917; it achieved a few excellent results; even though Russia was still dependent on foreign capital, the professional achievements of her small but growing middle class were at times quite remarkable. But no matter how promising its intellectual and even social stature, the structure and the political power of this enterprising Russian bourgeoisie were too weak to survive the storms of 1917. What Lenin, Trotsky, and Stalin inherited was still a vast peasant empire. Its industrial transformation had already begun; but its new masters could not really develop the material foundations laid by a class whose power they had destroyed until their political transformation of power was complete.

Thus in 1920 the success of American Industrial Capitalism coincided with the collapse of liberal democracy and with the Communist assumption of power in Russia. After the First World War, America was the wealthiest and Russia the poorest among the great nations of the world. Material prosperity was spread through the society of the first to an extent hitherto undreamed of; the enormous Empire of the latter was struck with misery and famine in conditions reminiscent of the Dark Ages many centuries before. Thus, in assumed theory as well as in recognized practice, American "Capitalist" and Russian "Communist" society in 1920 provided a contrast greater than at any time before or after.

4

The principal domestic purposes of the Communist regime during the past fifty years may be summed up in these two phrases: the enforcement of ideological conformity and the promotion of the industrial transformation of Russia. While Lenin, Trotsky, Stalin, and Khrushchev may have at times harbored variant ideas about the first, there has been little disagreement about the desirability of the second of these aims.

The great Soviet achievements in this respect are obvious. We know how Lenin himself once "defined" Communism, the Soviet goal, as "socialism plus electrification"; we know about the successive stages of Five-Year Plans and of impressive technical establishments. The evolution of a strong peasantry (a force about which Lenin was uneasy and which Trotsky affected to ignore with Jewish and cosmopolitan revolutionary disdain) was broken by Stalin through the dull dreadful collectivization of the countryside in the early 1930s. An empire of sullen peasants was transformed into an empire of factory workers, and instead of the vastness of the snowy steppes it is now the vast glow of gigantic Soviet furnaces that impresses the world. It was not until about 1950 that the Russian nation and people could reap some of the benefits of this long enforced industrial transformation. I need not recount the evidences. Russian living standards and educational opportunities have risen, even though they are still far behind those of the West. Russian steel production grew beyond that of Britain and of Germany, and it passed the halfway mark of that of the United States. The great wealth of the Russian earth is being extracted more energetically and more efficiently; at least in military technology the Soviet achievements have been impressive. Meanwhile in the 1950s the new rulers of

Russia, and particularly Khrushchev, deliberately dropped the previously almost unilateral emphasis on state and military production; gradually the goods, the clothes, the houses, and the general welfare of the Soviet peoples improved.

At the same time, keeping in mind the tremendous extent, the great wealth, the large population of the Russian Empire, we must ask the question whether the Communist "system," with all of its totalitarian pressures, was really the decisive factor in the present industrial might of Russia. Is it not reasonable to assume that, barring extraordinary conditions of enduring chaos, this powerful nation with its great resources and energies was bound to emerge during the twentieth century as one of the leading Powers of the world, no matter what her government? It would have been strange if she had not done so. At any rate, the building of Russia's industrial might was erected by Lenin and Stalin on foundations laid by people like Witte or Bessemer or Ford at least as much as by Engels or Marx.

At the same time we must also keep in mind that statistics of production and consumption tell us but little about the real developments of society that are inseparable from its concepts, ideas, and aspirations. And here the Soviet industrial transformation led to developments that are far from being Communist and that are not even typically Russian but rather world-wide. I said that Lenin and Stalin transformed masses of sullen peasants into masses of factory workers; but the typical Soviet citizen has not become that Vanguard of World Revolution, the class-conscious factory worker: he is a somewhat uneasy member of a new, amorphous sort of lower middle class. It is the irony of historical development that what Stalin and Bolshevist industrialization created were the foundations of a large and growing Russian middle class (whose weakness, as we have seen, was the main cause of the success of the October Revolution); and even though this new kind of middle class (as in many other places in the world) is quite different from the older "bourgeois" pattern of habits and aspirations, its desire for social status and for private possessions is evident indeed. By the 1950s the Soviet leaders themselves boosted the increasing quantity and quality of the private possessions of Soviet citizens; they boasted how this would soon surpass American standards. Whether the new masters of Russia recognized it or not, this was just what the egalitarian founding fathers of Marxism and Bolshevism would have contemptuously called a "petty-capitalist" or "petty-bourgeois" mentality.

Meanwhile within Russian society distinctions of position, income, education, and even of social status have increased. First in the technical industries, in the Army, and in certain specialized sciences and professions but lately in more and more fields an administrative and managerial bureaucracy has been growing up, at the top of which there exists a new kind of service aristocracy, whose positions and aspirations, however, depend on privileges of status rather than on land or money.

We shall see how this evolution of large administrative classes is perhaps a main symptom of our times. Let us but notice here that with the industrialization and the consequent administrative bureaucratization of life, Soviet society from the very beginning has developed along certain lines that are not very different from those of the United States, albeit starting from different conditions. Industrialization and "Fordism" attracted the admiration and the ambition of the Soviet leaders from the start; the speeches of Bolshevik leaders in the 1920s are full of exhortations to "Americanize," to create a new Soviet manager type with "American" characteristics. Whether this Russian emulation of the United States is still conscious or half-conscious is beside the point, at least here. The important thing is that the industrial transformation of the Soviet Union brought about social developments that follow, by and large, a world-wide rather than a Communist pattern; and this, rather than the otherwise impressive increase of Russia's industrial production, is the main reason why today, nearly fifty years after the Revolution, the similarities of Russian and American society are gradually increasing.[2]

5

The transformations of American society have been more gradual but no less paradoxical.

Forty-five years ago, after the World War and the Russian Revolution, the American government could withdraw into relative isolation and the American people could pursue their industrial and commercial prosperity within the confines of the United States along the customary patterns of private financial enterprises. Increasing complexities of financial speculation affecting large sections of the American people then led to the financial crash and panic of 1929, whose depressive consequences were exceptionally wide and deep. The reaction of the American people, requesting governmental intervention to solve the dreariness and hopelessness of the existing situation, was obvious and expectable. What was not obvious at the time was how, under the genial leadership of Franklin Roosevelt, the great economic and administrative transformation of the New Deal could solve these awesomely accumulated problems without revolution or even undue bitterness.

[2] We must say something here about the extraordinary extent of juvenile delinquency that prevails in Russia, Eastern Europe, and in the United States. The causes are obvious: the weakness of family authority and of other essential social bonds (together with the relative inefficiency of municipal police forces) in large technological societies employing rootless people whose residences within their communities are impermanent.

The reforms of the New Deal and the consequent extension of American industrial activity during the war brought new prospects of employment to the American working classes. Within the United States, victorious and undamaged by the Second World War, these developments continued to create new conditions of domestic prosperity and a new kind of an increasingly classless and affluent society. The ephemeral glamour of stainless steel, wire, and glass in the cheery standard houses of American workers may be superficial and vulgar at times; but in this respect the standard Russian (and European) criticism of "American materialism" is nothing but sheer envy. The achievement of the domestic American standards of popular prosperity stand out in history as something unique.

By the 1950s, however, it was obvious that this kind of popular prosperity existed together with a weakening spirit of free enterprise. Already by 1933 it was obvious that the nineteenth-century era of the domination of largely private enterprise was coming to an end, that governmental intervention was necessary (and requested by the people themselves) in order to rectify undue inequalities and privations. What was (and what is still) not so obvious is why the American people even now refuse to recognize that the United States has become a Welfare State.

For more than thirty years now governmental administration, supervision, and intervention in large areas of life in America has become an accomplished and accepted practice. We cannot, and need not, describe it in detail, save to point at the tremendous growth of bureaucracy, at the obvious growth of taxation, at the extraordinary growth of government "supports" given to agriculture, industry, and education, and at the consequent withering not only of private enterprise but also of the true functions of local and state governments (which have been, after all, the foundations of American republican democracy). What is even more important is that by now an American generation has grown up that takes this kind of governmental administration, intervention, and support for normal, proper, and granted. I do not deny that many of the reforms of the New Deal were needed and perhaps even salutary; I do not insist that we should officially recognize the United States as a Welfare State; I am saying that this large transformation from Legislative to Administrative Government has been developed by Republicans as well as by Democrats, that governmental intervention has become an accepted part of American life.[3]

Nor should we believe that all of this started suddenly in 1933 and that it is consequently attributable to Roosevelt's New Deal. I have said earlier that social democracy as much as political democracy, that equality as much or perhaps even more than liberty, had been part and parcel of the American national development long before this century. Beginning with the Puritans, but again not exclusively attributable to their influence, a certain extent of social conformity has been characteristic of American life and society throughout. In the United States, therefore, we may speak of "the socialization of souls" as a powerful tendency that long

[3] 24 April 1960. Two items from today's edition of the New York *Times*. (1) The presidents of American universities agree that government support to their institutions in the form of "research" is desirable. (These are the same heads of the same universities that used to produce so much pompous prose about Academic Freedom.) (2) Political reporters reveal that in certain key states where enormous aircraft and rocket plants now exist, the masses of workers are not concerned with any political issue, with Russia, or with disarmament; but they are worried about disarmament in the sense of whether the next President would maintain these plants and, consequently, their jobs. (Thus whereas in the past it was a few unscrupulous capitalist manufacturers who at times promoted armament programs, nowadays these are promoted by Labor and demanded by popular clamor—an ominous development, full of worrisome political portents, especially in our age of Democracy.)

preceded the actual establishment of the Welfare State.[4] It was but strengthened and extended by the arrival of millions of homeless immigrants and, most of all, by the standardization of communications and possessions, of words and habits of life, brought about by industry, technology, and mass production.

For, while it is the ironical paradox of Communism that it leads to middle-class habits and standards, it is the ironical paradox of Industrial Capitalism that its very success almost inevitably leads to governmental intervention and to the extension of socialist patterns of life and thought. It was not so much the evidence of fraudulent collusion and corruption among the industrialists and financiers but the very complexities of mass production that made it necessary for the American government to supervise the production and the distribution of certain goods around the turn of the century, in order to protect such essential things as the health of the American people: the Pure Food and Drug Act of Theodore Roosevelt is but one outstanding example.

But there is more to this. What has not been foreseen either by Communists or Capitalists was the fantastic burgeoning of administrative occupations that follows the successful phase of industrial transformation. We have seen that in 1920 the United States, uniquely rich, was far ahead of the rest of the world because of the energy and of the success of her industrialization. But by 1956 for the first time more Americans were employed in administration than in production. Thus the United States, now the leader of the free world, was ahead of the world in bureaucratization. This is an alarming development. It indicates the problems of growing inefficiency within American business that now for the first time is beginning to compromise the hith-

---

[4] Both countries are basically socialistic, wrote the perceptive Count Keyserling in the 1920s: "But America expresses its socialism in the form of general prosperity and Russia in the form of general poverty."

erto astounding achievements of American industrial production. Certain branches of American industry, facing for the first time serious European competition in the 1950s, were experiencing such effects. Just as government, with its cancerously growing number of civil servants (and the less visible but more ominous growth of the number of people indirectly and partly employed by the government), suggests the transformation from the Legislative to the Administrative State, similar developments have taken place in every kind of enterprise and in wide areas of American life. The administrator rather than the producer has become the typical (and respected) American occupation.[5]

The reasons for this social transformation have been manifold. To a large extent, as I have suggested, this is but part and parcel of the world-wide development of industrialization and technology (which at least suggests the question whether Industry and Technology themselves are not the main instruments of the transformation of human societies in a totalitarian direction). In different ways, in the Soviet Union as well as in the United States, the development has been from an Agricultural through an Industrial to an Administrative Society. "Administration" nowadays covers a multitude of sins; at any rate, in the United States, as in the Soviet Union, the interests of the managers of corporations are no longer the same as the interests of owners.[6] This emergence of a post-capitalist society—origi-

[5] This, too, corresponds closely with residence. In 1920, for the first time, more Americans were employed in industry than in agriculture; in that year, for the first time, the typical American was no longer living in the country but in a city. (The rural population of Russia declined, too, but in 1958 it still amounted to about 51 per cent). In 1956, for the first time, more Americans were employed in administration than in production; and for the first time the typical American was living in a suburb.

[6] The term "Managerial Revolution" is misleading; it suggests the existence of hard and determined Managers

nally revolutionary in Russia, evolutionary in America —has been consequent to governmental intervention but also to the decay of the spirit of personal enterprise that comes with the large scale of organizations. At any rate, this is not a particularly American but a world-wide development. The rise of social democracy throughout the world is one of the principal developments of the twentieth century; but it is social democracy not in the Marxist sense but more or less along the American pattern. In this sense we may speak indeed of the Americanization of the world.

Thus, just as certain American social and national characteristics had made American industrial prosperity unique, propelling it ahead of the rest of the world, there are certain American tendencies and conditions that now unfortunately propel the bureaucratic development of American society, too, ahead of the rest of the world. Among them are the previously suggested socialization of the American spirit, the ritualistic practices of American business and of American education, the maintenance of full employment often at the cost of obvious inefficiency, and, beneath all of them, a certain unrealistic American habit of reasoning and rhetoric, a tendency to substitute vocabulary for thought. They mark the transformation of the habits of a previously sparse, thrifty, and pragmatic people at the expense of common sense, of plain speaking, and of the recognition of the obvious.

Thus, just as the middle classes absorbed a large portion of the aspiring poor on the one hand and the few remaining fragments of a patrician upper class on

---

equipped with iron will, foresight, and determination, a class entirely separate from the rest of the workers. But the managers of our modern societies, with few exceptions, do not conform to this neo-romantic and neo-machiavellian picture envisaged by Spengler and by Burnham; they are themselves anxious conformists, servile followers of Publicity and State.

the other; just as the suburb, originally conceived to be a healthy middle ground between city and country, grew formlessly to devour both, the function of middlemen has developed into vast administrative functions at the expense of production and consumption. Consider only how in recent years such non-productive "industries" as advertising, entertainment, packaging, have registered the greatest growth. The means has become the end; indeed, administration rather than production absorbs the energies and creates the occupations of most Americans by now—all of which suggests the increasing regimentation and standardization of society and life.[7]

Thus, while in Russia we may recognize the transformation of society in a middle-class direction, within the United States we may recognize the emergence of a largely classless society where social distinctions are those of status rather than of ownership, a society where distinctions of education, employment, and credit mark the decline of distinctions of wealth and the endurance of private property, a consumers' society where the actual role of money is dwindling; a society whose industry, whose intellectuals,[8] and whose institutions are

[7] For example, in the 1950s American manufacturers were justifying the rise of the prices of their products "because of rising production and *advertising* costs"; American "liberals" greeted with enthusiasm the merger of the two already gigantic AFL and CIO labor unions, while "conservatives" hailed the extension of investigative and police powers of the federal government.

[8] We must say something here about the role of the intellectuals. We are witnessing all over the world the intellectualization of life. This is, of course, obvious: for administration is a more typical intellectual activity than is production. At the same time we should note that as the older class distinctions dissolve, recognition of professional intellectual status becomes more and more important; and in the so-called "anti-intellectual" United States, society and government, as in the Soviet Union, are more and more dependent on professional intellectuals. The world is thus mov-

more and more dependent on so-called government "defense" contracts (these by now are said to amount to about one third of the industry's current orders), where consequently the employment of more and more people depends indirectly on the government. This is the transformation of American society in an increasingly regimented, standardized, military, and centralized direction. While in Russia Khrushchev proclaimed that his people would soon surpass American production (and thereby unconsciously indicated his wish to emulate the American pattern of society), in the United States industrialists in the name of Free Enterprise clamor for more and more government orders for their own enterprises in order to "catch up" with Russian technology and military production.

Until very recently this kind of reciprocal and jealous emulation went but one way; the Soviet imitation of the United States, while largely unconscious, was unilateral. But now, as certain American and Russian social developments converge, we can see that American society, equally unconsciously, tends toward the Soviet governmental pattern. Let us, at any rate, bypass the tragic question whether the development of an American police state may not be the price of this American "catching up" with the Russians in military technology,

---

ing toward the recognition of intellectual elites; but this development (like so many others that they have wished for) is by no means as salutary and propitious as intellectuals have thought. The very word "intelligentsia" came to the West from Russia, denoting but a small and isolated segment of people; so did the usage of the noun "intellectual." This rather senseless category implies that the majority of people are *non*-intellectuals: strange, indeed, when we consider how many Americans, for example, are college graduates now. But what are they, then? The shoe is on the other foot. We are now learning how universal literacy and universal education did little to raise or even to maintain standards of reason and of culture; we may yet have to learn that an increase in the number of professional intellectuals may further depress certain moral and rational standards.

in the education of thousands of engineers, in the regimentation of the world-wide effort to surpass them in Martian exploits in state-sponsored circuses, or in massive victories for athletes at Olympic contests. Let us bypass the question whether a future American generation that knows only the experience of the welfare state and the propaganda of the cold war may not be willing to pay such a price. Let us but conclude by observing that even when American and Russian society are becoming more and more alike—this has not really influenced their mutual misunderstandings and the hostile attitudes of their governments at all.

CHAPTER XIII

The Two Societies:
The Tendencies of Their Political Theories

(The Ideological Element:
The Development of Marxism)

1

Now in these times of mass democracy the organized lives of two gigantic societies of the American Democracy and of Soviet Russia were growing more alike; but their suspicious hostility did not really abate. The main reason for this seeming paradox seems to be immediately at hand. The two societies have differing conceptions about the world; and they have hostile ideas about each other.

It is a great mistake to believe that ideas are superstructures of life. There is a widespread, common, scientific, and vulgar tendency to conceive of human life as if it were basically a mechanical function, that consequently ideas, culture, poetry, and art are but eventually refined superstructures of civilization. This is not so. For human beings (and for human beings alone) life is inseparable from the idea of life; ideas, conceptions, theories, are permanent and frequent formative factors of life and history. Their actual influence on history is often indirect and complex, but always important when they endure in the long run; but in the short run, too, the actual influence of their popularized and recognizable versions remains important. Like every basic human experience—like pain or pleasure, for instance, which exist even though they are not measurable, while their existence is inseparable from their recognition—the important thing, always in the short run, and especially in democratic ages, is not so much what happens but what people think happens. And especially in the long run, tendencies and aspirations are more important than material data and positions: it is more important what people want to be than what people actually are. Thus the history of ideas is more important than the history of routine life. Thus the conflict between Communism and Western Democracy is more important than the material comparison of Russian and American societies—as long as Communist Russians believe it to be their duty to strive toward the transformation of this world into a perfect and total Communist pattern (even though no such perfect and total transformation is ever possible, even though historical developments force them to depart over and over again from their original concepts and ideas).

2

Five, six, seven generations ago for the first time in history huge gloomy squares of factory buildings rose around the cities of England, the new towns of America, and the old towns of Western Europe; the smoke of ten thousand factory chimneys besmirched the sky. It was around that time that money "talked" louder and with more power than ever before (or after). The tendency of money economy, or of so-called Capitalism, was nearing its peak. The so-called Industrial Revolution had begun.

Like every great social movement, it produced painful disruptions and new problems in the beginning. Almost immediately it produced a wide and beneficial increase of material standards of life. In its great gray wake came, too, increased waves of crime, vice, disease, despair, and poverty. It was a new kind of poverty that cannot be defined along the line of material comparisons with the awful poverty of earlier centuries, since this was a new, more rootless, and unfamiliar condition of poverty. More important, in this new phase of a dawning Age of Democracy, it was recognized by poor, rootless, dissatisfied people themselves.

For millions of people have suffered through history; but their sufferings (as, indeed, any material condition) become historic only when they recognize their condition, when their dissatisfactions crystallize around and are formulated into ideas of protest.

There were, of course, people who already during the seventeenth century were seriously and politically concerned with the condition of the poor; who were as much, if not more, concerned with social than with political equality. Before the beginning of the Industrial Revolution, toward the end of the eighteenth century, this spirit again coagulated in a renewed spurt of protestant metaphysics: in England the principles of an idealistic materialism were being formulated by the new puritans of the Evangelical Movement on one hand and by the first metaphysical and scientific proponents of Economics and of utilitarianism on the other. A generation later these religious and intellectual concerns appeared in France and also elsewhere on the Continent. By the second quarter of the nineteenth century there were scores of radical thinkers who attempted to formulate principles, programs, and systematic theories about these seemingly new problems of society. Because of a combination of circumstances the reputation of Karl Marx towers above all of the others up to the present day.

There is no need in this book to sum up Marx's life and his writings or to explain the distinctions between Marx, his friend Engels, and the other socialist, anarchist, or Communist radicals of Britain, Europe, Russia, and America (even though attention should be drawn to the German, Jewish, and scientific tendencies of Marx that are more characteristic of his person and of his ideas than the more abstract characteristics of his radicalism, internationalism, and Communism). Whether in the *Communist Manifesto*, written in 1847, or in *Das Kapital*, published in 1867, or, indeed, in almost all of his writings, the foundation and the basic principle of Marxian thought is economic determinism.[1] According to him, just about every human and historic phenomenon is determined by economics. It is a pious and fraudulent error to believe that history consists of political or religious or spiritual struggles; these are, according to Marx, only rationalizations; at the bottom, every struggle goes on about material things; every struggle is of an economic nature. If, then, the main problems of life, history, and society are economic, the solution must be economic, too. Thus it is economic conditions that must be corrected, transformed, and radically equalized; and especially now when the critical stage of Capitalist Economy is approaching, this must be done through revolution whenever necessary. This destruction of Capitalism and of class distinctions will, then, lead to conditions of a just economic order that, in turn, will mean the abolition of political struggle and of political authority in a rational and scientific world.

I know that this is a shorthand and perhaps imprecise summary of Marxism; but it is not necessarily untruthful or inadequate. Let me mention, then, those few virtues of Marx that may appear in retrospect. It is, after all, the life and the dedicated theory of a man who was sincerely concerned with poverty. It is, after all, the work of a man in whom, even though he had renounced his religion and his ancestors, there burned a Jewish spirit reminiscent of the Old Testament, seeking for a systematic proposition of Justice in this world. Unfortunately the shortcomings and the vices of Marx-

---

[1] It is symptomatic that *The 18th Brumaire*, one of his few really brilliant writings, is the only indirect and relative exception.

ism are much more numerous. They are spiritual and moral vices; intellectual and historical shortcomings. The Marxian ideas are atheistic, materialist, mechanical, utopian, pedantic, arrogant; and, as a system, generally nonsensical. Marx denied the existence of God. He refused to admit the spiritual nature of human beings. He affected to ignore the superbly complex character of human aspirations. He failed to realize that life is not merely mechanical and that history is not really logical. And he proposed a utopia that is not only extremely utopian but contingent upon brutal process of revolution.

I know that this is a brief summary; but from any reasonable summary of Marxism we may perceive an essential condition that is pointed out all too seldom, even though it reflects basic characteristics and the paradoxical limitations of its creator. This seemingly modern, radical, revolutionary, anti-bourgeois, anti-German, and fearlessly progressive ideology is, in reality, a very passé, very nineteenth-century, very Germanic, and very naïvely scientific system. For Marx, this atheistic and anti-Prussian prophet, really reveals his pedantic and German-Jewish self in his attempt to construct his ideas into a system. His ideology is an intellectual system often grievously and disparately divorced from life and from history, conceiving them in the vulgar-scientific manner of the nineteenth century as if life and history were but mechanical and scientific propositions. It is in this respect that Marx, like Darwin or Mendel or Comte or Maxwell or Bury—but unlike the truly great thinkers and makers of history, who stand out precisely because they transcend their times[2]—is a

[2] That is: had Marx (or Darwin or Edison) not existed, there is reasonable evidence to assume that during the nineteenth century someone would have come up with a theory of economic determinism, Evolution, or with a working electric bulb. But had Tocqueville (or Nietzsche or Debussy or Bismarck) not existed, there is no reasonable evidence to

prototypical intellectual representative of his century: a bearded intellectual prophet, the professorial radical, working on a systematic theory of society under the gaslights of the library of the British Museum—a recognizable and well-known and altogether bourgeois picture.

3

Karl Marx died in 1883. Within a decade's distance from that year Stalin, Roosevelt, Mussolini, and Hitler were born, men whose impact and influence determined most of the course of world history during the crucial second quarter of this century, whose actions determined the origins of the cold war and whose achievements, incidentally and seldom consciously, disproved almost all of Marx's original theories and predictions. For I am not dealing here with Marx in the abstract; I am forgoing even the basic philosophical or moral arguments. They are no longer really necessary. The failure of Marxian ideas has been accomplished and revealed by history itself, even though this is still far from being adequately recognized. We have before us the record of more than a hundred years.

The year after the *Communist Manifesto*, in 1848, a republican revolution in Paris was followed by the first modern working-class and partly Socialist uprising. It was crushed. In 1871, in the wake of France's chaotic defeat, another republican transformation was followed by a radical revolution in Paris that entered history under the name of the "Commune": that, too, was destroyed by remnants of the French Army, accompanied

assume that someone else would have described the essence of Democracy, proclaimed the fate of Godless Man, written music about the sea, or united Germany quite as had Tocqueville or Nietzsche or Debussy or Bismarck.

by the hostility of the overwhelming mass of the French people.

Marx's actual influence on contemporary events was very small. It is the influence of his ideas—or, rather, not so much their influence as their reputation—that has been very great. During the three decades stretching from his death to the First World War, Marxist and other Socialist ideas attracted a growing number of political intellectuals. All kinds of Socialist parties and movements emerged and grew in Europe, Britain, Russia, and America. But the Marxians had already split. Almost everywhere the more moderate and evolutionary Social Democratic and Labor parties and movements had a far larger following than the radical and revolutionary Marxists, even though the distinction between Communists and Socialists (or in Russia between Bolsheviks and Mensheviks) did not become clear until around the First World War. At any rate, the power of international Socialist ideas (or the internal fortitude of most Socialist leaders) proved far from being effective in 1914: they were swept away by the national passions and pressures of the war. In Germany, where the Socialist movement was strongest, in August 1914 the party deputies voted for the war in the Reichstag, while the masses cheered the Kaiser on the streets; in Italy a few months later the most brilliant and popular young leader of the Socialists broke with the party and started a nationalist social movement that was to make him, Mussolini, the master of Italy within less than a decade.

Thus in 1914—two generations after the *Communist Manifesto* and the first Parisian Socialist revolution, one generation after *Das Kapital* and the first Commune—Marxian, Socialist, and radical ideas were still not powerful enough to influence the actions of the working class at a decisive moment. This is at least remarkable when we consider that by 1914 the working classes were no longer dumb and passive forces; in Western

Europe and in America universal manhood suffrage had been extended to their large ranks; for the first time in history their great majority knew how to read and write. In 1914, at a time when the smug class distinctions and social injustices of high finance capitalism were still apt to smother the personal freedom of a working man at every turn of the city road, the masses of industrial workers followed the call of the upper classes into the war with attitudes ranging from passivity to actual enthusiasm. With very few notable exceptions, they struggled through the four terrible years of the war without protest. It was in Russia, and in Russia alone, that by 1917 a radical and revolutionary Marxist party rose to power.

Why did this happen in Russia, in a country that Marx had despised and where, unlike in Western Europe, according to his system conditions for a Socialist Revolution did not exist? The answer to this complex and difficult question must be broken down into two parts. Russia was ripe for revolution in 1917—we have seen this in the first part of this book—because of the war, because her government was inefficient and corrupt, because the Russian people were dissatisfied and suffering. But why was this revolution a Marxist one? This is the question that concerns us at this point though even this question is somewhat imprecise, for we must stretch and possibly tear the blanket sheet of Marxist theory quite a bit here and there to cover the Russian events of 1917–21, the events of a revolution and of a civil war that was more typically a *Russian* than a Marxist revolution. The question, therefore, may be narrowed down to this: why did the leaders of this Russian Revolution call themselves Marxist? why did they believe that they were Marxists? why did, consequently, the red flag triumph in Russia while it failed everywhere else in Europe? *Why* is always the most difficult question in history (and especially in Russian history); the answer to such difficult questions is always necessarily suggestive (though not merely tentative) and imprecise (though not necessarily untruthful). In the first place we must consider the specifically Russian historical conditions of a society where, unlike in Europe, bourgeois, patrician, capitalist traditions were not only very weak but alien, without much of a historical past; the Russian concept of private property, for example, was different from the Western European one from the very beginning of Russian history.[3] In the second place —and this is more important, since we are concerned here with the attraction of ideas—we must consider the often neglected Russian intellectual penchant for radical and German ideas. This has little to do with the affinities and the relations of the Russian and German peoples; it even transcends the condition that Russian intellectual Francophilia was flourishing and creating vivid and refined expressions of high culture and art just before the Revolution. It is, simply, that Germany was the first great European nation bordering on Russia; that most European concepts and ideas filtered into Russia through the thick German sieve; that the Russian educational system since Peter the Great largely followed German models; that the German tendency toward the extreme systematization of ideas has a certain powerful attraction to thinking Russians, who are attracted by intellectual and scientific systems since these stand in contrast to the emotional and unsystematic characteristics of Russian genius. Of all political ideas around the turn of the century Marxism seemed the most radical, the most revolutionary, the most logical, the most systematic, the most "Western," and the

---

[3] Thus, just as I suggested in the first chapter of this book about the politics of the Russian Revolution, where the weak resistance of the ruling classes in 1917 may have been at least as much of a factor as the "dynamism" of the Leninists, it may be said that the weakness of the bourgeois ideas was perhaps more decisive than the attractions of the Communist ones.

most "European." Hence their appeal to Lenin (and also to the many Russian Jews who were the intellectual cohorts of the Revolution).

But Lenin was no German (even though his mother was of German origin); he was far from being Germanic in temperament (even though most of his ideas had come from Germany);[4] he was not at all a German agent (even though the Germans sent him back to Russia, he made peace with them, and he hoped for a revolutionary alliance with them). Certain Tatar characteristics of his person appeared even before the semi-Oriental peasantlike features of Stalin cast their shadow over the vast Russian scene. In 1918, when it seemed that the Revolution rose, in Churchill's early angry phrase, from "the gutters and ghettos of Eastern Europe," speaking in German, Yiddish, and Russian accents, the disillusioned comment of a German-Jewish Marxist was already closer to the truth. The German-Jewish Parvus, the most intelligent and active agent of the Bolsheviks during the war, who could have been a sort of an Alexander Hamilton of the Russian Revolution, the man who was mainly responsible for the decisive German support to Lenin in 1917, wrote in March 1918: "The new state the Bolsheviks try to establish is not socialism but a Chinese peasant state which is bound to lead to a new Tsarism. The intellectual inspirer of Lenin is not Karl Marx but Pobedonostsev."[5] Somewhat exaggerated but largely true; certainly true in view of the development of the Russian Soviet state.[6]

[4] Next to his reading of Clausewitz, his reading of the German Hilferding's *Finanzkapital* played a very important part in the formation of his ideas and policies.

[5] Pobedonostsev: the dogmatist of Russian absolutism.

[6] Exaggerated: but only because of the impassivity of the Russian peasantry. As late as 1940, when most Russians were still peasants, not one of a dozen Russian villages had a Communist cell. Since that time the Communist Party organization of the Russian countryside has obviously increased; but it is since that time, too, that the meaning of

I think I need not explain how the state of Lenin, Stalin, and Khrushchev departed from the original Marxian doctrines; how a state arose that was dictatorial but not egalitarian, managerial rather than proletarian, reactionary rather than revolutionary, Judaeophobe rather than cosmopolitan, nationalist rather than internationalist; how Marx, had he lived to come to Moscow in 1918, would probably have sooner or later shared Trotsky's fate, at best.

But in this chapter I am dealing with the history of ideas, not of states. And at least within Russia the principle of Marxist theoretical foundations continued to be upheld, with one important modification: Lenin's political success and the mere quantity of his intellectual efforts, speeches, and writing led to the adoption of the new term "Marxism-Leninism" (and later, of "Leninism-Stalinism"), which was to provide the ideological, intellectual, political, and systematic foundations of Soviet Communism in all of its phases, as if Marxism had been further refined, developed, and extended by a great Russian Founding Father. Yet we must not accept this ideological category at face value. In reality, the contributions of Lenin (not to speak of Stalin) to Marxist, or, indeed, to all historical or economic thought, are virtually nil. Lenin was a brilliant revolutionary leader; also, undoubtedly, a man of considerable intellectual capacity; his ideas and theories, however, are nugatory, unimportant, and insubstantial; he added nothing to the Marxist system that is original, interesting, or enduring—even though millions are told to believe that he did so.

Still, we must keep in mind that the orthodoxy of Marxism is maintained within the Soviet Union at least in theory; and that even in practice there remain certain fields of endeavor where its doctrines are still being

Party membership (like the meaning of union membership in the West) has decreased.

observed and followed. I repeat: at least as important as what happens is what people think happens. What happened in Soviet Russia for a long time did not really affect the power and the prestige of Marxist ideas elsewhere. Let us look, therefore, once more at the world-wide history of Marxism, Socialism, Communism.

4

When in the spring of 1918 Lenin, in the Treaty of Brest-Litovsk, paid the enormous price for Bolshevik survival within Russia, surrendering large European portions of the Russian Empire to Imperial Germany, he said to his cohorts that this price was worth paying: for Germany would soon collapse anyhow and a Communist revolution would rise on her imperial ruins. The first part of his calculation came true (mainly because of the massive strength of Capitalist America on the Allied side); the second did not. Revolutions broke out all over Central and Eastern Europe as the imperial scaffoldings came down in 1918; but they were not Communist revolutions. Certainly conditions were never riper for Communist revolutions than in Germany or Austria in 1918–19, in these bitter, ravaged, disillusioned, shivering countries. But the Communist revolutions did not come; and in the few places where they were attempted, they usually failed in a matter of days or weeks because of a lack of popular support. (Besides, the Russian basis of Communism made the latter especially repugnant to the peoples of Central and Eastern Europe.)[7] After 1920 Lenin shifted his attention to

[7] "Had Germany and not Russia turned Communist after the First World War, the prestige of Communism would have been much greater." John Plamenatz, *German Marxism and Russian Communism*, London, 1953, page 331. Also, page 187: "It was precisely because of the conditions that Marx thought necessary for a successful proletarian revolution did

Asia; but there, too, in Turkey, Persia, Afghanistan, and China the Communist movement failed to develop or when it developed, it was crushed by nationalist revolutionary forces. Certainly, according to Marxist theory, conditions were ripe for a radical Socialist revolution during the world crisis of Capitalism during the Great Depression of the early 1930s: but the revolution did not come in either of the two countries where the economic crisis was deepest; in America the masses followed Roosevelt; in Germany they hearkened to Hitler. With very few exceptions, the Communists did not succeed in gaining noteworthy popular support anywhere; between the two World Wars the Marxian historical system and Communism attracted not the masses but a portion of intellectuals and a number of political idealists.

Thus we must keep in mind two important historical facts that are obscured in the now prevailing forests of intellectual confusion. The first is that until the end of the Second World War—that is, almost one hundred years after the birth of Marxian Communist dogma—the Soviet Union was still about the only Communist country in the world. The second is that even though the number of Communist nations increased immediately after the Second World War, this was not due to successful Communist revolutions but simply because the victorious Russian Army installed pro-Russian puppet Communist regimes in a number of countries adjacent to the Soviet Union. (The four exceptions to this general rule are Cuba, Communist Albania, Mao's Communist China, and Tito's Communist Yugoslavia, but the two last exceptions are only partial ones: it is very questionable whether Tito or Mao could have become the full masters of their respective countries without the victorious advance of the Russian armies toward the

---

exist in Germany that there was no desire to make it; and it was also because they did not exist in Russia that Lenin was able to seize power in the name of Marx and the proletariat."

end of the Second World War. On the other hand, it is evident that their lack of total dependence on the Soviet Union led to political and ideological divergences from Moscow very soon: the character of the regimes in Havana, Belgrade, Peiping, Tirana, though avowedly Communist, is different from that of Moscow. It is *Cuban* and Communist, *Yugoslav* and Communist, *Chinese* and Communist, *Albanian* and Communist. The national element again emerges.)

Meanwhile we have seen that, no matter how large-scale the social advances to the benefit of the working classes, Communism remains unpopular, shunned, and even despised throughout the Eastern European sphere of forcibly Communized nations. This is one of the principal factors in the cold war. To this we should add that, even in Asia and Africa, Soviet instigation and support did not really pay off: up to now, as after the First World War, not the Communists but the nationalist leaders have gained almost everywhere the upper hand. Meanwhile, belatedly but surely, it has become apparent that the Marxian doctrines no longer have a dominant appeal among intellectuals in the West. And among the evolutionist and moderate Socialists of Western Europe we find that the British Labour and the German Social Democratic Parties are at last officially admitting what, in reality, they have been doing for a long time: they are abandoning basic ideas of Marxism partly because they realize their outdated nature, partly because they realize their wide unpopularity among the masses of the working class.

Thus, at least in Europe and in America, Communist and Marxist ideas have decisively failed. Thus, from the historical experience of a century, we may sum up the main historical failures of the Marxist predictions.

In the first place, Marx predicted that in the critical phase of Capitalism, economic, social, and class differences would dramatically increase; but we have seen that the very opposite happened: almost everywhere the rich have become relatively poorer and the poor richer. In the second place, Marx predicted that the Communist revolution would occur in the most industrialized countries of the Western world; but we have seen that the very opposite has happened, that the Communist parties and movements have proved weakest precisely in the most industrialized nations of the world, in Britain, in the United States, in Germany. In the third place, Marx despised Russia and consistently implied that of all the great countries Russia was least ripe for a Socialist revolution;[8] but we have seen that the only internal and successful Communist revolution perhaps in the entire world occurred in Russia alone; and we have seen how the spirit and the institutions of the new Russia developed very differently from Marx's projections and predictions. In the fourth place, Marx predicted that Communism would succeed because of the struggle between classes; but we have seen that all over the world the internal Communist revolutions and regimes collapsed everywhere and almost every time except where and when they were installed by the military force or upheld by the military pressure of Muscovite armies. In the fifth place, Marx proposed Communism as the only truly radical massive movement of the future; but we have seen how from Mussolini and Hitler to Perón and Nasser political movements based on emotional and national sentiments and dogmas have been much more successful than Communist movements with their systematic, economic, social, and intellectual doctrines: we must keep in mind, for instance, how in the 1930s the following of Nazi- or Fascist-type movements was often popular and spontaneous and that their success did not always and necessarily depend on their forceful installation by German or other armies. In the sixth place, Marx predicted that the in-

---

[8] Except for one instance toward the end of his life, when he admitted the possibility of a Russian revolution in the introduction to a Russian translation of his book.

dustrial proletariat would form the vanguard of the Revolution: but we have seen that even when the reputation of Marxist ideas was strongest, it appealed not to class-conscious workers but to rootless people and to intellectuals whose own records and reminiscences reveal that they were attracted to Marxism not because of economic or social but because of psychological or spiritual motives.

On almost every basic issue Marx has been proven wrong. There would be every reason, consequently, to dismiss Marxism as largely, and perhaps even totally, bankrupt. History, however, is not governed by logic. Unfortunately, therefore, we reach the added paradox: not only are its failures still far from being adequately recognized but the foundation of Marxist beliefs, economic determinism, has been generally, though not always consciously, accepted by the entire Western world, and especially by the United States.

5

The political theories of Americans came, with few exceptions, from the British Isles, mostly derived from Puritans in the seventeenth, Commonwealthmen in the eighteenth, Whigs and Liberals in the nineteenth century. Through most of these ideas runs a strong social and democratic concern, an evangelical temper together with an intellectual inclination to think in legal, mechanical, economic, and scientific terms. The extraordinary intelligence of the Founding Fathers provided the American Republic with a Constitution whose framework, together with the English and Celtic racial heritage of pragmatic political sense, kept American politics practical rather than ideological. By about 1890, however, German and other European influences began to penetrate American intellectual and educational habits. The influence of European ideologies and

the general intellectualization of life began to comple-
ment the earlier puritanical habits of idealistic materialism. Together they inclined toward economic determinism. While most Americans rejected the Marxist and
Communist teaching of revolution—the Express Eleva-
tor in the blueprint of the Marxist House of Mankind—
they tended, and still tend, to accept its basic foundation, that life is primarily, if not exclusively, a scientific
and politics an economic proposition; they also tended
to accept the idea of the Utopian Penthouse, the possibility of achieving a Garden of Eden in this world.

There is no need to criticize this American tendency
at this point. It is not an exclusively American, but a
general tendency in our times.[9] Besides its deeper historical roots there are specific historical reasons for its
American existence. Consider, for example, that the
greatest crisis involving the lives of most Americans in
this century was not a world war but the economic Depression of 1929–34. Even though Americans have recognized the complexity of spiritual, ideological, political, and military elements in the world-wide conflicts
of this century, they have excessively inclined to see the
decisive factor in economics. Consider, for example, the
Morgenthau Plan, the Marshall Plan, Point Four, different policies adopted at different junctures of the contemporary world crisis, proposed by different men, flowing from different (and not always conscious) passions,
but all of them resting on the proposition that economic
conditions produce political conditions, and not the
reverse.[10]

[9] It is, in any case, a symptom of the spiritual as well as
of the rational poverty of our times that the economic interpretation of any historical or the scientific interpretation of
any human phenomenon is equated with intellectual insight
or even with common sense.
[10] There is a revealing dispatch from the British Ambassador in Washington to Churchill, dated 7 July 1945, in
which we may sense the first whiff of the Marshall Plan—
indeed, of the whole evolution of American policy after the

It is important, on the other hand, that the open recognition and avowal of Marxist, Socialist, or Communist ideas in America have been largely restricted to the circles of an often indirectly influential but in politics not very potent minority of professional intellectuals and misguided idealists. There were times, during the quarter century before the Russian Revolution, when the Populist Party and the Progressives in America seemed to be on the verge of becoming large radical and even socialistic movements; but their influence declined, largely because of the parochiality of their provincial leaderships. There was a time, around 1914, when an American Socialist Party seemed to be on the verge of becoming, like Labour in Britain, an important Third Party (it won a number of important mayoralties, showing strength not only among the millions of immigrants but in the State of Oklahoma, of all places), but within a decade this Party fell to insignificance, destroyed as it was partly by the intrigues of the tiny unscrupulous fledgling American Communist movement and largely by the great tide of American popular anti-Communism that swept through the Republic soon after the Bolshevik Revolution.

Still, the American tendency to think about politics and history in terms of planning, along with the consequent inclination toward economic determinism, was an important element in the 1930s and 1940s. It provided the widespread, though vague, ideological foundation of the policies of the Roosevelt era toward Soviet Russia. There was this broad inclination to think of America and Russia as two young pioneer nations, ahead of the rest of the world in new and progressive policies of so-

---

war. The Americans, wrote Lord Halifax, may some time later "stand up with us against Russians." But he expected "the Americans in dealing with us to be more responsive to arguments based upon the danger of economic chaos in European countries than to the balder pleas about the risks of the spread of Communism."

cial and economic welfare. This was reflected by the wartime political tendency in Washington to see the United States somewhere in the middle between the Soviet Union and Great Britain, moving somewhere in the middle between the older Anglo-Saxon legal and constitutional tradition and the new radical progressive requirements of a technological world. This influential and widely fashionable attempt to create an American ideology did not recede, especially among intellectuals, until the cold war was well beyond its first phase.

On the other hand, even in the 1930s, even at the height of the popularity of the New Deal era in America, as in Europe, greater inchoate popular inclinations gathered around men like Huey Long or the Rev. Charles Coughlin—movements that, somewhat euphemistically, could be (and indeed were) called Fascistic or Right-wing; more precisely, these were anti-Marxist, *national* socialist movements. Because of the great popularity and political adroitness of Franklin Roosevelt and again also because of the relative parochiality of their potential leaders, these movements dwindled by about 1936, but the sentiments they had expressed continued latent. They burst out again as the cold war developed a decade later, gathering momentum and crystallizing powerfully for a while around the person of Joseph McCarthy. I shall come back to this problem of national socialism later;[11] here I must only mention in passing this new and strong combination of nationalist, indeed, of ideological anti-Communism together with the acceptance of the socializing practices of the Welfare State that had, and still have, so large a potential support among the American people, and by no means least among the American working class.

We are now coming upon a very important question. Why is it that, unlike in Russia, the Communist appeal never succeeded in America?—even though there has been this strong American inclination to formulate ideas

[11] See below, Chapter xvi, sub-chapter 3.

in social and economic terms, even though we may speak in America of a long tradition of a "socialization of souls," even though Marxism has had a unique appeal to American intellectuals, even though the United States has evolved toward a socialized Welfare State. A large portion of the answer to this question has been given a few pages earlier: it lies in the American virtues of common sense as well as in the practical failures of the principal Marxist dogmas. But, strangely enough, these virtues and those failures are far from being clearly recognized by Americans. Thus we must observe that together with the massive American social tendency to spurn not respectable ideas such as Socialism and Communism there has existed a strange lack of inner confidence that has pushed American anti-Communism into rather extreme misconceptions. For there are probably more Americans who believe that Communism is a dreadfully effective conspiracy than there are Russians who really believe that a dreadfully effective Capitalist conspiracy exists against Russia. The illusion of American Omnipotence and the belief in an Omnipotent Communist World Conspiracy often coexist within the same people. We have seen how, at the height of the cold war, the McCarthy crisis revealed how many Americans held extremely unreasonable notions of this Communist Conspiracy Theory. Even now such opinions are by no means extinct.[12] There has been a steady and unhistorical American tendency during the cold war to conceive world history as if its main movement has been the awesome and conspiratorial

[12] This does not mean, of course, that Communists in America did not, at times, exercise a pernicious influence far in excess of their number. They represent a potential danger, however, not when they act as revolutionary agitators but when some of them are potential Russian agents. It is not the successes of the Communist idea but only the occasional successes of Russian espionage in this country that require Americans to be on guard against the infiltration of Communists.

forward march of Marxism ever since 1848—a theory that conveniently disposes of the First and of the Second World Wars of this century, among other things; a theory as nonsensical as the Marxist theory about the conspiracies of Capitalism.

Since this kind of Anti-Communism, like Marxism, is a powerful and world-wide phenomenon despite its misconceptions, I must, as with Marxism, list some of these evident misconceptions. In the first place, the standard doctrine of Anti-Communist ideologies is that the idea of revolutionary Communism represents the greatest danger to Western Civilization: but we have seen that the greatest danger to the West is represented not so much by the idea of Communism but by the great power of a potentially aggressive Russia, by the growing power of a hostile China, and by the fact that Russian armies are stationed in the middle of Europe. In the second place, it is contended that the infiltration of the Communist idea represents the greatest danger to the United States: but we have seen how even during the catastrophic Depression in 1932 the Communists did not get anywhere. In the third place, it is asserted that the main purpose of Soviet Russia is to extend the rule of international Communism all over the world: but we have seen how the spreading of international Communism has seldom proved to be the primary purpose of Russia,[13] whose rulers, rather, aim to establish and maintain the maximum extent of power and security for their country—a sufficiently ambitious requirement, at that. In the fourth place, it is said that the international Communist conspiracy made it possible for Russia to enslave a whole chain of satellite countries in Europe: but we have seen that the cause of the deplorable division of Europe was not Communism but the Second World War, in which the nations of Europe

---

[13] We were assured that Stalin's *Problems of Leninism* was always on Dulles' desk. We may be sure that it was not on Khrushchev's.

tore each other apart and from which Russia was to profit by external and military conquest. In the fifth place, it is propounded that through Communism Soviet Russia has achieved tremendous advances in Asia: but we have seen that it is China that has advanced while Russia retreated in the Far East. And in the sixth place, it is proposed that Communism appeals especially to people suffering from economic distress: but this hardly explains why the distressed Germans in the Depression voted for Hitler, why in some of the poorest countries of Europe Fascist parties are often stronger than Communist ones, or why in the poorest sections of the United States there was not a single Communist at a time when Communists were not hard to find in Hollywood or even on Park Avenue.

As with the ideas of Communism (or of Vegetarianism or of Anti-Vivisectionism), so with the otherwise normal and more reasonable ideas of Anti-Communism: when human ideas are formulated into a rigid systematic theory, when the ideas of transient men of this world are illegitimately elevated to the level of principles, cruelty and nonsense result.[14] This is the truth of moral levels and not of relativity. The moral principles of our civilization must be neither Communist nor Anti-Communist: they are the Ten Commandments and the teachings of Jesus. This does not mean, as so many compromisers and "anti-anti-Communists" believe, that

[14] At this point it would seem from my interpretation of history that ideas are only a superficial part in the process of history, which is moved by stronger and deeper factors. On the contrary, it is my conviction that the role of ideas in history and in life is greater, stronger, and profounder than most people (including most historians) think. But when I say ideas, I do not mean officially recognized, categorical ideas, like the idea of Communism, for example, frozen into a gigantic block by its admirers and detractors alike. Such recognized categories of ideas in our times no more preempt the real history of ideas than the activities of recognized professional intellectuals pre-empt the sphere of creative mental activity.

the correct course of mankind is somewhere in the middle, halfway between Communism and Anti-Communism; nor does it mean, as so many radical Anti-Communists believe, that an anti-anti-Communist is logically a pro-Communist of a sort. Life, and the human spirit, transcends the logic of mathematics. Between two opposite doctrines of different falsity[15] the truth often is not in the middle: it is above them.

6

We have seen in the previous chapter how during the cold war Russian and American social and economic systems have begun to approximate each other. It would seem, then, that if ideas are more important in history, the causes of the cold war struggle are on that deeper level: between the Russian Communist and the American Anti-Communist ideas. There is much truth in this, though it is still far from the entire truth. For though on one hand ideas are inseparable from life, life is invariably stronger than theory. It is ideas that are part of life itself; it is theories that are often only superstructures. And the conditions of life—more precisely, the unwillingness of the leaders of Russia and America alike to risk their lives in a hydrogen war— have already led to a gradual approximation of their ideas and not only of economic and social policies. Even though Russians and Americans (the former because of the Byzantine and Marxist, the latter because of the Puritanical, Celtic, and Germanic elements in their intellectual inheritance) have a somewhat similar inclination to separate images and ideas from realities for a

[15] For Communism is not, as we are often told, a Half Truth. It is a Lie. The Half Truth is ideological Anti-Communism; and it is in the character of Western Civilization that Half Truths may be more deceptively dangerous than are obvious Lies.

long time, to postpone the recognition of the latter as long as possible; even though Russians as well as Americans, despite their utopian inclinations, have a strong fatalistic streak in their hearts, they have, after a while, begun to refashion cautiously not only their institutions but their recognized and official theories. Thus, for example, the Russian leaders have officially modified the thesis about the inevitable world-wide victory of Communism through war; thus, for example, Khrushchev's speeches propose a kind of future Russian prosperity more and more along American social patterns. On the other hand, the programs and policies of the Eisenhower Republican Administration, for example, have surpassed most of what had been the sectarian and radical demands of Socialists only a few decades before. It is true that this happened only in the wake of the already existing institutions of the American Welfare State; but the intellectual recognition of its development, too, proceeds.

Still, the gradual approximation of the Russian and American societies and their theories will neither explain the causes nor solve the problems of the cold war. For these institutions and theories are only representations and expressions of the greater reality of two powerful states and nations: were Russia, no matter how doctrinaire and Communist, a smaller and weaker country, like Yugoslavia, there would be no cold war between Russia and America today.

CHAPTER XIV

The Two States:
The Development of Their National Interests

(The Political Element: The
Tendencies of Their Imperial Relations)

1

Throughout their history America and Russia have represented very different political theories, very different political and social institutions, and very different ways of life. Yet, except in marginal or episodic instances, their vital interests did not come into conflict with each other until 1945. The cold war between America and Russia began as the advancing forces of this great transoceanic and of that great transcontinental Empire met each other in the middle of Europe. Then, in the momentarily powerless vacuum of a defeated Germany the bodies of these two tremendous Empires came into close contact. Sensing the breath of each other, they immediately felt the dangers of such a heavy and colossal proximity. The closeness of their contact suggested the conflict of their interests.

For the factor of geography, involving national interest, may be more decisive than differences in social systems and in political theories. Had Stalin, asserting Russia's domain over Eastern Europe, proclaimed himself Tsar Joseph I in 1945, the Russo-American conflict over Europe would not have shaped up much differently at that time; something like the cold war would have developed right away. Had Stalin withdrawn his forces from Europe at the end of the war, concentrat-

ing instead on a further radical transformation of the
Soviet Union into an orthodox Communist pattern (a
much less likely alternative than the first), such an
internal transformation, no matter how brutal, crude, or
shocking, would not have deeply involved the national
interests of the United States: the issues of foreign
policy would have shaped up quite differently, and the
cold war might not have developed at all.

Like life and the idea of life, foreign and domestic
affairs are intimately entangled, inevitably connected in
the history of nations. Perhaps the very term *"foreign
policy"* is misleading, with its implication of something
external and foreign. It is a mistake to think that foreign policy, save on certain critical occasions, is nor-
mally something very different from, extraneous to,
and secondary to the main, domestic and internal business of the nation. But there is even more to this.

Just as the character of a person is best revealed in
his dealings with others, the character of a nation is
often best revealed by its actions and attitudes toward
other nations. This is the stuff of history: the relationships of men, of nations, of states with others. There are
no isolated nations, just as there are no isolated persons.
Think of a single human being. He has three kinds of
overlapping relations: with God, with himself, and with
others. But we can neither judge nor fully understand
another person's relationship either with God or with
himself; we can only judge that person's relationship
with other persons. And even though national interest is
essentially somewhat different, less organic than personal interest, that is why its expression through foreign
policy is a primary, and not a secondary, historical
factor.

2

Five hundred years ago, as the Middle Ages were
coming to an end, at the time of the golden sharp

Mediterranean outburst of the Renaissance, just before
the Protestant eruption and the Western European discovery of new continents, the Principality of Moscow
comprised a small, irregular, isolated, wooden, semi-
barbaric territory beyond Europe. Two hundred and
fifty years later, two hundred and fifty years ago, that
Muscovite state had become a Russian Empire that
was to become a factor in European affairs; its enormous territory, stretching from Chinese to Polish frontiers, already comprised the by now proverbial Russian
one sixth of the land surface of the globe. One hundred
years later, by 1860, the Russian Empire extended from
the Pacific to Prussia, from Vladivostok to beyond Warsaw. In other words, until recently the expansion of the
Russian Empire was swift, relatively easy, and untrou-
bled by the other Great Powers of the globe. The reasons are obvious. Muscovite Russia, like the United
States but unlike the European Powers, could rush
ahead in vast and largely uninhabited lands. Only relatively recently was she brought into direct and permanent contact with the more crucial, more compressed
and traditional sphere of states. Her conflicts with her
European neighbors, with Sweden, Poland, Turkey,
Austria, then resulted in smaller but much more important accretions to her national domains.

Despite their already vast and still thinly inhabited
imperial territories, the masters of Russia frequently,
though not always consistently, wished to extend their
possessions even further. Their motives, as the motives
of every ambitious statesman, have been of course complex: but we must mention those peculiarly Russian
motives that distinguish them from the more customary
and traditional European ambitions of national or imperial expansion. In the first place, more than in the
history of other nations, suspicion has been a main inner
motive force of Russian expansion: Russia, with her
vast and not immediately defensible frontiers, labored

to hold on to the largest possible bolsters of lands between her vital central organs and the external world.
In the second place, Russians on occasion convinced
themselves of their pretense of Orthodox religious
uniqueness, attempting to influence, liberate, govern,
and conquer various Slavic and Orthodox peoples in
Eastern Europe and in the Balkans. Since, however,
Pan-Slavism was an effectively radiant force at best
only at certain occasions, its influence—as the influence
of the newer so-called "messianistic" influence of Communism—has been often overrated.[1]

Thus, in the history of Russian expansion, the defensive motive of fear and the aggressive motive of
messianism are mixed. They are mixed deeper and
worse than in the history of other civilized nations; let
us keep in mind how, through the alchemy of human
souls, insecurity may indeed find expression in brutality, and uncertainty in aggressiveness.

We have seen, then, that during the First World
War, Russia, on whose massive military partnership the
Western Allies so badly depended, exacted large territorial promises from them that were to be honored at
the time of victory. Her recognized ambitions included
portions of Eastern Europe, of Asia Minor, and even the
long-coveted prize of Constantinople. Then the Bolshevik Revolution swept all of these prospects away.

It is in the nature of great revolutionaries to believe
that their victory has brought a fundamental change in

[1] At some time or another every Slavic nation, from
Bohemia to Montenegro, and every Eastern Christian people, from Armenians to Abyssinians, came to depend on
Russian help. But despite these racial and religious affinities
more often Greeks came to prefer British, Bulgarians German,
Czechs and Serbs French friendships to Russian ones. The
cases of Slavic Poland and of Greek Orthodox Rumania are
even more obvious. They indicate clearly how Russia
alienated her Slavic neighbors when her own territorial and
national ambitions superseded her pretended religious and
racial loyalties.

the relations of the reborn nation with the rest of the world. This belief and attitude, exemplified in Trotsky's famous proclamation of November 1917, addressed to All the Peoples of the World, led the world to believe, and still makes the world believe, that in 1917 History Changed Gears, that something entirely new had begun. Certainly the new Communist regime proclaimed itself unhampered by the traditional bourgeois practices of diplomatic intercourse. Of course it intervened in world affairs, not only in relations with the governments of states but also through the new instrument of international revolutionary propaganda directed to specific groups and classes. Surely Trotsky, Chicherin, Litvinov, and even Molotov, Vishinsky, Shepilov, and Gromyko are not just Russian Foreign Ministers continuing a long line of Nesselrodes, Gierses, Gorchakovs, Milyukovs, and Wittes. Obviously the *Soviet* Union, *Communist* Russia are qualifying adjectives and not just ephemeral and meaningless labels.

Yet when a person informs the world that, because of a radical new experience or through a spiritual conversion, his character has changed, we are entitled to take such proclamations with a grain of salt. And even a change in the concept of human nature does not mean that human nature itself has changed. Very soon the Bolshevik leaders, no matter how revolutionary, were forced to learn to take into account elementary and basic conditions of Russia's situation: Russia was still Russia, occupying a certain place on the globe, bordering on certain nations, affected by certain enduring geographical and national conditions.

Historical life is stronger than historical theory—especially when that theory, like Marxism, is fundamentally unhistorical. Soon after the Revolution it became apparent (even though this, again, is far from being adequately recognized by Communists and anti-Communists alike) that, especially when it came to

Russia's relations with her neighbors, continuity was stronger than change.

True, the Russian Revolution made it possible for Finland, Estonia, Lithuania, Latvia, Poland, and Rumanian Bessarabia to tear themselves away from their previous Russian imperial bondage. But we have seen how none of these newly liberated nations became Communist; how thereafter Lenin and his colleagues hoped to conquer them with the help of the Red Army; but there, too, they failed. Consequently by 1921 the new Soviet Russia had to acquiesce, willy-nilly, in the independence of these new non-Communist border nations. Having had to retreat in Europe, the Communist leaders, in the old Russian manner, turned their expansive view toward Asia; but we have seen how, between 1921 and 1927, Russian hopes to see Communism established in Turkey, Persia, Afghanistan, and China came also to fail.

There are two pronouncements by Lenin that are being cited at every possible opportunity by doctrinaire Communists and even more by doctrinaire anti-Communists. First, Lenin said that the Revolution must at times follow a Zigzagging Course, meaning that the Communist movement must on occasion refrain from attacking temporarily stronger opponents head on and must execute Tactical Retreats instead. This is such an obvious truism that one may wonder why up to this day Experts on Communism and on Russia eagerly pounce on this statement, pursuing the obvious, as Wilde would have said, with the enthusiasm of shortsighted detectives. They dismiss every Russian retreat as insincere, devious, and dangerous. Tactical: but, let us ask, is not every kind of retreat, everywhere and always, a Tactical one? The other pronouncement, made allegedly by Lenin in 1920 at Baku before a revolutionary congress of Asian nationalities, reads: "The shortest way to Paris is via Peiping." This has been cited innumerable times by people who wish to see therein a statement worthy of a diabolical genius who foresaw the Communist victory in China. But Lenin was supposed to have said this after the gates of the road leading to Paris had been slammed in his face at Warsaw (besides, now, the Russians have arrived neither in Paris nor even in Peiping). From Moscow through Peiping to Paris: let us consign this alleged pronouncement to the category of rhetorical round trips. Otherwise it would reflect poorly not merely on the political but even on the geographical knowledge of this Bolshevik Founding Father.[2]

Often the Communist leaders of the new Russia fomented, of course, revolutions in neighboring as well as in faraway countries of the globe. We cannot ignore the historical influence of Communist relationships in world affairs. A new international revolutionary organization, the Communist International, sat in Moscow; its proclaimed dissolution by Stalin in 1943 was only a little more than window dressing. Besides the regular apparatus of Russian diplomacy for handling international affairs, the Soviets could count on occasion on the international collaboration of manifold Communist affiliations, on a clandestine network. There were occasions —China in the 1920s, for example—when the Russian leaders took steps in the interests of world Communism considerably beyond the national interests of Soviet Russia. Yet these occasions were few and relatively unimportant. The history of Soviet Russian foreign policy is studded with innumerable examples when considerations of Russian *national* interests clearly proved more important than the interests of *international* Communism, at the expense of the latter. This was especially true of Russia under Stalin (and this was, of course,

[2] Bismarck, who recognized the primary importance of Russia's European relations, was a better political realist. He told a British diplomat who had been worried about Russian ambitions in Afghanistan that "the Afghan Question ultimately depended on the situation at Tauroggen," that is, at the German-Russian frontier.

the core of the conflict between Stalin and Trotsky); but it was already evident under Lenin. Ever since Brest-Litovsk examples abound, especially in Russia's relations with Germany.

Seldom did the rulers of Russia allow international Communist interests to supersede what to them seemed the immediate national interests of their Russian Empire. The integrity and the defense of that Empire has remained the primary consideration in their minds from Lenin to the present day. For this purpose they collaborated on occasion with Prussian generals, African nationalists, American industrialists, Persian Shahs, Italian Fascists, British Tories, German Nazis, French conservatives, Japanese imperialists; they made political and strategic alliances with Mustapha Kemal, General Von Seeckt, Pierre Laval, Eduard Beneš, Adolf Hitler, Winston Churchill, Chiang Kai-shek, Franklin Roosevelt, Mao-tse Tung; they discussed alliances with and proposed divisions of spheres of interests to Mussolini, Stresemann, De Gaulle, and Nixon. Moreover, the leaders of Soviet Russia generally tended to get along much better with British Tories than with British Labourites, with American industrialists rather than with American labor leaders, with resolute and conservative Finnish patriots such as Marshal Mannerheim rather than with the avowedly Communist Tito in Yugoslavia—because, far transcending all ideological or social affinities, they saw how the different interests of different nations represented by these different national leaders at certain times and occasions accorded with the national interests of Soviet Russia.[3]

[3] We are often reminded, and with reason, of the record of the Soviet government in ignoring previous treaties. But we must keep in mind that such a record is not unique. And, instead of enumerating those treaties that the Russians did not keep, it would be an interesting exercise to enumerate those commitments that they did keep, recalling perhaps the words of Samuel Butler: "The world will always be governed by self-interest: we should not try and stop this: we

At any rate, the primary conception of national interests, though evident from the beginning, reached its
full fruition under Stalin in 1939. We have seen how
after the Revolution the European borders of the Russian Empire receded and the European influence of
Russia remained limited for twenty years. In 1939,
then, Stalin, having dismissed the Jewish Litvinov from
the Commissariat of Foreign Affairs,[4] stepped forward
to negotiate secret treaties with Germany, Italy, and
Japan that differed from earlier examples of Russian
imperial diplomacy perhaps only in the brutal character
of their execution. At the time when German Communists, the last true German followers of Lenin, were
herded and tortured in Hitler's concentration camps,
Stalin drank a champagne toast in the Kremlin to Hitler, "the great and beloved leader of the German nation." At a time when the Communist revolutionaries
of Europe were living in dreary apartment buildings in
Moscow ("the beggars of the Mokhavaya," Stalin called
them contemptuously), he and Molotov openly proposed that the principal aim of Russia was to recover
the territories and the influence that Tsarist Russia possessed in Eastern Europe in 1914. Stalin's concept of
national interest thus led to his Treaties with Hitler at
the expense of European Communism; the same concept, at the expense of Chinese Communism, led to his
Treaty with Japan, assuring the vital condition of war
on one front only.

This is the principal theme that runs through the
history of Russian foreign policy during the next crucial
decade. The partition of Poland, the incorporation of

---

should try and make the self-interest of cads a little more
coincident with that of decent people."

[4] We should note that not until May 1941 did Stalin
name himself the equivalent of Russian Prime Minister; and
until 1939 he, officially only the Secretary of the Communist
Party, did not receive Ambassadors—except, on occasion, the
Ambassador of the United States.

the Baltic States, the attacks and pressures on Finland, the Russian policies in Bulgaria and Yugoslavia, Stalin's early insistence upon the Curzon Line, the evidence of his secret tentative negotiations with Germany during the war, the Russian territorial demands at Yalta, all illustrate and confirm the existence of this tendency. To this were added the fruits and the consequences of the Russian victory in the Second World War: a ring of satellite nations along the western borders of Russia, a buffer zone separating the Russian homeland from the rest of Germany, Europe, and the American alliance system, a new extended concept of Russia's strategic interests in which a principal element is to avoid the rebirth of a strong and united and eventually ambitious Germany allied with the United States. We need not insist further that these are Russian and national rather than revolutionary and Communist concepts.[5]

And yet this does not mean, of course, that the Russian Communist leaders are simply cynical nationalists who keep on using the Communist terminology only to deceive the Russian people and the world. Life is not like that. It is not only that people may say one thing and do another; it is not even that people may believe in one way and act in another; it is that they may not admit even to themselves the obvious inconsistency between their acknowledged ideas and beliefs and their actions. Not even Stalin would admit to himself how typical a Russian national leader he had become; but while he may not have consciously admitted this, we

[5] In his book about Russian war aims during the First World War a judicious American historian observed that what Sazonov, the last intelligent Foreign Minister of Imperial Russia, wanted was "basically a Western Europe dominated by Britain and France, an Eastern Europe dominated by Russia, and a weak Germany as a buffer in between." (C. Jay Smith, Jr., *The Russian Struggle for Power: 1914–1917.*) Altogether this was very similar to Stalin's (and also to Khrushchev's) wishes.

can recognize it from the evidence of his own words and actions.

At any rate, had Talleyrand, Metternich, Castlereagh, and the other statesmen of the Congress of Vienna reappeared in 1945, they could have been briefed on the Russian Problem in about five minutes. They would have understood it at once, whereas it is doubtful whether a much longer briefing about Marxism would have made much sense to them at all. The instruments of power, the material conditions, and the personal representatives of 1945 would, of course, have seemed very different from the world of 1815; but the European problems posed by the territorial ambitions of Russia would have been quite familiar. At any rate, to find many a clue to the patterns of Stalin's behavior we would do better to read Herberstein rather than Marx, Custine rather than Lenin—just as the age-old Chinese pattern appears so much better from the actual history of such things as the Taiping Rebellion than from the dreary theoretical texts of Mao.

At any rate, from the murk of the past, from the murky gallery of Russian history, the monuments of Tsars—and not only of Peter the Great—emerge anew. It was Stalin who in 1940 spoke of the restoration of Russia's border provinces in the West; it was Stalin who in 1945 justified the Russian war declaration on Japan as the historic opportunity "to efface the shame of forty years before." It was Khrushchev who in 1958 spoke of the historic friendship of the Tsars (they were not "exploiters" or "colonizers," he said) toward the peoples of the Middle East, it was Khrushchev who in 1959 said that of course he had to suppress the Hungarian "counterrevolution," for had not Tsar Nicholas I in 1849 done the same thing? Had Stalin really known what the Bolshevik Founding Father had said in 1905, he might not have used such words in 1945 (for Lenin had welcomed the Japanese victory over Tsarist Russia in 1905); had Khrushchev known his history better, he might not have blundered into so grossly mistaken a statement (for it was in the very name of reaction and counterrevolution that the Tsar in 1849 had helped the Imperial Hapsburgs crush the Hungarian Republic). But just because Stalin and Khrushchev may have had their history wrong, this does not mean that history did not influence their lives. It did; it did very much, indeed. I have said before that history does not repeat itself; but historical circumstances do; and, as Santayana said, it is the people who do not know history who may be condemned to repeat it.

3

The history of American foreign policy is the history of American expansion, too; and yet the two stories are almost always treated separately from each other. The reason for this, of course, is that for a long time the adversaries of American expansion were natural obstacles and savage tribes, not established and civilized nations. Yet even before the establishment of the United States the expansion of the American frontier involved forests, rivers, and Indians at times together with the interests of European Empires; and, indeed, a principal cause of the American Revolution was the unenforceable limitations set up by the British government against the rapid and ambitious westward movement of the American pioneers.

Progress and expansiveness are American characteristics; but the exploration of those motives of American expansion that flow from certain religious components of the American character does not belong in this chapter. Let us but mention that even in our times American expansion, to many Americans, is synonymous with the expansion of law, democracy, order, civilization. The expansion of the United States, like its motive sentiments, is a complex and not always a conscious move-

ment. At least since 1776 the two threads of anti-
colonialism and of expansion run together in the history
of the Republic: at times one or the other is dominant,
but more often they are entangled with each other in
the very hearts and minds of the American people.

Throughout their history the American people have
stood for the abolition of colonies, of slavery, for the
extension of democratic freedom. There have been
times when this sentiment was running low; there have
been times when it was running high; there have been
exceptions to it, here and there; but these universal
democratic sympathies never have been wholly excluded from American political advocacy. Since the
very first winter of the War of Independence, when an
American military column moved into the St. Lawrence
Valley to promote a Canadian insurrection (indeed,
since 1769, when Americans extended sympathy and
help to a short-lived French "Republic of New Or-
leans" that attempted to detach herself from French
royal Louisiana) the united American colonies actively
sympathized and supported anti-colonial, anti-absolut-
ist, anti-royalist, nationalist, and democratic revolutions
in Latin America; and also in Ireland, Norway, Poland,
Hungary, Greece, Italy, Spain, Korea, the Philippines,
India, Israel, and China.

Still, it was more than mere democratic sympathy
that governed the extent of American support of foreign revolutionary movements. It was in the interest of
the American Republic to promote the decline and the
collapse of the older European Empires on the American continent. Thus for a long time the American Republic, not unlike Bolshevist Russia a century later, in
the eyes of conservative European statesmen like Metternich incarnated the radical and revolutionary forces
of upheaval. On the other hand, as certain British
statesmen as well as Tocqueville saw it, the ambitions
of the American Republic, unlike Russian ambitions,
did not conflict much with the vital interests of most

European states. Certainly some of the ideas proposed
by radical democrats and by republican expansionists in
America seem shockingly crude even in retrospect.[6]
Certainly some of the expansionist policies of the United
States at the expense of Indians and Mexicans, and directed at Santo Domingo and Cuba (and even at Canada as late as in 1911), deserve criticism and closer
scrutiny by historians. Still, the westward expansion of
the United States, like the eastward expansion of Imperial Russia, occurred in largely uninhabited and savage territories that other nations could not effectively
govern and civilize. Nor were the often so aggressive
and extreme desires of American expansionists always
followed by the Department of State.

But now we have to draw a geographical line. Until
the 1890s American expansion as well as active American assistance to foreign revolutions involved only the
Western Hemisphere. Between 1890 and 1917, however, the previously free and largely formless concept
of American national interests began to crystallize into
a global form that is now geographically recognizable
in retrospect.

It is what we may call the Theodore Roosevelt, or the
Two-Ocean, concept: the concept that the Atlantic and
the Pacific are the two gigantic moats protecting the
United States from eventual enemies; that, consequently, the power of the American Navy must be
predominant in Atlantic and Pacific alike; that the
United States must possess naval bases and friendly
ports throughout the Atlantic, Caribbean, and Pacific;
that the United States cannot, in her own interests,
permit the domination of the eastern Atlantic (and all
of Western Europe) or of the western Pacific (and all
of Eastern Asia) by a single Power. Here, on a vaster
and global scale, we may see a similarity with the earlier British concept of national interests. What the

[6] See below, Chapter xv, pages 367–68.

Channel was for Britain, the Atlantic has become for America. What the Lowlands were for Britain, Britain and Western Europe is for America.[7] At any rate, it is this geographical concept that explains so many things, from the conquest of Hawaii through the Spanish-American War, the building of the great Two-Ocean Navy, the Panama Canal, and American involvement in the First and Second World Wars to NATO.

But, while the explanation of a policy may be simple, its motives may not be. As with the age-old British policy of a Balance of Power, the actual practice long preceded its intellectual explanation in retrospect; and in its formulation imperial, political, commercial, rational, and religious motives were mixed. In America, too, the formation of tendencies more or less consciously in the direction of imperialism developed in the 1890s out of a variety of motives, among which perhaps most important was the desire to adapt and emulate the then seemingly successful policies of colonial expansion practiced by certain European races and nations. The conscious promoters of American public opinion in this direction were a group of very intelligent people, among whom Captain Mahan and Theodore Roosevelt stand out. Let us, then, look at the record of this new kind of American expansion from 1898 onward.

In 1898 the United States provoked a war with Spain over Cuba. During the next thirty years she became not merely the central but the tutelary Power over the Caribbean area. The United States conquered Cuba and Puerto Rico by war; in 1903 she acquired the Panama Canal through an ingenious *coup d'état* that involved the creation of an artificial republic (a practice to which the Soviet Union was to resort later on several occasions); in 1917 she bought the Virgin Islands from

[7] Whether this means that Britain has now become a "Second Holland" is still, to some extent, an open question. (Written in 1959. It is hardly an "open question" any longer: 1965.)

Denmark under some duress; the United States Marines intervened in Mexico and Nicaragua (and, since this was written, in the Dominican Republic); they were stationed for years in the latter and in Haiti. More significant is the history of American expansion in the Pacific, involving island groups far removed from the American mainland. The acquisition of Hawaii (achieved through a fraudulent *coup d'état*), of further Pacific islands of the Samoa type, and of the Philippines in the Spanish-American War were but steppingstones in the construction of an American Pacific Empire. They were justified by a now complex sheaf of nationalist arguments, in which the earlier strands of Manifest Destiny were mixed with the newer ones of the White Man's Burden, of Liberation, with that of International Policemanship.[8]

Still, there were sufficient strong sources of American political idealism that would react against the often only crudely varnished ambitions of imperialist expansion. President Cleveland refused to countenance the *coup d'état* in Hawaii. Liberals, patriots, Progressives, Democrats, certain conservatives, and influential public figures protested against the American suppression of the Philippine guerrillas and against many instances of Caribbean intervention. Waves of pragmatist idealism rose in the early 1910s and then again from about 1928 onward. These led to the improvement of relations with Mexico, to new Latin-American policies, to the withdrawal of the Marines from Nicaragua and from Haiti, and to the Congressional abrogation of the so-called Platt Amendment in 1934, promising the withdrawal of American forces from Cuba except for a naval base;

[8] Whatever the moral shortcomings of Theodore Roosevelt's arguments, the United States as well as the free world must still honor his name. His understanding of world history and of sea power provided the foundations for the security of American victory in two world wars and even for America's strategic position today.

in 1946 followed the recognition of Philippine independence (even though American air and naval bases were to remain in the islands). Meanwhile several international experiments, beginning with the International Court of The Hague through the Kellogg Pact to the United Nations, received liberal American support.

The sentiments of American anti-imperialism and of American national interests have been nevertheless sufficiently entangled to make it quite impossible to delineate two camps of conflicting American opinion. Often it is more difficult to disentangle American than Russian realities: the relationship between American political ideologies and American national interests is more complicated than that between Russian national interests and the official Soviet ideology. I must attempt to disentangle some of these sentiments and inclinations in the next chapter; but here I must return to the historical evolution of American expansion during the Second World War.

When the Second World War began in Europe, American memories were still sufficiently impressed with the horrible and, to Americans, disillusioning story of the First World War. The desire not to get involved was still overwhelming, even though public sympathy was beginning to be impressed with the atrociously aggressive record of Germany and Japan. We have seen the chain of great events that during the leadership of Franklin Roosevelt gradually wore down this popular inclination toward neutrality; we have also seen how the expansion of American possessions even before Pearl Harbor began to bring the mightiest Republic into the decisive area of the war. From Iceland through Greenland, Bermuda, the Bahamas, and the Antilles a whole chain of Danish and British territories became American military outposts in 1940 and in 1941. These were understandable defense measures,[9] taken in full agree-

[9] Less excusable was the arbitrary removal of Japanese-American citizens from the west coast after Pearl Harbor. The historical and strategic significance of this governmen-

ment with the governments of Denmark, Canada, and
Britain; in the Atlantic Charter, signed in 1941, and
thereafter the American government frequently and
sincerely denied any American desire for territorial ag-
grandizement. Still, it was apparent even before the
end of the war that the United States would now
emerge as the mightiest nation of the world; already
during the war President Roosevelt prepared the establishment of American bases in faraway places, from
Saudi Arabia and Libya to Okinawa.

Thus by the end of the war, in 1945, we may detect
the coexistence of two overlapping currents of American
sentiment. On one hand, the expectable and widespread sentiment to bring home the far-flung sons of
ten million American families prevailed; on the other
hand, the feeling that world leadership belonged to
America was already widespread, evident in many different facets (among them the establishment of the
United Nations in New York). Evidently American isolationism was dying—if, indeed, it was ever a real ideology rather than an imprecise blanket term for anti-
European currents and xenophobe opinions.

4

In the first part of this book I traced the conflict between Russia and America as it developed through the
history of the cold war. At various points during that
narrative I had to draw attention to the evolution of a
new kind of not always conscious American imperial
expansion, seldom recognized by politicians and expert

tal security measure (one of those quick reflex actions that
reveal essential national concepts of self-interest in a flash)
corresponds with the Russian removal of the Volga Germans
to Siberia during the same year. The American action was,
of course, executed in a much more humane fashion.

commentators but foretold twenty years before 1945 by an American poet, Robinson Jeffers, in his lines about the boiling American heavy mass, "thickening to empire." Thus the relatively recent evolution of American expansion need not be retold again. Yet it is at this point that a parallel geographical survey of the status and of the recent fluctuations of the Russian and American domains during the cold war is warranted, even though there is no parallel in the often so benevolent methods of this American expansion and the brutal methods of Communist Russian conquests.

The Russian state forms the core of the vast Eurasian continent. Officially called "The Union of Soviet Socialist Republics," in theory and to some extent in practice it is, like the United States, a federal union of commonwealths (States in the United States, Republics in the U.S.S.R.). Of its fifteen component Republics the largest and most important is the Great Russian one, dotted here and there by so-called "Autonomous Republics" and districts (somewhat like Indian reservations in the States of the American Union).

The frontiers of the Soviet Union are not unduly overextended. They are not very different from the frontiers of the Russian Empire of a hundred years ago. In Europe during the Second World War the Soviet Union incorporated the three small Baltic Republics, took a slice of Finland, the eastern provinces of Poland, a sharp small segment of East Prussia including the port of Königsberg (now Kaliningrad), the provinces of Bessarabia and Bukovina from Rumania, and the Trans-Carpathian province of Ruthenia (Carpatho-Ukraine), which belonged to Czechoslovakia before the Second World War and to Hungary before the First. In Asia, Stalin regained the southern half of Sakhalin Island from Japan and added the southern Kurile Islands to the Russian domains.[10]

[10] In addition to the small Central Asian province of

Yet we must keep in mind that most of these territories had been part of the Russian Empire before 1914; and most of them were inhabited by Russian, Byelorussian, and Ukrainian populations. (For a hundred years before 1914 most of Poland and all of Finland were Russian provinces; today Warsaw is the capital of Poland and Finland an independent nation.) During the nineteenth century Russia's imperial frontiers extended further into Europe than they do today.

At the end of the Second World War, Russia overextended herself not so much in her national territory (which, all Communist solidarity notwithstanding, is still separated by barbed wires and mine fields from her satellite neighbors) as in her jealous and aggressive control over a ring of buffer states in Europe, consisting of the satellite republics of Poland, Czechoslovakia, Hungary, Yugoslavia, Rumania, Bulgaria, and Albania in Europe; in Asia she kept tight control over her vassal state of Mongolia and established another satellite state in North Korea. Beyond this ring of subservient vassal states the Soviet Union maintained military zones of occupation in East Germany and eastern Austria; she occupied naval bases on the Porkkala-Udd Peninsula in Finland, in Port Arthur and Dairen in China, while over the Manchurian railroads and in Sinkiang a Sino-Russian condominium existed.

Now let us look at the fluctuations of these domains during the twenty years of the cold war. In 1948 Yugoslavia broke away from the Russian satellite system. In 1955 the Russians evacuated eastern Austria. They returned the Porkkala naval base to Finland. In 1960 they abandoned their submarine base in Albania. In Asia they relinquished their control over Sinkiang; they returned Port Arthur and the Manchurian railroads to China. In 1948 they removed their troops from North

---

Tannu Tuva. (See above, page 86. See also page 89, note 6.)

Korea, since that country was transformed into a full-fledged Communist satellite state; but in consequence to the development of the Korean War, China rather than Russia exercises predominant influence in North Korea now; and recently even in the oldest of Russian satellites, in the Outer Mongolian vassal state, currents of independence together with Chinese influences have begun to grow. We have seen, moreover, that the Russians suggested the eventual withdrawal of their troops from East Germany, too, if, in turn, American troops would leave West Germany; and they proposed that they might return some of the southern Kuriles to Japan in exchange for Japan's loosening of her tight military relationship with the United States. Meanwhile in Europe, even though Russia succeeded in re-establishing her influence over her satellites after the, to her, dangerous and chaotic events of 1956, the sovereignty and the independence not only of Poland but of virtually all other Communist satellite states has significantly increased.

Despite mutual professions of friendship, offers of Russian alliance, and the dispatch of Russian technical missions to new and unruly nations throughout the Middle East and Africa, up to now not one Russian base has been established beyond the Russian sphere;[11] and no alliance has been concluded with any nation beyond it.

Thus during the last twenty years, Russia has reduced the extent of her domains. Of course, the reason for this Russian recession is not an upsurge of Russian modesty. The reductions of these imperial outposts were calculated to promote corresponding concessions or advantageous impressions; they were not the consequences of external pressure; but we must understand the condition that in 1945 Russia, especially in Europe, may have bit off more than she has been able to digest.

"We have not sought an inch of territory after the

[11] With the erratic—and temporary—exception of Cuba, about which, however, see above, Chapter IX.

last war," said President Eisenhower on several occasions; yet, without doubting either the sincerity or the benevolent intentions of this President, it is the historian's duty to point out the necessary qualifications.

Let us begin with the great metropolitan core of the American Empire, providentially separated from other continents by the two largest oceans of the earth, virtually unconquerable by armies from other continents. This territory has been the same for more than one hundred years, since 1853. The forty-eight States first formed an unbroken block in 1912, at the very time when the American frontier was closing, when the United States became a Two-Ocean Power and the United States Navy was dominant in the Pacific as well as in the Atlantic. In 1959, for the first time in forty-seven years, for the first time since the Russian Revolution, and for the first time after two world wars, two new States, Alaska and Hawaii, were admitted to the Union. The admission of the latter, the addition of a multiracial group of islands, situated thousands of miles out in the Pacific, certainly marks a departure from the traditional territorial composition of the United States.

Further outward, then, beyond the component States of the Union, there is a garland of islands and territories, outer defense posts of the Republic in the Atlantic and the Caribbean, from Greenland to Puerto Rico and Panama; and in the Pacific there are scores of isolated corally island groups that became American domains during and after the last war. They include the Carolines, Marianas, Marshalls, and even the islands of Okinawa and Ie Shima, former possessions of Japan, on the very western edge of the great Pacific Ocean. The retention of these islands conquered from Japan is, to a considerable extent, dictated by interests of American national security. They mark the transformation of the Pacific into an overwhelmingly American strategic lake; and consequent to the Second World War in Europe the North Atlantic, too, has become largely, though of course not exclusively, an American strategic lake.

In 1945 the United States retained many of the strategic bases and territories which she had taken over during the war in agreement with the other North Atlantic nations: American bases remained in Greenland, Iceland, the Azores. During the cold war, from 1948 onward, the number of American military enclaves and air bases multiplied: in addition to the above-mentioned places in the Atlantic and Caribbean, the United States has acquired, erected, or maintained military enclaves and air bases in Britain, Spain, Italy, Germany, France, Morocco, Libya, Saudi Arabia, Turkey, Greece, South Korea, Japan, Formosa, the Philippines, Vietnam. In addition to these places, the United States has military missions and may use military bases in Norway, Denmark, Holland, Belgium, Luxembourg, Portugal, Iran, Pakistan, Australia, New Zealand, Siam. Even this list is not quite exhaustive: there are a number of other countries where the United States maintains missions of a technical nature whose existence is of course, also connected with American national interests.

There are exceptions to this general movement of American military extension, too. They are the withdrawal of the American garrisons from western Austria in 1955, the withdrawal of the revolutionary government of Iraq from the so-called Baghdad Pact in 1958, the withdrawal of American forces from Lebanon in October 1958 after the earlier landing of the Marines in that year, the later evacuation of air bases in Morocco and the promise to Japan of restoring some of the Ryukyus to Japanese rule.

There is no question that many of these new American establishments abroad are obvious consequences of America's own strategic position in the world, that they are necessary and reasonable defense measures, warranted by the central geographical position and the potentially aggressive power of the Russian Communist

Empire. Still, the very extensiveness of this new list of American domains and bases abroad suggests at least the development of a new and not merely temporary conception of American national interests, representing a departure from earlier American traditions. I have already implied, in Chapter VII, how this world-wide extension of American bases and colonies abroad has affected a new American generation, introducing new elements into the historical development of American society and politics.[12] Here, however, our concern is not with the future of American society but with the conflict of American and Russian national interests.

5

Even with their world-wide extension, even in this age of diminished distances, the national cores of the Russian and the American Empires are still far away from each other. Thus with the exception of the peak period of the cold war, 1952–56, they have treated each other's vital national interests with considerable caution and even respect. The Soviet Union has interfered little with the American position in the Western Hemisphere. Even in the bitterest and most suspicious beginning phase of the cold war, in 1947, the Russians agreed in the United Nations to the American trusteeship over vast areas in the Pacific; they did not protest

[12] From the daily Bulletin of the U. S. Department of Commerce of 29 April 1965: Wanted: "Service and materials to perform a RESEARCH STUDY ENTITLED 'PAX AMERICANA' consisting of a phased study of the following: (a) Elements of National Power; (b) Ability of selected nations to apply the elements of National Power; (c) A variety of world power configurations to be used as a basis for the U.S. to maintain world hegemony in the future. Quotations and applicable specifications will be available upon request, at the Army Research Office, 3845 Columbia Pike, Arlington, Va., until 1 May 1965."

against the incorporation of Alaska or of Hawaii into the
Union; and even when local unruly revolutionary governments were causing evident trouble in America's
own tropical Caribbean back yard, the Russian government acted with unusual circumspection, at most protesting by word or extending some economic support to
Mexico, Guatemala, or Cuba. The United States, too,
by and large followed the policy expressed as early as
1920 by the then uncompromisingly anti-Communist
Democratic Secretary of State, Bainbridge Colby, that
it was not in the interests of the United States to promote the partition or the dissolution of the Russian
state proper. It is true, on the other hand, that the
United States has not recognized the Russian incorporation of the Baltic Republics, that at times semi-official
and Congressional authorities have made statements
about the desirability of an independent Ukraine or
even of other traditionally component parts of the Soviet
Union, but these were not the official policies of the
Department of State.

Thus we can see how geography is still a basic factor
in international affairs: the United States protests but
does not intervene in Tibet (or even in Hungary); the
Russians protested but did not intervene in Guatemala
(and they withdrew from Cuba).

Thus we must keep in mind that there is little *direct*
conflict between the Russian and American Empires.[13]
Except in the Arctic region the two states do not border
on each other; except at certain points in the Far East
and in Europe, their respective alliance systems do not
border upon each other either. The cold war arose not
because of Russian ambitions directly aimed at the
United States but because of Russian ambitions in Europe and specifically in Germany. From the history of

[13] Hence the feasibility, and the historical significance,
of the Treaty recognizing the international (or, rather, supranational) character of Antarctica, signed by the United
States and the Soviet Union in 1959.

Russian foreign relations and from the contemplation of certain geographical realities, therefore, certain conditions emerge.

First, that there is relatively little conflict between Russian and American national interests in the Orient. There these two nations of the white race are marginal Powers with sparsely inhabited territories and far-flung outposts arching over from the north over the teeming and turbulent scene of the Far East. Consequently, the relations of Russia and America naturally improve whenever a Far Eastern power becomes powerful and aggressive. Thus in the 1930s Japanese expansion brought their interests closer together. Thus nowadays a similar situation may be developing because of China.

In the second place, the central area of the Russian-American conflict is not really that of the "uncommitted" nations of the world, not even the Middle East or Africa: there the Russians may be now learning the lesson that economic aid may really not get them very far. The center of the conflict is still in Europe, and particularly in Germany—so long as the United States insists on a fully rearmed and united Germany allied with the West, so long as the Russians insist on the recognition of a permanently Sovietized East German regime. We have seen that Central and Eastern Europe may be the principal theater of history in the twentieth century; it is there that the First and the Second World Wars broke out; it is there that the subsequent peace settlements were woefully insufficient, having sowed seeds of future conflicts; it is there that Russia feels her vital interests involved. This was why Khrushchev flew into a rage whenever Eastern Europe was mentioned by the Americans; for example, he almost upset the Applecart of Coexistence during Vice-President Nixon's visit to Russia in 1959 because of a thoughtless as well as harmless routine endorsement of "Captive Nations Week" by the United States Congress. This is why the Russians are restive about the continued existence of West Berlin in the middle of East Germany; this is why they have become a *status quo* Power; this is why they have given up their attempts to subvert or conquer West Germany or Western Europe while they are supremely anxious to insure the international, and particularly American, recognition of the *status quo* in Eastern Europe, perhaps preferably before the Germans possess atomic weapons.

It is in the interest of the world to understand this Russian position, resting upon geographical realities. But this understanding need not mean acquiescence in the permanent division of Europe. It is, in any case, in the interest of the world to seek some Central and Eastern European solution before Germany becomes powerful and dominant again.

For the relations of Germany and Russia are perhaps even more decisive than the relations of America and Russia in the twentieth century.[14] A German-Russian alignment, leading nearly inevitably to the partition of large portions of Eastern Europe, is the supreme danger not only to Eastern Europe but also the West. We have seen that, had Germany and Russia been allies, they might have won either of the two World Wars; had he not attacked Russia, Hitler's Germany might have been unbeatable. And yet this does not mean that it is necessarily in the interest of the Western Powers to promote hostility between Germany and Russia. As bad as a truculent German-Russian alliance is the situation when the Atlantic Powers tacitly give a free hand to either Germany or Russia in Eastern Europe: for this is what Chamberlain did at Munich and Roosevelt at Yalta. Meanwhile neither America nor Russia feels that she could let all of Germany slip away from her sphere of influence; and we have seen how by now both of them, as well as France and perhaps even Britain, prefer the present division of Germany rather than the at-

[14] Like the relations between America and Britain. See below, pages 381–82.

tempt to risk the unification of Germany at the price of mutual withdrawals. Even the Germans may accept this state of affairs for a while. Or they may not.

It all seems like a neat series of geographical and strategic equations. The Germans cannot oppose America and Russia at the same time; against the Russians they need the Americans. The British need either America or Russia against Germany; they need either Germany or America against Russia. The Japanese can confront China or Russia or both only when they have America's support. China may be able to struggle against either Japan, America, or Russia alone, but not really against any combination of two of them. The Russians can hold their own against China, Japan, Germany, or even against the United States, but never against any combination of three of them. None of the Powers, except perhaps for the United States, can afford the prospects of a struggle on two main fronts. Of all the Great Powers, the United States alone could face the last World War on two vast fronts, conducting them simultaneously, concluding them victoriously. She may do so again. Or she may not.

6

At this point it may seem that we have reached the realities and the causes of the cold war on the level of geography. It is as if there were some kind of Newtonian Rule of Gravitation among the Great Powers of the world. America and Russia, two great distant Empires, growing up unnoticed, expanding gradually, involved in two World Wars, bumping at each other in the vacuum created by Germany at the end of the Second World War. It all sounds very logical, this kind of politico-geographical Newtonism, like the above-mentioned Power-Balance Equations, like the rules often proposed by Experts in the Science of International

Relations—except that in science it is always the rules that count and in history the exceptions; for history, like life, is neither scientific nor logical. There is much truth in the proposition that geography determines the relations of the Great Powers—much, but not all.

Nor does technology. Communications and new weapons develop; but human nature does not really change. Sometimes man may alter the face of the earth: but the building of the Panama Canal was a consequence, not a cause, of American expansion; and the building of the Trans-Siberian Railroad, a consequence, not a cause, of Russian expansion, involved the timing, but not the main national motive, of the Japanese attack on Russia. In America the technological progressive view of history made "isolationism" finally disreputable. Americans tend to regard history as if it were but the Story of Progress. They have many reasons to regard the development of communications as if this historical development would by itself have caused America's involvement in the wider affairs and areas of the world. American history textbooks have little charts that show how the Atlantic has "shrunk"; in 1620 it took six weeks to cross that ocean, in 1820 three weeks, in 1920 six days, in 1960 six hours . . . Obviously today, in the age of the submarine, jet plane, transoceanic rocket, hydrogen bomb, America is more vulnerable than she was in the past. Of course technical developments have deeply involved the destiny of the United States.

And yet, as we survey American history, we may see that American involvements in the wars of Europe do not at all follow such a clear pattern of progressive increase. In the seventeenth century America was not much involved in the great wars of the European Powers; in the eighteenth century, until 1815, America was involved virtually in every European and world war; in the nineteenth century the Union was not involved; in the twentieth she chose to be involved again. Note that I said "chose": for the factor of these fluctuations may be varied: geography, strategy, technology, are important elements, but ultimately it is not blind Fate but human choice that decides.

Does the progress of technology alter the relations of nations? To some extent, yes; essentially, no; consider, for instance, how in 1914 the United States was safer from the danger of foreign invasions than one hundred years before, when a British force could stream into Washington and burn the White House. Does the diminution of distances mean the diminution of ignorance with which the peoples of the world regard each other? To some extent, yes; necessarily, no; consider how in this century millions know something about other nations, other millions visit other nations as tourists, but does this tremendous increase in communications correspondingly decrease misunderstandings among nations? As in the relations of persons, proximity may lead to understanding or to contempt, to enmity or to friendship. For it is not the instruments but the tendency of the relationship that counts; it is *not the technical conditions of distance but the direction of sentiments* that ultimately determines the relations of human beings.

Thus Washington's Farewell Address, forgotten and qualified nowadays as if it had been a noble but by now impractical admonition against the involvement of American sentiments in the affairs of the nations of Europe, at closer reading remains as timely as ever. For the sentiments and opinions of peoples remain the main motive force of nations. It is these sentiments that are formulated into conceptions of national interest; for national interest is not a fixed, constant category that automatically adjusts to ratios of geographical proximity and military power. National interest, like self-interest, tends to produce its own rationalizations; but national interest, like self-interest, is the product of sentiments, inclinations, tendencies, ideas. Thus again we find that though on one hand life is stronger than theory, on the other hand ideas are part and parcel of life itself: for national interest is what people think it is. There is more to it than meets the eye.[15]

[15] This is the main, though seldom observed, condition of Ranke's concept about the primacy of foreign policy in history. We must understand the inner life rather than the abstract principle of a State. *"Unter dem Prinzip des Staates haben wir nicht eine Abstraktion der Meinung, sondern sein inneres Leben zu verstehen."*

CHAPTER XV

The Two Nations:
The Development of Their National Character

(The National Element: The Tendencies
of Russian and American Nationalism)

1

We still live in an era of national states. The principal
motive of their decisive actions is still national interest.
But to say this is not sufficient; to leave the argument
at that is not enough.

We find the same problems with this concept on the
individual level. The main motive factor in the actions
of individuals is self-interest: but this is a truism. Take
such different modern thinkers as Machiavelli, La
Rochefoucauld, Bentham, Stendhal, Tocqueville, Marx,
Freud—yes, of course, this is what all of them say. But
the better thinkers among them (Stendhal rather than
Bentham, Tocqueville rather than Marx) do not leave it
at that; they see deeper motives: fear and greed, guilt
and ambition, all entangled; the best of these men see
vanity (a forgotten word nowadays) as the most basic
of human motives. For what is self-interest, after all?
Its formation comes from the concept of the self: an
entangled thing, a complex thing, a tendency rather
than a category, an aspiration rather than a constant.

The character of a person is formed as well as revealed by his own concepts of self-interest.

These are concepts that change with time. They are
often formed by the influence of other persons. Except
in rare instances they cannot be accurately defined; but

they nevertheless exist. So it is with the interest of a nation; the character of a nation, too, is revealed by its own concepts of self-interest, by the nation's own image of itself, by its own concept of the place it would like to occupy and of the figure it would like to cut in the world.

Thus the geographic situation of a nation to a large extent defines its foreign policy—the conduct of which, in turn, is largely formed by the nation's character. Thus the history of a state is formed by its concept of national interest, which, in turn, reveals certain dominant elements in the character of the nation. Take Britain, for example. Her geographical situation is obvious; but the conduct of British foreign policy also reflects the willingness to mediate, to compromise, the inclination to pragmatism and the racial self-confidence that are recognizable elements in the British national character. Take France: the French desire for natural frontiers, France's concepts of national security, from Henri IV to Clemenceau, from Richelieu to De Gaulle, reflect recurring characteristics that transcend the changing conditions of politics as well as the merely physical conditions of geography: the French penchant for security, precision, clarity, the peculiarly French kind of dashing selfishness, the peculiarly Gallic kind of egocentric logic, are all reflected therein.

"The peoples of the world," wrote Gustave Le Bon, "are governed not by their institutions but by their characters." "The life of nations," said Proust, "merely repeats, on a larger scale, the lives of their component cells; and he who is incapable of understanding the mystery, the reactions, the laws that determined the movements of the individual, can never hope to say anything worth listening to about the struggles of nations."

These national characteristics are by no means extinct in our day. Today, while the internationalization of the world proceeds, in a countervailing development nations are also becoming more homogeneous than ever before. Consider only the political eclipse of cosmopolitan ruling classes, the infrequency of intermarriage between various races and peoples despite the popularity of mass tourism, the development of national prototypes and habits in this era of mass communications, promoted by the standardization of life and of thought. Consider even developments behind the iron curtain, even in nations whose societies were so badly torn by war and so forcefully remade from top to bottom. Consider the Hungarian Revolution. Did the Hungarian people rise in 1956 because of their economic conditions? No. Did they rise because they wanted to do away with the nationalization of their industries; did they want to restore Capitalism? No. Did they revolt because of their sense of deep injuries to their national interest? Yes. And was not their very concept of their national interest, dissatisfied with the initial Russian concessions, expressed in impulsive, at times heroic and even unrealistic demands? Yes; for these very actions reflected typical Hungarian national characteristics. The Hungarian Revolution turned out to be the way it was not because it was post-Socialist, national-Communist, crypto-Fascist, or what not, but because it was a *Hungarian* Revolution—just as the Russian Revolution in 1917 was a Russian and the French Revolution in 1789 a very French Revolution.

National interest would be a constant factor, geographically ascertainable, strategically predictable, if human beings would be the same everywhere. And human beings *are* essentially the same—except that their actions and reactions are different when their standards and aspirations are different.

Thus these concepts of national interest are not always constant and not always consistent: the same isolationists in America who in 1940 strictured their government for extending support to Britain, in 1958 supported another Administration as it sent Marines into Lebanon.

And national character may be also tempered and conditioned by historical experience: the otherwise impulsive, romantic, feckless Poles in 1956 acted in a different manner from their revolutions in the past.

We must understand this important condition: national character is a tendency, not a category. A person is born with certain characteristics; he inherits tendencies; he acquires inclinations through life. Some of these are strong and enduring, others are ephemeral. For life consists of constant tensions: a person is formed, pulled, pushed by characteristics inherited from his father, by others inherited from his mother, as well as by his acquired personal desires, vanities, ambitions, obligations, loyalties, and fears consequent to his position in the world. So with the history of nations. Human (and historic) life is a succession of choices, which every conscious human being has to make every moment. At times these choices are of decisive importance; and the very quality of these choices will often reveal that person's character and decide his fate. But that fate is by no means prescribed: for he may go beyond his inclinations, inherited as well as acquired ones. The decision and the responsibility is his: for he is a free moral agent, responsible for his actions.

It is here that the analogy between the nature of persons and the nature of nations breaks down, even though there are great similarities between persons and nations, even though a nation is a more organic phenomenon than a state. Still, apart from the persons and groups that compose it, a nation has no life of its own. Thus, while a person is responsible for his actions, a nation is responsible only in part; for a nation has but a halfway sort of claim to immortality. Men die and disappear from this earth, whereas nations do not die for a long, long time; but whereas the soul of a man is liable to Divine Judgment and is immortal, the soul of a nation is not.

2

We have seen how the Empire of the Russians expanded at times westward, at times eastward, following varying lines of least resistance. When the European gates seemed closed, the Russians tried in Asia; when they met with congealing resistance there, they often turned back to Europe. This is a pattern that may be discerned throughout the centuries, including the Soviet period: Lenin trying in Europe until 1920, then in Asia in the twenties, then Stalin on the European border from 1939 to 1949, switching his support to the Chinese Communists finally when he abandoned the blockade of Berlin.

But these often alternating movements are part of the larger historic movements of the Russian pendulum. The seventeenth century, from Ivan the Terrible to Peter the Great, was, by and large, an "Eastern" period, when Poland and Sweden blocked Russia from Europe. A "Western" period, lasting two hundred years, followed from Peter the Great to Lenin, as the Russian Empire grew into Europe, when Russia became a member of the European group of Powers.

It is rather evident, this Russian position in the world: a mighty nation straddling Eurasia, the vastest of the continents, attracted by two directions, its national, racial, religious, political, cultural characteristics and habits revealing European as well as Asiatic strands.

The roots and sources of this Russian duality between West and East derive, of course, from the remote past in the history of Russia. They are particularly evident in the history of the Russian Church and religion, Byzantine from its beginnings. For religion forms as well as reflects the most important characteristics and inclinations of a nation; and the history of the Russian Church is full of significant things. The origins of the iron curtain are there in the schism between the Eastern and Western Churches, going back almost one thousand years; but the schisms *within* the Russian Church, too, particularly its crisis during the dark seventeenth century, are full of significant details.[1]

During the nineteenth century, then, the dual tendencies crystallize around two opposing movements of thought, "Westernizers" and "Slavophiles." Originally the names of two literary schools, they represent the two poles around which the creative talents of nineteenth-century Russia gather. The "Westernizers" are the pro-Europeans, those aristocrats, liberals, intellectuals who believe that Russia is hopelessly backward, that she must shake off the remnants of a barbaric and Asiatic past to catch up with the more free and more advanced culture and institutions of Europe. The "Slavophiles" are the anti-Europeans, at times profound men who believe that the nations and the churches of Europe are rotten from within, that Moscow is really the Third Rome, and the Russian people, leaders of all Slavs, the Chosen People of God, uncorrupted by the rest of an immoral and heretical Europe. Toward the end of the century the war between these ideological schools of thought flickers out; the Westernizers seem to have the field for themselves. Yet the tendencies remain; and they furnish an important clue to Russian history up to the present day.

It is a history full of paradox. In 1914 the leadership, the institutions, the intelligentsia, the upper-class cul-

---

[1] The emergence of the "Old Believers," for example: an Orthodox faction, puritanical, fundamentalist, intensely national and revivalist, it survived until the present day. Some of its inclinations reveal a similarity with certain American fundamentalist sects and tendencies.

ture of Russia, seem more Western, more European than ever before. Virtually all the important movements are progressive, anti-Asiatic, Western, including the Bolsheviks, who, after all, got their ideology from the West. With their atheism, materialism, progressivism, they seem on the surface the most extreme anti-Asiatic movement of all. But there is that tendency in the history of ideas: when you push something to its extreme, you arrive at its very opposite. The Revolution came; the Bolsheviks won; but the Russia that congealed and consolidated around them was full of anti-European, Slavophile characteristics. The alliances with France and Britain, with those most advanced and Western nations, were rejected; Russia refused Europe; she turned away from Europe; she separated herself from Europe by an iron curtain as early as in 1921. Very symbolic was the removal of the Russian capital from Petrograd to Moscow, from the cosmopolitan port and capital newly built by Peter, from "the window to the West," back to old Moscow, to that sprawling and formless metropolis in the middle of the Eurasian plain, with its Old Believers and occasional Tatar countenances. From Petrograd to Moscow, from Winter Palace to the closed fortress of the Kremlin: indeed, the modern history of Russia may be divided into Petrograd and Moscow Periods, roughly corresponding to Westernizing and Slavophile phases. It was as if after two hundred years the United States had decided to move her national capital from New York to Chicago; as if American history, consequent to great revolutions, would fall into alternating New York and Chicago periods.

Consider the struggle between these two opposite personalities, Trotsky and Stalin: it, too, will reveal how differences in national characteristics are often at the bottom of it all. "Self-interest": did they struggle over economics; were they jealous of each other's material benefits? Obviously not. Was the struggle ideological;

did they represent clashing political systems and theories? No, not really; both of them were avowed and convinced Communists (it is true that they accused each other of ideological heresy, but let us keep in mind how such exaggerated theoretical attributions are hardly more than rationalizations of the deeper personal divergences). The struggle between Trotsky and Stalin was, at bottom, the struggle between the brilliant, cosmopolitan, intellectual Jewish world revolutionary and the cunning, suspicious, Judaeophobe, semi-Asiatic peasant master of Russia. All of their ideological and theoretical differences (the one thinking primarily of world revolution,[2] the other thinking primarily of Russia) flow from these differences in personal character, with their inherently different national inclinations. It is not at all surprising that Stalin won, even though he was born in Georgia, even though he was a Communist tyrant: he was the more typically Russian of the two.

The writings of Lenin are full of the usual invectives against the old Russian regime, "an Asiatic regime," he writes, the most pejorative of all adjectives in the Russia before the Revolution. "Why do you say that we do not understand you?" said Stalin to the Japanese Foreign Minister Matsuoka in April 1941. "We are Asiatics, too."

It is possible to divide outstanding representatives of Russia into two groups: for beneath the expectable categories of rich and poor, conservatives and radicals, religious and anti-religious people, there is this deeper and more enduring division of relative Westernizers and relative Slavophiles, pro-Europeans and anti-Europeans. Peter and Ivan, Chaadayev and Khomyakov, Turgenev and Dostoevski, Witte and Pobedonostsev, Milyukov and Rasputin, Trotsky and Stalin, Litvinov

---

[2] His concept of Permanent Revolution meant primarily revolution in Europe. (The young Trotsky once called the Bolsheviks "Slavophilizing Marxists.")

and Molotov, Pasternak and Sholokhov—very different persons, with very different backgrounds and ideologies, but, still, they represent these respective antipoles.

3

But, again: life is stronger than theory. These are powerful tendencies rather than categories: the categories do not always fit everyone, and they are never complete. The mixture and the dual attraction of the two strains is there most clearly in Tolstoi, about whom the Marquis de Vogüé wrote that he was a mixture of chemist and Buddhist,[3] but the duality is there, too, in Herzen, Bakunin, Lenin, even in Khrushchev.

Peter the Great was the great original architect of Westernization. But his person, too, was complex; thus no matter how "Western" his purposes, his methods were often Oriental to the extreme. On the other hand, Stalin is our modern prototype of isolationist, anti-European Russia; but he never really attempted to question the dogmatic validity of Marxism; no matter what he did in practice and no matter how he extolled the Russian origin of modern inventions, it never occurred to him to slow down the technological and industrial transformation of Russia, emulating European and American patterns, inventions, and institutions in practice.

We should, moreover, observe the relative attractions of two opposite movements to each other: for this is often a reliable indication of their enduring strength. By about 1900 Westernization seemed to have triumphed over Slavophilism, reasonably enough, for the latter seemed to have been reactionary, dark, inconsistent, and useless. Yet a closer look at the nineteenth

---

[3] A phrase that Chesterton borrowed as he coined the stronger one: "the mixture of an inhuman Puritan and a presumptuous savage."

century will reveal how many more outstanding Russian personalities had become Slavophiles after having started out as Westernizers than the reverse: Dostoevski may be the most outstanding example. The Slavophiles were at least the more consistent ones throughout: for the *idées reçues* of the Westernizers changed throughout the century, dependent on the principal intellectual and radical political currents of Europe, while the *idée mère* of the Slavophiles remained largely the same. And at least in one important respect the Slavophiles—with all of their otherwise inconsistent, often fraudulent, semi-Buddhist mysticism—reflected an insight superior to that of the Westernizers: they recognized the enduring and supreme importance of religion in a century when, almost without exception, the Westernizers echoed the progressive European schools of thought that proclaimed the advance of mankind away from religion and tradition into the final progressive phase of an age of reason and science.[4]

Around the time of the Revolution there developed a Russian school of thought that for some time flourished within Bolshevik Russia as well as within the circles of the émigrés, formulating a philosophy of "Eurasianism." Its proponents looked at Russia as if she belonged neither to Europe nor to Asia but formed a continental civilization of her own. The intellectual influence of this doctrinaire school was short-lived; but it expressed a tendency that has been, consciously or unconsciously, represented by many personalities of modern Russia.

Then came Stalin's Oriental isolation from Europe, with his Oriental patterns of rule, of treachery, of suspicion, reminiscent of the isolationism of pre-Petrine

---

[4] The outstanding exceptions are Chaadayev and, a century later, Pasternak. Chaadayev's inclinations and his later conversion to Catholicism are significant, while insufficient attention has been drawn to Pasternak's religious philosophy that is existentialist rather than dogmatic, and Western and Catholic rather than Eastern and Orthodox.

Russia or of Japan after the seventeenth century; he also gave some new support to the Russian Orthodox Church.[5]

After the Battle of Stalingrad the Russian armies began rolling westward; and no matter how strong were Stalin's anti-European inclinations, no matter how strident his new nationalism, no matter how rigid his iron curtain, there is reason to believe that Russia's new and extensive entry into Europe could not remain a purely strategic development. Despite the awesome weight of her power, Russia's Communist ideology remained unpopular and unattractive; and less than a decade after 1945 it was already evident that European culture attracted Russia much more than Russian institutions and ideas attracted Europe. Many things in Russia still reveal the powerful hold of the old, peasant, Slavic, puritanical, and anti-European traditions and currents; on the other hand, together with the gradual lifting of the iron curtain, the uneasy Russian feeling about the growing pressure of China may have been moving the Russian spirit again in a European direction. There is certainly reason to believe that, in the long run, the Westernizing movement introduced by Peter the Great still continues; that here, too, despite the move back to Moscow, despite Stalin's Khanate, continuity has been stronger than change; that, after all is said, Russia is still more a European than an Asiatic nation.

But this is no ground for an easy over-all optimism. Some of the most successful Westernizers, from Peter the Great onward, brought Russia closer to the West at

[5] The following dates are significant: under Lenin, in 1922 the great Orthodox monastery at Zagorsk was closed and made into a Center of Bolshevist Studies. Under Stalin, in 1946 it was returned to the Orthodox Church; its buildings were splendidly restored; in 1948 its seminary was opened; in 1950 pilgrimages to Zagorsk were resumed. Under Khrushchev this policy was maintained; by 1960, however, articles in *Pravda* criticized the monks' "exploitation" of the great popular attraction of that shrine.

the expense of certain Eastern European nations. And Russia may be influenced again by European ideas: but by what European ideas? For the past half millennium European ideas, good and bad ones, have been streaming out into the world and into Russia. The abolition of slavery, parliamentary government, the Red Cross, the discovery of the cause of tuberculosis, were European ideas; so were Marxism, Fascism, and the Hydrogen Rocket. Here we must observe that even the isolationist Slavophiles got their original ideas from Germany;[6] the folkish sentimentalism and the nationalist romanticism of German thinkers of the Fichte type in the early nineteenth century formed the very foundations of the Slavophile ideology.[7]

This does not mean that the Slavophiles were politically pro-German (though many of them were). But it means that, because in history and in life the national element is more profound than the ideological one, there may be some justification in observing the inclinations of persons and of nations toward other persons and nations representing national and cultural prototypes. Dostoevski's Francophobia and Turgenev's Francophilia are not superficial or accidental but reflect important inclinations of their character. To some extent this is also true of the opposite inclinations of a Litvinov and a Molotov in relation to Germany and Britain; or of the relative pro-Americanism, of the envy and admiration for the United States, represented by such people as Mikoyan and Khrushchev, as well as by the new masters of an industrialized Eurasian Empire.

[6] Like the Marxists, of course. The very name of the original Marxist Party in Russia, the Social Democratic Workers' Party, was borrowed from the German model.

[7] The influence of German literature on Dostoevski has hardly been recognized. Like so many Russian writers, he, of course, never acknowledged it even though he cribbed entire plots from E. T. A. Hoffmann and the German Gothic-tale tellers.

4

America's Slavophiles are the Isolationists; America's Westernizers are the Internationalists. The terms are relatively recent, but the origins of their dichotomy go far back in the history of the Republic. American, like Russian, isolationism was largely due to geography, to the uniquely isolated situation of the Republic; it also had a strong formative religious factor, flowing from the condition that many of the earliest settlers of North America were adherents of radical religious sects coming from the fringes of an otherwise baroque and bourgeois Europe. As in Russian history, the religious element is there from the very beginning. It is the concept of the Chosen People, an evangelical inclination that prevails throughout American history even though Church and State are separated in the American Constitution. The Puritanistic, Hebraic, Old Testament-inspired inclination to regard the United States as a unique nation in the whole history of the world, the people of a New Jerusalem with a universal, divine mission to reorganize mankind, has been echoed through American history. Especially the nineteenth century is full of startling examples of this kind of messianistic rhetoric, of such revolutionary and revivalist proclamations. Later it is there in the fundamentalism of the Populists in the 1890s and in the withdrawal from Europe in the 1920s (which so curiously corresponds with the Russian isolationism of that time, with its Slavophile elements); it is even there in the reformatory zeal of the early Progressives stretching into the New Deal years, and it is an element not entirely absent from the rising sea of American Catholic political sentiment carrying the vessels of an ideological anti-Communist crusade.

Yet during the history of American expansion, the

Isolationists are not always consistent; and when it comes to the history of American concepts of national interest, we cannot clearly distinguish among the tumultuous voices in America's political camps. There is no clear division of concepts, no consistent opposition of ideas between Isolationists and Internationalists, conservatives and liberals, Republicans and Democrats, progressives and stalwarts, Protestants and Catholics. In the 1850s Southern Democrats pressed for Caribbean annexations; in the 1870s, Northern Republicans. In the 1860s there were Northern Democrats who called for the annexation of Canada; in the 1890s, certain Republicans. Not only Southern expansionists but the abolitionist Bancroft suggested annexing portions of Mexico (he wrote from London that it "is safe as well as philanthropic" that the United States "rescue a large part of Mexico from anarchy"); but the radical and populist Walt Whitman, too, exulted in the sight of the manly "chastisement" of Mexico, while "our divine mission to clean up Mexico" was later proposed by Representative Dies, the founder of the Un-American Activities Committee, in the 1920s. The slogan of Manifest Destiny was first broadcast in the 1840s by O'Sullivan, a Midwestern Irish-American Democrat, a radical newspaperman; but it was the so-called "conservative" Republican McKinley who in 1899 said that "we need Hawaii as much and a great deal more than we did California; it is manifest destiny"; and it was the "liberal" Wilson who in 1919 advised Congress to accept the providential mission of American world leadership, "surely the manifest destiny of the United States." Theodore Roosevelt engineered the Panama *coup;* but it was his temperamental and political opposite Wilson who sent the Marines into Vera Cruz and who suggested the establishment of an American protectorate over Armenia. "America does not want any additional territories," said Wilson in 1916; within a year he intervened with Denmark to relinquish her West Indian

islands. The isolationist and "conservative" Coolidge
sent the Marines into Nicaragua and kept them in Santo
Domingo at the very time when his Secretary of State
proclaimed the Policy of Latin-American Solidarity and
the absolute unwillingness of the United States to "intervene or govern" in any Latin-American Republic.
Coolidge, who in his inaugural address said that "the
legions that the United States sends forth are armed,
not with the sword, but with the cross," later called on
America to assume the role of an International Police-
man while his friend Eaton, a Republican Congressman,
said that the United States must help "solve the problems" of neighboring nations, "because our Nation is the
big brother in the family."

On the other hand, throughout American history conservatives as well as liberals, senators as well as poets,
idealists and realists, and on occasion Isolationists as
well as Internationalists protested against crude concepts and policies of Manifest Destiny. The other side
of the coin of national expansion is that American trait
of national generosity that led to expansive civilization
rather than to brutality whenever the American flag
was planted further afield. There is no need to list here
the outstanding examples: the American feeding of
starving millions within Bolshevik Russia in 1921–22,
at the height of the isolationist period, is only one
example.

Obviously Isolationism ceased to be respectable after
Pearl Harbor. Some of its best orators, such as Senator
Vandenberg, passed into the internationalist camp by
1945. Of course this marked more sophisticated concepts of American interests, a more sophisticated approach to world affairs. Yet, again, we may ask whether
this development has been profound rather than superficial and even whether it has been so clear a gain at
all?[8] We have now seen that Internationalists, too, were

[8] De Gaulle on Roosevelt: "It was true that the isolationism of the United States was, according to the President,

often imbued with the sentiment of a Chosen People; as in Russian history, not all Isolationists or Slavophiles were Beasts and not all Internationalists or Westernizers Angels. We have seen how "conservative" and "isolationist" Republicans in 1951 called for American military intervention in China, in 1956 for "the establishment of American bases all around the world"; in 1958 their most prominent spokesmen, Senators Knowland and Bridges, strenuously supported American intervention in Lebanon, in an area of the world that, to them, had become directly related to American national interests. On the other hand, those Internationalists and "liberals" who were the most vociferous advocates of a global crusade against Nazi Germany in 1945 condemned the entire German people in the name of Democracy while they remained for a long time callously indifferent to the establishment of Soviet rule in Eastern Europe.

Thus the two camps were, and still are, inchoate and seldom consistent. Like "Slavophile," the term "Isolationist" is imprecise and inconsistent: the Slavophiles were no friends of Slavdom when it came to their enemy Catholic Poland; the Isolationists were not isolationists at all when it came to expansion westward, for they have been among the most vociferous proponents of American expansion—in the direction of the Pacific and of Asia. As among the Slavophiles, there is at least this lasting factor within the Puritanical philosophy of the isolationists, from Cotton Mather to Robert A. Taft: it is a distrust of Europe. Here, then, is an enduring and principal problem of the American national character: the still undecided question whether America and Europe form the same civilization or not. We shall have to return to the more profound implications of this question: here we must observe that it transcends

---

a great error now ended. But passing from one extreme to the other, it was a permanent system of intervention that he intended to institute by international law."

the political division of Isolationists and Internationalists. Judicious commentators of American literature observed this division, proposing the two categories of Palefaces and Redskins: the first, those American writers, seers, artists who, while recognizing the peculiar qualities of American innocence, longed for the traditions and institutions of a civilization that America did not possess; the second, those who exulted in the pristine, rude, manly uniqueness of a frontier civilization. Palefaces and Redskins in America, like Westernizers and Slavophiles in Russia: Bancroft, Mark Twain, Vachel Lindsay—Redskins; Prescott, Henry James, F. Scott Fitzgerald—Palefaces.

But, unlike in Russia, the categories fit very seldom. Only a minority of outstanding Americans, and only a very small minority of American statesmen, would fit into them. Especially in the twentieth century, in the characters of most outstanding Americans, of artists and statesmen alike, from Theodore Roosevelt to Eisenhower, the two divergent strains are deeply entangled. Every American Paleface was a bit of a Redskin; every Isolationist a bit of an Internationalist; every idealist a bit of an imperialist—and the reverse. The problem consists not in the proportions of the mixture but in the quality of the person; for the ingredients are essential, mixed at the bottom, inseparable.

Thus it may be argued that American statesmen in this century—Wilson, Coolidge, Franklin Roosevelt, Eisenhower, Kennedy—were idealistic moralists; that, no matter what their errors, these flowed from the unique quality of American idealism; that therefore they stand out in comparison with their older and more cynical European counterparts. And it may be argued, with equal cogency, that these Presidents were imperialists, imperialists of a new sort, covering up their concepts of national ambitions with high-flown moralistic oratory, eminently successful imperialists of a new kind. The two arguments are contradictory; yet both of them are true. How is this possible? Is the answer to be found in mere hypocrisy: that these men were idealistic moralists on the surface but determined imperialists in their hearts? This is what the enemies of America may say; but this is not true at all. To be hypocritical, one must be conscious of the contradiction between words and deeds, between image and reality; but in the case of these Americans, this is seldom so. The two tendencies are only contradictory to outsiders on occasion, or to us in retrospect; they were entangled within the hearts and minds of these very people.[9]

For Americans are not a simple people, really: with all of their wonderful energy, youthful willingness, faithful dedication, they often do not really know what they want. And all the exhortations of the best American public philosophers in favor of an American public purpose are voices not in the wilderness but rather voices in the void: for the national purpose of the United States will not become sufficiently clear until the American national character becomes sufficiently consolidated.

Where, then, may we find the traces of the differing concepts, the main hidden lines of the national dialogue, that, through their tension, generate the power and provide the choices that govern the course of the American ship of state? Where, then, may we find the sources of certain American characteristics, of that peculiar mixture of individualism with conformity, of self-confidence with fatalism, of generosity with inward fear? There exist deep emotional currents of suspiciousness together with a fatalism and with a hidden lack of

[9] This, then, demonstrates the point that human beings are governed by deeper truths, the logic of which transcends mathematics. I did not say that each of the two arguments are half truths, 50 per cent truths; I said that both of the statements may be true. The truth is not in the middle between these two seemingly contradictory statements; it is above them, encompassing them both.

national self-confidence[10] that mark the uneasy relationship of the United States and of Soviet Russia and
that, in turn, may have critical consequences in dangerous moments fraught with suddenly condensing risk of
war. What, then, are the sources of these American
complexities? We are close to the core of the American
national problem.

5

"Of all historical problems," said Henry Adams, "the
nature of national character is the most difficult and the
most important." It is especially difficult, especially important, in the history of the United States. For the
American national character has not yet sufficiently
crystallized, coagulated, jelled.

[10] This American inclination to fatalism is one of the few
worrisome enduring marks of the American character.
Though its manner and its origins are quite different, Puritan
rather than Oriental, it curiously corresponds to the deep-
seated fatalism within the Russian character. It certainly
counteracts the refreshing characteristic American belief in
individual will power and enterprise. Possibly the American
inclination to accept the determinism of science (for example, intelligence quotients determining the mental capacity
of persons; technology determining the progress of history)
is only a modern version of this deep-seated fatalistic tendency that reaches far back in American history, leading to
false rhetoric and revealing sometimes terrible pessimism together with a lack of belief in Free Will. Thus Lincoln: "I
claim not to have controlled events; I confess plainly that
events have controlled me." McKinley: "The evolution of
events, which no man could control, has brought these problems upon us." (About the Spanish-American War.) Also
John Hay at that time: "We could not escape our destiny."
And Senator Beveridge: "Fate has written our policy for us;
the trade of the world must and shall be ours." Wilson in
1917: "Matters lying outside our own life as a nation and
over which we had no control . . . despite our wish to keep
free of them, have drawn us more and more irresistibly into
their own current and influence." (Second Inaugural.)
Kennedy's favorite quotation (from Hemingway): Courage

But is it not true that there exist very specific American characteristics? "What, then, is this American, this New Man?"—have not these traits of a New Society of Equal People been described by intelligent foreign observers from the very beginning, from Crèvecoeur through Tocqueville to the present?

Yes: there are specific, observable, typical, and even historical American characteristics. But they are intensive rather than extensive; they are social rather than national; they involve the relations of Americans with each other rather than their relations with other nations. For many of the specifically social characteristics and democratic institutions described by Crèvecoeur or by Tocqueville are also largely true of Canadians, Boers, Australians, New Zealanders, of non-aristocratic, egalitarian, largely Protestant, and of transoceanic white people with a Western European cultural heritage.[11] And this history of the cold war (or, at that, any history that goes beyond the domestic history of American society) must be concerned with characteristic tendencies that are American rather than egalitarian, national rather than democratic.

But we cannot simply say that there is no such thing as the American national character. We must, instead, observe some of its problems, among which the first is that from the very beginning the American concept of nationality was unique.

The nation—evolving from *patria* and from *natio*—is in many ways a uniquely European historical phenomenon. Its roots are feudal, traditional, particular as well as linguistic, cultural, residential. The ingredients of a traditional nationality are common language, common institutions, common culture, the sameness of race, the

---

is "grace under pressure." It is not. It is one's own capacity to overcome one's fear.

[11] We must keep in mind that Tocqueville wrote his book, as he himself said, about Democracy rather than about America.

THE TWO NATIONS 375

consciousness of national limits, the ties with ancestry, the permanence of residence. The first three exist in the United States; the last four do not.[12]

From the very beginning of American history it appeared that to be an American is something slightly but fundamentally different from being an Englishman, Frenchman, Pole.

Somewhat like Russian nationalism, the American concept of nationality has been populist rather than traditional, ideological rather than patriotic, universal as well as particular. *Nomen est omen*—the United States of America, like the Union of Soviet Socialist Republics, is a general and open term; it does not refer to a national society but it has an implicitly universal meaning;[13] like "Soviet citizen," "American citizen" marks adherence to a political principle rather than nationality; there is theoretically no limit to what it may include.[14]

[12] *All* of these seven ingredients existed two hundred years ago. Then the greed of the slaveowners increased, dragging hordes of hapless Africans in filthy ship bottoms across the Atlantic. The seeds of a terrible conflict were sown, and the end is not yet. *Most* of the seven ingredients still existed one hundred years ago. Immigration together with limitless expansionism at home as well as abroad (I am referring to real-estate developers in the broadest sense, from city planners through frontier land speculators to imperialists) compromised the rest. Thus do the sons pay for the sins of their fathers. The racial riots in 1964–65: they are not "firebells in the night" (Jefferson's 1820 phrase); they are, rather, smoldering mattresses underneath the surface of urban life in Northern America.

[13] Professor Richard Van Alstyne: "Franklin used the terms 'nation' and 'empire' interchangeably. The imperial state, that is to say, was the national state."

[14] The recent American reaction to the granting of statehood to the Pacific island group of Hawaii reveals how even today Americans (overlooking whether Hawaii belongs to "America") believe that admission to the Union may be the supreme fortune that may attend any place or nation of the world. This is not unlike the official Soviet propaganda about

From the very beginning the sentiments of uniqueness and of universality have been mixed in American hearts. "It is not in physics alone that we shall be found to differ from the other hemisphere," wrote Jefferson. "I strongly suspect that our geographical peculiarities may call for a different code of natural law to govern relations with other nations from that which the conditions of Europe have given rise to there." A new American concept of international relations, yes; but, still, dependent upon specific geographical conditions. For the Founding Fathers of the Republic could be supreme realists; and thus the concept of American national interest began to take form, leading to the Monroe Doctrine: that the United States must be the leading Power in the Western Hemisphere. Thus, even though the word "nation" does not figure either in the Declaration or in the Constitution (the concept did not become current until the nineteenth century), the concept of national interest existed. Even though American nationality was something different from European nationality, the crystallization of an American national character was taking place. After all, the people of the new Republic had certain racial and cultural and religious traits: they were predominantly Anglo-Saxon, democratic, and Protestant.

Now the institutions of the American people are still predominantly Anglo-Saxon, democratic, and Protestant. But meanwhile the character of the American people has changed.

In order to illustrate this, let us observe for a moment two of the most basic reflections of character: face and language. It is easy to distinguish an American from other people by his clothes, by his speech, by

the "admission" of conquered territories (the Baltic nations, for example) into the U.S.S.R. Unlike the Soviet propaganda, however, whose very insincerity reveals an uneasy half consciousness covering up a hoary multitude of sins, the American attitude is sincere and generous.

his attitudes, by his gestures, by his very bearing, by his haircut, by his glasses: but not by his face. Take a series of photographs of typical national faces: you can see the English face from the Italian and even from the German or from the Irish; but is there such a thing as an American face? There was something like it more than a hundred years ago: think of Lincoln or of Uncle Sam, the latter a symbol whose very facial countenance was at least as representative as that of John Bull. But this is no longer true today: for the very physiognomy of the American people has changed.

It is a truism that speech and language reflect character. It is true of persons, and it is true of nations. Now, there was every reason to believe that, as time went on, the American language would become more and more different from the English. This desire for an American national language was expressed by Noah Webster at an early time, and thirty years ago, contemplating the then promisingly fresh outburst of American literature in contrast to the then pale, heavily Latinized literary language of England (the contrast between, say, a Hemingway and a Galsworthy), H. L. Mencken could propose that an American language already existed, a language that was more manly, vital, direct, and clear than the English literary tongue, that would gain in contrast as time progressed. And yet today we may see that Mencken was wrong. It is true that in accent, rhythm, spelling, vocabulary, and tenor the American popular language becomes ever more different from its British counterpart; but it may no longer be argued that American slang is sufficiently direct, clear, and vital to form the American language; instead, our everyday language has become encumbered, Germanic, artificial, bureaucratic, inorganic.[15]

[15] President Eisenhower in London, September 1959: "Our nations, with common traditions and almost a common language . . ." Those who are acquainted with Eisenhower's language from the record of his news conferences may, then,

It may not be exaggerated to say that by now American writers face but two alternatives: write English, or write gobbledygook.[16] This is not merely a literary problem. For the literary language forms the popular language as much as the reverse.

It would be perhaps exaggerated to say that while there is an American people and an American state, there is as yet no such thing as an American nation. But it is not exaggerated to say that the absorption of a mass of immigrants by the young American nation may not have been such an unqualified success story as we are generally told. Both mass immigration and the American frontier—the two most important developments in the history of America after the Civil War—closed around the First World War; but their tremendous impact still continues, gradually and underneath the surface of American political life. Its indirect effects are still going on: and two or three more generations may have to pass until truly American national characteristics may emerge anew among the great-grandchildren of earlier Americanized immigrants who will share a feeling of affinity with the very history and not merely with the ephemeral and superficial and popular habits of their United States.

Let us remember that the overwhelming majority of immigrants brought little cultural baggage with them. Their "Americanization" was, therefore, an almost ab-

---

ponder the following defense of his way of expression by his Press Secretary, Hagerty (*Saturday Evening Post*, 21 May 1960): "The American people understand him. He talks the same way they do."

[16] Here, too, the Redskin element was insufficient to create an American tradition. Not only Mencken but Ezra Pound, too, tried to develop an American language: the result was tragic, often ludicrous, at times beautiful, but generally Chinese. (It is probably significant that Mencken and Pound were Anglophobes.) At any rate, only the Paleface alternative remains: now the question is whether the English or the German Paleface version will prevail.

solute success—but at the cost of a transformed concept of American nationality.[17] The kind of American *patriotic* nationalism that, despite its crudities, was beginning to coagulate a hundred years ago around a new prototype of an English-speaking nation thereafter changes into a newer kind of *ideological* nationalism where the "patriot" is distinguished not by his adherence to tradition but by his adherence to the current and popular brand of publicized national ideology.[18]

It is at any rate significant that it is usually the immigrant, and often the second-generation immigrant, who most strenuously asserts radical concepts of American national interest. Probably this inner sense of national insufficiency may explain the more strident concepts of Manifest Destiny touted by publicists and congressmen during the earlier part of the nineteenth century, when the American nation had not yet lived for more than a generation or so. Surely there have been crucial occasions when American diplomatic commitments and foreign policies have been unduly influenced by organized pressure groups of diverse immigrants. Certainly the exhortations of an ideological, as distinct

[17] The history of the word "Americanism" is instructive. Though it originated earlier in the nineteenth century, it became widely current only around 1900, when "Americanization" meant the teaching of the basic concepts of American citizenship to the masses of alien immigrants. Subsequently, the adjective "Un-American" gained currency. Thus, ironically enough, patriotism came to be equated with adherence not to traditions but to current political ideas, and a word connoting an immigrant education program acquired universal meaning.

[18] *Only in America* was the title, in 1958, of a sentimental best seller by a Jewish newspaperman who exults—and largely rightly—in the thoughtless generosity of America in accepting immigrants of diverse races who conform to its basic patterns of rapid civilization; yes, only in America would university students in 1958 give Dr. Wernher von Braun, the German ex-Nazi rocket maker, the award of Patriot of the Year.

from a patriotic, nationalism have been a product of relative immaturity, of people who are not sure of themselves and of their position in the world.[19] And yet— none of these things equal the really tremendous contribution that the millions of immigrants have made not only to the industrial power of the United States but also to the quickening of the American spirit.

The American national character is still mobile, restless, uniform in ephemeralities but manifold in deep unrevealed sentiments and occasionally revealed inclinations. This involves the very relationship of America to European civilization. The race and the religion of the American Indians is almost extinct; the overwhelming majority of Americans are of European stock, Palefaces: but what kind of Palefaces?

Here, then, is a partial clue to the evolving problem of American national interest and character. It is to be found in the inclinations of Americans toward other nations. I have said earlier that the character of a nation, like that of a person, is revealed most clearly in her relationship with other nations; consequently, the formative component of these relationships may be revealed in the relative attraction toward certain national prototypes. We have seen how different concepts of national interest may develop along the lines of national and ideological attractions and aversions; and though

[19] It may be symbolic that among the myriad Experts of International Relations who have been berating and advising the American people ever since the beginning of the last World War, Americanized immigrant professors have played a large role: they have fashioned, defined, and proposed new kinds of American National Interests, of an atomic *Realpolitik* tailored to what they state are America's needs. Before me lies one of these incantations by a Director of a Foreign Policy Research Institute, consultant to the Government and Pentagon: "For the next fifty years or so, the future belongs to America. The American empire and mankind will not be opposites but merely two names for the universal order under peace and happiness. *Novus orbis terrarum.*" I regard this kind of thing not merely pompous but impertinent.

the two elements are mixed, the national element is again the more tangible of the two.

As early as the 1790s, for example, it was evident that most of the Federalists were Francophobes at least as much as they were conservatives, while most of the Democratic-Republicans were not only liberals but Anglophobes. Hence the enduring wisdom of Washington's anxious parting admonition against American entanglements with *sentiments* involving certain European nations. Now we find something similar about the different concepts of American national sentiments during and after the last World War. For it may be argued that there was a division not so much between Isolationists and Internationalists, Old and New Americans, conservatives and liberals, Republicans and Democrats, as between relative Anglophobes (most of whom were, consequently, Germanophiles) and relative Germanophobes (who were, consequently, Anglophiles)—a division that, as certain significant manifestations during the McCarthy period indicated, persists up to the present day. Thus the majority of those who opposed American aid to Britain in 1940 were Anglophobes rather than Isolationists; thus recently the more extreme forms of American Anti-Communism correspond with Germanophilia rather than with Russophobia. It is true, of course, that such respective inclinations are strongest and most evident among certain American population groups of certain national and racial origins. But on the other hand, they persist deeper beneath the surface of American political life; these are tendencies that transcend these often parochial inclinations, reflecting the greater currents of world affairs.

So far as American culture, American institutions, and the very language of Americans go, throughout history the relationship between the United States and Great Britain has been enduring and crucial. So far as world affairs and the course of America among the Great Powers in this century go, the relationship between the United States and Great Britain is the key. From the turn of the century onward every British government has recognized the primary importance of securing American good will for Britain: for nothing could be so disastrous for her than the hostility of the American giant. Conversely, various American governments have recognized the usefulness of an Atlantic alignment with Britain from 1900 onward, at a time when the older American nationalist and Anglophobe sentiments of twisting the Lion's tail had already waned.

We have seen how a person's character may be very well revealed in his relationship with his important neighbors. Thus Russia's concept of national interest (and the very reflection of her national character) may be often seen best in her relationship with Poland (and Germany), while the key of American national interest in this century is often the American relationship with Britain (and with Germany). We have seen how, because of geography, the United States and Russia are still sufficiently far away from each other so that they are able to understand each other's immediate sphere of national interest; we have also seen how tragic are the consequences of misunderstandings between the United States and Great Britain. The conditions of the cold war arose because of such misunderstandings between Britain and America about their respective national interests even though Roosevelt was not an Anglophobe; we have also seen how, at least under Dulles, the United States regarded, for the first time in this century, Germany rather than Britain as her principal ally. Earlier in this chapter I tried to illustrate the complexities of the American concept of national interest by drawing attention to the complex character of Wilson; I may now illustrate my point about the formative importance of respective national inclinations with the case of Dulles. He was a Republican; but so were Theodore Roosevelt and Taft. He was a moralizer; but so was Wilson. He was a lawyer; but so was Acheson. He was a relative conservative; but so was Charles Evans Hughes. He was an Internationalist; so were all of his recent predecessors. He was also pro-German, a tendency that he revealed on a number of occasions throughout his life; and I believe that of all the above-mentioned categories the last tendency stands out as the formative element in his personal character and in his foreign policy.

I wish to make it clear that I am not asserting new categories of Germanophilia or Germanophobia as if these were to mark the deepest present divisions of American politics and of the American national spirit. The American support to Germany in the cold war has been, after all, the obviously reasonable result of strategic considerations, the reaction to Russian aggressiveness at the beginning of the cold war. What is more, the older kind of Anglophobia has been weakening now in America even among the Irish, the traditionally most Anglophobe of all American national groups. We are dealing with tendencies, not with categories; not so much with a conscious transformation of the concepts of American national interest but with the effects of transformations within the American character that are still going on (and whose effects on American diplomacy and strategy are indirect rather than direct).

Before 1860 the United States was overwhelmingly composed of people who had come from the British Isles.[20] Thereafter American habits, the American temperament, and even the American physiognomy began to change; and all of this involved a certain trans-

[20] No matter how different the religion, the race, the temperament of these peoples, they were English-speaking people—consider, for example, how admirably the Irish character is suited to the poetic and imprecise and noncommittal character of the English language. That is—blood is thicker than water; and speech may be even thicker than blood.

formation within the American character. In the last
fifty years the spirit of American culture, ranging from
the heavily intellectualized and professionalized university learning to the mass culture of the movies,
changed, so that today for the first time there may be
more in common between Americans and Germans than
between Americans and the inhabitants of the British
Isles. For the first time Americans are beginning to
look and think more like Germans than like Britons;
that their sons are more at home in Germany than in
Britain was already obvious during the last war.

Thus, while the institutions of the American people
are still Anglo-Saxon, the character of the people has
become more Germanic.[21]

It was in the 1890s that for the first time Germans
overtook the Irish as the largest single immigrant group.
But I must insist that what I am speaking about is
something different from the actual influx of the German race. For the German influence in the formation
of the American national character has been cultural
rather than racial. The influence of Central European
ideas and of forms of thought that in American higher
education and in popular culture began to replace the
up to then predominant Anglo-Saxon and Celtic habits
of learning was often promoted by people who were
anti-German and anti-Nazi in two World Wars. What
has happened is that most of the immigrants during
the last hundred years, including Jews and Eastern
Europeans, were more familiar with cultural patterns
and more inclined toward intellectual habits of the Ger-

[21] It is significant that the first two American Presidents
whose ancestry did not come from the British Isles or Holland, but from Germany, were Hoover and Eisenhower; they
were, too, the first two Presidents born in the West. (It is a
curious, and perhaps symbolic, coincidence that Lenin's
mother as well as Eisenhower's paternal ancestors had come
from the same central part of the world, from cramped and
still feudal German lands in the middle of Continental
Europe.)

man than of the English type. In a way this has been a world-wide phenomenon, this emulation by the upper middle classes of English and by the lower middle classes of German ideas, styles, and culture. I repeat that this has little to do with the German race or with Nazism. The transformation of the American character in a German direction has developed often (though not always) quite separate from a political Germanophilia. This transformation, furthered as it was by immigrant influences, is a cultural rather than a racial phenomenon: for the character of a nation, like that of a person, is formed by culture as much as by race.

In other words, the American people are no longer predominantly Anglo-Saxon and Protestant.[22] During the cold war this transformation has had its effects on the ideological currents of American anti-Communism; but this is a transformation whose ultimate effects we cannot project with any degree of certainty now, when the American national character has not yet crystallized into durable historical forms.

There is, as yet, no general resolution about the limits or the position of America's place in the world, about the limits or the purposes of American national interests. Still, such a clarifying resolution may be slowly forming in our times. The formation of the American national character was disrupted by expansion, internal and external expansion: by the restless-

[22] The number of American Catholics roughly doubled between 1930 and 1960. It is significant that this increase, too, has been a later and indirect rather than the direct consequence of mass immigration. American Catholics are already the largest single religious group in the United States. Though the effects of this on national politics are much more subtle and much less direct than commentators right now believe, this has already had a certain effect on the American national character. Even keeping in mind the often tenuous and imprecise nature of religious statistics, the figures demonstrate the superior vitality of the American Catholic population.

ness of the frontier, by the expansion of industrialization, by mass immigration, by imperial and strategic
expansion abroad. And yet it may be that this American expansion is coming to its end; that the American
spirit, instead of coursing even further abroad, may yet
come back to concentrate upon itself. For the history of
mankind is not really the story of the expansive explosion of Progress; it is, rather, philosophy teaching by
example; and these examples are furnished by people
and by nations.

The historic formulation of America's place in the
world, begun by the Founding Fathers and promoted
one hundred years later by the clear-sighted Theodore
Roosevelt, may now, under the pressing conditions of
the cold war, be entering its third phase. Despite some
of these disturbing developments that suggest the
transformation of the Republic into a centralized military empire obsessed with the inhuman sphere of space,
there is still evidence that youthfulness, resilience,
adaptability, and the idealistic inclination—all traditional American social characteristics—continue to exist
and that, in their proper context, they may play a
beneficent role in the world history of nations.

6

Peeling away layers, one by one, I have now attempted to approach the core of the great Russian-
American world conflict. I have tried to describe, in
consecutive order, the movements of two peoples, of
their political ideas, of two empires, of two nations. In
other words, I have tried to demonstrate, in successive
chapters, the contrast and the conflict of these two
great societies on the economic, on the ideological, on
the strategic, and on the national level; I have moved
the focus of attention from material to political to geographical to deep-seated national factors.

The concept of this history will, by now, appear to the reader. It is a concept rather than a thesis; an approach rather than a method.

Each of these factors is, of course, important. At the same time they overlap: the movements flow into each other. But my argument has been that the economic element, with its material factors, is less important than the political element, with its categorical ideologies, which, in turn, is less important than the geographical element, with the strategic factor of national interest, which, in the end, is involved with the complex elements of national character. Russian industrial statistics are less important than the condition that the masters of the Soviet Union are Communists; but that, in turn, is less decisive than the fact that they are Russians, the masters of a long-standing Empire and the children of a long-standing nation. The development of politics is more important than the routine life of populations; but the national interest of states is more important than their official ideologies; and the concept of their national interest depends not only on their geographical circumstances but on their national characteristics.

Let me illustrate this evolving argument for the last time. When I first wrote these lines (9 May 1960), the fantastic story of the American spy plane shot down over the Urals had broken upon the world. Was that airplane sent over Russia for economic reasons? No. For ideological reasons? No. Because of the present strategic concepts of American national interest? Yes. The emphasis is on the *present:* for Russia, Communism, and even Atomic Weapons have now existed for a long time; and yet it was only in recent years that such clandestine flying missions were organized by agencies of the American government. Thus this recent concept (suggesting, for instance, that the United States had the right to fly over any country in the world), its very origin (suggesting the increasingly dangerous complexity of direct and indirect military authorities in American government), and the very reaction of that government reflected characteristic tendencies that diverged from the American traditions of the past, and they were, of course, also different from the way another nation would have handled this curious affair. Conversely, Khrushchev's reaction, his boasting, crafty, uneasy, loud self reflected historic Russian national characteristics rather than Russia's economic or technological or ideological position.

At the same time this brings us back to the technological interpretation of history. Obviously it has become important to gather intelligence of a highly technical nature: but this should not obscure our view of the basic motive factors of human events. In the history of human reason the story of the Scientific Illusion of Progressive Objectivity has become a sorry tale; and nothing is sorrier in it than the modern belief that the farther we remove ourselves from the object, the more accurate our knowledge of it. The purpose of human knowledge is understanding rather than accuracy. Every experienced aerial intelligence officer will tell us that just because from high up one can see more, this does not necessarily mean that one can see better; and every serious student of history will attest that a ton of external information may not equal an ounce of introspection. With electrified whizzing satellite machines in the sky one day we may photograph the entire Soviet Union every five minutes. Some of their information may be useful; but, after all, what will we see? *All* of the Soviet Union—and yet only a tiny portion of the truth. What really counts is not a photograph of all of Russia but what goes on in Russian hearts: and the partial clue to that may lie not so much in scientific studies of Soviet mechanical logistics as in old history books.

I have said in this book that the really important elements in this history of the cold war ought not to be sought in world economic movements but within con-

tinents and nations and ultimately within the hearts of
persons in the midst of nations. Thus I seem to have
narrowed the focus deeper and closer, peeling away
the layers, getting down in the end to a very old-
fashioned, narrow sphere of national character of persons: an approach that was not telescopic but micro-
scopic in its direction. But the mysterious and divinely
created nature of human beings is such that now, close
to the dark recesses of the human heart, we find universality again. For the human heart is a microcosm in
itself, reflecting the universe. "No man is an island"—
these words of a poet, cited so often by superficial internationalists, have a meaning only because of the
spiritual condition of man. The body of a man may be
confined to a solitary island; but his heart and mind are
not. A nation occupies a certain confined place in the
world; but the origin and the effect of the ideas that
form its conduct are ultimately supranational.

Thus we come back to the history of ideas. There
is no such thing in history as an isolated material condition. The condition of human existence is such that
there is no purely material factor in life. Thus, in the
end, the spiritual factor is the truly formative one. Life
is stronger than theory; but life is inseparable from the
idea of life. The life of nations is more important and
more enduring than their systematic ideologies; but the
life of nations in itself is influenced by current ideas of
life that form the character, the institutions, the tendencies of nations: and these ideas contain religious and
cultural elements that are, by their very nature, more
universal than national. The spiritual as well as the material development of Russia and America in this century has been consequent to national conditions but also
to certain universal developments that are already discernible in retrospect. I must now attempt to sketch
their emerging outlines in the last chapter of this book.

CHAPTER XVI

Conclusion:
The Great Historical Movements of Our Times

1

The great overlapping historical movements of our times are biological, racial, social, political, cultural, moral—in order of ascending significance. From the merely quantitative point of view their order is the reverse: the problem of overpopulation obviously seems greater than the future of poetry or of theology. But this may be a crude illusion: the very word "great" has not only a quantitative but a qualitative sense. Historical life is spiritual as well as material; let me repeat, once more, how in the long run the spiritual factor is that which counts. Overpopulation is less important than race, which is less important than society, which is less important than politics, which is less important than culture, which ultimately depends on its religious concept of human destiny and on its moral concepts of good and evil.

There is now reason to believe that the expansion of scientific knowledge may lead either to a hitherto unknown increase and prosperity of the world population or to the hitherto unknown destruction of the major part of mankind.

Meanwhile there is reason to believe that the struggle of races may supersede the struggles of nations. There is reason to believe that the movement toward social democracy, involving the dissolution of distinctions of birth or of wealth, continues throughout the world. There is reason to believe that the main political tendency of our century is national socialism. There is reason to believe that the main historical problem of our times is still not the future of Asia or of Africa but the relationship of Russia and America to Europe. There is reason to believe that the essence of this problem is not merely military and political but cultural, as it involves the future of Western Civilization; religious, as it involves the future of Christendom; moral, as it involves the future of mankind threatened by arrogant and weakling scientists. These are the matters that I must illustrate now.

2

The world, we are told, is threatened by overpopulation. The white race is threatened by a rising sea of colored blood. America is threatened by the rise of Communist millions. We are acquainted with these arguments, illustrated as they are by certain purposeful statistics. Yet we must sum up some of the contrary evidence.

In the first place, since history is not governed by logic, its development has already refuted the otherwise seemingly logical gloomy predictions of the Rev. Malthus. All over the world living standards have risen, the span of life extended, infant mortality fallen during the last two hundred years; and in Europe and in America, at least, the highest standards of material welfare are to be found in the most densely populated regions.

In the second place, the figures do not bear out the ominous predictions about the decline of the white race. It rather seems that the population ratio between the Western and Eastern worlds has changed little through the centuries. Between 1900 and 1960 the population of the world nearly doubled, from 1.5 to 2.75 billion, but the proportion of the white race remained approximately the same: 36 out of a 100 inhabitants of our world were whites in 1900, and 35 in 1958.

In the third place, one of the most encouraging signs of vitality is the continued increase of the population of the United States (in great and good contrast to the dire predictions of scientific demographers of two decades ago):

IN MILLIONS

	UNITED STATES	U.S.S.R.
1900	76	130
1940	132	190 (including annexations)
1960	182	208 (including annexations)

Thus, in two decades, the population of the United States increased by almost 40 per cent, while that of the Soviet Union increased by less than 10. Even if we consider the losses of the Soviet people during the war, these are significant figures.

It is also instructive to note the distribution of the respective populations. There has been a strong westward movement in America and an eastward movement in the Soviet Union. In 1940 in the United States 70 per cent of the people were living east of the Mississippi; in 1960, 67 per cent. In 1940, 76 per cent of the population of the Soviet Union was living in the "European" portion, west of the Urals; in 1960 less than 70 per cent. Thus the movement of the populations away from Europe and away from the relatively densely inhabited regions has been greater in Russia than in America.

In Russia, of course, the government itself encouraged and at times enforced this eastward movement into thinly populated Siberian lands. For the movement of populations may be connected with political and strategic factors. And demographic figures indicating the relative biological vitality of nations do not stand alone:

they are involved with the race, with the culture,[1] with the religion of peoples.

This does not mean that in the future, with the extension of medical and other improvements throughout Asia, the proportion of the white race may not decrease further and faster. Still, Russia as well as America are even now relatively "underpopulated" nations. In different ways, however, they are beginning to feel the pressure of colored races. Whether these pressures will bring them together or not is an open question; anyhow, the pressure on Russians is greater than on Americans.

3

We cannot avoid the problem of race: for it involves the very problem of national character in these two great nations.

We have seen that the Bolshevik regime was established in that most European and most cosmopolitan of Russian cities that was subsequently renamed Leningrad. The first capital of the United States, too, was the cosmopolitan city of New York; the subsequent capital, too, bears the name of the Founding Father of the Revolution. But the American Revolution did not get its start in New York; unlike in Russia, there are no New York and Chicago periods in American history; and Washington is neither New York nor Chicago.

It did, however, become transformed in our lifetime into the political and strategic capital of the world. This transformation of the character of the city of Washington not only symbolizes but marks perhaps better than any other place of the Union the recent transformation of the American Republic in an imperial direction—this transformation of a slightly provincial, middle-sized Southern town into an expensive, malicious, cosmopoli-

[1] See below, page 405.

tan, occasionally brilliant, resplendently white, military metropolis, overgrown and formless, its sky crisscrossed every minute by military airplanes, with its influx of sullen Negroes,[2] with its recently erected great Mosque dedicated to visiting and transient Arabs, with its principal landmark the impassive Egyptian shaft erected in honor of Washington, with its gigantic Byzantine shrine erected by contributions of forty million American Catholics, with its vast and central Pentagon—an American Persepolis rather than an American Athens, an American Tokyo as well as the American Rome.

And Moscow, too, despite its old-Russian origins, has become the most modern metropolis of the Russian Empire, the largest city on the Eurasian continent, the capital of an enormous centralized bureaucracy: to Moscow flock not only civil servants but young Russians full of aspirations; and though the character of Moscow has become more "American," as visitors attest, its streets are also dappled with the face of a hundred thousand representatives of a dozen different races.

For we must keep in mind that the Soviet Union, like the United States, is a multinational as well as a multiracial Empire. It is inhabited not only by Russians but by Ukrainians, Bessarabians, Tatars, Estonians, Finns, Latvians, Lithuanians, Kazakhs, Armenians, Georgians, Turks, Tajiks, Mongolians, Uzbeks, and two-score different Siberian and Central Asiatic peoples, each numbering more than a million, apart from the different races in her outlying satellite possessions. Apart from the different races around the outposts of the American strategic empire, too, the United States and her territories are inhabited by Negroes, Indians,

---

[2] Reflecting a national problem that cannot be solved by legislation. It is a national problem visible to (and often falsely misunderstood by) the outside world. Thus already in 1850 the Congress of a divided nation was sufficiently aware of considerations of international prestige to legislate accordingly: the abolition of slave trading in Washington was one of the points of the California Compromise.

Mexicans, Japanese, Chinese, Hawaiians, Puerto Ricans, forming about one fifth of the American population. It is only now that the entire United States, and not only the South, is beginning to experience those problems of race, whose solution is so difficult; it is only now that the Soviet Union is beginning to experience national and racial problems of her own.

Both the United States and the Soviet Union stood against colonialism and against slavery; both preached the principle of racial equality for a long time, the United States rather generously, the Soviet Union rather cynically. But cynicism is seldom a good and durable policy. The rising sentiment of nationalism (again a political idea that spread from Europe all around the world) and of racial consciousness has already begun to affect the Soviet Union. The repressive Tsarist policies of pro-Russianism were cast aside by Lenin, who in 1921, with certain world revolutionary implications in mind, transformed the constitution of the new Russian Empire by granting cultural autonomies to a variety of republics and sub-republics. Stalin, then, returned to the older pattern of Russian primacy; and his successors have found themselves on the horns of a lasting dilemma. They face the evidences of rising nationalism, occasionally breaking out into violent, though quickly subsiding, riots in Georgia, Armenia, Kazakhstan; their return to the federalist system of Lenin, after all, promotes those very opinions of *national* Communism that they fear most of all; and behind them on the vast Russian frontier inhabited by Mongols and other varicolored races rises the sullen monster of China. Indeed, the Soviet Union is one of the largest colonial systems in the world; and this is one of the reasons why its rulers, emulating the United States, propose to buy time and good will by promoting the independence and the welfare of newly emerging colonial peoples throughout Africa and Asia. Whenever this, however, conflicts with what the Russian rulers conceive to be their national interests, there is no question that the latter consideration is dominant.

But China, on the other hand, has no such scruples or dilemmas. And, because of racial, national, cultural differences, the picture of Peiping and Moscow grows more and more different. This transcends categories of official ideology. Coming from Europe travelers still attest to how they sense a touch of Asia at the first Russian frontier station; but coming back from China, as they cross from one Communist Empire to another, they feel a sudden ease, an inner lightening of the atmosphere: there, in the Far Eastern depths of Siberia, they feel that they are coming home again.

There are certain affinities between America and the Far East, too; consider only the Oriental element in the cultural climate of California or the widespread Japanese influence in modern American architecture and art. But, like those enduring Russian affinities with Oriental habits of thought and even of religion, these are fragmentary considerations.

Toward the end of the last century Bismarck said that the most important factor in the next century would be that Americans, after all, spoke English. The most important factor in the second half of this century may be that, after all, the Russians are white.

It is, sadly enough, at least possible that throughout the world the struggle of races may be beginning. But we shall see that more is involved here than just the color of skins. The problem is cultural as well as racial. Consider only the ambiguity of the term "white race" when it comes to the mixed racial populations of South America. Consider the curious human inclination to attribute prestige to the lightness of skin among the colored races, too: for the cruelest racial prejudices exist among these races themselves. Consider that one hundred and fifty years ago, during the Santo Domingo Rebellion, during the first successful rebellion of Negro slaves against their white masters, the previously freed

Negroes and the mulattoes sided with the whites: their regard for their social status was more decisive than were their racial affinities.

4

Meanwhile the movement toward equality, the advance of social democracy, continues throughout the world. It is perhaps the most universal of the movements of our century; it is happening everywhere. What I described in Chapter XII about the gradual transformation of American and of Russian societies: the socialization of possessions, the disappearance of class distinctions, the emergence of the administrative state, the centralization of power—these, all, are consequences of a world-wide movement of social democracy. Throughout the world during this century equality has risen, while liberty has generally declined. This progress of equality has obviously brought certain important benefices; but some of its less fortunate consequences have also become obvious. The advance of equality, the mechanization of life, and the centralization of government have often resulted not merely in a decrease of liberty but in a decrease of the very taste for it. Hence, for one thing, the emergence of totalitarian states in this century. These have been essentially different from other tyrannies in the past: not only because of their widespread powers and efficiency but because the dictators have been often actively supported by large masses of the population.

Most of these evils of centralized government and of a new potential kind of tyranny by majorities were foretold more than a century ago by Tocqueville; but his noble soul nevertheless refused to despair of Democracy, in which he saw a greater Providential design. Though no one described so clearly as Tocqueville the often inherent conflict of equality and liberty, he did not say that they must necessarily conflict, always and everywhere. He saw that the advance of social democracy may assume a thousand different forms, dependent on the historical conditions of different peoples. At any rate, "a new science of politics," said Tocqueville, "is indispensable for a new world."

This admonition has been often quoted, but seldom really thought through. But it must be considered nowadays when the old categories no longer fit: "conservative," "liberal," "radical," "rightist," "leftist," "democracy," "socialism," are, all, words connoting categories that are rapidly losing their meaning (while the older national realities of "Russian," "American," "British," and so on, have remained more intact). The advance of democracy throughout the world has been tremendous; and yet its influence has not been accordingly formative. For this has been, by and large, a movement too general and too seldom conscious to have influenced more than the routine lives of peoples. The socialization of life and the centralization of government have been promoted not only by Communists and Socialists but by Nazis, Fascists, monarchists, conservatives, liberals, radicals. In differing ways and to varying extents, Hitler as well as Stalin, Mussolini as well as Lenin, De Gaulle as well as Blum, Roosevelt as well as Eisenhower, Nehru as well as Franco, whether conscious or not, have been agents of the broad movement toward socialism of this century. But we have seen that man does not live by bread alone; that in history even more important than what happens is what people think happens; that it is only in science that what is routine counts, while history is principally concerned with the unique. Consequently, we must look at the more or less conscious national varieties of this world-wide social movement; it is there that we may detect certain general features.

5

So far as Western Civilization is concerned, the main totalitarian movement of this century has been not Communism but National Socialism. This may be surprising: and yet it is true.

During the first half of the twentieth century we have seen four kinds of dictatorships: the Communist, the prototype of which has been Russia; the National Socialist, the prototype of which was Hitler's Germany; the Fascist, the prototype of which was Mussolini's Italy; the authoritarian, *a* prototype of which may be Salazar's Portugal.

Though these categories are neither perfect nor exclusive, two fundamental considerations emerge from them. The first is that not every modern dictatorship is totalitarian, since in some of the authoritarian regimes there remain important segments of private life that are excluded from the interference of the state.[3] The second is that Hitler was not really a Fascist and that there is an essential distinction between Fascism and

[3] Something like this may be happening in Russia now: but I think it would be wrong to call the present Soviet regime "authoritarian" (a term which is applicable to Franco's Spain or to Salazar's Portugal or to Mussolini's Italy). It is, rather, "post-totalitarian": which, however, does not mean a return to the older, nineteenth-century political liberties.

The converse question of our times is then this: there have been non-totalitarian dictatorships; may we not see the emergence of totalitarian democracies? By this I mean democracies where universal popular suffrage exists but where the essential and earlier basic conditions of political freedoms, of freedom of speech, of the press, of assembly, are hardly more than theoretical benefits to the average citizen, whose life and ideas, whose rights to privacy, to family autonomy, and to possessions are regimented by the state and rigidly molded by mass production and by mass communications.

National Socialism. The original doctrines of Fascism were cruel, lucid, rational, Latin; the postulates of Hitlerian National Socialism were crude, turgid, emotional, Germanic. The Mussolinian ideal was a neo-Renaissance one, reminiscent of Rienzi as well as of Machiavelli, with an important residue of aristocratism; the Hitlerian emotion was strongly reminiscent of the anti-Renaissance fury of Luther, with a powerful populist appeal. This distinction has been recognized by a few historians here and there, but the confusion of "Fascist" with "National Socialist" persists even now, flowing from the general and erroneous attribution of the "Fascist" adjective to *all* "Rightist," or non-Communist, dictatorships.

It is significant that the confusion of these two terms has been promoted by Soviet propaganda. Ever since about 1932 the term "National Socialist," or "Nazi," has been prohibited in Russia; the approved terms were "Fascists" and "Hitlerites." This blanket employment of the "Fascist" term immediately took root among the commentators and journalists of the West, particularly in Britain and America. But why did Stalin insist already in 1932 on suppressing the term "National Socialist"? The answer is there in the historical development of his own Soviet Russian state; it lies in what may be called the common ideological denominator between the three main totalitarian systems. Speaking of the Communist, the Fascist, the National Socialist: which one influenced the others more? This is an important question, for the comparison of their respective and reciprocal influences will indicate which was the strongest and the most enduring of the three.

The results of such a comparison will be remarkable. It is obviously nonsense to call Stalin a Fascist or Mussolini a Communist; yet the National Socialist term fits both rather well. As the years advanced, Stalin became less and less internationalist and more and more nationalistic and even race-minded; so did Mussolini.

This is why Stalin back in 1932 proscribed the National Socialist term; it fitted his evolving Russian state only too well.

Thus, while of the three dictators Hitler was the one who seems to be most repudiated by posterity and perhaps even by his own people, we find that it was his National Socialism whose impact on the other two prototypical dictatorships steadily increased and, in the case of Stalin's Russia, even survived Hitler's death. This is at least one reason why we may assert that National Socialism did not die with Hitler.

And national socialism, in one way or another, became the common denominator not only of the totalitarian but even of many of the authoritarian and of the democratic mass movements of the twentieth century. There are great differences among Mao, Mussolini, Tito, Trujillo, Castro, Stalin, Perón, Hitler, Khrushchev; but in one way or another all of them are national socialists. (To a considerable extent so was the late Joseph McCarthy.) What we see throughout the twentieth century is the fading of the earlier appeal of international socialism: the leading socialist prophets become old, respected, solitary figures, a Norman Thomas, an Attlee, a Blum. At the same time a similar thing is happening to another old-fashioned matter: to patriotic (as distinct from ideological) nationalism, with its traditionalist, military, and semi-feudal tinge. Consider the fading of the type of MacArthur, eclipsed by the nationalist image of a McCarthy, or of old Prussian generals, whose most typical representatives were brutally eliminated by Hitler. Instead of old-fashioned internationalist socialism and of old-fashioned patriotic nationalism, it seems that the merging concept of nationalism with socialism has become the dominant ideological constellation at least up to now in this century.

Still, we must keep in mind the distinction between national socialism in general and the Hitler variety in

particular.[4] Not every manifestation of national socialism will necessarily conform to the Hitlerite ideology:
anti-Semitism, for example, is not necessarily a part of
every national socialist movement or state. In the larger
sense of the term, McCarthy as well as Tito may be
considered national socialists; but, then, so could Gomulka or Bevan. The category is too broad. But is it so
broad as to be entirely useless? I do not think so; for
there is at least one main conclusion that we may draw
from recent historical experience.

It is that, all superficial appearances notwithstanding, our world in this century, including Russia and
America, has moved in a "rightist" as much as in a
"leftist" direction. Even though the two categories of
"Right" and "Left" are rapidly losing their meaning,
we may still observe that in this age of mass equality
and of mass communications, emotional, religious, national, and racial sentiments continue to exist and to
attract. On one hand, furthered as it is by the practices
of our technological civilization, the bureaucratized
Welfare State exists practically everywhere in the
world. On the other hand, what Hitler first sensed fifty
years ago has proven true in many places since then,
that the appeal to national, popular, racial, or religious
ideological emotions may carry the modern politican
further than the intellectual socialist appeals to international brotherhood. I have sketched the failures of
Marxist predictions in Chapter XIII of this book; here
let me say that it may not be an exaggeration to say
that the world has been going steadily in the direction
of anti-Communism.[5] Meanwhile even in China and in

[4] National Socialism was in many ways a German phenomenon; on the other hand, Hitler was less typical of Germany than Stalin was of Russia.
[5] I am bypassing here the fascinating speculation whether
the very organization of our societies, too, is not unconsciously moving in a "rightist" direction, away from Capitalism toward older, medieval institutions. Consider only the
movement away from money economy, the dependence of

Russia we see the continued emphasis on the national element.

Is it not true that Russian nationalism rather than orthodox Marxism forms the domestic currents of opposition that Khrushchev had to face? Isn't anti-Semitism, for example, such a popular current in Russia that Khrushchev could not afford to discount its existence? And when he came to America, the police felt that he had to be protected much more from the industrial workers of Pittsburgh than from the capitalists on Park Avenue.[6] Two generations ago, when the Russian Tsar visited Paris, the police had to round up radical Communists, Socialists, anarchists; in 1960 Khrushchev had to be protected from the eventual assaults of radical anti-Communists. In 1853 radical American mobs pelted a visiting Papal nuncio in Midwestern cities with stones; in 1959 the same kind of people in the same cities threw stones at Mikoyan, the visiting representative of the Workers' State. There was a time when the radicals among the masses were internationalists and Communists; now they are nationalists and anti-Communists. This is especially true of America; but it is true, to a large extent, of the entire Western world and even of Eastern Europe: witness the sentiments of the workers in Poland and in Hungary.

Still, we are dealing here with sentiments, not with recognized categories. But it is through ideas that senti-

_____

the citizen's position not upon birth or wealth but upon his function: a status rather than a contract society, and so forth.

[6] It is not the capitalist *Herald Tribune* and not even the *Wall Street Journal* but the New York *Daily News* whose anti-Communist line is the most violent—because its editors think that this is how the American working masses think and that this is what they want to read. And Congress scurried out of Washington, adjourning in haste, just in time not to have to meet Khrushchev. Politicians are sensitive to mass currents of opinion. They wished to avoid meeting Khrushchev in public: they were worried not that the American rich but that the American working masses might see them photographed together with a Communist.

ments become recognized and crystallize into historical forces: and the ideas that move the world—Communism as well as National Socialism, science as well as religion—have come, and are still coming, from Europe.

6

The cold war has come out of the Second World War and the Second World War came from the First. But both of these World Wars were primarily European wars, begun by Europeans, because of Europeans, wars in which the nations of Europe inflicted wounds in each other's flesh and division in each other's souls. It is the paradox of history that no one was as responsible for the advance of Communist Russia into Europe as Hitler, the self-appointed creator of a New Europe and the Crusader of Anti-Communism.[7] I have said in the very first page of this book that neither America nor Russia wanted the Second World War; but the theme of this book is, then, that their consequent conflict arose because of their clashing concepts of Europe. Thus that small continent is still the center of the world—and not only because of the cold war, not only politically so.

The religions, ideologies, discoveries of Europe are still the predominant ones. It is not only because of strategic and political but because of racial and cultural, not only because of material but because of spir-

[7] Here, again, we meet spectacles of historical paradox, flowing from the ultimate discrepancy between human intentions and of their consequences. In 1914 Mussolini received French monies for his nationalist propaganda pushing Italy into the war; in 1917 the German General Staff expedited Lenin's journey back to Russia; in the 1930s certain Prussian generals, certain British capitalists, and certain German conservative industrialists supported Hitler. They, all, succeeded in the short run; but their success led to their own disaster in the long run.

itual conditions that the relations of America and of Russia with Europe count foremost.

Despite the weakness and the division of Europe, Russians and Americans have been forced increasingly to recognize that they are Europeans in a sense, after all; that not only their race but that their culture is originally European. It is already evident that neither Soviet Russia nor modern America could altogether tear herself away from Western and European Civilization. For there has not been sufficient substance either in the Eurasian elements of the Slavophile or in the Redskin elements of a Far Western tradition to create and maintain a great civilization.

We have seen, for instance, that the vertical movement of the masses toward social equality is still going on; indeed, it has become world-wide. Meanwhile the horizontal, geographical mass movement of European migration to America and to Russia may have largely come to an end, though the movement of the American population westward and of the Russians eastward still continues. But while we must remember that both of these movements began before 1776 and 1917, before the American and the Russian Revolutions, they are also slowing down. Already fifty years ago the American frontier era was largely over, and mass immigration was turned down into a trickle. Though the westward movement of the population goes on, there is reason to doubt that the large but arid American West would ever attract a sufficient quantity and quality of people to become a center of history. And in Russia, too, notwithstanding the strenuous efforts and exhortations of her rulers, the young and ambitious people gravitate to Leningrad and to Moscow.

"Europe," wrote General MacArthur in 1944, "is a dying system. It is worn out and run down. . . . The lands touching the Pacific with their billions of inhabitants will determine the course of history for the next ten thousand years." Perhaps *in* ten thousand years; but not yet.

Russia, America, China, Japan: they all are powerful, dynamic nations, more dynamic than the old nations of Europe. Yet it is not dynamism but *resistance* and *resilience* that mark the health of a living human organism, a lesson that modern medicine is now learning anew. This is where the crude Darwinian theory of the survival of the fittest goes wrong. For who are "the fittest"? I have argued before that when it comes to human beings and to their societies, there is no such thing as an isolated material or biological factor, that every material condition is a spiritual condition as well. The experience of Nazi concentration camps, of Soviet terror prisons, and of Korean prisoner camps has shown that religious men and philosophers survived better than dockworkers and pugilists. To argue, therefore, whether the Swiss or the Russian, whether the Dutch or the Chinese nations are "fittest" is nonsense.

When it comes to human life, then, the supremely important element of *radiance* enhances the factors of resistance and of resilience. By radiance I mean that spiritual factor of prestige that is not devoid of latent historical consequences, when a man, a nation, a church, a civilization, exercises a spiritual and cultural influence far beyond its actual domains. One of the most astonishing evidences in this cold war is the condition that, Communism notwithstanding, Russia is not radiant.[8] Her influence does not even pervade her own

---

[8] A Swiss journalist talks with Communist delegates in Moscow, 1964: "Now they sat in the hotel coffee-shop, at small, uncleared tables piled with dirty dishes, and earnestly sought explanations and excuses for all the inadequacies and wretchedness which pervade the everyday lives of even the privileged classes in the USSR. Some found reasons in the two world wars, some blamed Stalin or 'difficulties of transition,' and when all else failed, the ancient domination by the Tartars was brought forth, an argument which the Russians themselves repeatedly raise. It is strangely moving

brutally clinched domains. The prestige of Russia and of Communism may be high in Indonesia or in the Congo: in Poland and in Hungary it hardly exists at all. Even before 1956, when the Communist masters of Poland rebuilt Warsaw from its ruins, they followed not Russian models but the architecture of the European eighteenth century. In this respect, too, the Eastern European events of 1956 fly in the face of all those gloomy prognostications about The Decline of the West.[9]

The decline of the bourgeois West, yes; the end of Europe, no; for, despite the iambic rhythm of the two words Decline and Fall, they are emphatically not the same.

This again shows how a Newtonian theory of gravitation does not quite hold in the historic life of nations. The tremendous Eurasian Empire of Russia, with its two hundred million people, had conquered and occupied Vienna, the capital of tiny Austria, for ten years; even now the armored frontier of the Soviet sphere stands but an hour's drive from that ancient capital: yet in Vienna it is as if the Russians had never been there. When Napoleon's Frenchmen occupied Vienna for a few weeks in 1809 (or Hitler's Germans for a few years after 1938), their influence left marks lasting for a hundred years.

Russia is in Europe but not quite of Europe. America is not really in Europe but of Europe. In a limited sense, both of these statements are true. And America should

---

that a nation of major world stature must justify, to friend and foe alike, the insufficiencies of its present-day economic and social system by involving the image of the Tartars of a bygone age." (Ernst Kux, in *Swiss Review for World Affairs*, 1964, IV.)

[9] There are two symbols that illustrate this best. In Vienna, *Stalin-Platz* is again *Schwarzenberg-Platz;* and Stalin's gigantic statue, pulled down during the short-lived revolution in Budapest, has not been replaced.

gain self-confidence from the evident condition that her influence, too, is more radiant than that of Russia.

I have said earlier that the best way to find the respective strength of influences is to compare their effects on each other: which one has influenced the other more? In the relations of Russia and America there can be no question about that. We have seen throughout this book how the masters of Communist Russia imitated American practices and adopted American ideas in hundreds of ways; we have seen that while few people in the world are as invulnerable to Communist ideas as are Americans, Russians are by no means as invulnerable to American ideas and practices.

This is at least one of the reasons why Russian expansion has reached its limits during the first decade of the cold war. This is the main reason why what is needed is more American self-confidence—instead of a race with the Russians about who will reach 1984 sooner.

In the Orient the short-lived Japanese victories have been enduring at least in the sense that the prestige and the formerly colonial power of the European nations may have been shattered beyond relief; but this is not true of American power and prestige, not even in Japan.

And in Europe, too—especially in Germany—the American impact far transcends any Russian influence. Together with a gradually increasing variety of European influences on American life we are witnessing, to some extent, the Americanization of the world.

7

But these considerations, though they are certainly not devoid of historical substance, cannot stand alone. The history of nations and of Empires is not formed by power alone; but, at least in the short run, it is not formed by prestige either. Power without prestige cannot for long endure unbroken; but prestige without power will not prevail in this world. The cultural supremacy of Europe's nations did not prevent their defeats in the past; the cultural inferiority of Russia did not prevent her expansion. If the new resilient and comfortable Europe is going to relinquish to America the very task of her own self-defense, her superficial "Americanization" may yet be a portent of doom not only for herself but for Western Civilization as it now exists.

We have seen that now Europe and America are closer together than ever before: yet the essence of their relations is still undecided. For it is not necessarily true that when great societies get in close contact with each other, they invariably borrow good things from each other. They borrow and adapt good and bad things alike. Europe is now learning American English; her nations are turning to the American practice of non-ideological two-party systems; her young people adapt American habits and entertainments; her national societies are becoming more democratic and egalitarian. America is now becoming more and more bureaucratic, military, intellectualized: but ultimately it is the quality, not the extent, of these transformations that counts.

But "Europe": the very concept of that term, referring to a civilization and not to a mere geographical category, is relatively new: it dates from the seventeenth century. Before that time what we call "European" was synonymous with "Western Christian." At that time neither Russia nor America really belonged to Western Christendom. And now Russia as well as America have become more European in spirit; but meanwhile the unity and the power of Europe declined until in 1945 Europe became divided along an artificial line; and who knows whether that line may not last longer than we think?

For the great question is this: Are there going to be two great confederations of the white race, a North Atlantic and an Eastern European one, stretching together around the world from Pacific to Pacific, encompassing most of the vital part of the globe, the Northern Hemisphere? An American confederation, stretching from Japan to Berlin; a Russian confederation, stretching from Berlin to Vladivostok; two confederations that meet in Europe but whose centers are not in Europe? *Eurasia* and *Euramerica*. Or will we really see a united Europe, between Russia and America, a superior middle ground reversing the tendency that prevailed up to now: is it possible that the Old World may step in to redress the balance of the New?

This question is still open: and it depends, of course, on Russians, Americans, Europeans, in increasing order of importance. So far as Russia goes, it seems that Russia may be bound to become more European because of the pressures of China and also because of the transformation of her own society; but also because under certain circumstances, the existence of a Europe not allied with the United States may be to her advantage. So far as the United States goes, the answer is not yet clear. With foresight and magnanimity, the United States supported the first steps toward a United Europe; but this United Europe is now bound to American purse strings and atomic power-lines. America's great hour of decision will come one day when the United States may have to decide whether to acquiesce in a truly united and a truly independent Europe, a Europe that may be even a powerful competitor of the United States in the trade of the world. It is at least a tribute to American generosity that we may not in advance answer this question in the negative. After all is said, Americans helped to save the freedom of Western Europe twice. Whatever their motives, these actions stand out in history. But, in any case, this question will be decided by Europeans themselves. It will depend on the quality of their determination to be free, on the moral quality of their determination to live.

In this respect again, the Germans, in the center of Europe, are in the center of the problem.

8

The history of nations is still more important than the history of technology; but the problem of morality already transcends national decisions not only in an ethical but in a practical way. During the last century Waterloo and Sedan were more important events than the invention of the steam locomotive or of the phonograph; in 1945 the defeat of Germany and of Japan were still more important events than the Atomic Bomb; and even in recent years the Hungarian Revolution was a more important event than the firing of Sputniks. But because of the awful weapons now at the disposal of the managers of great nations, the future of war and peace has already become a moral problem in a practical, and not merely in an abstract, sense of morality.

It is therefore that ultimately it is the quality of America's stewardship and of Russia's adaptation of the European heritage that counts. This, even more than the technological race into space, is bound to involve the future of the Russian and of the American peoples. These deeper tendencies are now becoming important and visible as the resilience of Europe, the potential danger of China, and the nuclear stalemate force the rulers to attempt negotiations on the highest level. But civilized mankind is now capable of destroying itself, not merely because of the existence of horrible weapons but because of the spiritual inadequacies of their constructors and managers.

From Europe to Russia and to America came the Christian saints, the discoverers, great art, the supreme ideas of justice and of truth. From Europe, too, came Communism, National Socialism, the Atomic Bomb. America and Russia: their power has been the product of the Modern Age; and the Modern Age has been the product of Europe. Loyola and Calvin, Shakespeare and Cromwell, Pascal and Newton, Dr. Johnson and Robespierre, Tocqueville and Marx, De Gaulle and Hitler, Heisenberg and Von Braun—all Europeans.

For five hundred years our view of the universe expanded as we built ever more powerful telescopes and microscopes until now the best of our scientists meet uncertainty and confusion at the two edges of our universe. While they are returning to a new recognition of older and deeper truths about human beings and about their inescapable spiritual condition, lesser men are still spreading confusion: masses of people are still told to expect Science to bring Paradise closer to Earth and Glory to their nation.

Glory to their nation: it is not that historic photograph of American and Russian soldiers meeting in April 1945 atop a ruined Europe that most saddens my imagination. It is the 1945 picture of the charnel house of Buchenwald, where icy experiments had been made with living human beings in the name of Science; and that other word picture, depicting the scene in the New Mexican desert on 16 July 1945, as one of the U. S. Official Scientists, an immigrant of European origin, jumps and shouts with glee, slapping the Chief Scientist on the back, as the first hot atomic bomb burst and darkened the sun in that desert dawn. There, in that prairie-dog dugout, we may see how sad it is when puny men who no longer believe in the virtue of imitating Christ arrogate to themselves the part of gods.

"Some day," Henry Adams wrote three generations ago, "science may have the existence of mankind in its power and the human race commit suicide by blowing up the world." But Henry Adams, that fine-spun American, was a fatalist of sorts; for no one commits suicide unless he wants to. Our danger comes from those men and women who are telling themselves that an Atomic War is unavoidable; but "unavoidable" is simply what people no longer wish, or dare, to avoid. In view of certain dangerous fatalistic inclinations in American and Russian souls,[10] it is this precious unique Christian doctrine of Free Will, leading to the will to live, that the European heritage may bequeath to both. For while it is true that in order to live a good life one must also know how to die, it is also true that, in order to die well, one must have known how to live; for, when it comes to the salvation of the soul, the willingness to die and the unwillingness to live are not at all the same.

[10] Joseph Conrad, in *Under Western Eyes:* "I suppose one must be a Russian to understand Russian simplicity, a terrible corroding simplicity in which mystic phrases clothe a naïve and hopeless cynicism. I think sometimes that the psychological secret of the profound difference of that people consists in this, that they detest life, the irremediable life of the earth as it is, whereas we westerners cherish it with perhaps an equal exaggeration of its sentimental value."

The American tragedy, then, is that to some extent—and only to some extent—this is true of Americans, too: but that is another book.

Index

Acheson, Dean, 63, 92, 94, 98, 109, 268, 383

Adams, Henry, 373, 412

Adenauer, Konrad, 72, 109, 110, 124, 125–26, 140, 173, 176, 178, 182, 188, 211, 255–56

Afghanistan, 25, 329

Africa, 13, 64, 199–201, 219, 221, 254, 271, 344, 391, 395

Aiken, Frank, 177n

Alaska, 12, 345, 348

Albania, 61, 79, 214–15, 220, 252, 312, 343

Algeria, 119, 202, 205

Algiers, 37

Allies' war aims in World War II, 41–42

America (U.S.). See United States

American-Chinese relations: during first half of 20th century, 83–84, 88, 90, 91; in Korean War, 97–100, 102

Americanization, 157, 290, 296, 378, 408, 409

American Revolution, 9, 10

American-Russian relations: early relations, 10–13; in 19th century, 15; in World War I, 15–16; between World War I and World War II, 27, 28; in World War II, 37; Dulles' role in, 107–28, 177n; Europe as main area of conflict, 108, 173, 218–19; and McCarthy, 115; and Eastern Europe, 147, 153–54; Hungarian Revolution as turning point in, 154; after 1956, 155–57; Chinese fear of improvement in, 170–71, 213; nuclear weapons race, 174–75; and Khrushchev, 180–84, 189; and Kennedy administration, 206–11, 257–60; crisis over Cuba, 216, 237–46; effect of Vietnam war on, 269–70; and expansionism, 347–50. See also Cold war

Anglo-French Plan, 223

Angola, 202

Annam, 265

Antarctica, 348n

Anti-Americanism of Castro, 232, 233n

Anti-Comintern Pact, 87

Anti-Communism, 28, 107, 114–15, 148, 152, 220, 244, 257–58, 262, 267, 275, 317, 318, 320–22, 367, 381, 402, 403n, 404

Anti-Nazi propaganda in U.S., 211n

Anti-Semitism, 160, 402, 403

Arab nationalism, 169

Argentina, 220

Armament race, 156, 222, 223–25, 273, 276

Armenia, 368

Asia, 13, 199, 219, 221, 254, 271, 391, 395

"Asia First" war policy of U.S., 98

Asian-African "bloc" in U.N., 201

Aswan High Dam, 135

Atlantic Charter, 44
Atomic bomb, 59–61, 76, 152, 172, 197, 270. *See also* Hydrogen bomb; Nuclear weapons; Rocket artillery
Attlee, Clement, 67, 68, 401
Austria, 54, 62, 72, 79, 109, 122
Austria-Hungary, 16, 22n
Austrian State Treaty, 57, 120, 122
Azores, 346

Baghdad Pact, 346
Bakunin, Mikhail A., 363
Baltic States, 33, 34, 44, 218, 333, 342, 348
Bancroft, George, 368, 371
Bandung Conference, 119
Bao Dai, 117
Bases, U.S., world-wide, 64, 102, 155, 161, 162, 165, 173–74, 185, 341, 346
Batista, Fulgencio, 229–32, 237n
Bay of Pigs affair, 193, 194, 235–36, 237n, 246
Beneš, Eduard, 331
Bentham, Jeremy, 355
Beria, Laurenti, 112, 158
Berlin Blockade, and Air Lift, 75, 109
Berlin Pact, 25
Berlin-Pankow, 75
Berlin question, 156, 176–77, 179, 183, 194, 206–8, 209–10, 217, 219, 254. *See also* East Berlin; West Berlin
Berlin Wall, 207–8, 211
Bessarabia, 34, 329, 342
Bevan, Aneurin, 402
Bevin, Ernest, 67, 68
Bismarck, Otto von, 16, 216, 330n, 396
Blum, Léon, 398, 401

Bohlen, Charles, 257n
Bolshevik Revolution (1917), 17–20, 23–24, 307–8, 327, 357
Bolshevism, 290, 306
Bonn, 75, 207
Boxer Rebellion, 84
Bradley, Omar, 102
Brest-Litovsk Treaty, 311
Brezhnev, Leonid, 263
Bridges, Styles, 370
Brink-of-war policy, 118
Britain: national character, 356; and Suez Canal crisis, 119, 135–37, 149
Buffer zone, 333, 343
Bukovina, 342
Bulganin, Nikolai, 121, 148, 158, 176
Bulgaria, 46, 62, 143, 214, 251, 333, 343
Bureaucracy, 162–63, 206, 290, 294, 296
Burma, 68

Cairo Declaration, 93
Cambodia, 117, 265
Capitalism. *See* Industrial Capitalism
Caroline Islands, 345
Castro, Fidel, 192, 220, 230–48, 401
Castro's Revolution, Myths and Realities (Draper), 238n
Central Intelligence Agency (CIA), 187–88, 210n, 234, 235, 237, 242, 243, 267
Chamberlain, Neville, 31
Changkufeng, 87
Chiang Kai-shek, 26n, 84, 85n, 86, 91, 331
Chicherin, Georgi V., 328
China, 85–86, 89, 91–92, 97–100, 102, 117, 155, 170, 171, 172, 268, 276

Chinese-American relations. *See* American-Chinese relations

Chinese Civil War, 67, 83, 87, 90–91

Chinese-Russian relations. *See* Russian-Chinese relations

Chou En-lai, 215

Churchill, Winston, 18n, 34, 35, 41, 42, 44–45, 46, 48–49, 55, 56, 58, 63, 64, 67, 112, 113, 118, 247, 250, 309, 331

Civil War, American, 14, 15

Clark, Mark, 75

Clay, Lucius, 208

Cleveland, Grover, 339

Coal-Steel Plan, 108

Cochin China, 265

Colby, Bainbridge, 348

Cold war: historical origins of, 3–39; crystallization of, 40–66; Russian acquisitions in World War II as source of, 43; geographical conditions of, 56–57; Stalin as principal architect of, 63; conditions of, as evident by 1947, 65–66; origin of term, 72, 273; effect of Dulles' rise on, 107; Europe as center of, 108, 173, 218–19, 276, 349; and 1950 nationalist revolutions, 119; crucial year of 1956, 129–54, 156, 249; phases of, 195, 216–17; decrystallization of, 249–72; or cold peace, 273–78. *See also* American-Russian relations

Collective leadership, 130

Collective Security, theory of, 27

Collectivization, 288

Colonial empires, disappearance of, 6, 199

Common Market, 108, 179, 203, 253, 254, 256

Communications, development of, 352–53

Communism, 28, 85, 86–87, 90–92, 93, 103, 109, 117–19, 129–30, 140, 220, 236, 237–38, 239, 252, 265, 271, 276, 287, 288, 289, 294, 301, 311–15, 318–22. *See also* International Communism

Communist Conspiracy Theory, 319

Communist Manifesto (Marx), 303, 305

Communist Party, American, 28

Congo, 200, 218

Conrad, Joseph, 413n

Constitution of U.S., 9, 376

Containment Policy, 69, 71, 78, 161, 167

Coolidge, Calvin, 369, 371

Cooper, Alfred Duff, 22n

Cosmonauts, 193

Coughlin, Rev. Charles, 318

Council of Foreign Ministers, 62, 70

Crèvecoeur, Michel, 374

Crimean War, 16

Cuba, 192, 193, 206, 218, 220, 226–48, 312, 348; missile crisis, 216, 237, 239–46, 254, 257

Cult of the individual, 130–31

Cultural exchange between East and West, 127

Currie, Lauchlin, 85n

Curzon Line, 33, 50, 333

Cyprus, 119

Czechoslovakia, 31, 32, 46, 62, 70, 73, 143, 214, 251, 343

Dairen, 52, 103, 343
Das Kapital (Marx), 303
Davies, Joseph E., 56n
Decline and Rise of Europe (Lukacs), 206n, 227n
De Gasperi, Alcide, 72
De Gaulle, Charles, 45n, 64, 67, 190–91, 203–5, 209, 236, 242, 250, 253–57, 260, 331, 398
Democracy in America (Tocqueville), 14
Denmark, 33, 64, 218, 339, 368
Depression of 1929–34, 24, 291, 312, 316, 320
Dictatorships, 399–401
Diem, Ngo Dinh, 265, 267
Dien Bien Phu, 117, 118
Dies, Martin, 368
Dillon, C. Douglas, 189
Disarmament, 108, 155, 171, 178, 189, 223–24
"Disengagement" in Central Europe, 177, 179, 210
Doctors' Plot, 105
Dominican Republic, 339
Dostoevski, F. M., 362, 366
Dulles, Allen W., 187, 193, 210n, 234
Dulles, John Foster, 106–7, 112, 117, 118, 119, 122, 124, 125, 128, 135–36, 140, 143, 147, 148, 150, 152, 162, 168, 173, 177, 181, 186, 210, 265, 266, 267, 382
Dumbarton Oaks Conference, 52
Dutch East Indies, 64

Earth satellites, 165–66, 193
East Berlin, 61, 115, 176, 207, 219
Eastern Austria, 220
Eastern Europe, 43, 44–49, 50–51, 52–53, 54, 61, 70, 116, 128, 132, 151, 155–56, 175, 213, 220, 250–51, 253, 257
East German Treaty, 208
East Germany, 109, 115, 143, 156, 175, 209, 212, 214, 251, 253
East Prussia, 342
Eaton, Congressman, 369
Economic determinism, 303, 315, 317
Eden, Anthony, 55, 122, 124, 136, 149, 150, 177n
Egypt, 119, 134–36, 146, 167
Eichmann, Adolf, 211n
18th Brumaire, The (Marx), 303n
Eisenhower, Dwight D., 47, 56, 104, 106, 110, 112, 117, 124, 147n, 148n, 149, 150, 176, 181, 182, 185, 188, 189, 190, 204, 224, 234, 265, 266, 277, 371, 377n, 384n, 398
Eisenhower Doctrine, 167, 168
El Alamein, 37
Engels, Friedrich, 289, 302
Equality, problem of, 397–404, 405
Erhard, Ludwig, 256
Espionage, 60–61, 85, 185, 186–88, 240, 243n, 258. *See also* Spy-plane affair
Estonia, 33, 329
Eurasianism, 364
Europe: division of, 3, 48, 57n, 65, 67–82, 107, 128, 173, 179, 195, 202, 210, 211, 250, 253, 275, 320; independence of, from U.S., 203–5, 253
European Advisory Commission, 54
European Defense Community, 110, 122

"Europeanism," 206n

European overseas empires, 6, 199

European Unity, 72

Evangelical Movement, 302

Expansion, national: of Russia, 326–27, 342–44, 354; of U.S., 65, 335–41, 345–47, 386

Fallout shelters, 207

Far East, 14, 25, 51–52, 89, 92, 93, 103, 120, 170, 349

Farouk, King, 119

Fascism, 27, 30, 232n, 314, 366, 399–400

Fatalism, 373n

Faure, François Félix, 124

FBI, 187n

Feisal, King, 168

Feudal tradition, 283–84

Figl, Leopold, 72

Finland, 11, 33, 79, 128, 217–18, 219, 220, 221, 329, 333, 342

First World War, 5, 7, 16–24, 285, 327, 404

Fitzgerald, F. Scott, 371

Five-Year Plans, 288

Ford, Henry, 286, 289

Foreign Affairs, 71

Foreign Ministers' Conferences, 94, 109, 121, 124

Foreign policy, 325, 332, 335, 354n

Formosa, 86, 91, 94, 102, 118, 346

Four-Power Trusteeship, 93

Fourteen Points, 22

France, 33, 109, 117–18, 135–36, 149, 202, 256, 356

Franco, Francisco, 202, 232n, 236, 398

French Revolution, 9, 357

Freud, Sigmund, 355

Fundamentalism, 367

Geneva Conference (1954), 118–19, 265

Geography, and international affairs, 348–51, 356

German Democratic Republic. See East Germany

German Federal Republic. See West Germany

Germanophobe propaganda in U.S., 211n

German Peace Settlement, 56, 65

German-Russian relations, 350; in the 1920s, 25–26; after Munich Crisis, 31–33; Non-Aggression Pact (1939), 33, 332; negotiations of Molotov, 34–35; German invasion of Russia, 35–36

Germany: division of, 3, 53–54, 80, 173, 179, 195, 202, 210, 211, 274; unification of, 109, 111, 125, 126, 127, 179, 209, 212, 351

Gerö, 140–41, 142

Ghent, Treaty of, 11

Gheorghiu-Dej, Gheorghe, 252

Gibraltar, 119

Goa, 218

Goldwater, Barry, 262–63

Gomulka, Wladyslaw, 134, 137–40, 204, 251, 402

Good-will visits, 180–84

Greece, 48–49, 61, 68, 69, 79, 119, 175

Greene, Graham, 266

Greenland, 36, 64, 346

Grillparzer, Franz, 123n

Gromyko, Andrei A., 241, 328

Guadalcanal, 37

Guantánamo naval base, 227, 236, 237n, 243n

Guatemala, 119, 235, 236, 348

Guevara, "Che," 247

Haiti, 339

Halifax, Lord, 317

Hammarskjöld, Dag, 201

Harriman, Averell, 257n, 260

Hawaii, 12, 36, 338, 339, 345, 348

Healy, Denis, 177n

Heer, Friedrich, 122

Herter, Christian, 181

Herzen, A. I., 363

Hiroshima, 60

Hiss, Alger, 77

Historical movements of our times, 390–413

Hitler, Adolf, 26, 28–29, 30, 31–35, 56, 259n, 305, 312, 314, 321, 331, 398, 401, 404

Ho Chi Minh, 117, 120n, 265, 271–72

Hong Kong, 64n, 86

Hoover, Herbert, 384n

"Hot line," 216, 259

Hoxha, Enver, 214

Hubertusburg Treaty, 8

Hughes, Charles Evans, 383

Hungarian Revolution, 141–47, 230, 249, 250, 251, 357

Hungary, 46, 62, 140, 145, 153, 214, 238n, 251, 343, 348

Hydrogen bomb, 76, 197, 222, 223, 366

Hydrogen war, threat of, 152, 156

Iceland, 36, 64, 346

Ie Shima, 345

Immigration, 14, 15, 286, 294, 378–80, 384. See also Movement of peoples

Inchon, 96

India, 68, 172, 184, 185, 213, 271

Indochina, 83, 116–19, 265–69

Indonesia, 83, 184

Industrial capitalism, 276, 285, 287, 294, 301

Industrialization, 197–98, 287, 290, 294, 295

Industrial Revolution, 197, 283, 284, 286, 301–2

Inner Mongolia, 92

Inspection, international, 124, 224

Intellectualization, 297n

International Communism, 25, 27, 147, 180, 320, 330–31. See also Communism

International Court of the Hague, 340

Internationalists, 356, 367–72

International Policemanship, 339, 369

Iran, 119, 346

Iraq, 168, 169, 346

Iron curtain, 25, 56, 58, 63, 116, 133, 155, 176, 195–96, 224, 250, 253, 273

Isolationism: in Russia, 24, 25, 31, 62, 78, 363, 364, 367; in U.S., 24, 30, 34, 62, 291, 341, 352, 357–58, 367–72

Israel, 68, 136, 150, 169

Italy, 76, 80

James, Henry, 371

Japan, 12, 14–15, 27, 36, 56, 59, 65, 99, 102, 223, 276, 332

Japanese Peace Treaty, 56, 102

Jaspers, Karl, 212

Jeffers, Robinson, 342

John, Dr., defection of, 126n
John XXIII, Pope, 217
Johnson, Lyndon B., 261–63, 267–69
Jordan, 168, 169
Juvenile delinquency, 291n

Kádár, János, 145, 251
Kaganovich, L. N., 158
Kassim, Dictator, 169
Katanga, 218
Kekkonen, D. Urho, 218
Kellogg, Frank B., 27
Kellogg Pact, 340
Kemal, Mustapha, 331
Kennan, George F., 71, 79–80, 161, 177n, 257n
Kennedy, John F., 190, 192–95, 206–10, 234–35, 237, 241–46, 247, 255, 256, 257–60, 266, 267, 371
Kennedy, Robert, 210n, 242
Kennedy (Sorensen), 235n, 236n, 257n
Kerensky, A. F., 19
Keyserling, Hermann, 294n
Khrushchev, Nikita, 112, 116, 121, 124, 129–34, 137–38, 143–47, 149, 151, 157, 158–59, 168, 171, 179, 182–84, 188–89, 190–92, 194, 204, 206–10, 215–16, 218, 223, 236, 239–46, 257–59, 263–64, 269, 277, 288, 289, 298, 310, 323, 334, 349, 363, 366, 388, 401, 403
Khrushchev-Kennedy correspondence, 216, 243
Kishi, Nobusuke, 185
Knowland, Senator, 370
Korea, 61, 86, 89, 90, 92, 93–94. *See also* North Korea; South Korea
Korean War, 94–101, 116, 268

Kosygin, Alexei, 263
Kozlov, F. R., 182
Kroll, Dr., Ambassador, 217
Ku Klux Klan, 263
Kurile Islands, 52, 89, 342, 344

Language, American, 377, 378n
Laos, 117, 194, 195, 213, 221, 265
La Rochefoucauld, François, 355
Latin America, 11–12, 229, 237, 239, 254, 339, 369
Lattimore, Owen, 85n
Latvia, 33, 329
Laval, Pierre, 331
League of Armed Neutrality, 10
League of Nations, 23, 26, 30
Lebanon, 113n, 168–69, 346, 358, 370
Le Bon, Gustave, 356
Lenin, Vladimir Ilyich, 10, 19–20, 21, 104, 264n, 287, 288, 289, 309–10, 329, 362, 363, 398
Leninism-Stalinism, 310
Lindsay, Vachel, 371
Lippmann, Walter, 72
Lithuania, 33, 329
Litvinov, Maxim, 27, 30, 32, 328, 332, 362, 366
Living standards, 288
Lodge, Henry Cabot, 149, 184
Long, Huey, 318
Louisiana Territory, 11
Lubin "Government," 50

MacArthur, Douglas, 93, 96, 97–100, 170, 223, 268, 401, 405

McCarthy, Joseph, 100n, 107, 115, 190, 262, 318, 401, 402
McCone, John, 210n
Machiavelli, Niccolò, 355
McKinley, William, 368
Macmillan, Harold, 181–82, 190, 254
McNamara, Robert, 268
Madagascar, 83
Magyar minority in Rumania, 252n
Mahan, Alfred Thayer, 338
Malaya, 117
Malenkov, Sergie, 112, 121, 133, 158
Maléter, Colonel, 144, 145n
Malik, Jacob A., 223
Malinovsky, B. K., 188
Malta, meeting at, 64
Malthus, Thomas, 391
Managerial Revolution, 295
Manchuria, 86, 89, 90, 92, 99, 103, 220
Manchurian Railway, 92
Manifest Destiny, 339, 368, 369, 379
Mannerheim, Marshal, 218, 331
Mao Tse-tung, 26n, 85, 87, 95, 170, 184, 312, 331, 401
Mariana Islands, 345
Marshall Islands, 345
Marshall Plan, 69–70, 109, 316
Marx, Karl, 247, 289, 302–4, 305, 306, 355
Marxism, 131, 290, 302–4, 305–11, 363, 366, 403
Marxism-Leninism, 233, 234, 310
Masaryk, Jan, 73
"Massive retaliation," 152
Mass production, 286, 294
Mather, Cotton, 370

Matsuoka, Foreign Minister, 362
Mencken, H. L., 377, 378n
Metternich, Count, 334, 336
Mexico, 339, 348, 368
Middle East. See Near East
Migration. See Movement of peoples
Mikhailovitch, Draza, 91
Mikoyan, Anastas, 131, 134, 142, 143, 158, 181, 245, 246, 258, 366, 403
Military technology, 288
Milyukov, P. N., 19, 328, 362
Missile gap, 165–66
Molotov, Vyacheslav, 32, 34–35, 55, 61, 76, 112, 122, 124, 158, 215, 245, 264n, 328, 332, 363, 366
Mongolia. See Inner Mongolia; Outer Mongolia
Monroe Doctrine, 12, 376
Montgomery, Field Marshal, 177n
Moon, race for, 197, 206
Morality, problem of, 411–13
Morgenthau Plan, 53, 316
Morocco, 346
Moscow, Treaty of, 33
Moscow Conference, 48
Mossadegh, Mohammed, 119
Movement of peoples, 13, 14, 57–58, 109, 145, 153, 238, 392, 405. See also Immigration
Munich Crisis, 31, 350
Murphy, Robert, 169, 183
Mussolini, Benito, 29, 30, 259n, 305, 306, 314, 331, 398, 401
Mutual Assistance Treaty, 92

Nagasaki, 60
Nagy, Imre, 116, 134, 141, 142, 144–45, 159

Napoleonic Wars, 10
Nasser, Gamal Abdel, 135, 150, 168, 169, 314
National character, 355–89
Nationalism, 313, 314, 355–89, 401, 403
Nationality, concept of, 374–86
NATO, 75, 78–80, 82, 122, 127, 177, 178, 204, 211, 217, 219, 253, 254, 255; NATO-SHAPE, 110, 217
Nazism, 27, 314, 400
Near East, 134–35, 150, 167, 344
Negroes, and civil rights, 263
Nehru, Jawaharlal, 398
Nerchinsk Treaty, 12
Neutrality Act (1937), 30
Neutrals' Conference (1961), 201
New Deal, 291–92, 293, 318, 367
New nations' "neutrality," 200
Nicaragua, 235, 339, 369
Nixon, Richard M., 182, 189, 190, 234, 331, 349
Nomonhan, 87
Non-Aggression Treaties, 32, 33, 34, 36, 88, 148, 332
North Atlantic Treaty Organization. See NATO
North Korea, 92, 94–95, 102, 220, 268, 343–44. See also Korea; Korean War
North Vietnam, 265, 268, 269, 271
Norway, 33, 218
Nuclear test ban, 224, 254, 260
Nuclear weapons, 155, 174 (table), 175, 177, 178, 189, 210, 211, 217, 222, 274

Oder-Neisse Line, 58, 178, 212
Okinawa, 64, 102, 345
Old Believers, 360n, 361
Open Aerial Inspection, 124
Open Door Principle, 84
Open frontiers, 283
Origins, historical, 3–39
Outer Mongolia, 27, 52, 86, 88, 92, 173, 211, 220, 258, 344
Outer Seven economic areas, 179
Overpopulation, 390, 391

Pakistan, 68
Palestine, 62, 68
Panama Canal, 14, 338, 352
Panmunjom, 100
Pan-Slavism, 16, 327
Paris, Congress of (1919–20), 24
Paris Summit Conference (1960), 188–89
Paris Treaty (1783), 8
Pasternak, Boris, 160, 363
Peaceful coexistence, 121, 148, 155, 260
Pearl Harbor attack, 36, 97, 185, 242
People's Republic of China, 92
Percentages Agreement, 48
Perón, Juan D., 220, 314, 401
Persia, 61, 329
Peter the Great, 362, 363, 365
Petöfi Circle, 133–34
Petrograd, 25, 361
Philippines, 63, 339, 340
Platt Amendment, 227, 229, 339
Pobedonostsev, K. P., 309, 362
Point Four Program, 316

Poland, 6, 11, 32, 46, 49–50, 51, 54, 55, 58, 62, 178, 204, 212, 214, 251, 329, 332, 342, 343

Polaris submarines, 218, 254

Police State, 298

Polish Revolution, 137–40, 250, 251

Political map of world, 199–200

Population, problem of, 391–93

Populist Party, 317, 367

Porkkala Peninsula, 128, 343

Port Arthur, 52, 92, 103, 343

Portsmouth Peace Treaty, 15

Portugal, 202, 399

Potsdam Conference, 56, 58, 60, 67, 81, 89, 93

Pound, Ezra, 378n

Poverty, 301–2

Power, and prestige, 198

Poznan riots, 133

Prescott, William H., 371

Problems of Leninism (Stalin), 320n

Productivity, and population, 198

Progressive Party, 317, 367

Proust, Marcel, 356

Prussia, 8, 11

Public opinion, 195

Puerto Rico, 338

Pusan, 96

Pyongyang, 96

Quebec Conference, 54

Quiet American, The (Greene), 266n

Raab, Julius, 72

Race, problems of, 120, 276, 390, 393–97

Radford, Admiral, 118, 265

Rákosi, Jenö, 115–16, 133, 134, 140

Rapacki, Foreign Minister, 140

Rapacki Plan, 171, 177n

Rapallo Pact, 25

Rasputin, 19, 362

Rearmament: of West Germany, 109, 110, 111, 124–25, 127, 156, 173, 175, 178; of Japan, 185

"Red Scare" of the 1920s, 114

Rhee, Syngman, 93, 94

Roa, Raul, 231n

Rocket artillery, 155, 159, 165, 174 (*table*), 175, 197, 223, 250, 254

Rocket bases, 175, 177, 239

Rokossovsky, Marshal, 138

Roman Catholic Church, 233n

Roosevelt, Franklin D., 26, 29–30, 32, 33, 35, 41, 42, 45–46, 55, 57n, 58, 64, 84, 88, 201, 259n, 291, 305, 312, 318, 331, 340, 350, 371, 382, 398

Roosevelt, Theodore, 15, 294, 338, 339n, 368, 382, 386

Rumania, 34, 46, 54, 62, 143, 175, 214, 251–52, 343

Rusk, Dean, 193, 268, 271

Russia: rise of, to 1945, 3–28; power and prestige of, after World War II, 4–5, 42, 219; in World War I, 16–19; American recognition of U.S.S.R., 26; in World War II, 35–36, 37–38, 39; take-over of Eastern Europe, 43, 44–49; enters war against Japan, 59, 89; Sovietization of satellites, 70; in Korean War, 95–96, 99, 101; domains of, in Far East,

Russia *cont'd*)
after Korean War, 103, 169–70; "Americanization" of, 157; declining power of, 219–20; Asian borderlands of, 271
Russian-American relations. See American-Russian relations; Cold war
Russian-Chinese relations: in first half of 20th century, 85, 86–87, 90–91; Stalin-Chiang Treaty (1945), 89; Communist Sino-Soviet agreements, 92; Mutual Assistance Treaty, 92; in Korean War, 102, 103; worsening of, 143, 159, 169–73, 184–85, 213, 215, 216, 250, 259, 260, 270–71; stages of conflict, 270n
Russian Orthodox Church, 16, 327, 359–60, 365
Russian Revolution. See Bolshevik Revolution
Russo-Japanese Pact (1941), 88
Ruthenia, 342
Ryukyus Islands, 346

Saar, 127
Sakhalin Island, 52, 342
Salazar, Antonio, 399
Santayana, George, 335
Santo Domingo, 369
Sarajevo, 17
Satellite states, 333, 343–44
Sazonov, S. D., 22n, 333n
Schlesinger, Arthur, Jr., 267n
Schuman, Robert, 72
Schuman Plan, 108
Second World War, 3, 4, 33–39, 46–48, 65, 404
Secret Service, U. S., 187n
Security Council, U.N., 52, 95, 148

Self-determination of nations, 24
Self-interest, 355–56, 361
Serfdom in Russia, 287
Shepilov, Foreign Minister, 133n, 328
Sholokhov, Mikhail, 363
Siberia, 12, 172, 392, 396
Sinkiang, 86, 92, 102, 220, 343
Sixth Fleet, U. S., 69
Slavery in U.S., 287
Slavophiles, of Russia, 360–66
Socialism, national, 294n, 318, 391, 397–404
Socialist movements, 306, 318, 323
Socialist Party, American, 317
Societies, American and Russian: tendencies of, 281–99; political theories, 300–23
Sorensen, Theodore, 235n, 236n, 257n, 267n
South Korea, 94–95, 101, 268. See also Korea; Korean War
South Vietnam, 265, 266, 267, 268
Soviet Union. See Russia
Spaak, Paul Henri, 178n
Space rocketry. See Rocket artillery
Spain, 119, 202, 227, 232, 253, 338
Spanish-American War, 338–39
Sputniks. See Earth satellites
Spy-plane affair, 163n, 188–89, 190, 258, 387
Stalin, Joseph, 10, 21, 27, 30–31, 32, 34–36, 41, 42, 43, 46, 53, 55, 58, 59, 60, 61, 70, 73, 74, 87, 89, 91, 93, 95, 104–5, 112, 264n,

Stalin, Joseph (*cont'd*) 287, 288, 289, 305, 310, 324, 332, 334, 361–62, 363, 398, 401; downgrading of, 131–32, 215, 264

Stalin-Chiang Treaty (1945), 89, 103

Stalingrad, 37, 38, 215, 365

States, American and Russian: national character, 355–89; national interests, 324–54

State visits, 180–84

Steel production, 288

Stendhal, Marie H. B., 355

Stockholm Peace Appeal, 101n

Stolypin, Pëtr A., 19

Strategic Air Command, 150

Strauss, Defense Minister, 178, 217, 218

Stresemann, Gustav, 331

Stürmer, Boris V., 19

Suez Canal crisis, 119, 135–36, 149–50, 249

Summit Meetings, 112, 113, 123–24, 157, 176, 182, 188–89, 194–95

Sun Yat-sen, 26n

Sun Yat-sen, Mme., 271n

Suslov, Mikhail A., 142, 143, 158

Sweden, 6–7, 79, 218

Switzerland, 79, 202

Syria, 167

Taft, Robert A., 370

Taft, William Howard, 382

Tannu Tuva, 86n

Technology, and international relations, 352–53, 388

Teheran Conference, 46

Teller, Edward, 222

Thomas, Norman, 401

Tibet, 86, 102, 348

Tibetan Rebellion, 172

Tito, Josip Broz, 51, 54, 61, 73–74, 91, 133, 145n, 148, 159, 201, 236, 312, 331, 401, 402

Tocqueville, Alexis de, 14, 131, 283, 336, 355, 374, 397–98

Tolstoi, Leo, 15, 363

Torgau, 3, 39, 55

Tourism, 127, 160, 253

Trieste, 54, 61

Trotsky, Leon, 10, 21, 27, 287, 288, 328, 361–62

Trujillo, Rafael L., 230, 236, 401

Truman, Harry S., 55, 56, 67–68, 69, 72, 90, 95–101, 170, 268

Truman Doctrine, 40, 69

Turgenev, Ivan, 362, 366

Turkey, 6, 11, 16, 61, 69, 79, 119, 329

Twain, Mark, 371

Twentieth Party Congress (1956), 130–31, 215

Twenty-Second Party Congress (1961), 215

Ukraine, 348

Ulbricht, Walter, 207, 217, 251

Un-American Activities Committee, 368

United Arab Republic, 167

United Europe, 410

United Nations, 52, 55, 61, 65, 94, 95–101, 128, 144, 145, 148, 150, 153, 191–92, 199, 201, 276, 340

United States: rise of, to 1945, 3–28; power and prestige of, after World War II, 4–5; in World War I, 21–23; in World War II, 36–37, 38–39, 340–41; post-World War II actions of, 64–65; de-

United States (cont'd)
fense perimeter in western Pacific, 94; in Korean War, 95–101; postwar forces in Europe, 110–11; foreign policies of, 111–12, 113n, 115, 186; and Communist advances in Southeast Asia, 117–18; and Suez Canal crisis, 135–36, 149–50; and Hungarian Revolution, 147–53; declining power of, 220–21, 256–57; in war in Vietnam, 266–69; continuing international involvement of, 276
United States-Chinese relations. See American-Chinese relations
United States-Russian relations. See American-Russian relations; Cold war
Urbanization, 295n
U.S.S.R. See Russia
U Thant, 245
Utilitarianism, 302

Van Alstyne, Richard, 375n
Vandenberg, Arthur, 369
Vera Cruz, 368
Versailles Treaty, 26
Veto power in U.N., 52, 61
Vietcong, 266, 267, 268, 269, 271
Vietminh, 117, 118–19, 266
Vietnam, 119, 265–69
Virgin Islands, 64
Vishinsky, Andrei, 76, 112, 328
Von Braun, Wernher, 222
Von Seeckt, General, 331
Voroshilov, Klimenty, 145

Waging Peace (Eisenhower), 147n, 148n
Wallace, Henry, 63

War of 1812, 10–11
Warsaw Pact, 127, 128, 143, 144, 149, 151, 204
Washington, George, 6, 9, 353, 381
Webster, Noah, 377
Weimar Republic, 59
Welfare state, U.S., 157, 160, 162, 292–93, 318, 323
West Berlin, 108, 176, 207, 209, 350
Western Europe, 65, 108–9, 212, 221, 253, 276
Westernizers, of Russia, 360–66
West Germany, 65, 79, 108, 122, 127, 175, 209, 212, 255
West Germany-U.S. relations, 109, 111–12, 124, 125, 173
White, Harry Dexter, 85n
White Man's Burden, 339
Whitman, Walt, 368
Wilson, Woodrow, 21–24, 26, 368, 371, 382
Witte, Sergei, 19, 289, 328, 362
World Crisis, The (Churchill), 18n
Wyszynski, Cardinal, 138–39

Xenophobia, 160, 341

Yalta Conference, 40, 42, 46, 89; Agreements, 50–53, 88, 89, 92, 93, 103, 350
Yugoslavia, 51, 73, 79, 121, 175, 214, 220, 252, 312, 333, 343

Zagorsk monastery, 365n
Zhdanov, A. A., 105
Zhukov, G. K., 112, 124, 148, 158
Zinoviev, G. E., 10, 88n

ANCHOR BOOKS

ECONOMICS

ANATOMY OF A METROPOLIS—Edgar M. Hoover and Raymond Vernon, A298

COMPETITION AND MONOPOLY—Mark S. Massel, A386

THE CORPORATION TAKE-OVER—Andrew Hacker, ed., A465

CORPORATIONS IN CRISIS—Richard Austin Smith, A475

ECONOMIC PHILOSOPHY—Joan Robinson, A415

THE ECONOMY, LIBERTY AND THE STATE—Calvin B. Hoover, A241

THE ERA OF TYRANNIES—Elie Halévy, Robert K. Webb, trans., A463

THE EXPLODING METROPOLIS—Editors of Fortune, A146

FREE MEN AND FREE MARKETS—Robert Theobald, A447

THE GUARANTEED INCOME—Robert Theobald, A519

INTERNATIONAL POLITICAL COMMUNITIES, A488

INTRODUCTION TO ECONOMIC REASONING, Fourth, Revised Edition—Marshall A. Robinson, Herbert C. Morton, James D. Calderwood, A338

THE MANPOWER REVOLUTION: Its Policy Consequences, Excerpts from the Senate Hearings Before the Clark Committee, ed. by Garth L. Mangum; Foreword by Senator Joseph S. Clark, A522

MARKETS IN AFRICA: Eight Subsistence Economies in Transition—Paul J. Bohannan and George Dalton, eds., N39

METROPOLIS 1985—Raymond Vernon, A341

THE ORGANIZATION MAN—William H. Whyte, Jr., A117

PRIMITIVE, ARCHAIC AND MODERN ECONOMIES—Karl Polanyi, ed. by George Dalton, A605

QUIET CRISIS IN INDIA—John P. Lewis, A383

THE RED EXECUTIVE: A Study of the Organization Man in Russian Industry—David Granick, A246

STRATEGY AND STRUCTURE: Chapters in the History of the Industrial Enterprise—Alfred D. Chandler, Jr., A461

TWO WORLDS OF CHANGE—Otto Feinstein, ed., A396

UNION DEMOCRACY—Seymour Lipset, Martin A. Trow, and James S. Coleman. With a foreword by Clark Kerr, A296

THE URBAN COMPLEX: Human Values in Urban Life—Robert C. Weaver, A505

DATE DUE
